WITNESS TO HISTORY
A Refugee from the Third Reich Remembers

Joachim von Elbe

The Max Kade Institute for German-American Studies
Madison, Wisconsin

B
Elbe

Published by the German-American Cultural Society, Inc., Madison, Wisconsin for the Max Kade Institute for German-American Studies at the University of Wisconsin, Madison.

ISBN 0-924119-00-4

Printed in the United States of America by Edwards Brothers, Inc., Ann Arbor, Michigan

Distributed by the University of Wisconsin Press

The book is a revised version of the German edition which was published in 1983 under the the title *Unter Preußenadler und Sternenbanner. Ein Leben für Deutschland und Amerika* by C. Bertelsmann in Munich, Federal Republic of Germany.

I HAVE SWORN UPON THE ALTAR OF GOD
ETERNAL HOSTILITY AGAINST EVERY FORM OF
TYRANNY OVER THE MIND OF MAN.

Thomas Jefferson

TO

MY BROTHER GUENTHER

IN MEMORIAM

Table of Contents

Foreword

The Max Kade Institute for German-American Studies at the University of Wisconsin, Madison, was founded in 1983 to research, document, and help disseminate the contributions of German immigrants and their descendants to the historical, political, and cultural life of their new homeland.

It is with great pleasure that we introduce the memoirs of Dr. von Elbe to the English-speaking public (the German version was published in 1983 by C. Bertelsmann, Munich). The memoirs give an account of an exemplary life spent in the service of the author's native country, Germany, and of his adopted country, the United States.

The book describes the demise of the Weimar Republic and the advent of Nazism, and sets forth a succinct record of the postwar developments that led to the restoration of German sovereignty after the catastrophe of 1945, and to the reentry of Germany into the community of free and peace-loving nations. The many favorable reviews which the book received stress the author's contributions to the reconstruction of the German legal and constitutional order and to the Paris Agreements of 1955—the continuing basis of Germany's membership in the Western Alliance. It may be added that the author is still serving the United States as an American justice at the Supreme Restitution Court in Munich. It is therefore fitting and proper that the subtitle of the German edition reads: "A Life for Germany and America."

The subtitle of the present book, "A Refugee from the Third Reich Remembers," refers to the fact that the author became the victim of a grotesque and generally less well known brand of Nazi racial madness, the fiction of a "mongrel race." In the Nazi view, a "Mischling" was a person who had a "non-Aryan" among his or her ancestors. The author belongs to a family that has given Germany artists, scientists, and generations of devoted public officials. In spite of that, the Nazis declared him unfit to continue serving his native Germany; it was through one "Jewish" grandmother that he became a person of "mixed blood" and thus racially unacceptable to the "pure Aryan" German society. It took foresight and courage to leave Germany in 1934 for the United States, to study law a second time in a foreign language and a foreign legal system under unaccustomed methods of instruction. His education in both German and American law put the author later on in a unique position to serve his country when this type of legal training was of vital importance to the American occupation authorities in their efforts to govern postwar Germany. In 1988 he was able to celebrate the 50th anniversary of his graduation from Yale Law School in the company of many of his former classmates.

Of great interest are the chapters dealing with Dr. von Elbe's youth. Time and events are reconstructed in an objective but loving recital of daily life during and after World War I. How fortunate that his mother saved his youthful diaries! It is with their help that the mature writer traces, with openness and a sense of humor toward his younger self, the development of his social and political consciousness.

The partly humorous and on the whole contented stories from the author's years in the humanistic high school are a welcome counterpoint to the dismal tales told of school by contemporary writers such as the brothers Heinrich and Thomas Mann. An educational system which, in teaching the Greek and Latin languages, points to classical heroes as guiding stars for a "good" life also inspires the student to embrace such virtues as love for one's country, hatred of tyranny, simplicity of manners, delight in nature, and to find satisfaction in the activities of the mind and in the service of the common good. It is this understanding of the classics which draws the connecting lines between the intellectual background of the European immigrant and the political concepts of the framers of the United States Constitution. Thus the words of Thomas Jefferson in praise of freedom and abhorrence of tyranny can become the motto of a life and a book.

The memoirs are filled with descriptions of friends and acquaintances—from the author's school days, university years, his professional life. I personally like the anecdotal style which tells what happened to the friends from both sides of the Atlantic.

A reader with a predilection for happy endings will find this an eminently satisfying book: Fortune lets the author return to the homeland that had rejected him. The ideals of service and commitment instilled in his German youth permit the mature American to help rebuild his defeated homeland. The very objectivity and the precise accounts of personal, German, and United States history and the instructive lessons in fine points of law do not hide, but rather highlight, the basic message of the von Elbe memoirs: that a passion for justice is central to both German and American society, and that the individual, in "struggling daily for life and liberty," must do so without rancor—within the law.

Charlotte Lang Brancaforte

Acknowledgments

The list of grateful acknowledgments is headed by William R. Tyler, former Assistant Secretary of State for European Affairs and Ambassador to The Netherlands. It was he who encouraged me to present my life story to the English-speaking public after it had appeared in German. His counsel and linguistic mastery were of inestimable value to me. His understanding and never-ceasing interest inspired me to see the work to completion.

And yet, there might not have been a book had it not been for Professor Charlotte Lang Brancaforte, Director of the Max Kade Institute for German-American Studies at the University of Wisconsin, Madison. She conceived the idea of incorporating the book into the program of the Institute. Her enthusiasm, her unflagging dedication and resourcefulness, aided by Professor John J. Nitti's expertise and technical apparatus, enabled the publication of the book. I am deeply thankful to all, including John O'Neill who did the data entry, for their generous support.

I am indebted to Dr. Catharine Rasmussen for her editorial work and, in particular, to Elio Brancaforte who contributed numerous valuable suggestions.

Special thanks are due to my niece Dorothea L. von Elbe for the design of the jacket.

The book is dedicated to my brother Guenther who appears on many of its pages. I owe him my spiritual and physical survival in the true sense of the word. Shortly before his death on April 4, 1988, I was able to tell him that the forthcoming book would constitute a lasting memorial to his brotherly love and to all he had done for me.

Introduction

In late November of 1918, the German First Army on its retreat from France crossed the Rhine at Neuwied on a hastily constructed pontoon bridge. Some of its units marched through the town with bands playing and regimental banners flying in the wind.

On December 6, the last troops of the retreating army left Neuwied. The spectacle of the disciplined combat soldiers had aroused in the people feelings of patriotic pride. It was a fleeting moment of self-delusion. With the soldiers gone, gloom and apprehension set in. A few days later "the Americans" were to arrive. Under the terms of the Armistice Agreement of November 11, 1918, the Koblenz bridgehead with Neuwied on the right bank of the Rhine had been assigned to the American army as a zone of occupation.

On one of those dreary December mornings—I was then sixteen years of age—I walked up to a window of the classroom on the third floor of the building before class had started and looked down upon the street. What I saw hit me like an electric shock. There on the street corner stood the "enemy," a stranger who seemed to be from another world, the first soldier of the American occupation forces. With a map in his hands he tried to get his bearings, apparently bewildered and uncertain. In the unfamiliar uniform he was a figure both fascinating and awe-inspiring, harbinger of an uncertain future.

Thirty years later, a uniformed American stood once again on the same street corner. The generation that had seen the collapse of imperial Germany became witness to yet another foreign occupation. This time the whole of Germany was occupied by the armies of the victorious Allies.

That American on the street corner was I. On a trip from my post in Berlin where I had been stationed since August of 1946 as a member of the Legal Division of the Office of Military Government for Germany (U.S.), I had come to Neuwied in search of my old home. I had not seen it for several decades. I had come to revisit the scenes of a happy childhood and of all my

years in school, the place where the foundation stones of my life
had been laid.

The window from which I had observed the first American of
my life was gone. The old school building lay in ruins, victim
of the battle which was fought around Neuwied in March of 1945
after the First American Army had crossed the Rhine at Remagen
on the still intact Ludendorff bridge and had raced down the river
to link up with Patton's Third Army in the Palatinate.

Neuwied, on the whole, had been spared destruction. I
walked through streets bearing familiar names. Many houses
evoked the memory of friends, but their present occupants were
unknown to me. I stood in front of the house where we had lived
for twelve years, my father's official residence as chief of the
county administration of Neuwied. Behind the rows of windows, I
visualized each room, its furniture and pictures, and remembered
the use it had served: the sitting room where the family gathered
after supper to read or listen to stories; the desk at which I did my
homework; my mother's drawing room with its crystal chandelier
and the stately rococo clock; my father's library. A piece of fresh
masonry in the basement wall marked the spot where, as I later
learned, three people had been killed by an artillery shell.

I looked for the faces of the people I had known, although
after so many years I might not have recognized old friends and
acquaintances just as they might not have recognized me. It
dawned on me that I had become a stranger in a world that once
had been my home.

The uniform of a civilian employee of the War Department
identified me as a member of the American occupation authorities
and as a representative of the supreme authority assumed in
Germany by the Allies. At that time, the fate of the German
people lay in the hands of the four occupying powers.

Speaking for the Americans, Secretary of State James F.
Byrnes stated in a speech at Stuttgart on September 6, 1946, that
it was the wish of the American people "to help the German
people to win their way back to an honorable place among the
peace-loving nations of the world."

How did it come about that I was destined to take part in this
task as a member of the American Military Government? The
answer lies in the labyrinthine course of my life which was shaped

by an epoch during which mankind underwent more fundamental changes than had occurred in ten previous generations.

Imperial Germany

Hamm in Westphalia where I was born in 1902 boasts of being Europe's largest railroad shunting station. Apart from its economic significance, the city shares with hundreds of other places in northwest Germany the distinction of being considered by archaeologists to be the site where, in A.D.9, Germanic tribes under the leadership of Arminius, prince of the Cheruscans, annihilated three Roman legions together with their auxiliaries (commonly known as the "Battle in the Teutoburg Forest"). The defeat forced the Romans to abandon forever the conquered lands east of the Rhine. Perhaps the spirits of slain Romans haunting the house of my birth inspired me to pay homage to them when in later years I wrote my book on *The Romans in Germany*.

In 1902, Germany was ruled by an emperor who presided over a motley variety of kings, granddukes, dukes, and princes. They reigned in twenty-two states. Together with three Free Cities and the "imperial land" (*Reichsland*) of Alsace-Lorraine, they formed the federated German Empire.

A few months after my birth, my father was transferred from Hamm, where he had been senior assistant to the county executive, to serve with the district government at Potsdam.

The city was a favorite summer residence of the emperor and his family, with palaces built by Prussian kings from the seventeenth to the nineteenth century and churches in Romanesque and Renaissance style. The wide streets were flanked by rows of two-story houses, their facades, by royal decree, ornamented with stucco designs. There were gates modeled on the lines of Roman triumphal arches and bronze and marble statues in the city's squares bedecked with flowers. All this regal splendor lay in a setting of woods and lakes, part of which had been turned into spacious parks with graveled walkways between shrubbery and trees. Horse-drawn equipages, the royal coat-of-arms emblazoned on the sides, liveried coachmen, lackeys on errands, soldiers in colorful uniforms standing guard at the palaces—all these signified that royalty was in town.

My parents lived with us five children in a house on a short dead-end street; there were only a few single houses, each one surrounded by a garden. We had a fountain in front of the house. It once proved my undoing when I fell in while trying to catch a goldfish. Considering my tender age, I must have cried furiously. The fish got away.

In the house across the street lived a family with three girls our age. Their father was an aide-de-camp to the emperor. In a magazine picture of a royal ball in the "White Hall" of the Berlin palace, he could be seen standing in a resplendent uniform near the emperor, amidst a glittering host of courtiers, bejeweled ladies in long-sleeved silken dresses, high-ranking officers in fanciful uniforms and civilian guests in tails. The girls were our playmates; we rode tricycles down the street or challenged one another at croquet. Once we were invited to their house when St. Nicholas paid a visit. Because we had been good, St. Nicholas rewarded us with apples and sweets; then he vanished from a balcony on a cloud. At least this was what happened according to my sister; she had seen it with her own eyes. I was lost in the shuffle and had not arrived in time to watch the spectacle. My disappointment at having missed this once-in-a-lifetime miracle remained with me for a long time. (Actually, one of the grownups had called the children to the balcony and had pointed to a cloud in the sky, telling them that St. Nicholas had just left on it.) The youngest of the girls achieved literary fame as a poet and novelist. One of the best-known novels of Marie Luise Kaschnitz entitled *Das dicke Kind* (The Fat Child) is an autobiographical account of her childhood in Potsdam.

On our daily walks we frequently passed the Russian Colony, a row of small wooden houses in Russian style with carved gables and balconies in the shade of huge chestnut trees. The name of the Colony and the foreign look of the houses intrigued us. We were told that the people who lived there were Russians whose forefathers had served in the Prussian army. We were, of course, too young to understand how all this had come about.

The Russian Colony was a settlement of Russian singers who had been made prisoners of war by the Prussian Corps of General von Yorck in 1812 (Prussia was an ally of Napoleon when he invaded Russia in 1812 and had contributed an auxiliary corps

Potsdam

1. A Street with Holy Ghost Church

2. Statue of Frederic the Great and the Garrison Church

3. The Marble Palace

4. Colony Alexandrowka

to Napoleon's "Grand Army"). Czar Alexander did not ask for the return of the prisoners after the war, but permitted them to be incorporated into the Prussian army at the request of the song-loving King Frederick William III. They were assigned as a "choir" to the First Guard Regiment stationed in Potsdam. After the death of Czar Alexander, the king founded the Colony Alexandrowka in 1826 for the surviving twelve choir members as an "enduring memorial of the bonds of friendship" that had existed between him and the czar. Each of the singers received a wooden house with a small vegetable garden. On a nearby hill called "Mine Hill" (in 1753 a powder mine for use in sieges had been tested on the hill), a chapel for the Orthodox faith was erected. Since that time, the hill has been called "Chapel Hill."

Close to the Russian Colony was the Bornstedter Feld, training ground for the Potsdam garrison. From one of our walks I still remember seeing a regiment of hussars on a galloping charge, enveloped in a cloud of dust, with lances tilted at an imaginary foe. The cavalry in those days was still trained in accordance with the military tradition of past centuries.

Situated south of the Bornstedter Feld was the Jägertor (Hunter's Gate), terminal station of a line of the "Potsdam Horse Tramway" established in 1880. We always watched with fascination when the car was turned around on its axle at the end of the line for its next run back to town. The line linked the Jägertor with the railroad station. At the intersection with Brandenburg street, one of the principal thoroughfares, the Jägertor line met the main line of the tram. Its cars were drawn by two trotting horses. They would approach the intersection with bells ringing in order to gain the right of way. Because of an incline in the street and the single horse pulling the car, the secondary line from Jägertor was forced to move slowly and to apply the brakes frequently. (In 1907, the horses were replaced by electric power.)

From our house we could easily reach the "New Garden," a beautiful park on the shores of a lake and one of the preferred goals of our walks. The name had been given to the park to distinguish it from the "Old Garden," the park of Sanssouci castle, summer residence of Frederick the Great. His nephew, King Frederick William II, had the New Garden laid out in 1786 in accordance with the rules of English landscape gardening. They had been developed in the reign of George II when "a growing delight in natural scenery ended the vogue of formal gardens, with their statuettes and yew hedges clipped into fantastic shapes." Shrubs, trees, lawns, and open spaces were arranged in such a manner as to combine the imitation of untamed nature with picturesque views.

In 1906, the German crown prince with his family stayed at the "Marble Palace" situated in the midst of the New Garden. While the royal family was present, the park was closed to the public, either entirely or in part. When the garden was closed only partly, chains were strung across the entrance to some roads or there was a soldier on guard. There was an aura of mystery about these obstructions. I wondered what might lie hidden behind them, what the bend in the road might hold. On one occasion the doubt was removed. A motor car came around the bend—one of those early vintage models with a body shaped like a bathtub high up on spoked wheels. A liveried chauffeur and a footman sat stiffly in front. In the back sat the crown prince, relaxed, the forefinger of his right hand lightly touching the visor of his white cuirassier's cap while we, at the urging of our governess, took off our sailor hats and made a deep bow.

Among the memories of my childhood in Potsdam is a visit to my granduncle, Oswald von Richthofen, brother of my paternal grandmother. He was, at the time, the secretary of state for foreign affairs. His official residence in Berlin was "the Villa," a large mansion in a park behind the Wilhelmstrasse.

I still retain the picture of my granduncle as he greeted us in the vestibule of the villa, clad in a black morning coat, his kindly eyes shielded by a pince-nez. After he had looked us over he retired to his study, leaving us to roam in the park and play with his dog—a friendly boxer fond of children. We had been met at the Potsdam railroad station in Berlin by a coach drawn by two horses. The glass marquee above the entrance was the first thing that caught my eye as the coach turned into the driveway of the villa. From that time on a marquee represented to me dignity and distinction.

More than a generation later I attended a meeting in the Foreign Office of the Federal Republic of Germany in Bonn as a representative of the American Embassy. The walls of the conference room were lined with pictures of all foreign secretaries from the middle of the nineteenth century up to the present. When I turned to see the pictures on the wall behind me, I noticed that I was sitting directly underneath the picture of my granduncle. He was portrayed in the same posture that I remembered from my childhood. This unforeseen meeting with the image of my granduncle made me realize what I had in common with him: the role of a diplomat striving to settle differences between nations by finding compromise solutions that would lead to an orderly and peaceful coexistence.

With its palaces and other signs of royal presence, Potsdam provided monarchical representation on a grand scale. We experienced a similar yet more modest spectacle, still typical of the time, in Neuwied-on-the-Rhine where my father had been transferred in 1906 to become the executive (*Landrat*) of Neuwied county.

The city was the residence of the prince of Wied and, as Goethe in his play *Torquato Tasso* had said of the city of Ferrara, it had become "great through its princes." In the Middle Ages a place called Langendorf was situated a short distance upstream from present-day Neuwied. During the Thirty Years War the town served as a bridgehead for various armies and in the process was almost totally destroyed. Five years after the Peace of Westphalia in 1648, Count Frederic of Wied, territorial sovereign of the region, "by leave of the emperor" founded the town of Neuwied not far from the ruined Langendorf. The town was laid out on a chessboard plan with wide streets. It was to be a sanctuary for all established and tolerated religious faiths.

The guarantee of religious freedom attracted followers of different faiths to the new town. In other territories princes made use of the right conferred on them by the 1555 Religious Peace of Augsburg to determine the religion of their subjects. People in Neuwied, however, whether they were Lutherans, Reformed Protestants, Catholics, Jews, Moravian Brethren, or Mennonites, lived peacefully together under the protection of the counts (after 1784, the princes) of Wied. The Mennonites were even allowed to build a small steeple on their house of worship, a privilege that was not granted them elsewhere. I grew up with my brothers and

my sister in an atmosphere of religious tolerance; with us it was a
matter of course that people adhered to different creeds.

Under the terms of the Final Act of the Congress of Vienna
of 1815, the Rhineland and along with it the Principality of Wied
were attached to Prussia. Because of his loyal attitude towards his
new overlord, the prince of Wied received special consideration.
By treaty with Prussia, he retained certain sovereign rights in
the fields of police and municipal affairs; the administration
of schools and church matters remained exclusively within his
domain.

At first the prince exercised these rights through his own
officials.   In 1849, because of jurisdictional conflicts with the
Prussian authorities, he discontinued the practice; the Neuwied
Landrat was named also head of the princely government. Thus,
when my father became *Landrat* in Neuwied, he acquired at the
same time the position of a princely official. Upon assuming his
post in Neuwied, his first duty was to pay his respects to his
princely master.   In 1919, when my father was transferred to
Berlin, the prince thanked him for his "efforts in performing the
police functions in the county of Wied." A law of 1920 abrogated
the prerogatives of the nobility; it also annulled the treaty of 1815
between Prussia and the House of Wied and thus did away with
this fanciful remnant of another era.

The Wieds appeared on the stage of international politics
in a short, dramatic episode.   At the end of the Balkan Wars
of 1912-13, most of the European possessions of Turkey were
distributed among the victorious Balkan states.   In the Peace
Treaty of Bucharest of August 10, 1913, the Great Powers
created the independent Principality of Albania. In November of
1913, Prince William of Wied, younger brother of the reigning
prince, was chosen by the Powers to be the ruler (*Mbret*) of
the new state—not without some prodding on the part of Queen
Elisabeth of Rumania.   A princess of Wied, she was known
in the literary world as a poet under the pen name of Carmen
Sylva.   To her it was obviously a pleasing thought to have a
close relative on a neighboring Balkan throne.   Count Czernin,
once Austro-Hungarian envoy to Bucharest and later minister of
foreign affairs of the Dual Monarchy, wrote in his *Memoirs* that
for the queen "in politics, next to King Carol, nothing mattered

Neuwied on the Rhine

5. Prince Wilhelm zu Wied with his Family

6. The Albanian Delegation with Prince Wilhelm
and Princess Sophie zu Wied in front of the
Princely Palace (February 1914)

7. The "Mbret" of Albania Prince Wilhelm zu Wied (1914)

except Albania." In a sentimental poem set to music by the Wied house composer August Bungert and entitled "Albanian Coronation March," the queen extolled the accession of her thirty-eight-year-old nephew to the Albanian throne. "Fairy land yearns for a king. . . ." I still can hear the solemn tune when I recall the first line of this long-forgotten hymn.

On February 21, 1914, a delegation of representatives of eighteen Albanian regions headed by General Essad Pasha appeared in Neuwied to offer the crown and throne of Albania to the prince on behalf of the Albanian people. Thus, for a brief moment in history, world attention focused on Neuwied. The whole town turned out to watch the arrival of the Albanian delegation. People stood several rows deep along the streets which were festooned with flags and garlands. I myself had found a precarious foothold in a dense crowd on the square in front of the railroad station where the cameramen of the German and international press had taken up positions. In a convoy of seven equipages drawn by magnificent horses from the princely stables, the delegates were escorted from the railroad station to the palace. There they were led to the ornate reception hall where the acceptance ceremony was conducted in an atmosphere of proud expectation.

At their departure the next day—a Sunday—the royal couple and their children were given a jubilant send-off. Clubs and societies had their members line the streets; a triumphal arch at the railroad station was illuminated by numerous electrical bulbs. Firefighters carried lighted torches.

The embarkation of the prince and his family in Trieste on March 4 took place under similar festive circumstances. The prince received a twenty-one-gun salute while large crowds gathered at the quay. The scene of joyful elation was repeated when the new sovereign was received at his residence in Durazzo. Albania had finally been freed from Turkish domination and seemed to be united in its enthusiasm for the prince as guarantor of a better future.

The festive overture was soon followed by a bloody drama. Unrest broke out among the Serbs and the Greeks in the north and south of the country. The weak police force was unable to cope with the disturbances. Though he had sworn allegiance to his new master in Neuwied palace, Essad Pascha conspired against the prince.   Neither the personal intercession of the prince—at the risk of his own life, he rode several times into the camps of insurgents to negotiate—nor the contingents of foreign volunteers helped to turn the tide.   With the outbreak of World War I in August of 1914, his situation became untenable.   The Great Powers which had created and collectively guaranteed the independent statehood of Albania were themselves at war with each other.   The prince waited in vain for the promised support. After a five-month reign, William I of Albania resigned, reserving all his rights.   At the beginning of September 1914 he left the country losing most of his personal belongings.   Albania drifted toward anarchy.   The land was left defenseless against incursions from abroad.   Italy seized Valona, Greece occupied northern Epirus, and Montenegro captured northern Albania.

I met the prince in later years in Neuwied and had discussions with him.   Although he had reserved his rights to the Albanian throne, he had no illusions as to his ability to return.   His wife died in 1936.   He himself lived for some time in Munich. In 1945, he died in Rumania under unknown circumstances.   He had moved to Rumania since the Wieds, through their relationship with Queen Elisabeth, had some property there.

We had been friends with his children.   Princess Marie Eleonora, known to us mainly by her nickname "Manina," was born in Potsdam in 1909, and her brother Viktor, in 1913.   In 1934, I saw the princess once again in Berlin.   It was shortly before my emigration to America.   She felt much sympathy with my plight.   Because of an outstanding academic record, she had won an American scholarship in 1932 and had spent several semesters at Oberlin College in Ohio.   She gave me letters of introduction to friends in the States.

After the death of her husband in 1941, the princess moved to Rumania to live with her father.   She was in Rumania when the Communists took over after the war and there she met a tragic fate.

Her attempt to escape to the West with British and Rumanian friends was betrayed.   The group was arrested.   In the spring of 1950, Manina was convicted of "espionage and sabotage for the West" by a kangaroo court and was sentenced to fifteen years of hard labor. After years of confinement under *Gulag*-type conditions and a slow physical decline, lacking bare necessities, Manina eventually succumbed to disease and died in 1956. The news of her death reached her relatives in Germany only after a delay of many months. On Good Friday in 1957, together with relatives and friends, I attended a memorial service in the Evangelical church of Neuwied. At the end of the service, while the church bells tolled, the pastor stood at the altar and slowly recounted the elemental data of her life.

Princess Manina possessed the engaging qualities that distinguished the female members of the Wied family; she had a profound interest in people, their characters and fates; she was sensitive and compassionate and showed graceful courtesy and consideration. "No better upbringing (*Kinderstube*) can be imagined than existed in the Wied family," Marie von Bunsen, a close friend of the family, wrote in her *Memoirs*.

Princess Luise, sister of William of Albania, embodied these qualities to the highest degree. We had known her since childhood. In winter-time we had often seen her at concerts, a tall figure dressed in white, a long scarf around her neck, her dark hair swept up into a crown. She entered the concert hall in the company of her sister Elisabeth who was paralyzed and had been confined to a wheelchair since girlhood. The musical interests of the two princesses drew ranking artists to Neuwied each year; among them were singers of the caliber of Sigrid Onegin and Lula Mysz-Gmeiner, the famous Rosé quartet, and the pianist and Beethoven interpreter Elly Ney. It was through these concerts that our tastes in music were formed.

Queen Luise of Prussia (1776-1810) was one of the great-grandmothers of the princesses. Her grace and beauty are preserved in a statue of her and her sister Friederike Wilhelmine by J. G. Schadow. Anyone who looked at Princess Luise was struck by her resemblance to the marble image of her ancestress.

Princess Elisabeth impressed people with her cheerfulness, her consideration and care for others, and her lively interest in the fine arts. Writing required special efforts and probably caused her pain. Shortly before I left Germany in 1934, my mother received a long, hand-written letter from the princess. She wrote that she had learned of my departure. She and her sister Luise were saying good-bye to me with a heavy heart. Her death in 1937 saved her from witnessing the Second World War and the total ruin of Germany.

I saw Princess Luise for the last time one year before her death (1965). Much of the old splendor of her residence, the Villa Monrepos at the rim of the Westerwald hills overlooking the valley of the Rhine, was gone. The garden in front of the terrace was overgrown. But the talk was as lively as ever. Presidential elections in the United States were soon to be held. The questions she asked in this connection showed how well informed she was about current events. Age had hardly changed her. She still presented the noble appearance we had known from childhood, and her bearing reflected gentility and kindliness in the best tradition of her family. A year later I joined a procession of mourners to the woodland cemetery where, together with other members of her family, she found her final resting place.

My Father

County Executive *(Landrat)*

Some of the splendor of the former sovereignty of the princes of Wied survived in the ceremonial glitter of the princely court. As the living embodiment of local history, the House of Wied occupied an honorable position based on loyalty and respect in the public life of town and county. Yet real political power resided in the "Royal Prussian *Landrat*."

The *Landrat* was both the representative of the central state government and the executive of the county, a self-governing public corporation. In this dual capacity, he was responsible for the security interests of the state and at the same time was the manager of the business interests of the county. This included the building and operation of hospitals, road construction, public transportation and public utilities (water, electricity). The administration of the economic activities of the county required managerial skills. In this respect, the *Landrat* differed from ordinary civil servants who were part of a hierarchy and subject to instructions. When, in later years, I attended meetings of *Landräte* where common problems were discussed, they impressed me as a special breed of men. They exuded self-confidence and independence. They were conscious of the fact that as executives of a self-governing body they carried special responsibilities toward the people whose confidence was essential for the conduct of their affairs. As state officials they were appointed by the king. However, the *Kreistag*, the elected representation of the county, had the right to propose candidates for the office. Thus, appointments were provisional and could become final only after the *Kreistag* had made use of its privilege. The *Kreistag* could also waive the exercise of this privilege. This happened in the case of my father. He was provisionally appointed *Landrat* on April 1, 1906, and took office after the *Kreistag*, by unanimous vote of August 13, had requested that the king appoint "the present holder of the office" as "Royal *Landrat* of the county of Neuwied" without nominating another candidate.

In the combination of state government with self-government of the county, an amalgam of authoritarian and democratic elements, lay the strength of the institution of the *Landrat*. The smooth operation of the administrative machinery at the county level made Prussia one of the best administered states in Europe.

In 1906, when we moved to Neuwied, there was neither an office building for the county government nor an official residence for the *Landrat*. Since 1851, when a member of the old established and highly respected family von Runkel had been appointed *Landrat* of the county of Neuwied, the baronial mansion of the Runkel family, called Haus Heddesdorf, had served both as office building for the county and as home for the *Landrat* and his family. The son had followed the father. This almost dynastic succession, coupled with the physical connection of the administrative apparatus of the county with Haus Heddesdorf, made the county appear to be a possession of the Runkel family. When my father replaced the last *Landrat* of the Runkel family, he became the first Neuwied *Landrat* who did not hail from the Rhineland. Perhaps for this reason *Landrat* von Runkel, upon his retirement, did not dissociate himself entirely from the affairs of the county. He had himself elected to the *Kreistag* in order to keep a watchful eye on that "stranger" from the eastern, primarily agricultural part of Prussia. Such a man would be unfamiliar with conditions in the industrial Prussian West, and as a consequence he and his family would have difficulties adjusting. In this, however, he was mistaken. My parents, although reared in Berlin and in the East, were soon on the best of terms with the people both in the city and the county of Neuwied.

The county administration had lost its seat with the resignation of *Landrat* von Runkel. This finally led to the construction of a county office building. It was completed in 1908. During the intervening years, the county administration used office space in rented private houses.

A spacious residence for the *Landrat* and his family was attached to the office building. I still remember the much-anticipated day when we were taken to see our new home for the first time. We were shown small black switches near the

Neuwied on the Rhine

8. My Father, the County Executive (*Landrat*) with his Family (1908)

Neuwied on the Rhine

9. Haus Heddesdorf, from 1851-1906 Residence and Office Building of the County Executive

10. 1908: The New Residence of the County Executive and County Office Building

doors of the rooms. Turning the switch would, as if by magic, produce dazzling brightness. The light sources in the house where we had previously lived had been gas and petrol lamps. To light them one needed matches, an article not available to children. Here we were able, without the help of grownups, to produce light ourselves—a miracle. Of all the wondrous things I was to encounter in later life, the electrical switches in my parental home, so far as my capacity for wonderment is concerned, belong to the enduring memories of my life. Since then man has gone to the Moon.

From newspaper articles and letters my father received upon leaving Neuwied in 1919 it became evident that the skepticism first felt toward the "Prussian official from Potsdam" had turned, in the course of the years, into a relationship of mutual trust. The confidence my father enjoyed among the people did not wane even during the trying war years of 1915-1918 when he had to carry out unpopular measures of the war economy, in particular enforce the distribution of food from rural areas to industrial centers. One newspaper wrote that by delivering food as ordered, the farmers not only did their duty toward the country but also discharged a debt of gratitude they owed my father for his years of devoted service in the interest of the farming population. From the wine-growing village of Leutesdorf whose products are now highly valued by connoisseurs came thanks "for the concern the *Landrat* had shared with the vintners and their problems. For years they had been struggling for their existence, but now they find themselves in excellent shape."

Neuwied on the Rhine

11. Prince Friedrich zu Wied (Back View) Arrives for the Inauguration of the County Office Building (1908)

Humanistic Education

The development of mind and character through learning began even before we entered school with "Fröbel lessons" (now known as kindergarten, but at the time not yet generally accepted as a mode of education). Under the guidance of our female tutor we modeled objects and figures from molding clay, wove designs by threading paper strips with folding needles through perforated sheets of multi-colored glazed paper, and did other handicrafts in accordance with the ideas of the educational reformer Friedrich Fröbel (1782-1852). Far ahead of his time, Fröbel had realized that in order to enhance man's creative powers, the "ultimate source of all culture," the mental faculties must be developed in early chilhood. He invented games and occupational materials designed to stimulate creativity and to meet the child's urge to be active.

After a short period of private instruction and one year of grammar school, I entered the *Gymnasium*, the German pre-college high school providing humanistic education. It was a proud day when I wore, for the first time, the black velvet cap of the *Sexta*, the lowest grade of the nine-year course of study.

The caps of each grade had their own distinctive colors. Black was followed by the sky-blue of the *Quinta*. Burgundy-red was the color of the next grade. Then came the two *Tertia*-caps in vermilion with silver and gold stripes to distinguish between the lower and upper grades. The dark-green cap of the two *Secunda*-classes was similarly trimmed, and the same held true for the white silken caps, the much-coveted and highly respected emblem of the top grade, the *Prima*. The yearly change of caps was as important to us as the advancement to the next higher grade.

The Neuwied *Gymnasium*, which offered nine years of Latin and seven years of Greek, provided the type of classical education then common in Prussia. Graduation from the *Gymnasium* conferred the right to enter a university.

Attached to the Neuwied *Gymnasium* was a second type of school called *Realprogymnasium*. It offered a six-year course of

mathematics, science and modern languages. It did not include
the three highest grades of the *Gymnasium* but stopped at the
lower fifth grade. (This education, incidentally, entitled the
successful student to omit one year of the two-year term of
compulsory military service.)

During the first three years both schools provided the same
curriculum, with Latin obligatory in both. In the fourth year
the two tracks separated and Greek became obligatory in the
Gymnasium. It was up to the individual student to state his
preference for one or the other school. With this choice the
student made a fateful decision; his future life might depend on
it. For many pupils who at the age of thirteen or fourteen
did not yet have a clear perception as to what they might
wish to accomplish in life, as well as for parents and teachers
to whom they turned for advice, the choice was not an easy
one. Classical education in those days was considered to have
more social prestige than the study of mathematics, sciences
and technical matters. A false assessment of a student's real
abilities, uncertainty as to the desired trade or profession and
considerations of prestige may have caused a student to embark
upon a battle with Greek grammar only to find out when it was
too late that the *Realgymnasium*, though less glamorous, would
have been better adapted to his faculties and talents.

For me the choice of classical studies was a foregone
conclusion. I merely followed family tradition and my own
inclination since early youth to become a public servant. This
choice required the study of law and hence a firm grounding
in Latin and Greek. Such utilitarian reasons aside, I felt that
learning Greek was exciting in itself. It meant starting at the
bottom with a new alphabet and new sounds before the spiritual
world of the Greeks would unfold.

Access to the poets and thinkers of antiquity was possible
only by plowing through the arid land of grammar. No generation
of students has escaped this ordeal. Of course, knowledge of
grammar is an indispensable requisite for the study of languages,
but grammar also trains the mind. The scientist Friedrich von
Weizsäcker conceded that in later life he never used what he
learned in school about the *consecutio temporum* and that he
may have forgotten it in the course of his life. "But the

mental processes I needed to go through in order to perform these grammatical exercises, and the understanding of temporal relations I gained have entered my life and continue working in it even now."

Yet exercises in grammar did not stop when we advanced to reading texts. We did less reading than construing of sentences. The nexus between the sentences was lost and also the relation of the text to what it was meant to describe. The classroom treatment of Caesar's *Gallic War* is, in retrospect, a classic example of the type of instruction that puts emphasis on form rather than on substance: "In school Caesar is not a man or an author, but an assignment. His legions are not armies; they are lessons" (John Mason Brown). Only much later did I realize that in Caesar we meet one of the greatest minds in the history of mankind. The words we read might have been written in an officer's tent, in the palace of a legionary commander, or dictated while traveling in a coach. The deeds and events they record made world history.

What also prevented students from really enjoying the texts and their meaning was the learning of vocabulary in a pedantic, obtuse way. Our teacher started his Greek lesson while still on his way to the classroom door. He literally "called on" a student to recite the ten words he was supposed to have selected as part of his homework from a text discussed in class and challenged him to recite "a few more as the dessert."

The reading of the texts proceeded in the same strict, military manner. Again, while still outside the classroom, the teacher would order a wretched student to translate. Usually the victim was one of the less successful scholars. If the student had not translated at least a few sentences before the teacher had seated himself at the desk, he would be urged to "get on with it. . . . You ought to have finished by now. . . . Time passes, death advances."

The teacher who spoke thus was the type of the "Prussian school monarch" not uncommon in those days. His appearance alone commanded respect—a slim, almost gaunt figure with a white, closely cropped beard wearing a broad-rimmed black hat and an old-fashioned coat. This was the sight he presented when he rode his bicycle through town.

The desk on the dais of the classroom was his throne from which, like Olympic Zeus, he would hurl his bolts of lighting at the students below him.

Teachers with less authority often had their classes enlivened by youthful pranks—a time-honored occupation of students who are bored with school. I distinctly remember one because of its ingenuity. It consisted in fastening a violin string between the top of the student's desk and the movable seat. By plucking the string the student produced a wailing sound when the seat was moved up and down.

Greek lessons passed without such playfulness. There were, however, incidents of a different kind. One of the older students, having been wounded in the first days of World War I, returned to school. During his brief military service he had formed the habit of answering *Jawohl* (Yes, Sir). This irritated the teacher who thought such military expressions were out of place in a humanistic *Gymnasium*. "Don't always answer *Jawohl*," the student was told. "*Jawohl*," came the answer. The teacher, exasperated, quoted from a poem by Schiller: "Yes, war corrupts the best." This remark caused the gallant veteran to advance to the podium before the class was dismissed. The class watched with bated breath when he addressed the teacher: "I must ask you, Sir, to desist from insulting remarks of this kind in the future." - "I, desist? Who do you think you are?" The teacher pounded the desk with the palm of his hand. "This desk is mine . . . .has been mine for thirty years. I, desist?" He could say no more; indignation had made him speechless. His authority had been challenged in a way that was impardonable. The student's behavior had made it appear as if he and the teacher were equals. This was unheard of. Students and teachers had always been separated by a wide, unbridgeable gulf. The incident proved, however, that under the impact of war, times were changing.

The teaching of classical languages during my school days failed to evoke a feeling for their reality as a means of human communication; it lacked vividness and imagination. The mother tongue of modern languages, Latin, could have been presented as a language used by living human beings in their dealings with one another and not just as a language of writers, poets, philosophers and scholars. Only in later life did I realize how a work such as

Cicero's *Letters to Atticus* might have helped us gain insights into Roman life through a text that mirrored the spoken word of its time.

In the immediate vicinity of Neuwied the Roman past has left striking relics. In the depths of the Westerwald forest, north of Neuwied, there are visible remains of the *Limes Imperii Romani*, the fortified frontier of the Roman Empire which stretched from a point between Bad Hönningen and Rheinbrohl in the county of Neuwied over a distance of 330 miles up to the Danube near Regensburg. Since the construction of the *Limes* in about A.D. 90 the Neuwied Basin (the tub-like expansion of the valley of the Rhine between Andernach and Koblenz) had belonged to the Roman Empire. Among Roman finds in the museum of Neuwied are charred pieces of wood from one of the bridges on which Julius Caesar crossed the Rhine at Neuwied in 55 and 53 B.C.

The aim of our Latin teacher, Professor Goerbig, was to make use of this Roman heritage. He was himself an expert on the *Limes*; he had described it in a monograph. He took us on hikes to the *Limes* and on an excursion to the Saalburg, a reconstructed Roman fort in the Taunus mountains near Frankfurt, rich in Roman antiquities. In the environment of the Saalburg it was not difficult to imagine that in the dim past Latin sounds had been heard there: orders given to the soldiers, barracks talk, merchants peddling their wares, wives of the soldiers in the nearby civil settlement quarreling with their children. And young officers sneaking out of the camp in the evening for a tryst might have had on their lips a line or two from Horace which they had brought along in their intellectual baggage to this faraway outpost in the northern wilderness:

Lenesque sub noctem susurri conposita repetantur hora (When evening shades descend rejoice to your heart's content at the gentle whispers at the appointed hour).

"Whoever reads *Antigone* as a student and is given only grammar and metrics and chafes under this type of instruction can still be deeply stirred when a text from antiquity lies before him." Karl Jaspers' words seem to go to the heart of humanistic education. "Cramming" grammar and words, "construing" sentences, and "preparing" translations may have been of little use toward understanding the beauty and nobility of ancient texts.

And facility in reading classical authors was not necessarily achieved by tedious dissection of texts. Yet we gained access to the cultural heritage of the classics. Their ideals and their worldly wisdom left lasting impressions on us and became guiding stars in difficult situations in life. Carl Zuckmayer, the famous German dramatist—he had been persecuted by the Nazis and found refuge in America—in a speech in 1962 before students of his *alma mater*, the *Ostergymnasium* in Mainz, admonished the younger generation: "So long as we wish to maintain what appear to us the higher values of our earthly life—freedom of thought, of inquiry, of conscience—we can never forsake the spirit of humanism; nor can we do without humanistic education."

As the valedictorian of my graduating class I voiced similar thoughts in April of 1920 before the students, parents, and faculty. I mentioned the values which the study of the spiritual world of antiquity had given us and which had become the basis of our intellectual existence. In keeping with the times, my speech emphasized what Hölderlin had called "the mightiest of spiritual forces, the lion-like love of the country," (*"O du der Geisteskräfte gewaltigste, du löwenstarke Liebe des Vaterlands."*)

The question as to the usefulness of the study of classical languages is secondary when compared with the real significance of humanistic studies, namely, the formation of character. There are, however, also practical rewards: Latin promotes linguistic discipline and enhances the ability for grammatical expression. This is of particular importance to lawyers who must formulate their thoughts clearly and precisely and draft contracts or treaties in logical sequence. Furthermore, a person with a knowledge of Greek or Latin will have a better understanding of numerous foreign and borrowed words. Otherwise these words remain dead letters, empty concepts. A knowledge of Latin also facilitates the learning of modern Romance languages.

It is difficult to predict which of the things we learn in school will be of use to us in later life and which will turn out to be simply useless cargo. That a treasure of memorized material can literally save a life was proven by my friend Eduard von Schwartzkoppen. He had been a banker in Germany, and after World War II was incarcerated by the Soviets in an internment camp in the Soviet-occupied zone of Germany. (More about him later.) During his five years of confinement under inhuman conditions—as an innocent man, moreover—he saved himself from spiritual and physical decline by repeating to himself and reciting to his fellow-inmates everything he had ever learned by heart—passages from the Bible, poems, maxims. He only regretted that he had not memorized more in his youth!

Besides the classical languages, my major interests were German and history. I was less inclined toward mathematics and deplored the necessity to spend so much of my time on mathematical problems during my senior year. At this stage in the evolution of his mind a student has become fully conscious of his major interests. The most recent reforms of the German school system allow the student to choose his or her major subjects in accordance with ability and inclination in the two senior grades of the *Gymnasium*. This innovation seems to me eminently suitable to individual educational needs. A similar method of promoting intellectual independence and of furthering a scholarly approach to studies did not exist when I went to school.

A feature which distinguished the Neuwied *Gymnasium* from many other schools of its kind was the emphasis on physical training. In addition to the prescribed course of gymnastics we could join a students' rowing and gymnastics club. This voluntary association was founded in 1882, long before physical education had become mandatory in the curriculum of the school. For rowers, the Rhine was ideal for exercise and recreation.

Traffic on the Rhine was at that time only a fraction of what it is today. Now whole squadrons of barges navigate this "artery of Europe" day and night in both directions. The transport of goods before World War I was limited to barges towed in rows of six to seven by large paddle-wheel steam tugboats. From the worm's eye view of the rower these black giants with their high funnels belching thick black smoke (they have been used on the Rhine since about 1840) presented an almost primeval, somewhat menacing sight. A favorite sport (frowned upon by our elders) consisted of fastening our boat, usually a four-oar or six-oar, to the last barge in the row of those going upstream, letting ourselves be pulled for a stretch, disengaging the boat, jumping into the river and then trying to steer the boat ashore as it drifted downstream. At the landing point we would reembark and row the boat back, taking advantage of the upstream current along the shore. Such a maneuver would be unthinkable today considering the heavy traffic and the pollution of the river.

Special care was required with regard to the large rafts which were used to float tree-trunks from the Black Forest down the Rhine to Holland. They were like swimming islands. In the middle of the raft was a small wooden hut which served as quarters for the crew. The raft was steered by means of rudders placed on wooden blocks at the stern and stem of the raft. Swimmers and rowers were warned to stay clear of rafts lest they be sucked under.

Some of the older teachers looked askance at our rowing activities. Their concern was with the rowers' homework which was likely to suffer, especially in summertime. This, however, in no way affected the devotion of the students to their favorite sport.

It is appropriate at this point to pay tribute to a teacher who had nothing in common with the type of dry schoolmaster so prevalent among the school's faculty. Dr. Hermann Ottendorff had been an active supporter of student rowing at various schools before he was transferred at Easter 1910 to the Neuwied *Gymnasium.* He was an expert rower and soon became the mentor and trusted friend of the students' rowing club. He himself owned a rowboat which he used for excursions with his family on the Rhine and its tributaries. His colleagues thought this type of sporting activity, in oarsman's dress, of course, unbecoming to a teacher at a *Gymnasium.* Occasionally he would invite us to a picnic on one of the islands in the Rhine, Urmitz or Hammerstein, where we were the only living souls. In the seclusion of this untouched wilderness we felt free as nowhere else. We roamed through the island's jungle of brush and undergrowth like the Indians of whom we had read in J. F. Cooper's *Leatherstocking* novels.

A sportsman and a lover of unspoiled nature, Hermann Ottendorff was a teacher, friend, and comrade to the students. He despised and disregarded the spiritual and psychological barriers that separated teachers from students at that time. His popularity with the student body, not just with the rowers, alienated him from his colleagues; he was treated like an outsider. He did not regret leaving the *Gymnasium* when he was asked to become principal of a girls' college in Neuwied. But even in his new position he remained the beloved mentor of the students' rowing club.

His later career was quite unusual for a teacher at a *Gymnasium*, yet was in keeping with his personality and his interests. In 1920, he was appointed director of a state school of gymnastics. Under his administration, the school was greatly expanded and became an academy of physical training. In 1930, he was appointed ministerial counselor at the Prussian ministry for science, art and education in Berlin. Two years later he suffered a breakdown and shortly thereafter he died.

At my time the Neuwied *Gymnasium* offered no courses in music. The school had a students' choir which performed at festive occasions. I remember the celebration of the emperor's birthday in 1915 because of its tragic end. I was a member of the choir. As an introduction we sang Mozart's *Ave Verum*. The choir was conducted by the school principal, a sensitive musician. He had come to the school only a few years before and had given new life to the somewhat neglected choir. We followed his conducting with close attention. Suddenly he stood motionless, the baton limp in his hand. We continued singing a few bars—then he collapsed and fell to the ground - a heart attack had ended his life. At the funeral service a few days later we sang the entire *Ave Verum* in his memory, as we had practiced it with him.

1914: On to Paris

The month of July was one of the most eagerly awaited times of the year. Much of the month was spent rowing and swimming in the—still unpolluted—Rhine river. At the end of July came the annual "Foundation Festival" of the students' rowing and gymnastics club, a festivity in which the whole school and Neuwied's citizenry participated. On the day before the event, the gymnastic apparatus of the school was taken from the gym to Nodhausen, a park with a hotel on the outskirts of Neuwied. In the afternoon of the festival day, the members of the club, preceded by a band, marched in squads to the park to compete in athletic events. At the end of the contests, in the presence of a crowd of guests and onlookers, the victors were awarded wreaths with ribbons in the red-white-green colors of the club. There were three prizes for each squad of gymnasts. In the evening the club marched home, in a torchlight procession, again preceded by a band. Upon arrival at the schoolyard the torches were thrown onto a blazing pile to the accompaniment of the students' song *Gaudeamus igitur* (Let us be merry).

The festival marked the end of the summer semester. We knew by then where we would spend our summer vacation. We always hoped that our parents would choose a vacation spot far away from home, which would impress our schoolmates. Where to spend vacations was a subject of never-ending discussion.

In July of 1914, the mood was different. On June 28, Archduke Francis Ferdinand, heir apparent to the Austro-Hungarian throne, and his wife were the victims of a bomb attack while visiting Sarajevo, the capital of Bosnia. There was reason to suspect that the deed was the result of a conspiracy aimed at separating Bosnia from Austria and attaching it to the Serbian state. The crime seemed to implicate the Serbian government.

I learned about the assassination in downtown Neuwied where I had gone with my mother. "Have you heard?", an acquaintance shouted at us from the other side of the street, "the Austrian crown prince has been assassinated." The shock and excitement of the grownups were also communicated to us children.   Unknown forces seemed suddenly to have been unleashed. The cloudless serenity of the summer was shattered.

Because of the severity of the crime and its political motivation which threatened the integrity of the Dual Monarchy, a sharp reaction by the Austrian government was to be expected. But nobody thought that war was imminent.   Up to that point, the frequent international crises, in particular conflicts in the Balkans, had always been settled by diplomatic means without embroiling the European powers in war—and this despite all manner of tensions within the community of European states where nation was pitted against nation and feelings of mutual hatred were not uncommon.

Even we children were not immune from such emotions. We had learned in school and had read in books that France was the "hereditary enemy" of Germany.   Indeed, the Rhineland where we grew up seemed to offer proof that this was a correct interpretation of history: To this day vestiges are visible of the destruction inflicted upon Germany by the "Wars of Spoliation" of Louis XIV. There are remnants of the Napoleonic epoch when the left bank of the Rhine belonged to France.   There is the "Niederwald Monument" near Rüdesheim on the right bank of the Rhine.   The bronze statue of Germania holds the imperial crown in her right hand symbolizing the unification of Germany; it had been achieved after the defeat of France in the Franco-Prussian war of 1870-1871.   Yet despite nationalistic fervor and friction here as elsewhere, there was a general belief that peace in the heart of Europe was not seriously in jeopardy.

On July 7, 1914, the emperor embarked in Kiel upon his yearly voyage to Norwegian waters.   The fact that he did not cancel his trip was considered to be a sign that diplomacy would succeed, as it had so often in the past.

The public learned next to nothing of the frenzied and ultimately unsuccessful efforts of the European cabinets to limit the conflict to the relations between Vienna and Belgrade.   We were therefore utterly unprepared for the dramatic events which followed each other in rapid succession at the end of July, and which culminated in catastrophe.

On July 25, from 6:00 p.m.   on—the hour at which the Austrian ultimatum to Serbia was to expire—my brothers, some friends and I stood in front of the house on Engerser Strasse where the hometown newspaper, the *Neuwieder Zeitung*, was published. After a short wait, a news editor appeared. He fastened a handwritten note to the wall. It stated (with a question mark) that Serbia had accepted all demands of the Austrian ultimatum. (In fact, the Austrian ambassador had rejected the Serbian reply as unsatisfactory, had announced the severance of diplomatic relations and had left Belgrade to return to Vienna.) Where did this optimistic but bogus message come from? Was it given out to the world because everybody expected this outcome? We don't know. But in retrospect it almost appears that the message of a peaceful settlement of the crisis expressed the collective hope of mankind that peace would prevail.

Convinced that things had turned out all right, we went home. But restlessness drove us once more downtown in order to catch the latest news. In the meantime, reports of the ominous turn of events in Belgrade and Vienna had reached the newspaper.

What followed was a week of feverish and contradictory news.

The events which led to the outbreak of the First World War have long since become history and need not be repeated here. However, a "Chronicle of Events" from my diary shows how a twelve-year-old boy reacted to the turbulent last week of July. My grandmother had advised me to start writing a diary. She had lived through the wars of 1864, 1866, and 1870-1871 and thought that at a time when history was being made one should record daily events as one experienced them for one's own recollection and for the benefit of future generations. I owe it to my mother's care that these records have survived the vicissitudes of the time. They are witness to my thoughts and feelings in the days when the world became disjointed, never to return to the secure order in which we had grown up.

The most important event which I recorded during the last few critical days of July was an "extra" of the *Neuwieder Zeitung* of July 26 reporting the "outbreak of the war between Austria and Serbia" and the return of the emperor from his cruise; there were patriotic demonstrations in the school and rumors about the possibility of war with Russia. On July 28, I wrote that the situation had calmed down amid reports that England had made a proposal toward mediation (Sir Edward Grey had proposed to submit the dispute between Austria and Serbia to a conference of ambassadors to be convened in London). The next item I recorded was an "extra" which reported that Germany had rejected the British proposal. (As revealed after the war, the German chancellor, in a telegram to the British foreign secretary, had stated that Germany could not let her ally Austria-Hungary be summoned before a European tribunal to consider her conflict with Serbia.) Then came news about military preparations in France and Russia. On July 29, Russia affirmed her commitment to peace. "The situation eases," I noted. On July 30, new tension: Russia mobilized her forces in four military districts. (The report was one day late. Russia's partial mobilization had been ordered on July 29 when the newspapers still carried reports of Russia's peaceful intentions. General mobilization followed the next day.) At the same time I took note of a report that the British navy had been declared ready for war. The headlines read: "German fleet returns to port."—"Secret conferences in Berlin and Paris."

On Friday, July 31, we had moved the gymnastic apparatus from the school to Nodhausen in preparation for the annual founding festival of the rowing and gymnastics club scheduled for the next day. I was at home at noon when my father came down the veranda steps into the garden. He held a piece of paper in his hands. It was an "extra". My father read the headline to us: "The emperor proclaims a state of imminent danger of war."

This was a measure preceding mobilization. It had the effect of transferring executive power to the military, and of suspending individual constitutional rights. Article 68 of the constitution empowered the emperor to take such action in the event of an imminent threat to the security of the federal territory.

At the time I was not aware of the far-reaching legal implications of the imperial decree. But the message sounded like a flourish of trumpets. For the first time since the outbreak of the great crisis an official German announcement had used the word "war" to characterize the danger threatening Germany. Now we became aware of the seriousness of the situation. Nothing else seemed to matter any more. The founding festival and the subsequent regatta of boats on the Rhine were canceled. The gymnastic apparatus was returned to the gym.

On the next day, large posters all over town announced the mobilization of the armed forces. Following the preprinted words "The first day of mobilization is . . . ." an entry in blue pencil read: "the second of August," and so forth, until the sixth day of mobilization.

On Sunday, August 2, the *Neuwieder Zeitung* appeared as an "extra". Under the headline "Mobilization", in boldface type, the proclamation of the previous day was repeated. Included in the issue were a number of military orders as well as political news under the following headings: "World War Threatens."—"No Declaration of War Yet; Mobilization Merely a Measure of Internal Security."—"Convocation of Parliament."— "The First Shots. Hostilities Opened by the Russians."—"Russia Attacks the Territory of the Reich."—"General Mobilization in France."—"Will Japan Create Difficulties for Russia?"—"General Mobilization in Switzerland."—"Demonstrations of German-Americans." From Berlin came reports of patriotic enthusiasm: "Immense crowds are milling about in the streets." The emperor, in the uniform of the Garde-du-Corps, so the reports went, had arrived in the capital from Potsdam in an open automobile, riding along the boulevard Unter den Linden. From the balcony of the palace he addressed huge crowds that had gathered in a mood of jubilation and national pride in the square before him. "The sword has been forced into our hands. . . The war will exact heavy costs from us in terms of lives and property."

Reports from Berlin about "cheering and enthusiastic crowds" were not exaggerated. The whole country was in the grip of patriotic exuberance. After the tension and uncertainty of the past weeks, people felt tremendously relieved that the die had been cast. One could sense that the nation was on the move. People were seized with a feeling of solidarity and of common destiny regardless of class and social position. The emperor had judged the situation correctly when he proclaimed in his speech from the throne on August 4 that he "recognized no parties, only Germans."

We youngsters, too, were deeply stirred by the wave of patriotic fervor; it carried us beyond our daily routine and beyond ourselves. We felt that we belonged and that we shared a common state of exultation. I have never again experienced with such

intensity this feeling of freedom, of being uplifted, of merging
with everyone else under the impact of a cataclysmic event.

What did we know about war? For almost half a century
Europe had lived in peace. The older generation knew war only
as a series of short victorious campaigns. From history books
we had learned that war was equivalent to glorious battles and
brilliant victories. It would be the same this time. We all
expected a quick, decisive triumph; faith in victory was as firm as
a rock. "On to Paris" was written in white chalk on the military
trains which rolled through the station of Neuwied in endless
progression, by day and by night.

Since we owned bicycles, my brothers and I followed a
call for volunteers, and reported to city hall to be enrolled
as "messengers." We were given armbands in the national
colors, black-white-red, bearing the stamp of the city's police
chief. Filled with pride in our mission, we rode our bikes
through the town delivering draft notices, guiding soldiers to their
quarters, or carrying messages from one agency to another. Each
messenger had a fixed station where he was on call. I was
stationed at the military district headquarters. It was housed
in one of the most beautiful and historic buildings in town, the
former residence and workshop of the famous cabinetmaker David
Roentgen (1743-1807).

In the first half of August, the town was filled with reservists
who assembled waiting to be assigned to units and shipped to
their respective reception centers. They often marched in groups
through the town, singing. One song in particular remains in my
mind whenever I recall those days. It was sung over and over
again and went something like this:

> On, on to battle. To battle we were born,
> On, on to battle for the fatherland.
> To Emperor William we were sworn.
> To Emperor William we give our hand.

(Little did we know then that after four years of war this would
become the marching song of the revolution. In November of
1918, demonstrating workmen sang to the same tune: "To Rosa
Luxemburg we were sworn. To Rosa Luxemburg we give our
hand." The soldier's song about loyalty to the emperor had

been turned into a hymn extolling the leader of the revolutionary Socialists. Again, in 1981, I saw a Communist rally on television, and the same melody was heard.)

The entire population, including the young, was seized with excitement. Indicative of this emotional state was the fear of "spies"—foreign elements allegedly bent on espionage and sabotage.

There was a rumor abroad that the French were trying to smuggle gold to Russia, their ally, in automobiles traveling through Germany. On the evening of August 3, excited citizens of Neuwied stopped a car on the outskirts of the town. Immediately the news spread that an automobile laden with gold on its way from France to Russia had been captured together with four Frenchmen, two of them disguised as women. The captives, so the news indicated, were at this moment being marched through the town. I was just in time to join a crowd of adults and youths who followed the "French spies" as they were marched, arms raised, to the military district headquarters by a detachment of soldiers with fixed bayonets. Upon their arrival the soldiers disappeared with their charges behind the high iron gates of the courtyard.

The crowd refused to leave. They repeatedly demanded to be told what had been done to the spies. Eventually a young lieutenant appeared and announced: "The spies have been executed." Some in the crowd affirmed that they had heard the shots. Satisfied that swift justice had been meted out, the crowd dispersed.

What had really happened? It was the mayor of a Rhenish town on his way back from leave with his wife and friends who had been set upon near Neuwied by a crowd looking for "French gold automobiles." Luckily a military patrol was nearby and could take charge. It would have done no good to explain the true identity of the travelers. The rumor of the French gold automobiles, absurd though it was, transcended all reason because it conformed to the image of war and its unknown dangers. In all likelihood the crowd would not have been moved to leave if the absurdity of the accusations had been explained to them rationally. Rather, they felt justified in their righteous rage, and were reassured when they learned that corrective action had been taken without delay.

On the evening of August 8—we were just having supper—a platoon of nine soldiers of the 28th Infantry Regiment appeared at our front door. The corporal in charge presented my father with a written order from the military authorities assigning billets for his men in our house. Our pride at having real armed soldiers under our roof was somewhat tempered by the realization that our house was no longer immune from outside intrusion. The compulsory billeting of soldiers was the first tangible evidence that war had profoundly altered the legal status of the civilian population.

Pictures I took with a simple box camera show the soldiers in different poses: they are lying or standing in front of a blackboard on which I had written "In memory of our billet in Neuwied." They are wearing field-gray uniforms and full battle-dress, spiked helmets covered with field-gray cloth (the steel helmet was introduced only in 1916), the rifles with fixed bayonets. I snapped pictures of them in parade formation or ready for combat, exercises they had practiced innumerable times on the drill ground and which they were now showing off with discipline and precision as though they were about to be inspected by an officer. The serious faces of the young soldiers seemed to express a sense of exaltation at belonging to an army which, as regards equipment, training, and discipline, was second to none among the standing armies of the time.

One morning, about a week after their arrival, the platoon suddenly disappeared. In our imagination we saw our friends marching through France from victory to victory.

Hardly a month had passed after the departure of the soldiers when we were confronted with the reality of war. On August 26, we "messengers" were asked to take stretchers to the banks of the Rhine. A hospital ship with casualties was expected. That same evening I confided to my diary what I had witnessed during the day: "One of the wounded had his right eye shot out. Others were wounded in the head, the arms, the legs. All were bandaged and were transported as quickly as possible to the hospitals on stretchers, by car or ambulance. I was appalled. It was my first encounter with the horrors of the war. The crowd gathered around the wounded behaved very badly. Despite all their efforts, the accompanying medical personnel and the police were unable to keep the curious away from the cars and the ambulances."

Only a few weeks earlier we had seen the field-gray columns march through town in serried ranks, acclaimed as heroes and future victors—now they were lying on stretchers, alone, battered and maimed, unable to move, the objects of morbid curiosity. I would see more of these scenes in the years to come. In my junior year I joined the Corps of Red Cross Volunteers. Among our duties was the transporting of wounded soldiers from hospital trains to hospitals in town. In a letter dating from 1917 I wrote: "We were alerted at 7:00 a.m. to unload casualties. Ninety-one badly wounded men from Arras. They looked terrible. I can't describe it. I had to move the wounded in the train from one bed to another and then carry them outside to a car. Another group was waiting to transport the wounded to the hospitals."

In the same month that the first casualties arrived in Neuwied we also saw the "enemy" for the first time. One early morning we learned that a train with French prisoners of war would pass through Neuwied. We managed to take up position near the tracks when the train rolled by. We could not see the officers in the closed coach compartments at the head of the train. These were followed by freight cars with open doors where the soldiers stood or sat, dressed in red trousers and big-skirted dark blue coats buttoned back at the corners, with red kepis on their heads. This was the uniform of the French Army of 1870 as we knew it from pictures of the Franco-Prussian War. Was this not a clear sign that we would be victorious also this time? (Herman Stegeman, in his *History of the War*, vol.1, p. 88, writes about French preparedness for war: "The lack of a proper field uniform turned out to be a gross omission. The troops went to the front in their colorful uniforms, and with their bright red and blue offered targets that could be seen over long distances while the German field-gray made the man almost invisible.")

Prisoners of war were used for important construction work. I saw British and French prisoners of war at the construction sites of the Rhine railroad bridges at Engers and Unkel in the county of Neuwied. The bridges were built in 1917 in preparation for the spring offensive of 1918. The "Crown Prince Bridge" at Engers

still stands today and, now known as the "Urmitzer Brücke", it
serves the railroad traffic between Neuwied and Koblenz.

The "Ludendorff Bridge" which connected the banks of the
Rhine at Remagen and Unkel became famous in World War II
when the First American Army, advancing toward the Rhine in
early March 1945, came upon the bridge which was still standing
intact. Tanks and artillery were moved across the Rhine, and
a strong bridgehead was established, an operation which was of
decisive importance for the outcome of the war. By crossing the
Rhine at Remagen the Americans had breached the last barrier
of German resistance in the West. The Germans called the
American move across the Rhine "the disaster of Remagen."
What an irony of history that Allied prisoners of World War I,
through their labor at the Ludendorff Bridge, had handed their
future comrades of World War II a tool with which to forge
their victory. The bridge later collapsed under the weight of
tanks. Today only the stone towers on both banks of the river
are preserved. One of the towers on the Remagen side has been
turned into a museum, the "Ludendorff Bridge Peace Museum."
An inscription on the tower reads: "Built for War—Destroyed by
War—The Tower shall forever remind us: Here soldiers of two
great nations fought. Here heroes of both sides died."

In the wake of the rapid advance of the German armies
in August of 1914 in the West, the imperial headquarters had
been moved forward to Koblenz, which is situated close to
Neuwied. Thus it happened that I saw the emperor twice when
I accompanied my father on trips to Koblenz—once the emperor
together with the King of Bavaria, and the second time when
he and Chancellor von Bethmann-Hollweg emerged by car from
the electoral palace, the emperor's headquarters. For those of
us who had grown up in the monarchial tradition, the emperor
was the symbol of Germany's might and greatness, the apex of
the political hierarchy which parents and teachers had taught us
to honor and respect. The annual celebrations of the emperor's
birthday with uniforms, speeches, choral hymns and a large
children's afternoon party were the highlights of the year. Now,
the emperor, as "Supreme War Lord," embodied the deeds of the
victorious German armies. The close encounter with this exalted
person left a deep impression on my youthful mind.

In the months of August and September of 1914, we were inundated with special reports of continuous victories in the West and the East. We were greatly excited by the news that the cavalry of the army of General von Kluck had reached the outskirts of Paris and had caught sight of the towers of the city. Were things not turning out as expected? Whenever great victories were reported, flags were unfurled, church bells rang, and schools were dismissed. "The triumphant progress of the German armies from Lüttich to Reims held the German people spellbound and caused flags to be flown from every rooftop. One more audacious leap forward, one more mighty upswing—and the impossible would become reality: the powerful French army smashed, England's field army destroyed. Luck would be grasped by the forelock and held forever." Thus wrote Hermann Stegemann in his *History of the War*.

The palm of victory seemed within reach, but the hand stretched out to seize it faltered. The western front which stretched from the English Channel to the Swiss border froze into a dense system of trenches and field fortifications. In battles which lasted for years, both sides tried to regain strategic freedom of movement by expending masses of war matériel and by unheard-of human sacrifices.

The notes in my diary were based upon the situation reports from Supreme Headquarters. From them I can still recognize how we gradually became aware of the transition from a war of movement to trench warfare. In September of 1914 I noted that "a battle is in progress near Paris." The next day I wrote: "The French have been stopped. Our left flank, however, had to be taken back across the Marne in the face of superior French forces." During the following days "the gigantic battle in France continues unabated." September 18: "No final decision in France. The British and French have gained no further ground in the battle of the Marne." On September 20, the situation is "unchanged." Further notes on the "titanic struggle" are lacking for some time. On October 20, the surrender of Antwerp is announced. On December 1, a sentence appears for the first time in my notes which would one day become the title of one of the most successful books about the war: "All quiet on the western front."

In the eastern theater of war the fronts remained in a state of flux for a number of years. After the liberation of East Prussia from the much feared "Russian steamroller," the danger of a Russian invasion had been eliminated. By 1917, Russia had been beaten and had ceased being a belligerent.

For us in the Rhineland, interest in the war centered on events on the western front. Since the victorious advance in August of 1914, the war had moved into the distant land of the enemy. Nobody gave a thought to the possibility that things might have turned out quite differently. French war plans called for an offensive against the central part of the Rhineland. Had the French plan succeeded rather than the German "Schlieffen plan" (named after the Prussian chief of staff Count Alfred von Schlieffen, architect of the German war plan in the West), at the beginning of the war, Neuwied would have been in the middle of the war zone, and we would have met the fate of thousands upon thousands of Belgian and French civilians who were forced to flee their homes before the advancing German armies.

The reality of the fighting was brought home to us by news of relatives and friends wounded or fallen at the front and by the casualties that were evacuated to hospitals in Neuwied. The only tangible evidence we ever had of a direct military threat was a lone French war plane which appeared in the sky over Neuwied on July 26, 1915. A rather exaggerated fear of possible future air attacks—Neuwied presented no military target—caused the principal of the *Gymnasium* to devise a plan to protect us against such danger. In a test run, the entire student body was marched into the low-ceilinged cellar where coal was stored. Except for the small entrance and a narrow staircase there was no other access to the cellar, and no emergency exit. Had an air attack occurred and the school been hit, nobody—not even a mouse—would have escaped the inferno of burning coal and poisonous gases.

In March of 1916, standing on the hills surrounding Neuwied, we could hear a continuous dull rumble, like a distant thunderstorm, when westerly winds prevailed. What we heard was the cannon fire of one of the bloodiest battles in world history, when the Germans were trying to break through the French defenses at Verdun.

For a brief moment the war had approached to within earshot. The battle affected us personally when we learned that a popular teacher had been killed at Fort Douaumont. We were proud of him. German war propaganda played up the seizure of the fort as a heroic deed unparalleled in history which, in reality, it was not (see German Werth, *Verdun: Die Schlacht und der Mythos*, 1979).

For years we lived in the shadow or, better, under the protection of the western front. A feeling of security made life continue at an almost normal pace. At Christmas time we sent gift parcels to the soldiers at the front. Our parents did what they could within limited resources to surprise us with the traditional Christmas tree and gifts, after we had helped celebrate Christmas at local field hospitals. At Easter time there were report cards, moves to the next higher grade, and new caps. I was confirmed at the prescribed time, underwent an appendectomy, and was sent to recuperate on a farm in the country. We spent vacations by the Baltic Sea, in the Bavarian Alps and with relatives who owned a large estate east of Berlin. The latter experience was new to me.

It was in the second half of August 1918 that I went east. In July, a large-scale German offensive on the western front had failed. French and American forces had broken through the German lines on a 27-mile-long front. This was the turning point of the war. Any hope Germany might have had to end the war victoriously was gone. From August of 1918 on, the German armies in the West were in continuous retreat.

I do not recall that we were aware of the seriousness of the situation. No official announcements had warned us that Germany was about to lose the war. On the contrary, there were signs that the German Supreme Command still considered itself in full control of the situation. As if nothing had gone wrong, on August 28 the emperor celebrated the thirtieth anniversary of his accession to the throne at his headquarters in Spa, Belgium.

In the train on my way east I met a former schoolmate. He was a lieutenant and was returning to the front. When I told him that I was ashamed to be going on vacation while others like him had to face the harshness of war, he replied that the army was proud to have offered the civilian population a chance to lead a normal life.

While I felt reassured by his remark, it seems inconceivable to me, in retrospect, that I could have spent a carefree summer in the country with Germany's collapse only three months away.

The house of my relatives was a modest one-story manor of a type frequently seen on estates in the eastern provinces of Germany. From a central section two wings extended toward the village street. The arbored courtyard was separated from the street by an iron fence and a gate flanked by stone pillars. From a patio in the rear of the house stairs led to a park full of oaks and beech trees.

The bucolic atmosphere ended at the door of the house. A different world opened up inside. An ancient Greek vase stood in a niche of the white-painted vestibule, and glass cabinets in the living room contained small Greek artifacts.

The master of the house, Dr. Felix Busch, was deputy of the Prussian minister of finance at the time of my visit and, in the estimation of his colleagues, one of the most brilliant minds of Prussian officialdom. He and his wife, a daughter of the leading Berlin banker Ernst von Mendelssohn-Bartholdy, were both great lovers of Greek antiquity. Dr. Busch belonged to a group of friends which called itself the *Graeca*. In wintertime the group would meet weekly to read classical authors in the original and discuss their works. Its members included the Nestor of Greek classical philology, Ulrich von Wilamowitz-Moellendorf, "the most renowned philologist of imperial Germany."

I passed the days of my vacation hiking through pine woods fragrant with sweet scent from the summer heat, rowing and swimming in the "Great Büssow," a lake deep in the forest, and trying help out with the wheat harvest. I discovered a new landscape of forests, lakes, and fields that stretched endlessly toward the horizon—so different from the narrow confines of the Rhine valley.

Far removed from the theater of war, school proceeded at its time-honored pace. Interruptions occurred when the *Landrat* ordered a holiday because of a victory on the front, or when the school building could not be heated in winter because there was no coal.

Some subjects were not taught at all because of the lack of qualified teachers. To make up for it we received "war lessons", when the teacher discussed the political or military situation with the class, or when the students gave talks on what they had learned about the war. Activities in support of the war effort were popular with the students since they always took time away from classes. At Christmas time parcels were packed in school for the soldiers at the front. Flags were painted on wooden boards and then covered with nails; each nail cost a small amount of money which was to be donated to the Red Cross. In Berlin, on the Königsplatz in front of the *Reichstag* building, a 36-foot-high wooden statue of Field Marshall von Hindenburg served a similar purpose. Gold, silver, and iron nails were available which the buyer could drive into the statue for the benefit of the "National Endowment for the Dependents of Soldiers Killed in the War." During a visit to my grandmother's in the spring of 1918, I myself "nailed" the "Iron Hindenburg," as the Berliners called the wooden colossus. A holiday from school was granted to the class which had collected a certain number of gold coins. No parent could resist pressure on behalf of such a noble cause.

The inventiveness of the military to spur the flagging support for the war knew no bounds. In the early summer of 1918, the entire student body of the *Gymnasium* was dispatched into the woods "to gather leaves." We were told that the foliage was needed as fodder for the horses at the front. It was even said that the collection of leaves was essential for the success of the offensive in the West. Thus we plunged into shrubbery, stripped leaves from trees and branches with patriotic zeal and competed with each other for the weightiest load. We never learned what happened to our harvests. In a poem I contributed to the commemorative "Festschrift of the Graduating Class of 1920," I extolled this epic happening in the style of the *Odyssey*, in particular the scene where "in accordance with the inscrutable ways of the Olympic Gods," a group of college girls appeared in the woods (there was no coeducation in those days) to join the students of the *Gymnasium* in the heroic task of defoliation for the sake of the fatherland.

Toward the end of the war a Young Men's Defense Force was organized. Those among us who were close to being drafted for active duty received pre-military training from war veterans. They gave each of us a military cap, and instructed us in close order drill and in shooting the standard army rifle. During the last few months of the war we also had to join the National Auxiliary Service, whose main purpose was to supply a work force to farmers. Along with some classmates I was assigned to a farmer who owned fields in the outskirts of Neuwied. We pulled beet roots from the soil, laid them out in long lines and decapitated the tops with an axe. One of the helpers was a Russian prisoner of war. He talked incessantly about the "white bread" of his homeland, the Ukraine; like all of us he had to be satisfied with a gray bread of dubious quality.

The field where we worked was near a cemetery. An epidemic called the "Asiatic flu" was rampant at the time. After years of malnutrition, people were dying like flies. I still remember the sight of the horse-drawn vehicles bringing caskets to the cemetery. After discharging their load they hurried back to town for a new one. That sad spectacle lasted for hours.

What brought us into closest contact with the war was our "daily bread." On December 1, 1914, I noted in my diary that a law had been passed which required that potato flour be added when baking bread. "The British hope to starve us out. If their calculations are right, we may win many victories, but in the end we shall be forced to surrender." I added that it was now a patriotic duty to tighten one's belt and economize on bread. These remarks reflect the first effects of the so-called "Hunger Blockade." On November 2, 1914, Britain had declared the North Sea a war zone. Access of neutral shipping to neutral coastal areas was made subject to a complicated system of controls which were enforced by the mighty British navy. The British measures were in contravention of the London Declaration on Maritime Law of 1909. If the rules of the Declaration had been observed, Germany might have been able to meet some of her requirements for consumer goods—in particular, foodstuffs—through trade with neutral countries. The "undeclared" blockade of the sea lanes prevented this. Germany had to rely on her own resources, which were inadequate even in peacetime. The war emergency presented the authorities with tasks for which they were woefully unprepared. This was the hour of the ration card. The rationing of food (bread, meat, butter, eggs, milk, etc.) and food distribution by means of ration cards provided people with the essentials of life and prevented mass starvation. The control machinery was directed by a central authority, the Office of Food Production and Distribution. It issued direct orders to the governments of the individual states; they, in turn, acted through their subordinate agencies.

At the county level the *Landrat* was responsible for carrying out the control measures. This highly unpopular task demanded that the *Landrat* adhere strictly to regulations in his personal conduct. He and his family were "sitting in a glass house". In order to supplement their meagre rations people made trips, called *Hamsterfahrten* (hoarding trips), to farmers. They were against the law and obviously out of the question for us.

Still, the *Landrat* was not immune from suspicion. Rumor had it that the cellar of our house was filled with sausages and hams. My father eventually saw no other means of countering these malicious rumors than to insert a notice in the local paper inviting people to inspect the cellar, and to help themselves to whatever they might find there. This put an end to the rumormongering.

In the winter of 1916-1917, owing to the shortage of some basic foodstuffs, we had to subsist largely on turnips. Everybody who remembers the war years will always talk about the cruel "turnip winter." Among the privations caused by the war, however, the most difficult one to bear was the scarcity of bread. It taught us to honor bread as man's basic and most precious food. The respect for bread has accompanied us throughout our life. Every member of the family received one loaf of bread a week; it was his or her responsibility to use this allotment economically. We did this by marking the number of slices we could afford per day on the bread crust. In so doing we followed the example of our ancestor, the philosopher Moses Mendelssohn (1729-1786). In the years of his bitterest need after he had come to Berlin as a boy of fourteen, he marked his daily ration of bread with such lines. Those were the limits he must not exceed; otherwise he would have nothing to eat at the end of the week.

Similar procedures were applied to other rationed foodstuffs. The weekly butter ration was kept in a small earthenware jar with everyone's name on it. When butter ceased to be available, the jars were used for various *ersatz* spreads such as artificial honey and turnip jam. In 1918, I noted in my diary: "If only we still had our individual jars. Now the whole family is reduced to one jar. We are urged to take as little as possible from it." In March of 1917, I wrote: "We no longer cook our lunch. There is nothing to cook. Food is provided by 'war kitchens.' A bowl of soup and some vegetables cost 60 pfennig per person. On certain days there is even a bit of meat. We haven't seen potatoes for quite some time."

There were, however, mitigating factors. Our small garden yielded fruits and vegetables. For a while a goat was kept for milk. We went into the woods to collect beechnuts from which oil was extracted, and a variety of wild plants such as nettles were prepared as "spinach." There were other *ersatz* foods—for instance, "meat" made from plants, as we were told. Many of these wartime substitute foods, however, provided no nourishment at all. An attempt to grow our own potatoes on a piece of leased land had to be abandoned because the fruits of our labor accrued to others who arrived at the unprotected field before we did.

During almost the entire war, a ship of the Netherland Steamship Company plied the Rhine. Since the German *Köln-Düsseldorfer Dampfschiffahrts-Gesellschaft* had discontinued service, the Dutch boat offered the only opportunity to take a trip on the Rhine. What made such a trip particularly attractive was the possibility of getting a real breakfast with butter and cheese aboard ship. There were, however, restrictions. I believe one needed a special pass which only officials could obtain. My father once took me along on such a trip, ostensibly for official purposes. The two neutral countries, Holland and Switzerland, were the only outlets Germany had to the non-belligerent world. The Dutch Rhine ships formed a link between these two states and were probably also used for less innocuous purposes such as smuggling and espionage.

1917-1918: Peace—Freedom—Bread

While the German armies in the West had fought the Allies to a stalemate and in the East had conquered the enemy, there was movement on the domestic front. Under the impact of the hunger blockade which had weakened the will of the people to resist, and as a result of disappointed hopes for peace, there were signs of unrest pointing to political changes. In Germany, President Wilson's peace efforts since 1916 had stirred up an impassioned debate about the aims of the war. As a result, the Coalition of National Unity which had existed since August 1914 had fallen apart. On the one side were the "annexationists," led primarily by the Pan-German League. They demanded the incorporation of the industrial basin of Lorraine as well as an expansion of Germany's colonial possessions. They were opposed by advocates of a "peace of reconciliation without annexations and reparations" which the annexationists disparaged as a "peace of surrender."

On July 19, 1917, the *Reichstag*, declared itself in favor of a "peace of understanding and permanent reconciliation of nations." The resolution was supported by the Progressives, the Center party, and the Social Democrats.

With this resolution the *Reichstag* asserted a claim to a major role in domestic politics and with its initiative took the first step toward a constitutional system of parliamentary control. Under the existing constitution, the government headed by the chancellor was appointed by, and was responsible solely to, the emperor. The Supreme Command, represented by Generals von Hindenburg and Ludendorff, was opposed to yielding to parliament. In July they forced the resignation of Chancellor von Bethmann-Hollweg whom they suspected of collaborating with the *Reichstag*. His successor, Chancellor Georg Michaelis, was appointed by the emperor with the express approval of the Supreme Command. In a speech before the *Reichstag*, Michaelis, while ostensibly accepting the July resolution, added the words, "as I understand it." This reservation practically negated his support and enabled the government to follow whatever course of action it might choose. The uproar created by the chancellor's remark, and his subsequent failure to prove his charge of treason against the Independent Socialist party convinced the Supreme Command that the *Reichstag* and the opposition could no longer be ignored. Michaelis was dismissed. His successor was the Bavarian Prime Minister, Count Hertling; he was still appointed by the emperor without participation by the *Reichstag*. Yet, for the first time in history, he took into his cabinet as vice chancellor a leading member of parliament, Friedrich von Payer, a member of the Progressive party.

I considered the July resolution a cause for alarm, and tried to grasp its meaning and possible consequences. The days of August of 1914 were still very much on my mind. Then it had seemed a foregone conclusion that victory would be won, followed by a glorious peace which would enhance the might and greatness of Germany while "punishing" the enemies of Germany for their "treacherous attack." It seemed to me that the action of the *Reichstag* was a threat to these aims. The Allied statesmen, so I confided to my diary, had nothing but victory on their mind, and, in this respect, were in perfect harmony with their peoples. We, on the other hand, talked about "understanding and reconciliation" although we held the pawns for victory, Belgium, Rumania and Serbia, in our hands. The July resolution, in my estimation, indicated to the world that we were a divided nation, and would thus have the effect of prolonging the war.

The Social Democrats, as the strongest opposition party, had been the driving force in the coalition which adopted the resolution. I knew very little about them, and therefore delved into the literature about their history and programs. In a paper I wrote for my father about the position of the Socialists with regard to Germany's foreign policy, I concluded that the Socialists as representatives of the workers ought to support the concept of a powerful empire because it assured an enduring high standard of living.

The trend toward democratization made me think about the best form of government for Germany. Not only were forces within Germany pushing toward parliamentary democracy, but there were equally strong pressures from abroad. In his reply to the peace initiative of Pope Benedict XV of August 1, 1917, President Wilson had spoken of a split between the "irresponsible

German government" and the German people. Inherent in Wilson's reply, I thought, was the demand for eliminating a government allegedly at variance with the will of its people. I considered this an attack upon the institution of the monarchy and thus capable of undermining the very foundations of Germany's national identity. I wrote another paper for my father in defense of the monarchy, and stated that the crown was a symbol around which the nation could rally and which assured Germany a respected place in the world. My opposition to the trend toward democracy and to a parliamentary system arose from the political concepts with which I had grown up, and which were rooted in the traditional values of my family. I was therefore ill prepared for what was soon to confront me.

At the beginning of 1918, it was rumored that in the spring the German army would launch a strong offensive in the West that would bring victory. The prospects seemed to be highly favorable. After the defeat of Russia the main force of the eastern armies was available for a breakthrough on the western front.

The great battle in the West began in March of 1918. Once again the German army was filled with faith in victory. At home we shared their confidence in success, and started to read the news bulletins of the Supreme Command again.

The first German assault on the northern front succeeded in carrying the German forces far beyond the Allied front lines. At the beginning of April, however, the offensive was stopped. In May, in a renewed attack on the central front, the Germans advanced as far as Château-Thierry on the Marne, and, as they had done in 1914, threatened Paris. As a result of decisive intervention by American troops, the salient was cut off. In July further German advances in the vicinity of Reims were checked by the French in fortified rear positions. This was the turning point of the war. From then on the Allies went on the offensive. The German armies began to retreat to the Siegfried line and to other prepared positions in the rear.

At the beginning of October the vast scope of the catastrophe in the West became apparent to us at home. After four years of privations and sacrifices, defeat stared us in the face with frightening suddenness.

The slogan "Peace! Freedom! Bread!" had first been heard in 1917 during strikes in Berlin and other major cities. Now it became the rallying cry for the masses in their demand for an end to the war. I was shocked when I heard young men in the street shouting: "Let the big boys fight it out among themselves. Count us out. We have had enough." This, I felt, was the voice of revolt.

The hopeless military situation sharpened the domestic political crisis. On September 30, 1918, the emperor announced by imperial decree that "men enjoying the trust of the people shall participate to the fullest extent in the rights and duties of government." This fundamental declaration in support of parliamentarianism and democracy was followed on October 3 by the formation of a government under the chancellorship of Prince Max of Baden, known for his liberal views and as an early advocate of a conciliatory peace. Two government departments, Interior and Labor, were filled by a member of the Center and Social Democratic parties respectively. Otherwise, the majority parties (Social Democrats, Center party, and Progressives) were represented in the government by secretaries of state without portfolio, that is, without specific tasks and responsibilities. On October 5, the newly formed government presented itself to the *Reichstag*. The previous day it had asked President Wilson to begin the peace process and to arrange for an armistice. This step was taken at the urging of the Supreme Command, since further military resistance was considered futile.

From the subsequent exchange of notes between the American and German governments, it became apparent that Wilson wished to exert pressure towards a fundamental change in the German constitutional system before entering into negotiations. His reply to the papal peace initiative of 1917 had already foreshadowed this aim.

Although it was never clearly stated, it seemed to us that Wilson's primary purpose was the overthrow of the German monarchy. He was obsessed, so we thought, by the conviction that the German imperial government was autocratic, not subject to control, acting in secret, and therefore a danger to world peace that had to be eliminated. The German government viewed Wilson's pronouncements as interfering with Germany's internal affairs, and as incompatible with the right of self-determination.

The transformation of the governance of the German Reich to parliamentary rule needed to be sanctioned by a constitutional amendment. The amendatory process was already under way before the German government had approached the American president. On October 28, the *Reichstag* adopted legislation subjecting the Reich chancellor and his cabinet to parliamentary control. The *Reichstag* could force the chancellor to resign by a vote of nonconfidence. The political responsibility of the chancellor was extended to include the emperor's military command as well.

In several notes, the German government tried in vain to convince the American government of the fundamental change that had taken place in the German constitutional system, and of the democratic legitimation of the present government for armistice and peace negotiations. We followed the exchange of notes between the German and American governments with a feeling of exasperation bordering on frustration. (This is an account of personal memories. I am thus describing the situation as we perceived it at the time.) We asked ourselves what else had to happen in the field of German domestic politics in order that the negotiating process might begin. We thought that the American side made no effort to understand the changed situation in Germany, but stuck to a preconceived notion that their German counterparts were "military rulers" and "monarchial autocrats," representatives of arbitrary power who had to be removed before negotiations could begin. It seemed to us that no notice was taken of the repeated assurances of Dr. Wilhelm Solf, the newly appointed secretary of state for foreign affairs, namely, that a government was in power in Germany that was supported by the popular will.

The exchange of notes did not clarify whom the American government would consider acceptable on the German side to conduct negotiations. The authority of the German government, at any rate, had been severely weakened.

The new German constitution was modeled along the lines of the British parliamentary monarchy. It lasted only ten days. The revolution of November 9 wrecked this last attempt to preserve the traditional institutions of the German Reich. The most striking sign that the old order had disappeared was the abdication of the emperor and his flight to Holland on November 9, 1918.

The news hit us like a bomb shell. A vacuum was created. Faith in the authority with which we had grown up, and respect for the achievements of our forebears began to falter. What were the causes of this debacle? Had the roots of the old regime been in such a state of decay that it was incapable of withstanding the strains of war? Had the true condition of the constitutional system and the competence of the persons who ran it been concealed from us? As early as the end of 1918, memoirs of statesmen who had borne responsibility in the empire began to appear: Hammann, press spokesman of the foreign office; Karl Helfferich, secretary of the treasury and vice chancellor; von Jagow, secretary of state for foreign affairs; von Bethmann-Hollweg, Reich chancellor; von Tirpitz, chief of naval operations; Count Pourtalès, ambassador to Russia and others. Their accounts were largely self-serving and selective. The blame for mistakes always rested with others, never with the author of the memoirs. I read them all in quest of answers to troubling questions.

In Neuwied the revolution proceeded without violence in an almost civil manner. Throughout Germany local workers' and soldiers' councils had been formed as the centers of revolutionary power. The initiative for setting up such a council in Neuwied originated with the owner of a furniture store, a friendly elderly gentleman who had been known for years to be a member of the Social Democratic party. Together with some of his political cronies, he published a notice in the local press on November 11 stating that, "following the example of other cities," the administration of the city of Neuwied would be "subject to the control of the Provisional Workers' and Soldiers' Council." The citizens were cautioned to remain calm. "Don't let yourselves be provoked to reckless actions." Guards wearing white armbands had to be strictly obeyed. Parents and guardians were urgently requested to keep children off the street. The notice further announced that any breach of the peace would be severely punished. "What matters first of all is to protect the property of the citizens against theft and looting, and to maintain peace and order."

Much to the relief of the citizens, the mayor had stayed in office. He let it be known that the city administration would continue to function. It was only the "supervision" of the administration and of the police of the city which, "in agreement with the Provisional Workers' and Soldiers' Council," would pass to the council's permanent successor.

In the evolution of the new order, cooperation of the revolutionaries with established political parties was by no means excluded. As early as November 11, representatives of the Center and Liberal parties met in City Hall with the workers' and soldiers' council to form a "Committee of Public Welfare." Except for its name, the committee had nothing in common with the notorious *Comité de Salut Public* of the French Revolution. Its exact functions were not stated. At one time it signed an appeal for donations together with the workers' and soldiers' council. The committee was composed of an equal number of members of the Social Democratic party and two non-Socialist parties.

The social order of the country and the way of life on the local level were little affected, if at all, by the rise to power of revolutionary forces. Illustrative of the survival of customary standards of behavior was the manner in which a workers' and soldiers' council was established in a community of farmers and small industrial enterprises near Neuwied. As reported in the local press, at a meeting held "under the chairmanship of factory owner E. B. in the large hall of the . . . Inn and well attended by the citizens," it was resolved that "in each village and town of the district of Heddesdorf two representatives shall be elected who shall meet jointly to form a workers' and soldiers' council"—a democratic procedure hardly in conformity with the concepts then prevailing for setting up a revolutionary organization.

The revolution presented a different face when the county building was occupied one day by a detachment of sailors who had spearheaded the revolution throughout the country. They wore red armbands and had rifles slung over their shoulders, the barrels pointing downward. We spent many anxious hours when the sailors took my father in the official county car to an unknown destination. I no longer remember the purpose of this "abduction." It might have involved some action for which the sailors thought they needed the authority of the *Landrat*.

In fact, the administrative machinery continued to function because the professional civil servants everywhere were willing to cooperate with the powers that be. Such accommodation averted the collapse of order, and maintained respect for the law. This was all the more important since the economic blockade instituted by the Allies during the war remained in force even after the conclusion of the armistice. Only through strict adherence to the existing system of controls was it possible to assure an uninterrupted supply of food to the population. In rural areas there was a widespread belief that the revolution had done away with controls. This dangerous attitude caused my father to warn the general public that controls and observance of regulations were essential in order to ward off starvation.

The schools were early targets for revolutionary reforms. Among the first measures was the introduction of student government at the *Gymnasium*. Its primary aim was to bridge the gap between students and teachers, to abolish the traditional hierarchy of "above and below", to create an atmosphere of mutual trust through open dealings with one another, and to strengthen the self-reliance of the students.

From the third grade on, each class had to elect a class spokesman, a secretary, and a monitor. The class spokesman was responsible for discussing requests of the class or individual students with the teacher, and "was to maintain inside and outside the school a spirit of order, discipline and good morals." All class spokesmen jointly formed the "Students' Committee." The chairman of the committee (and thus the representative of the entire student body) was the spokesman of the ninth and final grade, an office to which I was elected by my schoolmates.

The committee adopted rules of procedure, conducted meetings in accordance with parliamentary proceedings, convened the entire student body on matters of general concern, and held discussion sessions.

In my opening statement at the first meeting of the committee I appealed to the sense of responsibility of my fellow-students in an effort to forestall tendencies among certain groups to turn the newly won freedom into a free-for-all of rule-breaking and rowdy behavior.

The establishment of a student government pursuing attainable goals prevented a radicalization of school activities as one of our schoolmates had envisaged. Because of his extremist views and rebellious attitude toward the teachers he had dropped out of school and had vanished—ostensibly to prepare for graduation through private studies. In December 1918, he suddenly reappeared as emissary of Dr. Gustaf Wyneken, cofounder of the "Wickersdorf Free School Community", a work and life companionship of students and teachers. Wyneken had been appointed by the Berlin revolutionary government as "State Commissioner for Western Germany" with the mandate to initiate reforms of the school system. Our friend, in particular, had been directed to see to it that a "Students' Council" was set up at the *Gymnasium* after the model of the council system that had become the form of political organization at all levels of government. The council was to have a say in all matters pertaining to the operation of the school, and was even to have the right to make decisions of its own, especially on questions of school discipline. For a while the young revolutionary had the run of the school; he browbeat the faculty and tried to spread his message by means of indoctrination sessions with the students. People were not yet ready to accept radically new educational concepts, however. Strong attacks in the local press upon his "subversive activities" forced the luckless would-be revolutionary to leave town without having achieved his mission.

Other attempts at interfering with the established school system proved to be political dynamite. Thus, the proposal to abolish mandatory religious education galvanized the Catholic Church. "We shall resist such efforts to the utmost" was the reaction among parents and clergy. Among their chorus of defiance were menacing voices which demanded "self-determination for the Rhineland", and even cried "Break away from Berlin!"

1918: Retreat

The political events of October and November had completely absorbed our thoughts and feelings. They were soon to lose significance with the imminent passage of German troops retreating from France through Neuwied, and the subsequent occupation of the Rhineland by the victorious Allies.

A first call for action in the face of this unprecedented situation came from our Latin teacher, Professor Goerbig. In his capacity as head of the "Association of Red Cross Volunteers" he issued an appeal for contributions: "Our heroic soldiers are coming home. Hundreds of thousands will pass through Neuwied within the next two weeks. Welcome them with open arms." He added that many trainloads of soldiers would have to be supplied with food. This reminded me of August 1914, when we had carried baskets full of sandwiches to the station, far in excess of what was actually needed; much of the food had spoiled in the summer heat.

Next came the task of preparing the population for the sight of a defeated German army in retreat. The Supreme Command was concerned lest it lose face in the public eye, and endeavored to soften the stark reality of military defeat. This was clearly the intent of an "Appeal to the People at Home" from the headquarters of Army Group Crown Prince. It was published in the Neuwied papers by the commanding general of the Eighth Corps in Koblenz, and countersigned by the workers' and soldiers' council. It read, in parts:

> Within a few days the forward divisions of our army will finally cross the frontier to return home. They will march through the towns with flags flying and to the beat of drums. These are the troops which, filled with unshakable faith and love for the fatherland, have endured the most harrowing hardships, have performed the most brilliant feats of heroism to shield our native soil from the scourge of the battlefield. It is now your responsibility to show them your gratitude for what they have done for you.

Everyone was urged to be at the service of the returning soldiers. "Post yourself at road intersections, give directions, show the soldiers their billets, illuminate the streets, grab the spokes of the wheels in the mountains when the horses are tired. . . . Keep order and protect the army against subversive and undisciplined elements. Stop gloom and dejection. Hold your heads high. Be proud of your army. Display flags as a welcoming sign for your heroes."

The appeal on behalf of the army was heeded. "To honor our heroes, Neuwied put on festive garb"—thus did the newspapers describe the manner in which the city welcomed the soldiers "returning home." While the general mood was not one of "frenzied rejoicing," the papers thought they should remind the people that "it is not the army in the field that bears responsibility for the collapse of Germany." In commentaries like these was born the legend of the "stab in the back." And the theme "unconquered in battle" (*Im Felde unbesiegt*) was to reverberate through German politics for years to come with disastrous consequences in the end.

Since the time of Caesar, armies of many nations have crossed the Rhine at Neuwied. The city was destined to play this role again in the drama that was about to unfold. "Between Weissenturm and Neuwied a bridge must be built to enable the army to cross the Rhine," the soldiers' council of Koblenz announced jointly with the *Landrat* on November 19. "Construction of the bridge is a matter of the highest priority if the harsh conditions of the Armistice are to met. Everyone knows how much compliance with the Armistice means to the fatherland. Workmen are needed." The people were asked to volunteer for the work in the national interest. Ten marks would be paid for a day's work, and free meals from army kitchens at the construction site were promised.

On November 26 the bridge was ready. The next day, the first contingents of soldiers—about 10,000 men—marched across the bridge. On the river bank where the soldiers entered the town, garlanded poles had been erected bearing signs with the inscription: "Welcome home." On the market place a military band played martial music.

The troops were the vanguard of the First Army retreating from France with 150,000 men and 60,000 horses. Its commander, General of Infantry von Eberhard, let it be known that he would be giving the orders within the area occupied by his army. He expected all military and civilian authorities to support him in maintaining order and peace. "The workers' and soldiers' councils will have to subordinate themselves to the military authorities. The wearing of red emblems is strictly prohibited."

I often stood on the river bank to watch the troops as they passed by, wearily, but in perfect military order. What a difference, I thought, from the days of August 1914. I still retained in my memory the image of the young soldiers fresh from the barracks, in their new field-gray uniforms, and their spiked helmets covered with field-gray cloth, carrying field packs and rifles on their backs, confident of the victory which previous historical experience had taught them to expect. After four years of fighting what was in the end a losing battle, the German soldiers were still a disciplined body of men, but their appearance showed the strain of endless marching; many wore just field caps and bore no arms. Heavily loaded covered wagons pulled by worn-out horses and dismounted cavalry units passed between the ranks of marching troops; horsedrawn howitzers rattled noisily over the wooden planks of the bridge. The lines were in constant motion, as if the marchers sensed the foe in pursuit, and knew the deadline for the evacuation of the Rhineland.

For a few days I was in bed with fever, suffering from the "Asiatic flu" that was rampant among the half-starved population. One morning a unit passed our house with the band playing the Prussian parade march. The tune has haunted me all my life whenever I think of the beaten German army passing through our town in the winter of 1918.

The county roads had not been built to sustain the massive weight of an army. The wheels of the wagons had left deep ruts in the roadways. One day my father took me on an inspection of the roads. It seemed inconceivable to me that an army could have made any headway under such conditions.

On December 6, the crossing of the Rhine by the First Army was completed. On the day before, General von Eberhard, on behalf of his army, had thanked the people of Neuwied for their efforts "to give his men a cheerful reception on their return home." The local press, for its part, gave the troops high marks for their "exemplary comradeship" and praised them for the "high morale" they had displayed. "It is with a heavy heart that we see them go. The last protective barrier has now been removed. . . . At the beginning of next week, Allied forces will enter our town." The last German soldiers to leave Neuwied were engineers charged with dismantling the Rhine bridge.

On his departure from the Rhine, General von Eberhard was reported to have thrown his sword into the river, a gesture reminiscent of a German heroic saga. He had received the sword as a gift from Empress Auguste Victoria in recognition of services he had rendered as a page in the imperial household while in military college.

The Americans on the Rhine

The city of Neuwied together with parts of the surrounding county belonged to the Koblenz bridgehead, which under the terms of the Armistice Agreement of November 11, 1918, was to be occupied by American troops.

The period between the retreat of the German army, and the entry of the Americans was used by the authorities to prepare the population for the "hard and trying times to follow."

The first order of business was the removal of all vestiges of the preceding weeks. Flags on the houses had to come down, garlands and decorations had to be taken away, weapons were to be surrendered. The collection point for weapons was the princely palace.

Political parties and the authorities issued instructions to the people on how to conduct themselves toward the occupation forces. They suggested "calm, restrained, dignified behavior." The *Landrat* appealed to the citizens "to face the foe with German pride." Only then could they expect to be treated with respect to which they were entitled considering the heroic deeds of the German army. "No flirting with the enemy," no "sycophancy." Such attitudes would only evoke contempt. In addition there was to be "no violence, nothing which might provoke the strangers. They come to us as victors. Show them that we are a people that stands for order."

From Trier where the Advance General Headquarters of the American Expeditionary Forces had been set up came the first reports about the Americans on their march into Germany.

"Correct behavior of the Americans," proclaimed a news item in the Neuwied press on December 7, 1918. This was followed by the account of a meeting between representatives of the Trier press with the chief of staff at the American headquarters. The chief of staff reportedly gave assurance that the American High Command wished to avoid any interference with the freedom of the press and the daily activities of the population. "Life should continue as though there were no occupation. The

American High Command expects the population, as heretofore, to conduct itself with dignity and without hostility."

On his return from Trier, a representative of the foreign office stated that the arrival of the Americans had caused no inconvenience to the civilian population. All Germans, from innkeepers to the man in the street, agreed that the conduct of the Americans had been above reproach. "Everything proceeds normally. American convoys are most considerate in not hampering ordinary traffic."

Among the officers at the American headquarters in Trier was John J. McCloy. Thirty years later, as United States High Commissioner for Germany, he was destined to play a decisive role in the reconstruction of Germany after the catastrophe of World War II.

On December 12, around 10 o'clock in the morning, about 15,000 men of American infantry and cavalry entered Koblenz, preceded by a military band. A German reporter who had watched the Americans was intrigued by the "odd" shape of their steel helmets, "round and flat like a bowl." The leather stirrups of the cavalrymen reminded him "of those of medieval knights."

In the afternoon of the same day, several American officers appeared at the Neuwied city hall to discuss details of the forthcoming occupation with city authorities. They announced that an American headquarters would be stationed in Neuwied. This meant that accommodations had to be provided for about 200 officers and 2,000 men. As a first step, a radio signal station was set up on the market square.

During the following days, motorized columns of divisions assigned to occupy the American bridgehead in the Westerwald passed through Neuwied. Personnel carriers with about fifty standing or sitting men drove through the town at considerable speed, and yet almost silently on their rubber tires. They were followed by heavy trucks, motorcycles with side-cars, officers' automobiles, ambulances, and signal corps vehicles. We experienced the spectacle of a motorized army—what a contrast to the German army with its endless lines of horse-drawn wagons and its soldiers marching on their wearisome retreat from France across the Rhine.

The Americans on the Rhine 1918

12. "The same flag of the United States that flew over the Rhine fortress of Ehrenbreitstein when it was the garrison flag of the U.S. 4th Division from 1918 to 1923 during the occupation following WW I, is again raised over the historic fortress in 1945."

13. John A. Lejeune Major General, United States Marine Corps
Commanding General, Second Division (Regular)

In the middle of December, Neuwied became the headquarters of the Second American Division. The insignia of the division, worn on the left upper arm of the uniform shirt, consisted of an Indian head on a white five-pointed star. The division is reputed to have been the foremost American division which stopped the German advance in June 1918 at Château-Thierry and thus saved Paris (see *The Second Division: American Expeditionary Forces, 1917-1919*, published by members of the division at Neuwied, Germany, February 1919). Its organizations included two regiments of Marines, regular infantry and artillery regiments, and engineers.

Commanding general of the division was John A. Lejeune, Major General, United States Marine Corps. I still remember the small, wiry figure of the general, as well as his springy gait as he stepped into his large eight-cylinder, beige-colored staff car. A Marine training camp in North Carolina bears his name to this day.

Among other units that occupied Neuwied for short periods of time was the 32nd Division from Wisconsin, a state which one day—though I did not know it then—would be my "home state."

With the arrival of the occupation troops, traffic became as heavy and hectic as in a big city. Military police with the red letters "MP" on black sleeve badges were posted at street intersections to regulate traffic with sweeping hand movements and signal whistles—a sight of never-ending fascination for us small-town people.

For every ninety inhabitants there was one American soldier. For the most part the troops were billeted in private homes. The German occupants were ordered to make room for the Americans, but were allowed to stay if this did not interfere with the needs of the military. There was no "anti-fraternization" policy; the soldiers were not forbidden to associate with the civilian population. They were merely warned not to become "familiar" with the people, and to use restraint in discussing politics.

Our school building had been seized and converted into barracks. The school principal, however, had been allowed to keep his office and share it with a captain and his aide who had set up their staff headquarters there, an indication of the considerate way the American occupation authorities treated the

civilian population. In the meantime, the students were moved
to the girls' college where instruction took place on a rotating
basis—the boys in the morning and the girls in the afternoon,
reversing the schedule the following week.

Although our home, the official residence of the *Landrat*, was
one of the most spacious buildings in town, we escaped, to the
amazement and disappointment of us children, the quartering of
American troops. Only a lone officer appeared at the house one
day and demanded two rooms as his quarters. We soon were on
friendly terms. The young captain explained the insignia of the
U.S. Army to my brother and me, and occasionally he would give
us chocolate.

When we learned that General Lejeune had been billeted
in Haus Heddesdorf, residence of the von Runkel family and
until 1906 the seat of the county government of Neuwied, we
thought we had discovered the reason why the American billeting
officer had passed us by. Obviously, the official residence of
the *Landrat* had been selected as the general's headquarters and
living accommodations from the beginning, but an old map of
Neuwied on which Haus Heddesdorf was marked as the *Landratur*
or county seat might have been used in locating the building.

The family mansion was still occupied by Frau von Runkel,
widow of my father's predecessor, and her granddaughter. In his
Reminiscences of a Marine, General Lejeune describes his first
meeting with the lady of the house:

> As I drove up to the semi-circular steps leading to the
> front door I saw an old lady of distinguished appearance
> standing on the landing at the head of the steps. She
> greeted me with great dignity and with fine courtesy,
> holding out her hand and saying, as I shook her hand,
> "You are welcome to my home, General. If you will come
> this way, I shall show you to your rooms." She took me
> into the dining-room and said, "This is your dining-room.
> The kitchen, too, has been placed at your disposal." Then
> we went up to the second floor. She showed me the
> drawing-room and the adjoining sitting-room and then the
> large library at the end of the hall. She said, "Either
> of these rooms is yours, but I think you would prefer

the library on account of the fine collection of books in English, French, Spanish and German." I told her that I would take the library. We then went up to the third story and, after inspecting three bedrooms, she said,"These rooms are for yourself, your Chief of Staff, and your aides. I think this one (pointing out a very attractive room) is preferable to the others. It is our guest room for my granddaughter's friends, and I feel that perhaps the furniture, the hangings, the ornaments, and the woman's touch would remind you of home. May I ask if you are married?" I replied that I was and that we had three daughters, one of whom was married and the mother of our grandson. She seemed interested and pleased."

What is remarkable about this scene is the attitude of the two principal actors. By the manner in which Frau von Runkel received the general she avoided the appearance of having been forced to let strangers occupy her house. This might have offended her pride. She opened her house to a "guest" as she had done many times in her life. It was she who assigned rooms to her guests. Yet the general came as victor. The house was at his disposal. He had the power and the right to decide what space he and his staff required, whether the whole house or part of it. Without objection, however, or any show of indignation, he accepted being treated as a "guest." The personality of his hostess had deeply impressed him. Frau von Runkel

. . . . was a very stately but a very kind *grande dame*. A member of a prominent German family, she was an aristocrat to her finger tips and thoroughly loyal to the old regime and to the Kaiser, except that she could not forgive him for having given up his throne and for having fled to Holland. A King, she felt, ought to be willing to die for his country and his dynasty.

The general was very comfortable in the "large country house," as he called his quarters. "It was a charming place in which to live. Immaculately clean and perfectly heated." Frau von Runkel's "corps of servants were well drilled and would have been the envy of any American housewife. There was discipline in the house."

The general had been greatly attracted by a photograph in the library. It showed "a gallant lad in the uniform of the Death's-Head Hussars. One day I asked the granddaughter who it was. She answered that it was her oldest brother and Frau von Runkel's grandson, and that he had been killed in Belgium early in August, 1914. She said her grandmother could not speak of him without breaking down, and asked me not to mention him to her."

Frau von Runkel, the general writes, was the only German with whom he had any but the most formal official dealings during the whole of his stay in Germany. This, he thought, was both advisable and desirable, for "we should not mingle with the people who are subject to our rule, as military government should be not only strict but impartial."

Lejeune had a sense of history and was accordingly well informed about the historical background of the country his troops were to occupy. "The crossing of the Rhine by American troops was a thrilling event to all who took part in it. Our minds reverted to the days nearly two thousand years before, when Julius Caesar built bridges and marched his conquering army across the river. . ."

The accommodations in Haus Heddesdorf soon proved inadequate. In the meantime the billeting officer obviously had learned of the real *Landratur*, and that it would provide ample space for the general and his staff. We were no longer isolated from the American occupation.

In February of 1919, an American officer appeared in my father's office to inform him that the residence of the *Landrat* was now to serve as the quarters for the general and his staff. "We had at our disposal," the general writes, "the large dining-room and kitchen downstairs and the entire second floor, including a reception room and the spacious ballroom . . . . for the weekly dances and the theatrical entertainments by our soldier troupes which became the vogue later on" (the general refers here to the assembly hall in which the county representatives, or *Kreistag*, met and which was connected to the living quarters of the *Landrat*).

The rooms, the furniture and all household goods belonging to my parents were seized; the Meissen china, the table cloths and the glass and silverware were to be used in the officers' mess which was installed in the dining room. In compliance with strict orders, the aide-de-camp, Captain Nelson, and my mother made a careful inventory of every article to guard against possible theft.

The "more commodious quarters in the *Landrat*'s official residence" allowed the general to house and entertain the many high-ranking guests who visited the Second Division during the first few months of the occupation. On such occasions an honor guard, their bayonets fixed, was drawn up in front of the house. A mounted squadron accompanied the guest to the house, where he was saluted with flourishes. Among the visitors were Secretary of the Navy and Mrs. Josephus Daniels and Assistant Secretary of the Navy Franklin D. Roosevelt. Who would have thought that a future president of the United States had stayed under our roof?

The family was restricted to living on the third floor. My mother told us that were we to encounter the general in the house, we should be respectful and greet him with a bow. The kitchen was used jointly by our cook and the American mess personnel. Occasionally this "symbiosis" caused friction. Until the signing of the Peace Treaty in June of 1919, the naval blockade of Germany remained in force. Soldiers of the occupying powers were prohibited from sharing food with the civilian population. The leftovers from the mess kitchen had to be thrown out rather than given away. (My younger brother once brought home some cans of food which he and some friends had salvaged from dumps in the Rhine under the eyes of amused GI's. My parents were not amused, since it was still army property, though abandoned as useless.)

The foreign occupation overwhelmed us at a most unpropitious moment in our life. We had been unprepared for the defeat of our country. After four years of want and sacrifice which we had endured with patriotic zeal in the belief of a better, more powerful Reich, the role of the vanquished which we had to face so suddenly was something we could not comprehend. Furthermore, under the impact of the military defeat, the traditional political order had collapsed; it was as yet uncertain what would replace it. On top of these events came the occupation and foreign domination. Small wonder that we considered the Americans to be "intruders," that we looked upon the occupation forces with a feeling of dislike, even defiance.

Everything about them was strange: their smell, which was a mixture of sweetish cigarettes, rubber, and gasoline; their high-necked, tight-fitting brown uniform shirt, folded cap, puttees, and boots with rubber soles which made their gait appear elastic and light, in contrast to the heavy step of German infantrymen in their hob-nailed boots; the khaki uniforms of the officers with shirt and tie and the diagonal shoulder strap of the "Sam Browne Belt;" the sight of black soldiers. Among other wonders were motorcycles with side-cars which were soon nicknamed "bathtubs;" the eight-cylinder staff cars which could be started with the battery—a mechanical device unknown to us; soldiers throwing balls to each other which were caught with a sharp thud in oversized leather gloves—a game we didn't understand as we knew nothing about American baseball. The sense of strangeness was increased by the marvelous things the soldiers brought with them in large quantities, items which we had not seen for years: oranges, chocolate, white bread, butter, other foods we could only dream of—and soap.

In the wake of the occupation so-called "souvenir shops" sprang up. Their merchandise consisted of German military paraphernalia, such as spiked helmets, war medals, parts of German uniforms—articles which only a short while ago had belonged to people we considered heroes. It seemed inconceivable to us that anybody would part with decorations for money. The shops were run by people from out of town. How they had managed to enter the occupied zone and open up business there remained a mystery. My brother and I wrote a letter to the local newspaper voicing indignation at activities we felt were almost sacrilegious. The editor informed us that censorship regulations of the occupation authorities prevented publication of the letter. He suggested, however, that we write to the police and complain about the shops as a public nuisance. This we did not do. The shops disappeared after a while, probably upon orders of the occupation authorities.

To entertain the soldiers, trips were organized on steamers of the "White Fleet," the excursion boats which plied the Rhine in the summertime. The boats were named after figures from German history or mythology, such as "Bismarck," "Barbarossa," "Lohengrin," and "Siegfried." Depending on which occupation troops the boat happened to be carrying, the Stars and Stripes, the Union Jack, or the French tricolor was hoisted at the stern. This was too much for us when we passed them in our row-boats. The flags of the victors on the "most German" of all German rivers! We would straighten up and sing the national anthem—a childish gesture of protest which we performed, however, in dead seriousness. The soldiers, if they noticed us at all, probably laughed at us.

What taxed our capacity of comprehension were the parades occasionally held to commemorate special events, such as the victory of the Second Division at Château-Thierry. The marches seemed to be a mixture of seriousness and buffoonery with soldiers dressed as clowns prancing around the procession in silly contortions. A dummy on a stretcher representing the Kaiser was a sight we could hardly view with equanimity.

As General Lejeune writes, no abuse or mistreatment of the inhabitants by the troops was permitted. "In consequence of this system we lived side by side with the civil population during the long period before the signing of the peace treaty without any serious disturbances or disorders, and, I believe, left behind us when we departed for home a reputation for justice, honor, and fairness that has never been excelled by any army of occupation in the history of the world." It is equally true that the American army interfered but little in the daily life of the people or in their relations with one another.

It was, however, advisable to stay home at night, even after the lifting of the curfew which had been imposed during the first few weeks of the occupation. Alcohol easily led to altercations, and the Military Police could not be omnipresent.

Tension developed between the army and the German population during the critical days before the expiration of the Armistice on June 24, 1919. In the event of Germany refusing to sign the Versailles Peace Treaty, a further invasion of Germany was planned. In preparation for the advance, three American divisions were deployed in the area of the Koblenz bridgehead. After June 18, troops in battle dress, among them French lancers, were seen passing through town. Rumor had it that upon resumption of hostilities all Germans between seventeen and fifty would be interned, and public buildings and factories would be destroyed. The contingent in our house also left for the front. Before leaving one of the soldiers told me that he would be back on June 24 provided "the Germans sign the peace treaty. If not, the Rhine will become French and the Germans will be in bad shape. We will just walk to Berlin."

Germany signed the treaty on June 28. The city reverberated with gunfire. American and French troops, back from the bridgehead border, roamed the streets. Extras were thrown from cars into the crowds proclaiming: "PEACE! PEACE!" in huge letters.

Upon the entry into force of the Versailles Treaty, the legal status of the occupation authorities in the Rhineland was governed by the Rhineland Agreement which was attached as an Annex to the Treaty. Parties to the Agreement were Germany on the one hand, Belgium, France, Great Britain and the United States on the other. The occupation of German territory west of the Rhine, including the bridgeheads of Cologne, Koblenz, Mainz and Kehl, was meant as a guarantee of the observance of the Peace Treaty by Germany. The duration of the occupation differed. From January 20, 1920 on, the northern zone was to be evacuated within five years, the central zone within ten, and the southern zone within fifteen years.

The supreme civilian authority of the occupation regime was the Interallied Rhineland Commission which had its seat in the electoral palace in Koblenz. The flags of the four Allied Powers fluttered over the palace where, only four short years before, I had seen the imperial standard fly.

The commission had authority to issue ordinances with the force of law when this was required to ensure the maintenance, security, and the fulfillment of the needs of the occupation forces. Military courts were established to deal with violations of Allied ordinances on public order and safety, and crimes against members or the property of the occupation forces.

In all other respects, however, the exercise of German sovereignty in the Rhineland was not restricted. In principle, German laws entered into force simultaneously in the Rhineland

and in the unoccupied parts of Germany. German legislation had to be registered with the commission which had the right to veto it within ten days after registration if the legislation endangered the safety or the maintenance of the occupation forces.

The Reich government was represented at the seat of the Rhineland Commission by a Reich Commissioner for the Occupied Rhenish Territories. The commissioner, for his part, was subordinate to a special Reich Ministry for the Occupied Territories.

The occupation was hardly noticeable to the ordinary citizen. The only visible interference with his private life was the obligatory proof of identity. Everyone above the age of twelve had to carry an "Identity Card" issued by the local police which bore the photograph and the signature of the holder. The cards were valid for three months and could be extended for another three months. Within the "territories occupied by the Allies," there was freedom of movement. All that was needed to move from one zone to another was a stamp of the "Allied Armies of Occupation" on the identity card. Thus, during Holy Week of 1919, my sister and I traveled to Bonn in the British zone to attend a performance of Bach's *St. Matthew Passion*. The concert took place in the Beethovenhalle which at that time was a wooden art nouveau structure with celebrated acoustics. The violin solo accompanying the contralto aria "Have mercy, oh God" in the second part of the *Passion* was played by Adolf Busch, who was then just a member of the Bonn orchestra. He was to become one of the foremost violinists of his day. As a refugee from Hitler he emigrated eventually to the United States where he died in 1952.

On a visit to Wiesbaden in the French zone we were startled by the sight of black Senegalese soldiers guarding the Rhine bridge at Mainz.

The American Senate refused to ratify the Versailles Treaty. On August 25, 1921, the United States concluded a separate Peace Treaty with Germany. In 1923, American troops were withdrawn from the Rhineland although it had originally been agreed that they would stay in Germany for ten years. With the withdrawal of its troops from the Rhineland the United States lost its power base in that part of the world along with its ability to exert influence on the future developments in Europe.

At the outbreak of hostilities, Germans had entertained
some strange notions about the United States' attitude toward
the war. In the first days of August 1914, newspapers carried
stories about "sympathy demonstrations of German-American
Associations" which expressed admiration for Germany's loyalty
to her ally Austria and wished Germany luck in the war. Rumors
had also existed about an "ultimatum" addressed by America
to England demanding the withdrawal of the declaration of war
against Germany within 24 hours. The report of an American
declaration of war against England even spread to the western
front as demonstrated by the letter of a fallen German soldier of
November 11, 1914.

News about U.S. shipments of ammunition and weapons to
France and England dealt the first blow to our illusions about
America's sympathy for the German cause. That America,
however, would lend military assistance to Germany's foes, that
American troops would appear in the European theater of war
seemed entirely unthinkable to us. All our misconceptions about
American sentiments and actions vanished with the American
declaration of war in 1917 in response to Germany's unrestricted
submarine warfare which mainly threatened American shipping.
Eventually, reports by the German Supreme Command about the
appearance of American forces on the western front opened our
eyes to the extent of the United States' commitment on the side of
England and France.

The occupation of German territory by foreign forces,
more than any other single factor, made us feel the depth of
Germany's fall. An exaggerated fear that Germany's military
defeat might lead to a general ostracism of German culture and
civilization gave birth to the idea among us young people that we
should awaken a consciousness of Germany's spiritual values and
national traditions among ourselves and give public testimony of
it. This, we decided, should be done through the medium of an
organization we called "German Youth."

Our organization was to include all classes and faiths. We did
not wish to tie ourselves to any party or ideology.

In public meetings to be held every two weeks, members of
the organization would discuss subjects from German literature
and history. In addition, evenings of entertainment with music

and theatrical performances, hikes, and visits to museums were planned.

We drafted a "program of activities" and had it distributed through leaflets which the local newspaper printed for us. There were no objections on the part of the occupation authorities. Obviously they did not consider our aims subversive in any way or in conflict with the interests of the occupation. Our program, like all printed matter, had of course been subjected to their scrutiny.

In the aftermath of the war and defeat, and the ensuing general state of emotional upheaval, the spontaneous movement of the "German Youth" was encouraging even to grownups, a glimmer of hope that also attracted the attention of the press. A newspaper report about a "Hermann-Löns Evening" (a neo-Romantic German poet who had been killed in the war) praised the speaker for having "depicted the life of the poet ably and lovingly . . . . with recitals from poems and songs. . . . One left the lecture with the conviction of having gained an insight into the truly German way of thinking and feeling of our young people, a ray of sunshine in today's dismal situation."

I quote these words of the newspaper report about the "truly German way of thinking and feeling of our young people" verbatim, because the speaker to whom they applied was a Jewish classmate of mine. In those days nobody had as yet heard about Hitler's mad racism which denied Jews even the capability of "German thinking and feeling."

University Years 1920-1924

At the beginning of 1920 my father was appointed justice at the Supreme Administrative Court in Berlin. In March 1920 I had graduated from the *Gymnasium*, having been exempted from taking the oral examination.

On April 6, the family followed my father to Berlin. On our way to Berlin by rail we had to travel via Koblenz to Giessen, where we were to connect with a train from Frankfurt.

"The journey became highly unpleasant," I wrote in a letter about the trip, "when the conductor told us that our train would not be allowed to cross the border (of the occupied zone) at Diez, and that the train from Frankfurt had been canceled owing to the occupation of Frankfurt by the French. The train which we nevertheless were able to catch in Giessen was the last one out of Frankfurt to the unoccupied part of Germany. A huge crowd at the Giessen station was waiting for the train."

On April 6, the very day we started on our journey to Berlin, French troops with artillery and tanks had proceeded without warning from Wiesbaden and Mainz to Frankfurt. They had occupied all public buildings and banks. A state of emergency had been proclaimed, and all German authorities had been placed under French control. All train traffic to unoccupied Germany had been canceled.

At that time the Versailles Treaty had already become effective. International boundaries, including zonal boundaries established by the treaty, were from that date on inviolable. The treaty not only gave rights to the victors, but was also meant to safeguard the position of the vanquished. The occupation of Frankfurt was justified by the French as a "sanction" against the brief entry of German troops into the Ruhr district, at that time in the demilitarized zone of Germany, to quell a Communist uprising.

At the end of April 1920 I became a student of law and political science at the University of Hamburg.

The university had been founded in 1919. Up to that time, Hamburg's connection with *academia* had been an Institute

of Colonial Studies. A university was something new in the
educational system of the city. Old-established citizens looked
askance at this innovation which seemed out of touch with
Hamburg's Hanseatic tradition as a premier seaport and trading
center. In bestowing the rank of a university town upon Hamburg,
after the military and political disaster of 1918, the shipowners
and merchants might have been motivated by the same idea that
caused the King of Prussia, after the defeat by Napoleon, to
establish the University of Berlin in 1810: that the state had to be
compensated with spiritual gains for what it had lost in material
goods. The new university was housed in the building of the
Colonial Institute, a gift of the Hamburg Senator Sievers.

Apart from the lure of a big city as contrasted to the
small-town life I had known during my school years in Neuwied,
the decision to choose Hamburg rather than one of the traditional
universities was based on practical considerations. A granduncle
of mine, brother of the previously mentioned State Secretary
Oswald von Richthofen, had offered me a room in his house in
Hamburg where I could live during my first semester. This
was an offer I could ill afford to refuse considering the difficult
conditions of the time.

After many years in South America, this granduncle had
established himself in the insurance business. He was proud of
his principal achievement, a "villa" in a quiet residential section
of the town close to the elegant Harvestehuder Weg (where,
incidentally, the American Consulate General is now located).
Above the door of his house he had affixed the coat-of-arms of the
Dominican Republic in his capacity as consul general of Santo
Domingo. On festive occasions he would raise the flag of the
republic on a flagpole in front of his house.

As a consequence of Hamburg's century-old tradition as an
independent state and its world-wide trade relations, the consular
corps had retained a quasi-diplomatic status even after Hamburg's
integration into the German Empire as a constituent state. My
granduncle had no qualms about making the most of his status
whenever it suited his purpose. He once told me how he had used
his position as consul general of Santo Domingo to save his house
from would-be looters during a period of unrest immediately
following the end of World War I. When the crowd appeared in

his street, he met them in front of his house. Pointing to the flag and the Dominican coat-of-arms he declared in a firm voice that he and his house enjoyed the protection of the mighty Republic of Santo Domingo. His government, he added, would know how to find and hold intruders accountable for any injury or damage to his property. He remained undisturbed.

On entering the university, I realized for the first time what was meant by "academic freedom:" the right to establish my own course of studies and be solely responsible for my intellectual advancement. After registering as a "citizen of the university" and enrolling in the Faculty of Law and Political Science, I was confronted with the task of selecting my curriculum for the first semester from the list of courses and lectures (*Vorlesungsverzeichnis*). I was overwhelmed by the variety of subjects the university had to offer. Everything seemed tempting. There were no restrictions either on the number of courses or subjects I might wish to take. I could even go beyond the confines of the law faculty. It was difficult not to overburden myself and yet satisfy my intellectual curiosity. I felt as though I were standing in front of a buffet laden with delicacies and being allowed to take only what the plate could hold.

My father had advised me to start my legal studies with Roman law. It would offer the best method, he told me, to train my mind in the art of legal thinking. In my father's library I had come across a copy of the *Corpus Juris Civilis*, the system of jurisprudence that had been compiled and codified under Emperor Justinian in A.D. 528-533. I would read it from time to time to test whether my school Latin would enable me to comprehend legal terminology. To my regret I found that it did not. Yet the glimpse I had gained of the thinking of the Roman jurists made me wish to advance to a full understanding of their writings. A further incentive to study Roman law was my interest in history. With her army Rome had built an empire; with her law a civilization. For half a millennium, from the Middle Ages to the beginning of the twentieth century when the German Civil Code was adopted, Justinian's Code was the law of the land in Germany, and modern German law has preserved many traces of its Roman past. The study of Roman law thus appeared to me like a hallway through which I had to pass to reach my final destination, a legal education, and I was prepared to follow this path.

In the days when I entered the university this was by no means the rule. Gustaf Radbruch, leading legal philosopher and criminologist, Professor of Law at Kiel University in 1921-22 and Minister of Justice of the Weimar Republic in 1923, told his students that since Roman law was no longer in force, it was a "conventional lie" to maintain that it still had educational value.

Radbruch's views were welcomed by a generation of students who had just returned from the war and were eager to complete their studies at the earliest possible date. Roman law appeared to them an unnecessary obstacle, a "useless burden upon the memory, a mass of words that had no relation to reality." A fellow student, in an article in the magazine *The Law Student* of August 5, 1920, thus expressed his aversion to Roman law. In the same issue, I advocated keeping Roman law on the curriculum. Since most of the legal systems of the Western world had at one time or another been influenced by Roman law, knowledge of its basic principles, I maintained, was an essential element in a lawyer's education. "Live honestly, injure no one, and give every man his due." Ulpian, the greatest of the Roman jurists, had proclaimed these to be the precepts of law; I believe they are worth being posted on the walls of every law office.

Gerhard von Beseler, an authority on Roman law and Radbruch's colleague on the Kiel Law Faculty, was quick to join the issue. To him, the study of Roman law was more than an intellectual exercise; it was an indispensable building block in forming a lawyer's personality. "He who has penetrated into the thoughts of the great Roman jurists acquires their spirit, their love for justice and order, if he is at all capable of such feelings," Beseler wrote in a pamphlet challenging Radbruch's thesis.

Among the scholars who were attracted to the new Hamburg University was Friedrich von Gottl-Ottlilienfeld, Professor of Political Economy at the University of Munich and considered one of the leaders in his field. I took a course with him because I thought that I needed it to supplement my legal studies. I soon discovered that I was far too inexperienced in this field of learning to grasp the professor's high-flying thoughts. To make matters worse, he expressed them in a complicated language of his own. What made me stay until the last lecture, however, was the attractive personality and incomparable showmanship of the professor. Together with my fellow students who filled the large auditorium to capacity I was fascinated by his elegant appearance and brilliant rhetoric. He would treat words and phrases as if they were balls tossed into the air, playing with them like a juggler while walking up and down the dais. He talked about "fate" and "sentiment" in economics, and the agony man suffers from the discrepancy between his boundless will to achieve and the limits of his existence.

Besides law and economics I took courses in history. Max Lenz, at age seventy among the most eminent of German historians, became my teacher. From my school days I had known his book *The Great Powers*. Now I would have a chance to see the great old man in person and come directly under the spell of his personality. Lenz had been a disciple of Leopold von Ranke. A chapter on the life and work of this Nestor of German historical science was one of the highlights of Lenz's lecture on the "History of German Historiography in the Nineteenth Century." Ranke's basic premise not to judge and teach but to describe what actually had happened should not be interpreted, Lenz told his students, to mean that Ranke was solely motivated by reason. "Nothing could be further from the truth than to ascribe to Ranke the coolness of objectivity. Because Ranke was intent on seizing an edge of the mantle of God, it was religion and philosophy which led him to history. He viewed the spirit of history with piety and respect for the given facts and with no other intention than to reveal the sight of God in history."

A different approach to history was taken by Professor Eric Wolf, then at the beginning of a brilliant academic career. In his course entitled "Introduction to the Philosophy of History" he attempted to explain historical events in terms of Freudian psychoanalysis. An unhappy, dissatisfied nation, for instance, might go on a rampage because it suffered from an inferiority complex. I had never heard of psychoanalysis up to that time and was intrigued by Professor Wolf's unorthodox thesis that history is shaped by forces of the human mind which Freud had been the first one to reveal.

The defeat of 1918 had been a traumatic experience for the Germans, and people were searching in past historical events for an explanation of this appalling disaster. A new insight into the course of history was presented in Oswald Spengler's *The Decline of the West* (*Der Untergang des Abendlandes*). The first volume appeared in 1918 and immediately became a bestseller. His morphological concept of the rise and fall of nations and cultures stood in contrast to the customary notion that history, as Spengler put it, is "a highway along which mankind plods, always in the same direction."

The sudden interest in Einstein's theory of relativity was also the product of a psychological situation in the years after the war when people eagerly seized upon anything uncommon that would lead them out of the misery of their daily existence. The award of the 1921 Nobel Prize in Physics to Albert Einstein caused a sensation and brought forth a spate of publicity for the laureate and his work. Newspapers and magazines all over the country acclaimed Einstein's theory as "the greatest event in the history of physics," "the greatest scientific triumph of modern times," "a discovery of world-shaking importance." Einstein, so the reports claimed, represented the beginning of a new epoch in the history of mankind.

Despite popular descriptions which swamped the bookstores, Einstein's theory remained a sealed book for the vast majority, including myself. Small wonder that I was electrified when I read an announcement on the bulletin board of the university that "Professor Albert Einstein from Berlin," at the invitation of the Faculty of Mathematics and Natural Sciences, would give a talk on July 17, 1920, in the Auditorium Maximum on the *The Foundation of the Theory of Relativity*.

The lecture was scheduled to begin at 6:00 p.m. I had posted myself two hours earlier at the entrance of the lecture hall and was the fourth one to be let in so that I could secure a seat close to the speaker's platform. Soon the room was completely filled; even the aisles were packed. It was a hot, sticky summer day; the air in the room became oppressive. There was agitated talk among the waiting crowd. I picked up snatches of conversation: "One hears that Einstein has very serious opponents." And then two sentences which contained what was then beyond my imagination, but would one day become terrifying reality: "Professor Hahn has found his postulate confirmed: the atom can be split;" "Nationalist students in Berlin booed Einstein."

Several gentlemen were greeted with stamping of feet (the academic way of applauding) as they took their seats on the podium: Hamburg's mayor von Melle; the rector of the University; faculty members; Professor Wolf, the historian, in ceremonial morning coat. Einstein was not among them. Shortly before six o' clock a severe storm with thunder and lightening broke loose. Suddenly, Einstein stood at the lectern. He began to speak in a soft voice: "Ladies and Gentlemen! I am supposed to tell you in a brief hour something about my theory of relativity." I tried to take notes, but I lacked the background to follow the speaker closely. Einstein used simple phrases; there were no mathematical formulae, and only occasionally would he draw a few chalk lines on the blackboard. Here are some of his key sentences: "Movement is a relative concept. It makes no sense to say the reference body is in motion and the other one is at rest. All we can say is that one body moves in relation to the other." Or, "the concept of mass is integrated into the concept of energy. Mass is nothing but energy which is stored up in a specified system." Einstein referred to the British expedition to Egypt in May of 1919 to observe the eclipse of the sun. "It found light rays that went past the sun." This proved Einstein's thesis of the curvature of light rays within the gravitational field of celestial bodies.

Einstein knew the limits to which he could go to keep his lecture comprehensible to his audience. "I have not told you anything about the most difficult problem, the invalidity of the Euclidean geometry. This is a complicated matter. I prefer not to talk about it tonight."

What mattered to me was that I had seen the man of the century. The night before the lecture I had scarcely slept.

In early March of 1920, Wolfgang Kapp, a high official in the provincial government of East Prussia, in collusion with General von Lüttwitz and groups of the radical right, attempted to overthrow the Reich government and establish a military dictatorship. The attempt failed because of the steadfastness of President Ebert and his cabinet, and the effectiveness of a general strike which had been called by the free trade unions and the three parties of the government coalition. The adventure was over in a few days.

Nevertheless, the unsuccessful coup led to Communist uprisings, particularly in the industrial Ruhr district. There were also riots in Hamburg, mostly around the harbor. For a brief period a state of siege was proclaimed. In the residential district where I lived, vigilante committees were formed. During my evening walks I met armed men patrolling the streets. My granduncle's insurance company accepted applications for insurance against looting and riots. Yet life went on as before. The university, although situated in the inner city, was not affected.

On June 21, 1920, while police in downtown Hamburg were battling insurgents, thousands of students marched to Friedrichsruh, burial site of Bismarck in the Sachsenwald, a large wooded area near Hamburg, to observe the solstice at Bismarck's grave. In an impassioned speech, the historian Professor Lenz, invoked the spirit of Germany's greatest statesman, unifier of the nation. Citing the Kyffhäuser legend about the medieval Emperor Barbarossa who, from his tomb in the Kyffhäuser mountain, would one day reappear to restore the ancient glory of the Empire, he made the students take a solemn oath that they would strive with all their energy to make this dream come true.

In a speech at Würzburg University of February 26, 1924, on the *Political Responsibilities of the German Youth*, Oswald Spengler sharply criticized this type of political romanticism, the blind, aimless, irrational fanaticism which in the years after the war had gripped parts of the German youth. "Youth has become enthralled with colors and badges, with music and parades, theatrical vows and dilettante proclamations and theories. . . . Never has politics been made with the heart alone. . . . Politics is the very opposite of romanticism, very prosaic, sober, and hard." He cautioned youth to "forego ecstasy and spectacles." It is their duty, he said, to acquire the necessary knowledge of the facts and forces which govern world politics through studies and unremitting industry. This alone, he emphasized, would enable them to be successful in politics; for "politics is not based on will, but on the ability to act, and this ability springs from the mastery of all fields which are the subject of political action."

Spengler's exhortation fell on deaf ears. The generation to whom he had appealed to educate itself so as to gain a sober, clear insight into the problems facing Germany and the world—this same generation let itself be swayed by demagogic forces into pursuing irrational schemes offered as a panacea for Germany's salvation. It was a tragic mistake; its consequences were destined to affect the whole world.

For the winter semester of 1920, I went to the University of Kiel which is among the oldest in Germany. It was founded in 1665 and bears the name of its founder, Duke Christian-Albrecht of Holstein-Gottorp. In contrast to modern Hamburg where student registration was but a formality, enrollment at Kiel was an act performed with academic solemnity in accordance with the traditions of an old university. In the registrar's office I was handed a copy of the constitution of the university. I was summoned to appear before the rector to vow, as stated in the enrollment certificate, that I would "loyally and conscientiously" observe the laws and regulations of the university. Having thus promised adherence to the constitutional order, I was accepted as a "citizen" of the university.

A similar procedure was followed two years later when I enrolled as a student at the Friedrich Wilhelm University of Berlin, except that the text of the enrollment certificate was phrased in Latin and bore the device *Quod felix faustumque sit*, expressing the wish that entry into the student body might bring me good luck and blessings. In both Berlin and Kiel, the signatures of the rectors were not stamped but written by hand. The rector of Berlin University was Professor Walther Nernst, renowned physicist and chemist, and winner of the 1920 Nobel Prize in chemistry. Nernst impressed me as a modest, affable scholar. He greeted the assembled students with a few friendly words before we all stepped up to him and, shaking his hand, promised to be loyal and to respect and obey the laws and authorities of the university. Registration as a law student also was certified by a document phrased in Latin and signed by the dean of the law faculty in his own hand.

It might be argued that these enrollment rituals were empty formalities, signifying nothing. For me the personal appearance of rector and dean at the ceremony had a real meaning. The involvement of the highest dignitaries of the *civitas academica* in the act of conferring academic citizenship was apt to strengthen the ties with the *alma mater*. At the same time, it impressed upon the student the fact that while enjoying certain rights as citizen of the university, he or she had also assumed certain duties. Freedom of education and of participation in all activities of the university was matched by the obligation to pursue studies in the chosen fields diligently and conscientiously, as well as the commitment to a decent and disciplined conduct within and outside the university. Formalities such as ceremonies and robes cannot by themselves generate a spirit conducive to the observance of the requirements of academic life. It is rather the product of common efforts by faculty and students; for it to become a living force all concerned must be willing to let themselves be guided by it.

The selection of Kiel for the continuation of my studies was motivated by the same situation that took me to Hamburg for my first semester. Relatives of mine had offered me a chance of staying in their house. For the next three semesters, from the winter of 1920 to the winter of 1922, I lived in the house of Professor Ernst Siemerling, husband of my mother's eldest sister.

Siemerling was a full professor of psychiatry and neurology at Kiel University. At the turn of the century he had been among the pioneers who established psychiatry as a separate branch of medical science.

His foremost contribution was the modernization of psychiatric hospital care. Prime target of his attacks had been the old-fashioned method of housing the mentally ill in prisonlike institutions where they were forcibly restrained. The psychiatric clinics of Tübingen and Kiel which he founded, became models for his concept of treating patients in small units within landscaped surroundings instead of in multistoried buildings. Colleagues of Siemerling considered his clinics masterpieces both of design and management.

The direction of my studies and, in the last analysis, of my future career were decisively influenced by Walter Jellinek, Professor of Public Law, and his course on administrative law. He was the son of Georg Jellinek, famous authority in the field of public and constitutional law. Because of his lively presentation, Jellinek's "Administrative Law" was among the most popular courses at the university. He mastered the art of elucidating abstract principles with descriptive court cases. For example, to illustrate the somewhat esoteric doctrine that "governmental acts are neither inferior nor superior in relation to each other" he told the story of the registrar of marriages who while in the process of marrying a couple was interrupted by a bailiff who tried to serve a document on him, whereupon the registrar unceremoniously threw the bailiff out. "Has the registrar committed a punishable offense? No, because both officials acted in the exercise of legitimate governmental functions."

The part of Jellinek's course which attracted me most was the law concerning the police. It was based on the jurisprudence of the Prussian Supreme Administrative Court, which Jellinek called the *viva vox iuris*—the living voice of the law. Over decades the court had developed a system of rules limiting the power of the police from a provision of the Prussian "General Code of Law" of 1794 which defined the function of the police to consist in "maintaining peace, security, and order and preventing dangers threatening the public or its individual members."

Of the numerous court cases which Jellinek cited to demonstrate how the court used the 1794 law in establishing the limits of police authority, one has stuck in my mind because of its whimsical nature. At the time when ladies still wore hats in the theater, female headgear eventually grew to such sizes that it obstructed the view of the stage. The police were asked to intervene. They promptly issued an order enjoining the ladies, under penalty of the law, to remove their hats while in the theater. Some of the ladies apparently felt offended and went to court. The Supreme Administrative Court ruled in their favor. The police had exceeded its powers as defined by law, the court held. The order was nullified because the wearing of ladies' hats in the theater "did not constitute a danger to the health or the life of the audience."

In its efforts to protect the citizen against arbitrary police actions the court also demanded that police orders and decrees be phrased in clear and precise language if they were to pass the test of legality. Police orders which prescribed that "chicken cackle must be reduced to a tolerable level" or which prohibited "staying in the vicinity of the factory premises" were held to be invalid because of imprecise wording.

One of the enduring lessons I gained from Jellinek's course was the realization that the citizen possesses a sharp weapon with which to protect himself against illegal infringements by the state upon his individual rights: a suit before administrative courts. In these procedures state and citizen are on a footing of equality; for the state must submit to the ruling of the court just as any other party to court proceedings. The subject of administrative jurisdiction held such fascination for me that I chose it for my doctoral thesis. The thesis was published in 1925 under the title *The System of Administrative Courts according to the Laws of the German States* by a publishing house in Berlin. Since plans for establishing a federal administrative court had made considerable progress at that time, the dissertation met with such interest that the small edition was soon exhausted.

In 1929 Walter Jellinek received a call to the University of Heidelberg to take the chair his father Georg Jellinek once occupied. In 1935 he was ousted from his position by the Nazis for racial reasons. In 1945 he was reinstated by the university and continued to teach and act as advisor to governmental and other agencies until his death in 1955.

In the years immediately following the war, students of economics were attracted to Kiel by a prestigious institution, the Institute for World Economics and Overseas Trade under the direction of Professor Bernhard Harms. The institute had been founded in 1911 when Germany's prosperity and standing in the world were at their peak. The name of the institute called to mind visions of global commercial relations, of oceans and of distant lands. This had a magic effect on the younger generation which felt cut off from the world through the consequences of the Versailles Treaty. Through his choice of the Harms Institute as a training ground, a student had already spiritually escaped the narrow confines of home. A doctoral degree earned at the institute was widely considered a guaranteed ticket to economic advancement.

The physical plant of the institute was in keeping with its reputation of sophistication and largess. Its offices, lecture halls, and library were located in a sprawling building at the southern end of the Düsternbrook grove close to the yacht harbor in the Kiel fjord. During the annual Kiel Regatta Week in pre-war days the building had served to accommodate the guests of the emperor. On the same premises was located the Imperial Yachting Club. With the abdication of the emperor the club had lost its identity and was dissolved. The clubhouse was taken over by the institute and became a "Faculty and Students Club." As a student registered with the institute I was a club member and received a key to the clubhouse. Its terrace offered a wide view of the harbor. Inside, appropriate furniture created an atmosphere of ease and well-being. Tea was served in the afternoon; newspapers and magazines were provided. Here students could meet professors over a beer. On Tuesday nights there were lectures and discussions. For German students a club of this type where students and faculty could meet in an informal atmosphere and establish personal contacts was an entirely new experience. The Harms Institute thus introduced into German academic life a feature which in Anglo-Saxon institutions of learning had a long-standing tradition.

As I had done in Hamburg, I went beyond the curriculum for law and political science in pursuit of my special interests. I did not yet feel the pressure of examinations. I attended a lecture by the biologist Professor Höber on "The Brain and the Soul," and was introduced to the fundamentals of philosophy by Heinrich Scholz. The most significant of the extracurricular courses I took was a seminar with Otto Brandt, at that time Assistant Professor of Modern History.

Otto Brandt had started his academic career in Kiel in 1919. As a pupil of Hermann Oncken and Max Lenz he had been educated in Ranke's method of historical research which stresses discovery and criticism of sources. Next to European and German history Brandt's special interest was the regional history of Schleswig-Holstein. He was the author of an outline of the history of Schleswig. In his book *Intellectual Life and Politics in Schleswig-Holstein at the Turn of the 18th Century* portraits of personalities, descriptions of intellectual and cultural life, and trends in domestic and world politics are woven into a composite and colorful picture. Critics acclaimed the book as the best work of German regional history. A scholar of penetrating mind, a stimulating teacher, and a warm-hearted personality, Brandt knew how to integrate the small group of his seminar students into a closely knit fellowship where, through mutual give-and-take, everyone gained spiritual enrichment.

Brandt was a friend of Paul von Hedemann-Heespen, a descendant of Wilhelm von Humboldt and an authority on the history of Schleswig-Holstein. Thanks to this personal relationship our seminar was invited to visit Hedemann's estate of Deutsch-Nienhof and, in particular, his library, one of the most modern and best organized private libraries in the country. On a summer day in 1921 we students together with our mentor traveled the nine miles from Kiel to Deutsch-Nienhof in horse-drawn coaches which the lord of the manor had sent to collect us. The trip took us through woods, meadows, past lakes and numerous hedges, called *Knicks*. These are walls of earth and stone overgrown with shrubbery, creating a chessboard pattern of greenery, a characteristic feature of the countryside in this part of northern Germany. After we had finished inspecting the castle and the library, our host placed his strawberry patches at our disposal, knowing full well that a group of students from the city would expect more substantial benefits from an excursion into the country than learning about the noble interior of a castle and its well-equipped library.

A short time after our visit, Hedemann gave a talk in the seminar about the historiography of the German states. In order to understand the history of Germany, he told us, one must know the history of the individual states, which is the backbone of their cultural autonomy. The speaker warned that the states be watchful lest they lose their cultural identity under the impact of the ever expanding aspirations of the central government.

In December of 1921, I had read a paper in the seminar on "Stein in Königsberg." It dealt with the mission the former Prussian Minister of State Freiherr vom Stein had undertaken in January of 1813, upon the direction of Czar Alexander I, to prepare the province of East Prussia militarily to fight on the side of Russia in its war with France which was bound to involve Prussia as well.

I had only one week for the preparation of the paper in addition to my other academic commitments. After the talk Brandt asked me to see him in his office. My talk, which my fellow students in their critique had called exemplary, had been an amazing accomplishment, he said. He added that my talents lay decidedly in the direction of historical studies and he regretted that I had not chosen to become a historian. This remark from a teacher whose judgment I highly respected created a dilemma for me. True, I had always felt a strong inclination towards history. I had been eager since my youth to know about the driving forces of history, and the contemplation of history inspired my imagination. What caused me, after a great deal of soul searching, to continue on my chosen path of a career in law, was a distaste for an ivory-tower existence. I wanted to work with people, to take an active part in the management of public affairs, and in the shaping of societal conditions. As a judge or administrator I would be able to do just that, but not in a life restricted to research and teaching in the field of humanities. I once read that a judge, when asked by a student for advice on the choice of a profession, said: "Interest in history and talent for historical studies may be taken as a hint that a person will find satisfaction also in jurisprudence."

The Kiel semesters included more than classes, seminars, and papers. I often attended concerts and listened to the beautiful voices of Emmi Leisner and Sigrid Onegin which I had already heard in Neuwied or enjoyed the piano recitals of, for instance, Eugene d'Albert. A disciple of Franz Liszt, he was the composer of the opera *Tiefland* (a favorite of mine) and one of the greatest pianists of his time. Edwin Fischer, himself a truly great pianist, said of d'Albert that "if we listen to him we garner the spiritual fruits of many illustrious artists." I still remember d'Albert's appearance: short and stocky, with hands on the grand piano described by Fischer as "elastic and explosively springy." Edwin Fischer was then at the peak of his art. Of his crystal-clear, subtle playing he himself had said: "One gets the feeling, it is not *I* who plays; *it* plays. . . . all is just right; as if directed by divine hands the melodies flow from the fingers." Joseph Pembaur was the direct opposite. His playing seemed to immerse the audience in a stream of spiritual energy. He was in constant movement involving his head, his arms, his whole body as if he were intent on bringing forth sounds from the depths, throwing them into the air, and then calming the turbulence he had created in a truly stupendous performance.

Among the guest conductors of the Kiel symphony orchestra were Hans Pfitzner who conducted excerpts from his opera *Palestrina* and music from the the tone poem *Das Käthchen von Heilbronn*, and Siegfried Wagner. I still remember Wagner's face, resembling that of his father Richard, and his stocky build. I was less impressed by his conducting; it lacked, as I remember, the spirited impulse, the suggestive force I came to admire in later years in the performances of such great conductors as Furtwängler and Toscanini.

The picture of my years in Kiel would be incomplete if I failed to mention the appearance at public gatherings of figures from the "heroic time of the war." They were invited by political parties or patriotic associations to revive and strengthen national consciousness and pride in the deeds of the war. There was Admiral Scheer, former commander of the German deep-sea fleet at the battle of the Skagerrak in 1916, and General von Lettow-Vorbeck, who with his small colonial force of 5,000 men, among them only 150 whites, had pinned down a British-Indian army of 120,000 men for four years in a brilliant campaign in the German colony of East Africa. He delivered his speech in the manner of a military commander talking to his troops. When, on relating an episode of the campaign, he noticed a sergeant in the audience who had served under him, he interrupted his speech and addressed him. "Isn't it true, sergeant? You were there and you could also tell them a thing or two."

Over the years I lost touch with most of the friends and acquaintances of my Kiel days. They gradually faded from my memory. Yet the thought of one family from my circle of friends will always be present in my mind whenever I recall the years in Kiel. The daughter was a frequent companion on visits to the theater and concerts; we met at dances in the homes of mutual friends. I visited her parents in their elegant apartment in the Esmarchstrasse, a wide, tree-lined avenue in an upper-class residential district in the western part of the town. The apartment was furnished with exquisite taste. Original paintings, rugs and period furniture were evidence of a sensitive, expert appreciation of art. The son was an art historian and had helped select the objects. The father was a justice at the Court of Appeals and as the author of books and articles on legal subjects was highly respected among his colleagues. Visitors were always welcomed with warm hospitality.

The family was Jewish. When Hitler came to power the son went abroad. The daughter stayed with her parents. As a Jew the father was dismissed from his judgeship. The family was eventually evicted from their apartment and forcibly relocated in a small flat in a rear building in the old, dingy part of town. The precious belongings were squandered and many of them perhaps looted by Nazi party bosses.

The family's misery ended one day when the daughter received an order from the *Gestapo* (the Nazi secret state police) to get ready for shipment to Theresienstadt, the notorious "reception center" from which the road led to the gas chambers of Auschwitz. The *Gestapo* order was disobeyed. When Hitler's henchmen appeared at the door of the flat to lay claim to their quarry the door had to be forced. Behind it lay three dead. Parents and daughter had poisoned themselves.

Between the semesters I either stayed with my parents in Berlin or I visited Gothard, an estate near Rotenburg on the railroad line between Hamburg and Bremen. The owner of the estate was Hartmann von Richthofen, the son of the previously mentioned secretary of state for foreign affairs during imperial times.

"Uncle Hartmann," as I called him, had the character of a rebel. This became evident in the selection of his career. He had a gift for politics, for the practical, creative art of statesmanship. This was not in keeping with family traditions. Members of the Richthofen family either became army officers or public officials when they entered government service.

My uncle had started out in the diplomatic service but quit to run for elective office. As a member of the National Liberal party he was elected to both the federal and Prussian parliaments. During World War I he was the Cassandra of his party. It did not take him long to realize that the war was militarily lost, and that a political solution was the only way to a tolerable peace. He strongly opposed the unrestricted submarine warfare whereby the Supreme Command, completely misjudging the real power situation, especially after the United States entered the war, tried to stem the tide of the approaching defeat.

In his efforts to bring about a negotiated peace he found an ally in Matthias Erzberger, a member of the Catholic Center party. After the 1918 Revolution, the National Liberal party had been dissolved. Together with its left-wing members, Richthofen participated in founding, in 1918-1919, the Democratic party (among its early supporters was Albert Einstein). The party favored a constitution based on the principles of parliamentary democracy. While aiming at a synthesis of individual freedom with social responsibility, it neither leaned towards, nor was it prepared to make concessions to, socialism. The first chairman and most prominent member of the new party was Friedrich Naumann (1860-1919), a theologian,and for many years associated with the welfare work of the Evangelical church. Naumann was also active in politics, and was instrumental in merging leftist-liberal groups to form the Progressive party which he represented in the pre-war federal parliament (*Reichstag*). Richthofen was a member of the Weimar National Assembly (1919-20) which drafted the constitution of the German Republic, and was also a member of the Prussian Diet. From 1924 to 1928 he was a member of the *Reichstag*. After leaving parliamentary life he devoted himself to political writing and in 1929 became editor of the *Yearbook of Foreign Policy*. Besides articles on the relations of Germany with other countries the Yearbook, similar to the British *Statesman's Yearbook*, contained historical and statistical information on all major countries of the world.

On August 26, 1921, Erzberger, Richthofen's partner in politics, was murdered by two former army officers while on a walk in the Black Forest; the perpetrators were members of the organization "Consul" of the radical right.

As one of the initiators of the peace resolution of 1917 and a signer of the Armistice Agreement of November 11, 1918, Erzberger, in the eyes of rightist extremists, belonged to the

"November criminals" who were blamed for the loss of the war and therefore deserved to be killed. For Erzberger, together with the majority of the *Reichstag*, the peace resolution represented an effort to achieve an honorable and tolerable peace for Germany. The chairmanship of the German Armistice Commission had been thrust upon him by the chancellor and the Supreme Command since no other politician, let alone a military man, was willing to associate his name with the instrument of Germany's defeat.

It was hardly a year before another political murder shook the German Republic to its foundations. On June 24, 1922, Walter Rathenau, the Reich Minister for Foreign Affairs, while traveling in his car to the foreign office from his home in the Berlin suburb of Grunewald was shot from a passing car by men armed with submachine guns and hand grenades. Again, right-wing extremists, members of the paramilitary "Erhard Brigade", were the perpetrators of the crime. Carl Zuckmayer, of whom mention has been made earlier, writes in his *Memoirs* that Rathenau was murdered "because he was a Jew." Before the day was out, the Reich president issued an emergency decree "for the Protection of the Republic" imposing drastic penalties on acts of terrorism. The following month the decree was adopted by the federal legislature and in an expanded version became a federal law. We did not know it at that time, but the murders of Erzberger and Rathenau foreshadowed events which were to bring about the total ruin of Germany.

For the summer semester of 1922 I transferred from Kiel to the University of Berlin.

Despite Germany's decline as a great power, despite unrest which threatened peace and order, and despite inflation of cataclysmic dimensions, Berlin had emerged from the war as a city pulsating with life. The restraints of war had been lifted, pressure and privation had been replaced by openness, liberality, liveliness. In all fields of intellectual activity, in literature, the arts, and sciences, creative forces had been set free which brought forth brilliant achievements and gave the first decade after the war the name of the "Golden Twenties."

The theaters in particular offered spectacular performances. I shall never forget the staging of Romain Roland's *Danton* by Max Reinhard in the *Grosses Schauspielhaus*. The building was

the former Circus Schumann (I had seen shows there in my
boyhood) which Hans Poelzig (1869-1936) had converted into a
giant, modernistic theater in 1918-19. For reasons of acoustics the
enormous dome had been fitted with a construction resembling
stalactites, which gave the auditorium the appearance of a cave.
The interior had preserved the circular shape of the circus. There
was no curtain. Shortly before the start of the performance the
theater was darkened. Then, as the light gradually returned,
the stage became visible. It consisted of a podium-like scene
surrounded by steps. In front of the scene, after the model of
the classic Greek theater, was a semi-circular orchestra around
which rows of seats were arranged. Stage and auditorium formed
an architectural unit. The spectators were under the illusion
that they were participants in the events on stage. This effect
was enhanced in the third act when Danton stood before the
Revolutionary Tribunal to defend himself. Actors had been seated
among the spectators in the balconies from where they heckled
the proceedings on the stage. The mighty circle of the playhouse
became the tribunal. All felt as though they had been present
when Danton was sentenced to death in March of 1794.   For
a performance of Shakespeare's *Midsummer Night's Dream* the
entire stage had been transformed into a "wood near Athens" and
the various scenes in the wood were illuminated as they followed
one another so that the action could proceed without a change of
scenery.

The *Grosses Schauspielhaus* had opened in 1919 with
a brilliant performance of Aeschylus' *Oresteia* which critics
acclaimed as a unique, trend-setting event in the history of
the theater.   The selection of plays suited for such a vast
stage was limited, and art and drama eventually gave way to
light entertainment.   Eric Charell's revues, lavishly produced
in American style with magnificent settings, glittering costumes
and enchanting dances on annually changing themes, became
the toast of the town.   Among the musicals produced in the
Grosses Schauspielhaus was Ralph Benatzky's *White Horse Inn
at the Wolfgang Lake*, which played for years to a full house.
I still remember the final act when the old Emperor Francis
Joseph (played by the Viennese actor Paul Hörbiger) disembarked
from a steamboat at a lakeside landing and was enthusiastically

welcomed by a huge crowd. The exultation displayed by the actors spread to the spectators in such a way that the whole house erupted in applause to salute the dignified old gentleman as though this were an event in real life. The behavior of the audience might have signified a still latent respect for crowned heads, and the old Austrian monarch was certainly a person the public had no qualms about applauding.

I could afford entertainments of this kind only occasionally. I had my sights set on finishing my law studies and taking my final examination at the age of twenty-one. I had only three more semesters at my disposal to make good this resolution. The examination was given by a board composed of university professors and justices of the Prussian Supreme Court (*Kammergericht*) and was considered to be particularly tough. It was a challenge which demanded discipline and unrelenting exertion.

At the time when I attended the Friedrich Wilhelm University in Berlin (the name was changed to Humboldt University after World War II by the authorities in the Soviet sector of Berlin), it was the foremost academic institution in Germany with the highest scholastic standards. All members of the law faculty were outstanding authorities in their specialized fields. As a body they represented the "Golden Age" of German legal science. To my knowledge there has never since been such a concentration of legal talent at one single university.

I can name here only a few of the professors with whom I came in contact through lectures, seminars, and practical exercises. Professor Joseph Partsch's scholarly pursuits encompassed a wide range of subjects. He had established his reputation as a scholar through studies of the legal history of antiquity, in particular through his research in the field of Egyptian papyri. He was an authority on comparative law, and was among the first to take a scientific interest in the law of the Versailles Treaty. He was teaching in Bonn when, in February of 1922, he received a call to join the Law Faculty of Berlin University. His call was connected with the establishment of a German Office of State Counsel to represent German interests before Mixed Arbitral Tribunals, an institution created by the Versailles Treaty to deal with claims of citizens of the Allied

powers arising from German acts of war. The tribunals had their
seat in Paris. Partsch was fluent in French and knew French law.
This made him the ideal choice for the position of state counsel.
He considered it his patriotic duty to accept the appointment. "We
must keep faith with the men who have died in the war. We
must continue to fight for our country to the best of our ability,"
he wrote to a friend. He added that a Frenchman had told him:
"La guerre n'est pas finie pour nous." This "continuation of the
war by other means" manifested itself on the French side by
attempts to increase Germany's financial liabilities through broad
interpretations of loosely worded clauses of the Versailles Treaty.
Partsch and his staff had to match the often brilliant moves
of high-caliber French lawyers with similar maneuvers. Partsch
devoted himself to this task with all his energy. His involvement
with proceedings before Mixed Arbitral Tribunals in Paris forced
him to be absent from Berlin for long periods of time. We thus
lost many hours of instruction by this highly respected teacher.

Partsch could warm up to a difficult legal problem and had
the gift of making his students participate in the mental processes
that led to elegant solutions. His dedication was such as to
arouse genuine enthusiasm for the study of law. A practical
exercise in civil law for which I signed up had attracted more than
300 students, an unusually large number for this type of course.
Partsch announced at the first meeting that students were to write
a major paper complete with footnotes and bibliography every two
weeks, and that anyone not feeling up to this task should drop the
course. As a result the number of participants was cut in half. The
rest stayed for the whole semester and greatly profited from this
rigorous exercise. I was gratified and reassured by the fact that
some of my papers received better than passing marks.

The lectures and practical courses of Professor Martin Wolff
also drew large numbers of students. Wolff was the author of a
textbook on property law which was considered a classic. He
was of small, almost frail build. When analyzing a court case
he would slowly walk from the lectern through the center of
the classroom, holding his audience spellbound. One had the
feeling that an intellectual giant was at work. Wolff did not
need a stentorian voice nor imposing physical stature to gain
respect and establish authority. The editors of a publication in

honor of Wolff's eightieth birthday described how his students remember this "master of civil, comparative, and international private law," this "most modest of all scholars." They write: "In their ears there still rings his voice which knew how to call ever so softly yet so insistently for sharp logic, careful reasoning, critical examination, independent thinking. They still feel his gaze which did not allow evasion but demanded a juristic decision." This aptly expresses my own feelings when I call to mind this exceptional teacher.

Martin Wolff was Jewish, but even the advent of the Third Reich could not detract from the high esteem and great popularity he enjoyed among the students. A day before classes started in the summer of 1933, an announcement on the university bulletin board had warned students to keep away from lectures by Jewish professors. Anyone disregarding this warning would put himself "outside the circle of German students." The following day the auditorium where Martin Wolff gave his lecture was crowded. Wolff was greeted with demonstrative stamping of feet. When attempts were made to disturb the lecture from outside by repeatedly opening the door, Wolff himself closed the door and finished his lecture undisturbed. Despite this spectacular success which revealed the true sentiment of the students, the rector of the university advised Wolff not to continue his lectures since large demonstrations were being organized against him. The authorities knew what to expect from Nazi rowdies. Thus, like many of his colleagues at Berlin University, Wolff eventually became a victim of Nazi racial madness. He emigrated to England (his wife was British) and found refuge at Oxford University. He was still able to carry on scholarly work—he wrote a textbook on private international law—before his death in 1953 at the age of eighty.

Professor Heinrich Triepel, the third of my Berlin teachers to whom I feel a special debt of gratitude, was more than a law professor at the University of Berlin. An authority on constitutional and international law, he had acquired a singular reputation among academicians in Germany and abroad because of his style of scholarship, a combination of legal analysis with the study of history and the political forces which shape the constitutional and international order. This sociological approach came to fruition in his last book entitled *Hegemony. A Book of Leading States*, which was acclaimed by critics as a monumental achievement. It was published in 1938 and deals with the phenomenon of hegemony from antiquity to modern times. In an opening chapter on "the leader", Triepel presents a thesis which directly challenges the fundamental Nazi tenet that there must be "racial identity" between a leader and his followers. Nowhere in history did such "perfect homogeneity" exist, Triepel states.

In a monograph published in 1942 under the title *Delegation and Mandate in Public Law* he dared to attack the Nazi method of legislation. It is a basic constitutional principle, he wrote, that the executive branch may not delegate its power to the legislature; nor may the legislature vest the executive with its power. This happened when the *Reichstag*, through the Enabling Act of March 24, 1933, abdicated its power and made the government the legislator so that its decrees had the force of law. Triepel concluded that since the legislation of the Third Reich rested on an illegal transfer of power, it had no basis in law and was itself illegal in its entirety.

During the last years of his life, Triepel suffered from a severe eye ailment. He died, almost blind, on November 23, 1946. Indicative of his character are the words with which, at the end of his term of office as rector of the university in 1927, he passed the ornate rector's gown on to his successor: "This gown is heavy and that is how it ought to be. One cannot easily trim it to the wind." For me Triepel remains the admired and revered teacher who decisively advanced my legal education through his critical support. When I left Germany in 1934, he lent me, through letters of recommendation, the authority of his illustrious name to help me on my way into an uncertain future.

At this point I feel duty-bound to remember two fellow students of my Berlin University years because of the tragic fate both suffered under the Nazi regime: Hans von Dohnányi, the son of the eminent Hungarian composer and pianist Ernst von Dohnányi, and Klaus Bonhoeffer, less well known than his brother Dietrich, the theologian, but like him a victim of the Third Reich.

Together we had taken a seminar with Professor Rudolf Smend on the protection of the citizen by administrative courts against illegal governmental acts. We shared the same fascination with this topic of individual rights versus the state and were impressed by the example of the French *Conseil d'Etat* and its role as guardian against governmental authorities exceeding their power (*excès de pouvoir*).

When still in his early twenties Dohnányi had contributed a lengthy article on the *Policy of Sanctions* to the *Handbook of Politics* (vol. 5 of 1922). It showed a wealth of knowledge and a high degree of intellectual maturity. He sharply criticized the sanctions which the London Conference of the Allied powers of February-March 1921 had imposed upon Germany: occupation of German cities east of the Rhine and extension of the customs area to the boundaries of the occupied territories. The Allied action was designed to force Germany to accept a reparations settlement that envisaged payment of forty-two annuities ranging from two to six billion marks, and as punishment for alleged violations of provisions in the Versailles Treaty on war criminals and disarmament.

Dohnányi argued that the Allied measures were justified neither by the Treaty of Versailles nor by general international law. His study was like the opening shot in the "struggle for law" which the German government and legal scholars waged with increasing intensity in the following years in an effort to break "the shackles of Versailles." Part of Dohnáyni's study was devoted to an analysis of the economic consequences of the Allied sanctions. He concluded that the London measures, in the last analysis, were counterproductive as they inflicted considerable damage on the economy of the Allies and neutral countries.

In this atmosphere of political and economic madness it strikes one as almost a miracle that Winston Churchill, then British Minister for the Colonies, could declare in a speech of June 8, 1921 (quoted by Dohnányi): "If we want to put Europe back on its feet, there is, in my opinion, only one way: There must be sincere peace between Great Britain, France, and Germany. There must be real cooperation between these powerful nations in order to rebuild on the ruins of the war and to restore the glorious unity of Europe." A statesman from among the victors was willing to grant the vanquished an equal role in the reconstruction of Europe. Had such statesmanlike foresightedness prevailed

among the political leaders of the time, the world would have
been spared untold suffering and misery.

After my university years I lost contact with Dohnányi. Only
decades later did I learn of his fate. As a high official in the
Federal Ministry of Justice at the time of Hitler's rise to power,
he was among the earliest and most determined opponents of
Nazi lawlessness. He became the central figure of a resistance
group. The *Gestapo* later charged him with having been the
author and spiritual leader of a movement to oust Hitler. He was,
rather, a leader in the struggle against Nazi crime. As early
as 1933, he started to collect documents on Nazi atrocities. In
April of 1943, the *Gestapo* arrested him. About his death in the
concentration camp of Sachsenhausen no reliable information is
available. In all probability he was murdered there in April 1945.

Klaus Bonhoeffer and I were fellow students of the same
tutor preparing for our finals in law. I often went to Bonhoeffer's
home in the Berlin suburb of Grunewald to compare notes.
Bonhoeffer liked to travel. From a trip in May of 1924 he
sent me a postcard in which he wrote: "After my brother [very
likely Dietrich] and I had fully enjoyed Italy and Sicily, we
now perspire in Africa. From Syracuse we went in steerage
via Malta in forty hours to Tripolis. Here one is in the
midst of the African Orient and there is little to remind one of
Europe as the [Italian] colony is still very young." Like his
brother-in-law Dohnányi, Bonhoeffer was appalled by the Hitler
regime's contempt for the law. He saw "the law, culture, and
honor of the German people sullied by a mob of hooligans." He
became chief counsel of the German airline *Lufthansa* and was
deeply involved in the plot to assassinate Hitler. After July 20,
1944, he was arrested and, on February 2, 1945, was sentenced
to death by the infamous "People's Court" of the bloodthirsty
Freisler. During the night of April 22-23, 1945, when the
Russians had already entered Berlin, Bonhoeffer, together with
other prisoners, was treacherously murdered by SS-guards in the
vicinity of the Lehrte railroad station at a street crossing on
the way from one prison to another. His brother Dietrich, as
a member of the "Confessing Church," was actively engaged in
the resistance against Hitler. His sufferings in Nazi prisons have

become internationally known. He was brutally killed by SS-men in April of 1945 in the concentration camp of Flossenbürg.

What the university was unable to achieve was to prepare the law student effectively for the final examination. After completion of three years of study the student was entitled to present himself to the examining board. The examination consisted of a paper on a legal case to be prepared within six weeks, written tests taken under supervision, and an oral examination on the legal system in its entirety. The students had gained only a fragmentary knowledge of the legal system from the courses they had taken. They were not trained to comprehend the various branches of the law (civil, commercial, criminal, administrative law and so forth) as a whole—an indispensable requirement on "judgment day" when facing the examining board. Here the tutor, or *Repetitor*, stepped in.

Usually an experienced lawyer with pedagogical talent, the *Repetitor* would discuss and explain the whole range of the legal system to small groups. He would rehearse the routine of oral examinations by asking questions from the various branches of the law. He would help students practice the technique of organizing and completing written tests under supervision within a fixed period of time. A particularly precious possession in the hand of the tutor were reports by grateful former students on the proceedings of their own examinations (so-called "Protocols"). From them one could learn the type of questions being asked and which board member might ask which questions. As the panel members changed it was important to find out who would officiate on examination day. The court clerk usually helped.

Despite many complaints on the part of the universities about the "tutor plague," nothing much has changed. The need for this type of instruction still exists. Without intense mental training geared specifically to the requirements of the examination, the large majority of candidates would not be able to endure the peculiar stress of the comprehensive finals.

At the end of August, 1923, I applied, with the blessings of the tutor, to the examining board at the Prussian Supreme Court in Berlin for admission to the examination (officially called "examination as candidate for the judicial and higher administrative service"). At the beginning of September I received a communication, by registered mail, outlining a legal case, along with the request to write a paper on it within six weeks. Shortly before Christmas I was summoned to appear on three consecutive days in January at the court building to take the written tests. On one of these days the Berlin transportation system was on strike. The tests began at 9:00 a.m. I had to walk the four and a half mile distance from my home to the court on streets covered with ice and snow.

On January 17, 1924, I passed my oral examination. For the examination certificate a fee was charged which had to be paid on the spot to the court clerk on duty. The receipt stated that I had paid to the treasury the sum of "one trillion five hundred billion marks" (in figures 1,500,000,000,000). It was the most expensive examination I ever took in my life. On September 7, 1923, I had paid an admission fee of 5,000 marks. On September 25, I was asked to pay "forthwith" an additional sum of 7,495,000 marks. The runaway inflation had made us within a few months billionaires and then trillionaires within a few months.

Following the successful examination I was appointed *Referendar* (junior assistant in the judicial service). On February 5, 1924, I appeared, in a cutaway coat as prescribed, before the President of the District Court of Berlin-Charlottenburg to take the oath on the constitution of the German Republic. The first stage in my career as a public servant had been completed. I had reached it, as I had vowed to myself, at the age of 21. Six days after my appointment further appointments of *Referendare* were stopped for reasons of economy.

During the time it had taken me to pass through the various stages of the examination, Germany had experienced a period of economic and political turmoil without parallel. It bordered on the miraculous that I had at all been able to conclude the examination procedure in due course. The economic chaos manifested itself in an inflation which threatened the political order. In a Munich beer hall during the night of November 8-9, 1923, the "unknown private first class of the World War," Adolf Hitler, had declared the Reich and Bavarian governments deposed and had proclaimed himself chancellor of the German Reich. At that time the Reich government was headed by Gustav Stresemann as Chancellor. The suppression of Hitler's "beerhall

Putsch" and the preservation of the unity of the German Reich has been considered the crowning achievement of Stresemann's brief chancellorship; it enabled the German people as a whole and all of us individually to continue on the path of progress in peace and security. I always felt that I owed Stresemann a personal debt of gratitude. I regretted that there had never been an opportunity of getting to know Stresemann personally. I saw him only once in the fall of 1929, a few weeks before his death. He was riding in an open car down Wilhelmstrasse in Berlin. His face was waxen, deadly pale, and his eyes staring rigidly ahead. This terrifying sight of a man with the mark of death upon him impressed itself deeply upon my memory. (Many decades later I was afforded an opportunity, in a talk with Wolfgang Stresemann, to voice my thanks to the son.)

I started my apprenticeship in the judicial service at the Municipal Court in Berlin-Charlottenburg. As a junior assistant I occasionally was given an independent role in court proceedings, sometimes acting as prosecuting attorney in minor criminal cases. On Saturdays the court dealt with a particular type of "client," prostitutes who had been picked up outside their allotted zones. I had the choice of asking the court either to assess a fine or impose a prison sentence, including detention in a workhouse, a measure of "security and rehabilitation" much detested by the errant ladies. The judge, as a rule, was less stern than the youthful prosecutor, who thought that he should always exact the maximum penalty allowed by law.

The French on the Rhine

Having reached the first rung on the ladder of my professional career I was eager to let my friends in Neuwied know what I had achieved since my departure in 1920. In August of 1924, I traveled to Neuwied. I wanted to renew old friendships, and I was also able to observe firsthand the French who had occupied Neuwied since the departure of the Americans in 1923.

At the time of my visit, attempts supported by the French occupation authorities to detach the Rhineland from Germany by establishing a "Rhenish Republic" had failed. The Ruhr district, however, which the French and Belgians had occupied in January of 1923 to enforce the delivery of coal, was still in the hands of the two occupying powers.

To enter the occupied Rhenish territories one needed an identity card issued by the police of the visitor's place of residence.   Furthermore, a *Sauf Conduit* of the Interallied Rhineland Commission had to be carried on one's person at all times while in the occupied Rhineland. The entire railroad system was operated by a French company, the *Régie des Chemins de Fer des Territoires Occupés*. One paid for railroad tickets in French occupation currency obtainable at the banks. It seemed that the French, in designing the occupation currency, had taken a leaf out of the books of the old Romans. The Romans used coins as a means of imperial propaganda. Portraits and inscriptions proclaimed heroic deeds, military successes, imperial benefits. Similarly, the one-franc note of the French Forces (*Trésorerie des Armées*) was made into a document to celebrate the reintegration of Alsace-Lorraine into France. The face of the note showed a woman in Alsatian folk costume. Children with outstretched arms greeted a French soldier rushing towards them, his right hand raised in greeting. One of the children held a laurel wreath; a dog jumped joyfully against the soldier. The one-franc voucher of the railroad company pictured "Father Rhine," holding a cornucopia, reclining against a silhouette of Mainz (the Rhine a French river?). Money issued by the *Mines Dominiales de la Sarre* identified the French state as the owner of the coal mines of the Saar.

All signs at the railroad stations were in French only. At the baggage checking counter (*Bureau de bagages*) I received a *Bulletin de dépot*. The French tricolor was ubiquitous. All public buildings in Koblenz flew it, and it was also hoisted on the flagpole of the Ehrenbreitstein fortress. Only recently had it replaced the Stars and Stripes.

In talks with friends and acquaintances I noticed a lingering indignation at the "separatist rebellion," as the attempt to create a Rhenish Republic was called. People spoke with pride of the "battle of the Ägidienberg" near Honnef on the Rhine where, in November of 1923, farmers of the Seven Hills region who had banded together in self-defense organizations slew 180 marauding mercenaries hired by the leaders of the separatist movement The *Landrat* told me how he had succeeded in preventing separatists from taking possession of the county building and flying a Rhenish flag, even though all offices along the street had been occupied by the French county administration which favored the separatist movement.

Small incidents were indicative of the insecurity and mistrust felt by the French occupation authorities towards the population. Thus, a protest was lodged by the French county administrator with the *Landrat* against a fire drill by the Neuwied fire brigade because it had the appearance of a militaristic exercise and hence was considered an affront to the occupation authorities.

There was considerable tension in the schools and in the city, the principal of the *Gymnasium* told me, at the time the French and the Belgians invaded the Ruhr. Innocuous festivities such as the annual founding festival of the students' rowing and gymnastics club were prohibited. Singing of the national anthem during music class could be risky. Many a student could not be certain that he would see his father upon returning from school. Two members of the faculty had been summarily expelled. Teacher L. received an order to leave while he was at work in the school. He was given only a few hours to depart. One of my former teachers summarized his views by calling the French "poor psychologists. They failed to gain sympathy with the people."

After the visit to Neuwied, my trip took me to Southern Germany. At Hoechst on the Main we had to pass through passport and customs inspection. As previously mentioned, the customs frontier between Germany and France had been advanced, in March of 1921, to the border of the occupied territories. This was one of the sanctions imposed upon Germany by the London Conference. It had been maintained despite far-reaching concessions on the part of Germany. In Frankfurt a mounted policeman on the square in front of the railroad station was the first sign of German sovereignty. The French forces which, in April of 1920, had occupied Frankfurt, had in the meantime been withdrawn.

I walked down the crooked, narrow lanes of the medieval city near the "Römer," Frankfurt's historic city hall. Hardly a ray of sunshine struck the cobblestone pavement between the tall, colorfully painted, high-gabled houses. Towering above the roofs was the mighty reddish-brown sandstone facade of the Gothic cathedral. From there I went to the Goethe house on Hirschgrabenstrasse to see the rooms familiar to me from Goethe's autobiography *Dichtung und Wahrheit* (*Poetry and Truth*).

In November of 1946, while on an official trip to Frankfurt, I stood at the same place once again. I was profoundly shocked. The old patrician house had vanished; it had become a victim of air raids. Hardly a trace was left. A few sculptured stone fragments from lower window sills were lying scattered on the street. A small fountain in the courtyard had escaped destruction. Between neighboring ruins and the gray sky there was nothing but empty space. (The house has since been reconstructed and presents its original appearance.)

Other impressions from my trip through Germany in August of 1924 which I noted in my diary were the sky-blue uniform and the Bavarian cockade on the cap of the conductor who checked the tickets while the train traveled through Bavaria. I was reminded of our vacation trips to Tyrol before 1914. At that time at Aschaffenburg, the Bavarian border crossing point, the Prussian conductor and his dark blue uniform were replaced by a Bavarian in an attractive sky-blue uniform with a large signal whistle on a silver cord. This changeover made us feel that we were entering a foreign country.   In addition to the railroad administration, Bavaria in those days also managed her own postal service—her stamps bore the image of the king. These peculiarities originated from special rights granted to Bavaria (and Württemberg) when the German Empire was founded in 1871—as compensation for the diminution of sovereignty that the unification of the German states entailed. Another field in which Bavaria retained a separate status was the military.   While all other German states were obliged to adopt the Prussian army organization, the command of the Bavarian army remained in peacetime with the Bavarian king.

On August 16, 1924, on my return trip to Berlin through Thuringia, I saw at the railroad station of Arnstadt "a group of Hitlerites wearing sports trousers, black leather leggings and red armbands with a black swastika on a white background.   In Weimar the houses were decorated with the black, white and red flag of imperial Germany and swastika flags. There were many followers of Hitler on the station platform. They probably had gathered to celebrate a Germany Day (*Deutscher Tag*).   The celebration seems to extend to the whole of Thuringia."

East Prussia

The short period of time I had spent in the judicial service had convinced me that I would not find satisfaction in this type of activity. The ways of justice seemed cumbersome, bureaucratic, routine, narrow, and rigid to me. "Initiative, action, freedom of decision, a latitude of discretion"—these were, in the words of my teacher Walter Jellinek, the essential elements of the administrative service. Together with the model presented by my father's professional life as a civil servant, these elements were the reason why I decided to apply for entry into the higher administrative service.

In those days legal training after the first state examination was divided into two courses, depending on individual preference. Individuals aiming at a career as a judge or practicing attorney underwent three years of training at lower and higher courts and in law offices. The candidate for the higher administrative service, after a stint of six months at a municipal court, was assigned for in-service training to a district government. For two and a half years he passed through various stations, acquiring a knowledge of the workings of the public administration by watching and assisting his superiors. After an introductory period at the "home" government where he learned such useful things as the handling of files, he proceeded to a county executive, and from there to the police department of a larger city, an internal revenue office, and a city government. Training both for the legal profession and the administrative service ended with a second state board examination and the appointment to a tenured position either in the judiciary or the higher administrative service.

Only a limited number of district governments were authorized to accept candidates for in-service training, and only ten of these candidates could serve together at any given time. For all practical purposes entry into the higher administrative service was subject to a *numerus clausus*. Several attempts for admission at various district governments having failed, I finally succeeded in being admitted for training at the district government of Gumbinnen in East Prussia. After a test at the district government of Potsdam to prove my aptitude for the administrative service, I was appointed, in January of 1924, by the president of the district government of Gumbinnen *Regierungsreferendar* (candidate for the higher administrative service) and was assigned to his government for training.

After World War I the journey from Berlin to East Prussia led through the so-called "Polish Corridor." This was the name for a strip of land which connected the newly formed Polish state with the Baltic Sea.

"Access to the sea" had been promised to the Poles by the victors of World War I. For this purpose Germany was forced to cede, without plebiscite, most of the provinces of Posen and West Prussia and one East Prussian county.

The corridor separated East Prussia from the rest of Germany. To bridge this gap Article 89 of the Versailles Treaty granted free transit traffic through the corridor to persons and goods. Details of the transit traffic were regulated by an Agreement between Germany, Poland and the Free City of Danzig signed in Paris on April 21, 1921. Danzig was included because the transit traffic between Germany and East Prussia also touched the territory of the Free City.

Among details regulated by the Paris Agreement was a provision "strictly prohibiting" the taking in or passing out of articles by the passengers while the train was in transit through the corridor. Passengers were not allowed to leave the train. The doors of the railroad cars remained closed and windows could stay open only on the aisle side. Polish guards on the trains enforced these rules.

To use the train to East Prussia I had to have a special permit "for transit between East Prussia and the rest of Germany" issued by the police of my place of residence.

At the end of January 1925, I left Berlin. At the German-Polish border the doors of the railway cars were sealed. At stops in cities within the corridor, Polish soldiers guarded the train.

In Gumbinnen I rented a furnished room in the apartment of a widow with the Lithuanian name of Maschuk. With motherly care she watched over her tenants, bachelors like myself who were connected with the district government.

The name of Gumbinnen is of Lithuanian origin and means "winding river." The small stream on which the city is situated bears to this day—to the embarrassment of newcomers—the Lithuanian name of "Pissa." Gumbinnen was founded by King Frederick William I of Prussia in 1724. Legend has it that the king, during an inspection tour of the province, at one point ordered his carriage to stop in an open field. Getting out he rammed his stick into the ground and exclaimed that here he would set up a district government "so that the fellows will work." Though not confirmed by historical evidence, there may be an element of truth in this story. The somewhat stark and sober environment of the city seems to be in tune with the royal call for diligence.

The ethnic composition of Gumbinnen's inhabitants reflected the history of the northwestern part of the province. In 1709-11 almost 300,000 persons, or about one-third of the population, fell victim to a plague brought in from the East. Ten thousand farms were abandoned; large tracts of land lay barren.

In order to reclaim the wasteland, royal patents were issued granting special privileges to resettlers. Numerous families came from Southern and Western Germany, from Brandenburg and Pomerania. French Huguenots, Swiss and Scots were also among the immigrants. Of the greatest political and economic importance to East Prussia and the Prussian State was the arrival of the "Salzburgers," people who had been expelled because of their evangelical faith from Salzburg, which at that time was an archbishopric bordering Austria. In 1732 the king of Prussia offered them refuge and land to cultivate. Of the 20,000 originally expelled from Salzburg, 16,000 finally made it to East Prussia. "In those days the image of Frederick William I had attained the nimbus of a hero, and the detractors who had scoffed at the crowned corporal and peasant grew silent."

Gumbinnen was the collecting point for the Salzburgers. From here they were sent to their new homes. Until recently (the city is now occupied by the Soviet Union) Gumbinnen was the spiritual center of the descendants of the original settlers and guardian of their cultural heritage. They had their own church and hospital. They were at times so numerous that there had been talk of naming Gumbinnen "New-Salzburg."

The settling of people from an Alpine region in the plains of East Prussia provided its share of problems. A good Salzburg name like "Kaeswurm" could hardly be understood in the new surroundings. Who would know that the name had nothing to do with "cheese" and "worm," but belonged to the farmer Wurm who had lived near a "Kaes" (glacier)? In the course of time his descendants acquired considerable property, including Puspern, a large estate in the vicinity of Gumbinnen. For the younger unmarried set of the district government and the officers of the Gumbinnen garrison, it became a focal point for social activities. The owner was untiring in arranging dancing parties for his daughter, who had reached marriageable age. He would send carriages to take us to his estate. After riding through the countryside in the brilliance of a summer day, we would arrive at the manor house in high spirits and full of expectations. The house was roomy enough to provide accommodations for the night. We would be taken back the next morning to be in the office on time.

Otherwise, the members of the district government kept largely to themselves. There was very little social contact with the citizens and even less with the officers of the garrison because the president had the reputation of being a liberal, which kept him at a distance from the military. One exception was the annual fancy dress party to which the garrison commander invited the citizenry and the officials of the various governmental agencies in town. I remember one of the parties. It had a theme: "A Carnival Night at the Friedrichstrasse Railroad Station in Berlin." The ballroom was decorated with a huge picture of the station. In real life the area around the station became at night a meeting place for a motley crowd of nightlife characters. One of the rooms of the officers' mess had been transformed into a tavern with drawings of Berlin family life in the manner of the Berlin humorist Zille; the drawings had been produced by a talented corporal. The Berlin scenery aroused nostalgic feelings in many guests. It had been a long-standing practice of the Prussian government to have people from the Western part of the country serve in the East and vice versa. The "Westerners" felt like exiles in this remote province, and the evidence of Berlin sights at the party enhanced their longing for the fast life and the cultural attractions of the capital.

Neither war nor revolution had brought about significant changes in the strict pre-war code of social behavior; customs of the time of the monarchy still prevailed. This applied in particular to the practice of visiting. In order to receive invitations for dinners or dancing parties in private homes—in view of the limited choice of entertainment in Gumbinnen a vital necessity for us bachelors—one had to present oneself in person at the homes of prospective hosts. Digression from this rule marked the offender as a social outcast. We were handed lists of obligatory visits which included all colleagues from the president of the district government down to such dignitaries as the local postmaster and the judge of the municipal court. Calling on industrialists and tradespeople was optional.

The prescribed formalities of the visits covered wardrobe and timing. Essential elements of the wardrobe were a top hat and white gloves. The time was Sunday after church. One appeared at the door and handed the maid one or several calling cards (depending on the number of grownups in the household) with a dog ear in the upper right-hand corner to signify personal appearance. As a rule "Mr. and Mrs. X" would have their regrets conveyed, a gesture by no means considered offensive but rather the height of discretion. Personal contact was established at the party for which an invitation would follow in due course.

Getting a top hat in Gumbinnen proved to be a major problem. I set out to acquire one with a colleague who also lacked this indispensable requisite for our social career. We first approached Mr. Moses, known to us as the purveyor of dress clothes. He regretted he could not help us and referred us to the firm of Boas. We were shown the collapsible type. As the sales clerk explained, it was very easy to carry. We insisted on the fixed hat. Reichel & Son were out of stock. The sales clerk at the "East Prussian Central Store for Hats" asked us whether we needed the hat for a fancy dress ball. We indignantly denied, whereupon she disappeared and upon return advised us that fixed top hats were out of fashion and no longer available. For this reason the store carried only the collapsible *chapeau claque*. We gave up and ordered the required headgear from a store in Berlin.

For dancing parties tails were obligatory. On an invitation to "Tea and Dance" for which a business suit was the proper attire, the host had noted: "Please no tails." He was afraid that without this warning his guests, heeding the strict dress code for dancing parties, might appear at the *thé dansant* in formal evening wear.

What the city had to offer in the cultural field was more than modest. The "Lithuanian Music Festivals," which had once been an established feature, had been discontinued after the war. Efforts of a local orchestra association to start regular concert seasons "with the help of the authorities," as their announcement promised, resulted in a few isolated events. One of these was a two-day "Orchestra Festival" produced in cooperation with the symphony orchestra of Königsberg, the provincial capital. The military band of the Gumbinnen garrison occasionally outdid itself with the presentation of "symphony concerts." Those who could afford it went to Königsberg for opera and theater. Berlin, the glittering, seductive metropolis with its abundance of art and amusements, remained the longed-for mecca for the migrants marooned in Gumbinnen's cultural desert. With such distractions mostly out of reach, we had to be content with social activities within the circle of friends and colleagues. We traded gossip about office affairs and personalities and relished what came along by way of scandals.

The in-service trainees were a mixture of budding public servants and students. They already had a title, *Regierungsreferendar*, and a coveted one at that because it indicated a candidate for the prestigious higher administrative service. They received a monthly allowance. Although not yet integrated into the hierarchy of the civil service, they were subject to its discipline. They had no fixed position. While they might occasionally substitute for a department head, their primary duty at headquarters was to keep up with the training program, attend courses and write papers. In that respect they resembled students working towards a university degree. A residue of the freedom they had enjoyed in their student years tended to make them sometimes disregard the social constraints imposed upon the members of the district government. Thus they had a glass of beer now and then at places shunned by their established colleagues. On other occasions they might seek female companionship outside the social circle of the district government to the displeasure of their superiors who thought they had first claim to their loyalty because of their potential as candidates for marriage. A "proctor," usually from the ranks of the younger officers, was responsible not only for their professional training but also for a moral education that would enable them to meet the high standards expected of a Prussian civil servant.

After I had been initiated into the workings of the district government during a three-month period, I was sent, in April of 1925, to my next station, the county government of Goldap headed by County Executive Hans Berner. He was to be my mentor for the next ten months. I could not have been put in better hands. *Landrat* Berner was a warm-hearted, intelligent, scholarly and utterly unbureaucratic person who took care of my professional advancement with exemplary solicitude.

Goldap—now belonging to the Polish-administered part of Germany's eastern territories—was at that time a small township of 7,000 inhabitants. Its appearance was cheerful and bright, in contrast to Gumbinnen whose chessboard layout presented a dull, uninspiring picture. Goldap's main attraction was its large market square, the administrative, economic and cultural center of the town. Such squares, comparable to Boston's "Commons," are a typical feature of most towns in East Prussia. Goldap's square was surrounded by rows of two- and three-storied houses, each painted in different colors, their ground floors concealed behind arcades. The bright colors and the string of arcades made the square look lively and diversified. In the center of the square stood the church, the courthouse, city hall, and the post office. The square, second largest in East Prussia, had been rebuilt after Goldap had been almost totally destroyed during the Russian invasions of August 1914 and in early 1915.

The construction of the county building, also a replacement, had been completed in October 1923 at the height of inflation. The total costs amounted to 22 billion marks which were fully paid by October 21, 1923. (A few months later, in January of 1924, I paid about seventy times this amount as fee for my examination certificate.)In the county budget of 1925, the building ended up with a book value of 335,000 gold marks. It was a simple, modernistic but pleasing structure: a three-storied central edifice with a colonnaded entrance and wings bent slightly outwards.

Goldap was situated in one of the most scenic parts of the province. To the south stretched rolling hills about 600 feet high, a rare feature in this predominantly flat country. To the north, only a few miles from town, lay the Goldap Lake, a large body of water alive in summer time with bathers and boaters. Adjacent to it was the vast expanse of the Rominter Heide, a huge, mostly virgin forest of pine and spruce intermingled with oaks and beeches. It covered almost one-third of the county area. The Rominter Heide and similar woodlands to Southwest are remnants of a primeval forest many miles wide. In the Middle Ages when the country was ruled by the Teutonic Order, the forests secured its southern and eastern borders against raids of neighboring tribes. Only a few roads led through this great wilderness; they had been pathways for military expeditions of the knights. Scattered throughout the woods had been outposts manned by natives familiar with the region; they served the knights as guides through swamps and marshes. The Rominter Heide was the native habitat of red deer. Before World War I, it was the hunting preserve of the emperor. His hunting lodge, called "Imperial Rominten," was built of wood in Norwegian style and was situated in the heart of the forest. (The appointment of my father as *Landrat* was signed by the emperor on September 25, 1906, "at the Hunting Lodge Rominten.")

In the spring and summer, the woods provided an ideal place for hikes. In the fall the forest reverberated with the calls of the rutting deer. In the winter we amused ourselves with sleigh rides, with bells jingling in the soft stillness of the deep snow. "Meeting place at 2:00 p.m. in Jörkischen, Freudenhammer Inn. Coffee at 4:00 p.m. at the Klausens. Bring a cake," read the invitation for a sleigh ride. The *Landrat*'s official trips during the winter were also made by sleigh; motor cars were of no use, and snowmobiles were unknown.

The county had about 40,000 inhabitants, mostly small farmers. Of the sixteen estates none was larger than 2,000 acres, and only three of them were of this size. Goldap was the only town in the county.

Learning about the county administration was the core of the training program for the higher administrative service. At the county level the *Referendar* could observe firsthand the full range of fields within the purview of the public administration.

As assistant and constant companion of the *Landrat*, I would, for example, keep records at meetings which the *Landrat* held with constituents in remote parts of the county to save them arduous trips to the county seat. Or I would accompany him to horse-shows, on trips lasting several days to inspect road conditions, on visits to model farms to judge the effectiveness of irrigation, or I would assist in proceedings to establish drainage cooperatives. We might even participate in shooting matches with the state troopers.

The *Referendar* could also be assigned duties for which he became solely responsible, including the right to sign public documents. Thus, I was appointed prosecutor in disciplinary proceedings against county officials. One such case involved the county architect who had been accused of having engaged in fraudulent schemes. In another case, one of the most prominent landowners in the county who also was police chief on his estate had been charged with "undignified behavior." I was to ask the disciplinary court for his dismissal from office. The accused was known to be a hot-tempered individual easily roused to anger. When an elderly sheriff appeared on the estate to attach some property, the owner-police chief chased him from the premises with a horsewhip. For this conduct "unbecoming to a public official" the accused had already been sentenced in criminal proceedings. In these circumstances I had no difficulty convincing the disciplinary court that the ruffian was unfit to be a police chief and that he should be dismissed from office.

In the east the county of Goldap bordered on Lithuania, at that time still an independent state (it was annexed by the Soviet Union in 1940 following the Hitler-Stalin Pact of August 23, 1939), and on Poland. As executive of a county with an international frontier, the *Landrat* was occasionally confronted with problems unknown to his colleagues in the interior of the province.

In January of 1923, there had been rumors of an imminent Polish attack on East Prussia in connection with the occupation

of the Ruhr district by the French.   A concentration of Polish
troops had been observed at the county border.   At a conference of
the executives of frontier counties at the district government of
Gumbinnen, plans had been made to assign escape routes for the
population and to establish reception areas for refugees.   While
the county executives were instructed to advise the population
not to flee in the event of a Polish invasion, they themselves
were ordered to withdraw as far as possible into the hinterland
to escape invading troops.   Upon their protest the order was
rescinded by the provincial governor but was reinstated two hours
before the Polish invasion was supposed to occur.   In the end no
invasion took place.   Discussions in the press about German-Polish
border questions were a continuing source of mistrust on the part
of the East Prussians towards their Polish neighbors.   Maneuvers
and marches through Gumbinnen by the garrison (one battalion)
in battle dress were staged occasionally to bolster morale and
allay fears.

Although there were never any major conflicts, there were
nevertheless occasional confrontations with Polish and Lithuanian
authorities.   One day we received a delegation of farmers from
the vicinity of the Polish frontier.   They had come to complain
that their Polish neighbors had refused to dredge drainage ditches
on their side.   As a result the fields and meadows of the German
farmers became inundated.   When in desperation the German
farmers tried to clean the ditches themselves, they were arrested
and charged with illegal border crossing. They were at their wit's
end and appealed to the *Landrat* for help.   An agreement between
the federal government and the Prussian state allowed local
authorities to settle minor border conflicts without diplomatic
intervention.   Acting on this authorization we got in touch with
our Polish counterpart, the *Starost* of Suwalki, and suggested a
meeting at the border to settle the dispute.

Several weeks passed before the *Starost* received instructions
from his superiors.   Eventually, agreement on the place and date
of a meeting was reached.   On the Polish side the frontier at the
meeting place was marked by a ditch, earth wall, and palisades
and was guarded by soldiers.   After a two-hour wait—our Polish
colleague had been delayed because his mode of transportation
was a horse-drawn vehicle—the *Starost* appeared accompanied by

the district engineer and a platoon of soldiers. After a ceremonial exchange of salutations, we offered the Polish delegation, among them the Polish farmers whose refusal to dredge had caused the difficulties, an ample breakfast which a young lady, daughter of one of the German farmers, undertook to serve. This greatly reduced the tension which we felt had built up on the Polish side because of the unauthorized action of the German farmers. When the *Starost* failed to persuade his people to relent, we offered the Polish farmers a pecuniary compensation in the form of shiny coins if they would allow their German neighbors to dredge the ditches on the Polish side. The offer as well as the money were duly accepted, and the problem was solved.

There was a remarkable difference in the state of cultivation on the German and Polish side of the border. On the German side the intensive utilization of arable land extended clear up to the border; beyond it most of the Polish land lay fallow. Never was the significance and effect of a boundary demonstrated more strikingly to me than at this spot.

In October of 1925 when the first snow had fallen, we received a report from the government in Gumbinnen that Lithuanian border guards had violated German territorial sovereignty while arresting smugglers at the German-Lithuanian border near Lake Wystiten, a part of the county of Goldap. The *Landrat* was instructed to investigate the incident in cooperation with Lithuanian authorities. Should the allegation prove to be true, he was to request the return of the seized contraband. In the meantime the smugglers had been released.

After preliminary negotiations with Lithuanian authorities had been completed, the *Landrat* and I proceeded to the agreed border crossing point in the county car, the official standard with the Prussian eagle on white ground affixed to the right front fender. There we were to meet our Lithuanian counterpart. Of youthful appearance, wearing a derby and spats, the Lithuanian county chief presented the studied image of the perfect city gentleman. He was accompanied by members of his staff and a detachment of border guards under the command of a police officer who, like his troops, wore a sort of sun helmet with an oversized golden star at the front. The troopers with their helmets and long-tailed coats—only the officer wore breeches and spurred high boots—looked like the "Keystone Cops" of early American movies.

The investigation of the alleged border violation at the lake proved difficult, because contrary to the rule that international boundaries at inland lakes run through the center of the lake, the boundary at Lake Wystiten was formed by the water level on the east shore and consequently was, in the true sense of the word, in a state of constant flux. Eyewitness accounts proved unavailing. As a result, we all agreed there was no evidence to show beyond reasonable doubt that German territorial sovereignty had been violated. This outcome satisfied everybody. It also saved us the embarrassment of having to request the return of the contraband.

In a relaxed mood the German-Lithuanian "Commission of Inquiry" set out for the nearby village. The car with the *Landrat* and the Lithuanian county chief was followed by a second car bearing the martial-looking police major and me. We were headed for the parsonage where our Lithuanian friend had ordered a luncheon. It had been the custom, we were told, in old Russia—and this had once been a part of Russia—that the local pastor undertook the function of innkeeper in small villages where there was no inn. In front of the parsonage the entire village population had gathered to watch the unaccustomed sight of a large police contingent and the arrival of German officials accompanied by their own masters.

The luncheon consisted of *sakuska*, the Russian type of hors d'oeuvre, roast duckling, and vanilla ice cream. In a toast the pastor extolled the memorable meeting of representatives of the German and Lithuanian governments in his house. After the meal, coffee, cake, cigars, and plenty of vodka were served. In these circumstances the drafting of the minutes of the negotiations presented considerable difficulties. The work had been postponed until this late stage. I had taken notes of the discussions at the lake and had drafted minutes in German. The Lithuanian county chief knew very little German, but some Polish. Our interpreter knew Polish, but no Lithuanian. Thus, the German minutes were translated first into Polish and then into Lithuanian. Occasionally, when it seemed impossible to reach a common understanding in the three languages, the wife of the pastor, when she appeared from the kitchen with steaming dishes, would be asked to help

East Prussia

Goldap

14. Market Square

15. Rominter Heide (Forest): Feeding of Red Deer in Winter Time

16. Castle of the Teutonic Order (1584-94/1705-12) and Coronation Church

17. The Cathedral (1297-1302)

out with Russian which at least the Lithuanian county chief could understand.

In none of these languages was there an equivalent of the title of my position. In the Lithuanian text of the minutes I had been referred to as "Jurist." This seemed to me to be too general and also did not satisfy the county chief. The police major saved the day by suggesting that I be called "Assistant-Adjutant," adding a bit of military flavor to my civilian status. He took such pride in his invention that he did not simply amend the Lithuanian text of the minutes where necessary, but copied the entire three pages again, word by word. While I watched him he repeatedly urged me to have a drink. "Mr. Assistant-Adjutant, you must drink. You did a lot of work." He raised his glass to me. "Boddenseh," he insisted. Although the words sounded like "Bodensee" (the German name of Lake Constance), they had no relation to water. What he meant was that I should empty my glass at one draft so that I could "see the bottom" of the glass. The *Landrat* had impressed upon me that I should stay sober and watch out for him. When I noticed that he had increasing difficulties responding to the numerous toasts of his Lithuanian colleague, I positioned myself behind his chair, discreetly took hold of the glass, emptied it with lightning speed into a suitable receptacle and returned the empty glass to him. He then presented it to his drinking companion, who had been unaware of this maneuver, with a proud smile as evidence of his ability to hold his liquor. This went on for a while. In the late afternoon we took our leave from our gracious hosts, the pastor and his wife, and from our Lithuanian friends. At the border the Lithuanian guards sent us off with military honors as we crossed into Germany.

In Goldap I completed my doctoral dissertation which I had started in 1924 during a leave of absence in Kiel. On May 29, 1925, I closed the last sentence with the final period. "The dissertation is now finished after fifteen months of labor. The moment I had often desperately longed for but which at times seemed unattainable has finally come. Instead of rejoicing, disenchantment, anticlimax. The strain makes itself felt," I wrote in my diary.

In November of 1926, I passed my oral examination for the degree of Doctor of Law before the Faculty of Law and Political Science of the University of Kiel.

In January of 1926, my time in Goldap was up. I returned to Gumbinnen to continue training in the affairs of the district government.

At the beginning of May in 1926, I was assigned to the Police Commissioner of the city of Königsberg to be initiated in the various branches of police work. I became acquainted with the city at the most beautiful time of the year when the shrubs and flowerbeds around the lake at the foot of the medieval castle were in full bloom and swans charmed the eye with their graceful motions.

I remember Königsberg as a bright, friendly city. Some of its sights have become firmly imprinted on my memory. In the center of the city stood the old castle, symbol and landmark of Königsberg, its slender, square, red brick tower with pointed calotte and corner turrets rising above the baroque gable of the main residential structure. This had been the residence of the Prussian dukes, successors to the Knights of the Teutonic Order; here the first King of Prussia was crowned in 1701 and later William I, who one day was to become German Emperor. On the corner wall below the massive roundtower of the castle, in the midst of milling crowds and the clanking noise of passing streetcars a bronze tablet inscribed with these words of Kant invited meditation: "There are two things which fill the mind with ever renewed and increasing admiration and reverence the more often and more persistently they are contemplated: the starry sky above me and the moral law within me." South of the castle, on Kneiphof Island, lay the center of the old city, the simple, two-story building of the university where Kant had taught, and towering above it the huge roof of the cathedral. A green belt, once the site of a ring of fortifications, encircled the city and served as a promenade.

It was the season when people took the Samland railroad line to Cranz and Rauschen, the popular seashore resorts on the Baltic Sea, to relax on the sandy beaches or find shelter and shade in nearby pine woods.

At Whitsuntide an excursion on a small steam boat took me across the Kurisches Haff (lagoon) to the ornithological station on the Kurische Nehrung, a long sand bar with famous drifting dunes which separates the Haff from the Baltic Sea. The director of the station had just returned from hunting with a falcon on his wrist when I visited the station. On the return trip I learned how treacherous this small inland sea could be. The ship ran into a severe thunderstorm and pitched and tossed mercilessly on the high, short waves in the gusty winds. Many a pretty summer dress was ruined by the churning waters. It was my first experience of a "sea voyage."

I had rented a room in a housing development not far from the police commissioner's office building. My hosts were an elderly couple who lived on a social insurance pension. They avoided personal contact with me. They let me know that they had lost all their property during the inflation and considered it almost a disgrace that they were reduced to supplementing their income by taking in a tenant. They belonged to the impoverished middle class who blamed their misfortune on the democratic state. In later years many of Hitler's supporters came from the ranks of these people.

The head of the passport and alien police division was on sick leave when I started work in the police commissioner's office. Without any warning I was told to take his place. I had to face a steady stream of visitors; everybody wanted something from me. Many spoke only broken German. I was addressed by a variety of titles, among them "Mr. Police Councilor" or simply "Mr. Secretary." A nobleman whose estate of 30,000 acres in Latvia had been expropriated without compensation wished to be granted German citizenship. A Russian woman dancer with soft almond-shaped eyes needed identification papers. A lady in shabby clothes asked for an exit permit for her daughter. Closer examination revealed that the daughter, if permitted to leave, would be held abroad as a prostitute. An elderly lady from an eastern country to whom I had addressed some comforting words wanted to express her gratitude by kissing my hand. For all of them, some uprooted, some even persecuted, but all victims of the slings and arrows of outrageous fortune, I had to play the role of destiny.

In the summer of 1926, the political situation in Germany
was dominated by the agitation of Socialists and Communists
who demanded a referendum calling for the expropriation without
compensation of the property of Germany's former princes and
rulers. Political passions of the days of the November revolution
of 1918 were revived. It happened that at the same time the
Soviet film *Battleship Potemkin* by the Russian film producer and
author Sergei Eisenstein was in the news. The film glorified the
mutiny of the battleship's crew while at anchor in Odessa during
the first Russian revolution of 1905. Through new techniques of
montage and the force of its imagery, the film had revolutionized
the art of film making. Because of its strong emotional appeal,
the question arose among the authorities whether in view of
the tense political situation a public showing of the film was
advisable. The exposed position of the province made it necessary
to avoid at all costs political unrest, which the authorities feared
might erupt under the impact of the film. In order to gauge the
effect of the film, it was shown in a preview to the members of the
the police commissioner's staff. Thus, I was among the first in
Germany to see the film.

There could be no doubt that the film carried a clearly
subversive political message. The existing authority of the state,
as represented by the officers of the battleship, is brutal and
inhuman. Violent resistance, a revolutionary uprising against
the established order is justified. The message is powerfully
expressed; its effect on the audience electrifying.

In judging the film there was agreement that its significance
as an artistic masterpiece and trailblazer would have to be the
prime factor in deciding whether or not the film was suitable for
public showing. A prohibition was rejected. As it turned out,
there were no disturbances when the film was shown in public.

At the beginning of July, I left Königsberg. I did not know it
then, but the centuries-old city had only twenty more years to live.
In 1945, a Soviet siege lasting several months reduced the city to
a heap of rubble.

After a few weeks of leave, I returned once more to
Gumbinnen to complete training in the remaining branches
of public administration (internal revenue, city government,

administrative court) and to prepare myself for the final examination.

From the human point of view I value as one of the most important gains of my years in Gumbinnen the bonds of sympathy and understanding with my superior, the president of the district government, Dr. Hermann Otto Rosencrantz. They were based on a relation of trust which manifested itself on two occasions.

When, in 1926, Germany's admission to the League of Nations was being debated, I had, on my own initiative, prepared a paper on the Statute of the League for the *Referendar* study course. The president, when he learned about the paper, had me read it to the members of his immediate staff and later on to the entire personnel of the district government in the main conference room. He was present both times. Through his attendance he wished to emphasize that all employees should keep abreast of political developments affecting the welfare of the nation. He was concerned that people living in the isolated world of East Prussia might lose touch with current events, especially in the field of foreign affairs. He appreciated that through my lecture I had set an example of political self-education, which he expected from all members of his staff.

After the lecture my colleagues nicknamed me "Mr. League-of-Nations-Councilor" ("Herr Völkerbundsrat"). Apart from informing my colleagues about a subject novel to most of them, the lecture had an effect I had never expected. On leaving the conference room, one of my colleagues told me that the lecture had given him "aesthetic pleasure." He had rediscovered, so he told me, the possibilities of the German language. This remark made me realize how fortunate we *Referendare* were compared with our "established" colleagues. While they were bogged down in the daily routine, caught in the bureaucratic machinery, we learners were free, even obliged to occupy ourselves with larger problems. This freedom also affected the language we used in our written work. We could express ourselves unfettered by "officialese."

In early September of 1926 Germany was admitted to the League of Nations as a permanent member of the Council. The speeches made on that occasion in Geneva were broadcast live and even made their way to far-off Gumbinnen. I can still hear

ringing in my ears when I recall this event the passionate words
of Aristide Briand, the French Minister of Foreign Affairs: *À bas
les canons! À bas les mitrailleuses!* ("Down with cannons! Down
with machine guns!")

The second time I came in touch with President Rosencrantz
was in connection with a problem of administrative reform. As a
result of Prussia's territorial expansion after the Napoleonic wars,
the post of provincial governor had been created to represent
the king and the central government in the provinces. As time
went by, the provincial governor assumed more and more of
the functions originally assigned to the district government, the
traditional authority at the provincial level. This development led
to overlapping responsibilities and professional jealousies which
impeded the smooth workings of the administrative machinery. It
was widely believed that the best way of eliminating the two-track
provincial organization was to abolish the district government.
Dr. Rosencrantz was strongly opposed to this idea. To buttress
his point of view he needed a thorough study of the problem. In
his capacity as chairman of a council of district presidents, he
chose me to prepare the study. I was granted a leave of absence
of several months to work on this project in Berlin libraries, the
only place where the pertinent material could be found. The study
was eventually published in a professional journal. In the end the
district governments were retained and survived all subsequent
reforms.

President Rosencrantz was a native son of the Gumbinnen
area. His family did not originate, as was sometimes assumed,
from Denmark where Rosencrantz in unison with Güldenstern
almost brought about the untimely demise of Prince Hamlet. The
family had emigrated from Hesse to East Prussia in 1725 pursuant
to the policy of King Frederick William I to resettle the province
which had been depopulated by the plague. After completing
his legal studies at the University of Königsberg and earning a
doctorate in law, he practiced law for a while before turning to
municipal government, which brought him back as Lord Mayor to
his home town of Insterburg.

In 1920, Rosencrantz replaced the president of the district
government of Gumbinnen, Baron von Braun, the father of the
rocket scientist Wernher von Braun (who went to school in

Gumbinnen). Von Braun had held the presidential post for several years before he lost it in March 1920 in the aftermath of the so-called Kapp *Putsch* mentioned earlier. Upon the recommendation of the Provincial Governor Winnig and the Commanding General von Estorff, Baron von Braun had placed himself at the disposal of Kapp, who for a few days had seized power in Berlin. Because of the isolated situation of East Prussia, von Braun had not been able to grasp the meaning of events in Berlin. He never actively supported the rebellion. In retrospect von Braun has described his situation at the time as follows: "After I had received the telegram from Winnig, what was I to do? Should I have set up a 'Republic of Gumbinnen', as it were, on my own without the means to pay the government employees and without backing by the military while there was unrest at our eastern border in Lithuania and certainly everywhere else underground?" Von Braun was dismissed from office, but received his pension since a disciplinary court found that he had had no connection whatsoever with the coup.

Rosencrantz' political philosophy was shaped by the East Prussian liberalism which had its roots in the spiritual world of the great East Prussian philosophers: Kant, Hegel, Herder, and Gottsched. As a convinced democrat, Rosencrantz was an outsider among his colleagues, mostly conservative Prussian civil servants. His outlook went beyond the narrow confines of his district and the province. It was in keeping with his basic liberal attitude that he endeavored "firmly and justly" to ease the differences between the political parties. He was open minded and tolerant. In the conduct of his official duties he was realistic and unbureaucratic. Among his principal achievements were the improvement of the road system, a task of vital importance in that remote part of the country, and the merger of various narrow-gauge railroad lines into a joint venture. Because he always acted with decency and honesty, and in the best traditions of Prussian officialdom, he was able to weather all the political crises of the Weimar Republic. The Nazis had no use for this upright and liberal East Prussian. In March of 1933, the Nazi government removed him from office.

For us *Referendare* public transportation offered the only means of exploring the country. To own a car—today almost a matter of course—was beyond our means. Excursions were time-consuming and expensive. Thus, except for the immediate vicinity of the places where I lived at a given time, I have seen relatively little of the scenic beauty of East Prussia.

I remember in some detail, however, an excursion to the Masurian Lakes which I took with some of my colleagues at Whitsuntide of 1927. Angerburg, a small town dating back to the the time of the Prussian dukes, successors to the Teutonic Knights, was our starting point. From there we took a motorboat across the Mauersee, one of the three largest of the Masurian Lakes. The boat stopped at the island of Uplaten, property of Count Lehndorf-Steinort. Centuries-old oak trees surrounded the castle that had been built at the time when the Great Elector (1640-1688) had ruled the province as a Prussian duke. We then went by steamboat to Lötzen at the northern end of the Löwentin Lake where history beckoned in the form of a castle of the Teutonic Knights. The next day we took a four-hour trip through lakes that were interconnected by canals and looked like river valleys. Dense woods extended inland from the shallow banks; they belonged to the vast expanse of partly primeval forests that stretched along the eastern and southern borders of the province. At one point in our journey the huge surface of Lake Spirding, one of the largest of Germany's lakes, glistening in the midday sun, came into view. Cranes, wild swans, herons and storks lived in great numbers in the meadows and waters. What we had seen on our trip was nature in its pristine beauty.

An invitation by the city of Tilsit to inspect communal installations and industrial plants took us to the lowlands at the estuary of the Memel river. Before the Memel reaches the Kurisches Haff, it splits into the Russ and Gilge rivers; the fertile lands between the two rivers are criss-crossed by canals reminiscent of Holland. Dikes protect the land from the tides of the Haff waters in the spring and the fall. To the north lie swampy meadows and woods, a haven for elk. When we visited the area in 1926, we were told that some 150 of the animals still roamed the wilds of the swamplands.

Tilsit, at the time the second largest city of East Prussia, is situated on the left bank of the Memel. The territory on the right bank, called "Memelland,"was formerly a part of East

East Prussia

Königsberg

18. Cathedral Island with Old University (1544)
where Immanuel Kant taught

19. New University (1844-1862)

20. Imperial Palace

21. Imperial Palace, Inner Courtyard

Prussia. It had been detached from Germany by the Treaty of Versailles and was administered by France on behalf of the Allies. Simultaneously with the occupation of the Ruhr district by French and Belgian troops in January of 1923, guerrillas from neighboring Lithuania invaded the Memelland. In 1924, it was annexed by Lithuania with the consent of the Allies.

The economic life of Tilsit was heavily dependent on the Memelland. The city's paper mills, its principal industry, received their raw materials from the Memelland woods. In the course of our visit we were shown the manufacturing process for paper, from the cutting and grinding down of mighty blocks of pine wood to the final product, colored tissue paper.

As a consequence of the Treaty of Versailles, the city had been separated from its waterworks on the right bank of the Memel. In order to visit them we had to cross into Lithuania—on the "Queen Luise Bridge" named after the Prussian queen who had tried unsuccessfully to persuade Napoleon to ease the harsh terms of the Peace Treaty between France and Prussia concluded at Tilsit in 1807.

During my Christmas vacation in Berlin in 1927, I was notified that the examination to qualify for the higher administrative service had been scheduled to be held in the Ministry of the Interior during the week of January 7 to 14, 1928. This meant that my time in East Prussia had come to an end. Except for one short trip to the Vistula frontier and to Königsberg in 1931, I have not revisited the land where I spent three years of my life, years that were rich in human experience and in professional and spiritual gains.

Institute for Foreign Public Law and International Law

On January 14, 1928, I passed my examination and was appointed senior assistant in the higher administrative service (*Regierungsassessor*). I was assigned to the *Landrat* of the county of Templin to assist him "in the management of the affairs of the county." In the event the *Landrat* was absent or unable to perform his duties for other reasons, I was to substitute for him to the full extent of his functions. In that respect my new position differed from the one I had occupied in Goldap. Except for the few cases mentioned earlier where I was specifically authorized to act on my own responsibility, I had been, as *Referendar*, subordinate to the *Landrat* at all times. I had signed papers "by order" only; the *Landrat* had remained fully in charge. As *Regierungsassessor* on the other hand, I was the deputy of the *Landrat* and his "alter ego" in law and in fact.

Templin was a small town at the western end of a sizable lake. It has preserved charming remnants of its medieval past, among them a number of fortified towers and gates and an ivy-covered city wall. A town hall in late classical style graced the market square. In 1912, the prestigious *Joachimsthalisches Gymnasium* founded in 1607 by the Brandenburg Elector as a "Princes' Academy," had been transferred from Berlin to Templin. As the seat of a scholarly institution, Templin occupied a special position among other towns of the region.

Here I was to start my career in the higher administrative service. But the love I had previously felt for my profession had—strange as it seemed to me—completely vanished in the meantime. I was neither proud of having reached a once coveted goal nor happy to be on the first rung of a ladder of offices; nor did the prospect of climbing this ladder appeal to me. I felt ill at ease in the narrow confines of the small town. Although I held a position of public trust for the first time in my life as the *Landrat*'s deputy, I felt as though I had returned to the days of Goldap. The new position failed to give me a lift; instead I was weary and uncertain about my future.

In this mood of confusion, halfheartedness and low spirits, there arrived, only a few months after I had moved to Templin, a completely unexpected letter which was to change my life.

Professor Viktor Bruns, Director of the Institute for Foreign Public Law and International Law in Berlin, wrote that he intended to entrust me with an extensive research project and that for this purpose he wished me to join the staff of his institute. Since the study he had in mind was also requested by a central Berlin agency (he meant the Foreign Office), my early transfer to the institute was a matter of some urgency. A bureaucratic hurdle was still to be overcome before I could respond to this surprising and highly exciting call. I had to ask for a leave of absence from the position I had just assumed. In view of the scarcity of trained administrators, it was by no means certain that the request would be granted. But the reference to a "Berlin central agency" in the letter of Professor Bruns helped. One week after I had received the letter, the Prussian Minister of the Interior granted me a leave of absence for one year with the proviso that it might be extended if necessary. This was done from year to year as my work at the institute expanded.

The founding of the institute in 1924 was a direct consequence of the lost war. Vanquished Germany had been saddled with heavy financial burdens. In addition to enormous reparation payments, the country had been made accountable by the Allies for pecuniary claims of their nationals arising from acts of war committed by Germany. There was no way to estimate the amount of these claims. They were a novelty.

No peace treaties in the past had granted war indemnities to individuals. Part X of the Versailles Treaty established a whole system of such claims. It had its origin in French and Anglo-Saxon legal thinking. For the adjudication of the claims the treaty provided for Mixed Arbitral Tribunals composed of a judge from the country of the claimant, a German judge, and a neutral president.

Germany was ill prepared both as regards substance and personnel to deal with the mass of suits that were expected to be brought against Germany under the provisions of the Treaty. The damage claims were governed by international law. German science in this field had concerned itself primarily with the question of war reparations among states; damage claims of individuals arising from acts of war had been ignored. What was lacking, in particular, was a comprehensive and centrally located collection of the widely dispersed material needed for handling such claims. Thanks to the initiative and foresightedness of Viktor Bruns, Professor of International Law at the University of Berlin, arrangements to settle this problem led to an institution which benefited not only Germany, but the scientific community at large.

The Institute for Foreign Public Law and International Law was an independent research organization affiliated with the Kaiser Wilhelm Society for the Advancement of Sciences, a holding company set up in 1910 at the suggestion of Emperor William II to support research primarily in the field of natural sciences.

The Bruns Institute was designed to promote the development of international law through a program which was both unique and ambitious. Bruns was convinced that international treaties, diplomatic correspondence, and decisions of international tribunals contained a wealth of legal principles that had never been tapped before. His first concern was to gather the primary source material from at least the middle of the nineteenth century up to the present time. The next step in the program was to analyze the material with a view to extracting legal principles and to arrange these principles systematically in accordance with the categories of international law.

Bruns brought to this task an exceptional gift for organization. He knew how to weld a staff of lawyers, judges, administrators, foreign scholars and Russian emigrants into a team that under his guidance pursued the aims of the institute with enthusiasm and unflagging zeal. Within a few years after its foundation, the institute had gained international recognition and a highly respected name both at home and abroad.

Much of this success was due to the personality of Professor Bruns. A cosmopolitan outlook and urbanity facilitated contacts with the outside world. Genial, broad-minded, and generous towards his staff, he combined a zest for life with calmness in the face of turbulence—a heritage of his native Swabia; he was born in Tübingen, the son of a professor of medicine. His mother came from the Weizsäcker family, one of the oldest and most prominent families of that placid and prosperous land. Upon his death in 1943 at the age of 58, Professor Edwin Borchard of Yale Law School said of him that "the world has lost one of its most constructive thinkers and doers."

The institute's offices and library were located on the top floor of the old imperial palace in the center of Berlin. Professor Adolf von Harnack, President of the Kaiser Wilhelm Society and eminent theologian, had his office on the ground floor. Upon joining the institute I was introduced to him and gave a brief account of my research project.

In order to arrive at the institute one entered the palace through the mighty dome-crowned "Eosander-von-Goethe" portal facing the national monument of Emperor William I on the right bank of the river Spree, crossed a courtyard and turned right to the main entrance. Here one was greeted by a dignified old doorman who had officiated in that capacity already in the days of the Kaiser. He would show very important persons like the director of the institute to the elevator, an electrically operated contraption that dated back to the beginning of the century and with increasing age was available only to the director by means of a special key.

My office was located in the attic, which had been turned into a row of offices along a corridor. Enormous wooden rafters presented a grave fire hazard and required constant attention. I soon got used to the firewatchers as they passed on catwalks outside my windows. After they had ended their rounds their rattling keys could be heard as they locked the heavy iron door which separated the attic from the corridor.

Not a single stone of the Berlin palace is still standing, although essential parts had escaped the bombs of World War II, in particular the famous Schlüter courtyard built by the sculptor and architect of the palace, Andreas Schlüter (1660-1740) in the Roman baroque style, a unique structure in Germany's architectural landscape. (I saw it still completely intact in the fall of 1946.) With other equally undamaged parts, the palace might have been restored as a monument to art, history, and culture. Instead, the Communist rulers in the Soviet sector of Berlin, for reasons of ideology, dismantled the structure to the last stone in 1950.

The nerve center of the institute was the library. It occupied a suite of rooms and was managed by a staff of several librarians under the supervision of Curt Blass, a native of Switzerland. Georg von Gretschaninow, a Russian emigrant, was the founder and keeper of an invaluable collection of source books on international law. He had a flair for rare books and maintained connections with antiquaries and booksellers all over Europe. This combination netted the institute a library considered among the best in Europe.

The work of the institute appeared in a number of distinguished publications. There was the quarterly *Journal of Foreign Public Law and International Law* (first published in 1929). Contributors included, besides members of the institute, foreign scholars from Europe and the United States who frequently published in their native tongue. Appended to the *Journal* was a section of official documents (treaties, diplomatic notes, and decisions of national and international courts relating to constitutional and international law and usually annotated). A series of monographs entitled *Contributions to Foreign Public Law and International Law* provided an outlet for comprehensive studies in these fields.

Foremost among the research projects of the institute, and unparalleled both in planning and size, was a documentary publication in German, French, and English called *Fontes Juris Gentium* (*Sources of International Law*). The work was planned in four series: (1) decisions of international courts and of the highest national courts concerning international law; (2) diplomatic correspondence; (3) opinions and decisions of international organizations other than courts; (4) treaty clauses.

The first volume dealt with the decisions and opinions of the Permanent Court of International Justice at The Hague during the period from 1922 to 1930. The basic principles enunciated by the court were reproduced and systematically arranged according to categories of international law, thus providing a handy tool for scholars and practitioners.

Next in line was a *Digest of the Diplomatic Correspondence of the European States* 1856-1871. The *Digest*, an unrivaled venture of truly monumental proportions, contained in several volumes systematically arranged excerpts from reports issued by governments of principal European states in connection with specific international events for the information of legislative bodies and designated by the color of their binding ("White Book," "Blue Book" etc.). Critics hailed the *Digest* as one of the greatest collections of documents that has ever been undertaken in the field of international law.

The main burden of this infinitely laborious and time-consuming work was borne by Professor Alexander Makarov, formerly professor at the University of Petrograd. Incorruptible scientific objectivity brought him into conflict with the Soviet Government, and he was dismissed from his post. In 1925 he emigrated to Berlin and in 1928 became a member of the institute. Until his death in 1973 he pursued an unusually fruitful and successful academic career in Germany, both as a teacher and author of articles and books. His principal field of research and teaching was the law of nationality. A stateless person who had never lost an emotional attachment to his native land, he felt a personal commitment to this body of law which was of vital importance to the ever growing number of refugees and expellees. His engaging, cultivated personality reflected the traditions of the European-educated, cosmopolitan middle class of old Russia. His warm-hearted loyalty towards his colleagues, his calm, considerate, objective attitude in dealings with junior members of the institute made working with him a professionally rewarding and humanly gratifying experience.

The "extensive research project" which Professor Bruns had mentioned in his letter to me concerned the question of territorial adjustments in international law, in particular the delimitation and changing of boundaries of European states since the Congress of Vienna of 1815. I was given the task of developing procedures and substantive principles governing the fixing of state boundaries from international treaties, minutes of international conferences, and diplomatic correspondence. The study was aimed at establishing a system of legal norms to serve as a basis of a German foreign policy that would bring about a peaceful change of the territorial order of the Versailles Treaty where it was clearly in conflict with justice and equity. In the context of this mandate I published several articles in the *Journal* of the Institute, in particular a comprehensive study on the *Restoration of the Balance of Power in Europe by the Congress of Vienna*. Other articles and a summary of legal principles compiled from these studies, although completed in manuscript, remained unpublished because of my emigration to the United States in 1934.

Together with four members of the institute I co-authored a *Fontes* volume—in English, French and German—entitled *Decisions of the German Supreme Court Relating to International Law 1879-1929*. It is fitting that I remember the friends with whom for several years I shared the trials and tribulations we had to endure to bring this work to its triumphal completion.

Ernst Schmitz, whom we called "the master" guided our labors. We readily submitted to his at times authoritarian rule. By his own conduct he exemplified the discipline and intensity of work which he demanded from us. His sense of fairness and justice, his meticulous attention to details, his objective approach inspired team work. His insistence on perfection helped us with our own work. Half-truths and imprecise thinking had no chance of passing the acid test of his judgment; he exposed such faults with relentless criticism. While stern in the performance of his duties, he was cheerful and given to conviviality and *joie de vivre* in the privacy of his home, qualities he owed to his Rhenish background. He never succumbed to the blandishments of the Nazi government, which was eager to enlist the services of such an outstanding personality. In 1936-37, as reported by Wilhelm Grewe (in later years one of the closest collaborators of Chancellor Adenauer and German ambassador in Washington during the Kennedy Administration), Schmitz initiated gatherings of like-minded patriots such as Berthold Graf Stauffenberg. The topic of the discussions was opposition to Hitler. Schmitz's death in January 1942 as the result of a skiing accident in the Allgäu Alps probably saved him from an infinitely worse fate that he might have suffered at the hands of the Nazis.

Berthold Graf Stauffenberg was a close associate of Schmitz and one of our teammates in the work on the *Decisions*. Like his brother Claus who planted the bomb in Hitler's headquarters on July 20, 1944, Berthold belonged to a resistance group which

had planned the assassination of the dictator. He was arrested
after the attempt on Hitler's life had failed, was placed before
the so-called "People's Court" of the notorious Freisler, and after
terrible suffering was executed in August of 1944.

I remember Berthold Stauffenberg as a person given to few
words, a quality which earned him the nickname "the taciturn
one." At staff meetings he seldom spoke. Even among friends
he remained somewhat aloof. His mind, however, was all the
more active. From his tall, lanky figure with the dark, searching
eyes, there emanated an aura of intellectual superiority. He and
his brother had been disciples of the poet Stefan George. The
"aristocratic-esoteric mannerism" which was practiced by George
devotees may have molded Berthold's behavior.

In 1930, Stauffenberg had been assigned to the Secretariat
of the Permanent Court of International Justice at The Hague
for several months. During that time he wrote the leading
commentary on the statute of the court in French. In World War
II he served on the staff of the Chief of Naval Operations. As
an expert on the law of naval warfare he endeavored to exert as
much influence as was possible under the conditions existing in
the Third Reich to keep Germany's conduct of the war within the
bounds of international law.

From official U.S. State Department documents published in
1979, it has become known that during a secret trip to Stockholm
in February of 1942, Stauffenberg informed the Swedish Foreign
Office of Hitler's plan to occupy Sweden before resuming the
German offensive in Russia. Sweden thereupon mobilized her
army and Hitler was forced to abandon the planned invasion.

Stauffenberg was one of the prime movers at the institute
and, together with Schmitz for whom he acted as deputy, was
among the small group who were awarded the title of "Scientific
Member of the Institute." Obituaries, which could be published
only after the war, stressed the high repute Stauffenberg enjoyed
both at home and abroad as an outstanding authority on
international law.

Among the colleagues who participated in the work on
the *Decisions*, Eduard von Schwartzkoppen was closest to me
as a friend; old ties existed between our respective families.
Schwartzkoppen's father had been Chief of Personnel of the

German Foreign Office at the time my granduncle Oswald von Richthofen was the secretary of state, and my grandmother (on my father's side), sister of the state secretary, had acted for her widowed brother as the Lady of the House. Schwartzkoppen had often heard his father mention the name of "old Mrs. von Elbe," as my grandmother was called by members of the Foreign Office.

Schwartzkoppen and I had attended the same *Repetitor* to prepare for the first state board examination. After we had passed the examination, our paths separated. Schwartzkoppen had chosen a career in the judicial service, and I had entered the administrative service. On the strength of his brilliant examinations, Schwartzkoppen became a teaching assistant at the law faculty of Berlin University and an associate of Professor Partsch in the scientific section of the German State Representation, a division of the Foreign Office, at the Mixed Arbitral Tribunals (mentioned earlier). In 1928, Schwartzkoppen and I met again when I became a member of the Bruns Institute. Schwartzkoppen had been among the founding members of the institute. At the beginning of 1931, he left the institute to become legal counsel to the *Berliner Handelsgesellschaft*, one of Germany's major banks. Its president at the time was Carl Fürstenberg, considered the foremost private banker in Germany; he was both famous and feared on account of his sharp wit. After Schwartzkoppen—then 28 years of age—had been introduced to him, Fürstenberg is reported to have told a confidant: "One of these days he will be my successor."

Fürstenberg's prediction became true. After many years Schwartzkoppen was named president of the bank. However, before he attained this position, he had to pass through years of incredible hardship. In May of 1945, at the end of the war, Schwartzkoppen was in Berlin. He had been able to send his family away to relatives in Western Germany, but he himself, although fully aware of the imminent attack of the Soviet armies on Berlin, had refused to leave. He had declared to a friend who had urged him to join his family that the staff of the bank had remained in the city and that it was his duty to do likewise. He was determined to meet his fate in Berlin, no matter what it might hold in store for him.

According to Allied planning Berlin was at first occupied exclusively by the Soviets. Among the measures taken by the Soviets to restore order in the city was the reopening of banks. To this end the Soviet authorities issued an order that all bank employees present in the city had to report to their former places of work on a certain day. Thus Schwartzkoppen, with all of his co-workers he could contact, turned up at his bank on the appointed day. The bank was largely undamaged. After a while Soviet officers appeared and declared everyone present under arrest. No reason was given. The prisoners were taken on military trucks to the former Nazi concentration camp of Buchenwald. There Schwartzkoppen was detained for about five years. He was not allowed to communicate with the outside world; nor could he get in touch with his family. On one occasion his sister, who had learned about his arrest and his whereabouts through a British officer, was able to send her brother vital drugs. This was accomplished under dramatic circumstances—riding in the engineer's cab of a train to the vicinity of the camp was by itself a fearsome adventure—and at the risk of her life by approaching people who were at work outside the camp.

The Nazis (before the Holocaust) had done away with prisoners in concentration camps by maltreatment and forced labor. The Soviets used more subtle methods towards the inmates of the "internment camps", as they called these installations. The prisoners were intentionally neglected. Everything was lacking, Schwartzkoppen told me later. There was not a piece of paper or a comb, to mention only a few items which one hardly notices in ordinary life but which assume enormous importance if one cannot have them. The Soviets refrained from physically abusing the internees; they just let them perish by slow decay. At night the prisoners lay on wooden planks, next to and above each other. Despite his strong physique, Schwartzkoppen eventually contracted double tuberculosis which became so menacing that he was kept in the so-called "death barracks" for months.

In February of 1950, in connection with the release of German prisoners of war which Chancellor Adenauer had negotiated with the Soviet government in Moscow, Schwartzkoppen was set free. He was literally the last one to leave, as he wrote me. After he had crossed the line into freedom, the door behind him was shut tight. About 2,500 of his co-prisoners were deported to another concentration camp, and were sentenced to long prison terms after mock trials. Schwartzkoppen added that he had endured the years of suffering "mentally unbroken."

I was able to verify the truth of that statement when I visited him in a sanitarium in the Black Forest where he had gone immediately after his release to cure his tuberculosis. How had it been possible to withstand the conditions of a Soviet internment camp for years and emerge unscathed? Is it not common knowledge that no one can survive innocent imprisonment over a long period of time without suffering irreparable mental harm? If ever the theory of mind over body holds true, here is an example. Schwartzkoppen's unshakable Christian faith, legacy of his forebears, gave him the strength to endure privation and hardship and to renew his confidence in ultimate liberation. Amidst all the misery around him his mind was wide awake and constantly at work. He drew up plans for the economic reconstruction of Germany without being able to put his thoughts into writing. One of his fellow inmates, a former official of the German Foreign Office and, like Schwartzkoppen, never a follower of the Nazis (he eventually died in the camp) surprised his companions-in-suffering every morning with a poem he had composed during the night. They were written in a serious or humorous vein, on a lyrical or religious theme or they recalled scenes of Berlin life. Schwartzkoppen kept these poems in his memory without losing a single line and wrote them down after his release. They fill a book. (Schwartzkoppen's eldest son is the keeper of this unique document, testimony of the indestructible power of the mind over bodily suffering.) From passages of the Bible and quotations he had learned by heart in his youth—too few, he once told me—Schwartzkoppen derived comfort which he could pass on to others. During the 28 years which were granted him after he had been freed—he died in October 1978—he was able to overcome his illness and restore his bank to its former pre-eminence as its president, just as Carl Fürstenberg had predicted in 1931.

Schwartzkoppen's personality was a blend of the best traditions of Prussian officialdom with the sturdiness and vigor of the landed gentry. In his scale of values, devotion to duty ranked supreme. His sense of justice and fairness earned him respect and authority, and his high intelligence gave him a superiority which, however, he never let others feel. He had a great sense of humor and knew many funny stories, especially about the whimsical weaknesses of some of his university teachers. He was an indefatigable traveler. Railroad timetables were for him what detective stories are to others; he read them at night in bed. Schwartzkoppen was the expert on all official trips of the members of the institute. From Marakesh which he visited on a trip to Morocco in 1930 he wrote: "The impression of the city is appalling. People live in horrible shacks and in filth beyond imagination. It is only natural that all kinds of diseases are frightfully rampant. Skin diseases, in particular syphilis from which the majority of the population suffers, find a breeding ground here. The sick run around among the people with their deformed, partly corroded limbs. Nobody thinks of curing them. (Allah wants it that way!)." A journey to the Black Sea in 1936 brought him to the Crimean Peninsula: "From the point of view of scenery, the Crimea, formerly the site of many princely palaces, is of indescribable beauty. It can easily compete with the French and Italian Rivieras. But the delight this sight evokes is dampened by a glimpse into the Bolshevik world. Perhaps half of this fertile land lies barren. There is no house without a damaged roof or window. Repairs, if made at all, are done with wood or paper. At night our ship was surrounded by unlighted patrol boats. They watched for people who might attempt to flee this paradise."

With the English text of the *Decisions*, we were helped by Abraham H. Feller, at the time a budding scholar of international law at Harvard University. In 1930 and 1931, Feller was for several months a guest research associate at the institute. He liked to be in Germany, and was fascinated by the abundance of cultural attractions which Berlin had to offer in those years. Feller admired the clean, newly reconstructed metropolitan elevated railway which ran frequently and on time. "If only we had something like that in New York," he once confided to me with a sigh of regret. He was impressed by the excellently equipped and superbly trained "blue" mounted police whom he had observed as they dealt with demonstrations. He considered them superior in appearance and conduct to the similarly organized New York police. In 1931, I went with him on a trip to Danzig and the German-Polish Vistula frontier. Stauffenberg also came along. The institute had arranged the trip to show Feller two glaring examples of areas of tension which had been created by the Versailles Treaty. The zig-zag course of the Vistula frontier was particularly absurd and had become an object of curiosity for sightseers. On our return trip we used the newly created shipping line across the Baltic Sea from Königsberg to Stettin.

In 1946, after a brilliant academic and governmental career, Feller became Legal Counsel and Personal Assistant to Trygve Lie, the first Secretary-General of the United Nations. "He soon was my closest adviser and during the first seven years in the history of the United Nations rendered invaluable services," Trygve Lie writes in his memoirs *In the Cause of Peace*. He added: "Abe Feller had been nearer to me than anyone else outside the circle of my immediate family . . . hardly a day passed at Headquarters when he did not come to see me—most days he would come several times. Whenever something was up, Abe was there, alert, discreet, full of energy and ideas. I had a deep admiration for his intelligence, and an affection for him which was strengthened by his own loyalty and personal regard."

In 1952, America was hit by a wave of persecution of alleged and bona fide Communists. It had been set in motion by Senator Joseph McCarthy from Wisconsin. In high government places a witch hunt was on for Communist sympathizers. The administration of the United Nations was also affected. American citizens who, like Feller, were in the employ of the United Nations, were exposed to ruthless persecution by reactionary elements. Feller saw how fundamental principles of fair play and orderly justice were violated. Concern for his co-workers put a strain on him that finally became unbearable. On November 13, 1953, he was found dead on a street in New York. He had jumped from the window of his twelfth-floor apartment. Feller's death, as Trygve Lie writes, was an "incalculable loss" for the Secretary-General as well as for the United Nations. A room in the United Nations Library was dedicated as "The Abraham

Feller Memorial Room" to the memory "of a great and loyal international civil servant and a great and loyal American."

Two other colleagues in later life attained fame as outstanding authorities on constitutional law and political science; I remember both with affection as close and valued friends. Gerhard Leibholz ranked already in the days of the Weimar Republic among the leaders in his field. After his return from exile in Great Britain which the Nazis had forced upon him for racial reasons, he resumed teaching at the University of Göttingen and became a member of the Constitutional Court of the Federal Republic of Germany. The high esteem which the court has enjoyed ever since it came into existence in 1951 is in large measure due to Leibholz's contributions. Ulrich Scheuner, after leaving the institute in the early 1930's, taught constitutional and international law at a number of German universities. He was a prolific writer and at times represented the federal government in proceedings before the Federal Constitutional Court. He decisively helped to shape the constitutional order of postwar Germany.

The Institute for Foreign and International Private Law was, like the Bruns Institute, an affiliate of the Kaiser Wilhelm Society for the Advancement of Sciences and also occupied rooms on the top floor of the imperial palace. Its director, Professor Ernst Rabel, lost his position at Berlin University under the Nazis, and as a "non-Aryan" emigrated to the United States where he continued teaching at the University of California at Berkeley. The two institutes were friendly neighbors. Their members met regularly for lunch which the janitor's wife prepared. The kitchen and the janitor's family quarters were located close to the rooms of the institutes. Presiding at these joint luncheons was Professor Rabel, respectfully called "Mr. Privy Councilor;" his arrival, sometimes delayed, was religiously awaited before luncheon was served.

One of the members of the Rabel Institute was Walter Hallstein, with whom I was on particularly friendly terms. I remember an episode which is characteristic of the *entente cordiale* between the two institutes. Professor Martin Wolff's wife, one of Bruns' closest associates, occasionally yearned for the glamorous atmosphere of metropolitan high life when the hectic pace of the institute became too much of a burden. In such a situation Hallstein and I took her to a *thé dansant* in the Hotel Esplanade, one of the more renowned hostelries of Berlin where the famous Hungarian violinist Bárnábás von Géczy and his orchestra provided the music. For years von Géczy was the toast of the town, the "Paganini of the five-o'clock-tea," as he was called. A small part of the hotel up to the first floor has survived the ravages of World War II. Its neglected condition is a sad reminder of a once glorious past.

I met Hallstein on several occasions in Bonn after the war. As secretary of state of the foreign office under Chancellor Adenauer he was one of the architects of Germany's foreign policy. A diplomatic doctrine designed to buttress the claim of the Federal Republic of being the sole representative of the German people in international affairs bears his name. As the first President of the European Economic Community (1958) he attained a position among the leading statesmen in postwar Europe.

The Bruns Institute was not devoted purely to research; we did not lead an ivory-tower existence. Professor Bruns was both an eminent scholar and a practitioner of international law. He kept in close touch with its realities. From 1927 to 1931 he was the German judge of the Germano-Polish Mixed Arbitral Tribunal. It dealt with claims of Polish nationals against the German Reich for damages caused by German war measures and with claims of German nationals for the restitution of property in former German territories which had been liquidated by Poland. In 1928, 1931 and 1932 Bruns was the national judge in litigations of the Free City of Danzig before the Permanent Court of International Justice at The Hague.

The Germano-Polish Mixed Arbitral Tribunal had its seat in Paris in the former Austro-Hungarian Embassy, the private property of the Hapsburg family located in the exclusive Faubourg St. Germain.

To the sessions of the tribunal Bruns used to take along members of the institute who had worked on pending cases. In May of 1929, I was among those chosen by Bruns for this mission. It was my first trip to the French capital. I was overwhelmed by what I saw. "He who has seen Paris in his youth," writes Stefan

Zweig, "carries with him throughout his life an incomparable memory of happiness."

Carlo Schmid, decades later the "grand old man" of the Federal Republic of Germany, was a colleague of mine at the institute and in the Bruns party at the May session in Paris. The language of the tribunal was French, truly Schmid's mother tongue, as his mother was a native of Southern France. His memos were written in elegant, impeccable French; as stylistic masterpieces and for their wealth of penetrating legal thoughts they were a joy to read. Knowing that I was a novice about everything French, Schmid was untiring in educating me about French life and the customs of the country, in explaining the sights of Paris and, as a connoisseur of restaurants, in introducing me to French culinary art. He taught me that at the end of a meal the proper drink with coffee was not cognac but armagnac and that the preferred cigarette was the "Gauloise jaune" because of its beneficial effect. With his broad-rimmed black slouch hat, a cigarette butt wedged nonchalantly in a corner of his mouth, he presented such a strikingly French appearance that we gladly let him guide us through the gastronomic wonders of Paris.

Pending before the tribunal at that time was the suit of Count Ulrich Wilhelm von Schwerin Schwanenfeld against the Polish state contesting the liquidation of his estate in the former province of West Prussia, a part of the "Polish corridor."

Count Schwerin had asked the tribunal to issue an injunction ordering the Polish government to desist from carrying out the liquidation. The Polish measure was contrary to commitments undertaken by Poland with respect to German property in the former German territory which had been transferred to Poland after the war.

One afternoon when the tribunal was not in session, I went with Count Schwerin to Versailles. On our walk through the park he talked about the false attitude of Germans towards the Poles. Although his own life had been profoundly affected by the territorial change, his main concern was that Germans and Poles should be on friendly terms and deal with each other fairly and justly. (His petition did not succeed. The tribunal ruled that it had no jurisdiction in the case. The question of German property in Poland was eventually settled by a German-Polish agreement.)

In August of 1946, when I had started service with the Legal Division of the Office of the United States Military Government in Berlin, during a briefing on conditions in the Third Reich I saw a documentary film of proceedings before the so-called "People's Court" against resistance fighters involved in the plot against Hitler of July 20, 1944. Suddenly a face I remembered appeared on the screen. The figure which emerged in the darkened room was Count Schwerin. I had little knowledge at that time about the German resistance and, of course, had not the slightest inkling that Count Schwerin had been involved in the resistance movement and that he would be among the victims who had to face the murderous Freisler. When asked by Freisler about his motives for joining the resistance, I heard Count Schwerin say in a low voice that he thought of the many "murders" (of Poles by the Nazis). "Murders?" Freisler shouted in a fit of rage. "You are a rotten scoundrel." (Count Schwerin was referring to the thousands of Polish Christians and Jews who had been slain by the Nazis in a gravel pit on his estate of Sartowitz.) I was profoundly shaken.

Count Schwerin, like many others who had risked their lives in the struggle to free Germany from Nazism, was killed by Hitler's henchmen in Plötzensee prison on September 8, 1944. In his book *My Mission in Danzig*, Carl J. Burckhardt, the last High Commissioner of the League of Nations in Danzig, writes about his connections with secretary of state in the German Foreign Office, at the time Freiherr von Weizsäcker, to whom he sent confidential reports from Danzig, especially about subversive activities of the Nazis. He communicated with Weizsäcker through middlemen. Burckhardt writes: "One of the most impressive people who called on me on behalf of the State Secretary was Count Ulrich Wilhelm von Schwerin Schwanenfeld, son-in-law of the President of the Danzig *Senat*, Sahm. Schwerin owned property in the Polish corridor. He belonged to the elite which later made common cause in the events of July 20, 1944, and for his noble-mindedness and purity of motives had to pay with his life."

Whereas litigation before the Mixed Arbitral Tribunals dealt with pecuniary claims of private individuals, the institute and its director entered the domain of high politics when Professor

Bruns was asked to assist the German government in the dispute
over the Austro-German customs union. In a Protocol signed at
Vienna on March 19, 1931, Austria and Germany had agreed
to initiate negotiations for a treaty "to assimilate the tariff and
economic policies of their respective countries" in accordance
with the principles laid down in the Protocol. The proposed
treaty amounted to a customs union between the two countries.
Apart from economic advantages Germany and Austria were to
derive from the treaty, the Brüning government hoped, through
this modest initiative in foreign policy, to blunt attacks by the
rapidly growing National Socialist party for alleged weakness
in foreign affairs. The planned customs union immediately
aroused strong French opposition. The customs union, it was
argued, infringed upon the independence of Austria and for
this reason was incompatible with Article 88 of the Treaty of
St.-Germain of September 10, 1919, whereby Austria undertook,
"in the absence of the consent" of the Council of the League of
Nations, "to abstain from any act which might .... compromise
her independence." Furthermore, under the terms of a Protocol
signed at Geneva on October 4, 1922, the Austrian government,
in exchange for a guaranteed loan by Great Britain, France, Italy,
and Czechoslovakia, agreed, in accordance with Article 88 of
the Treaty of St.-Germain, "not to alienate its independence."
The four other signatories, on their part, declared that "they will
respect the political independence, the territorial integrity and the
sovereignty of Austria."

The touchy French reaction was obviously dictated by the
fear that the Austro-German customs union might be the prelude
to a future German-Austrian political union (*Anschluss*) as the
Zollverein (Customs Union) of 1834 had been a step toward the
political unification of Germany. This was considered a threat to
French hegemony in Europe.

The idea of a German-Austrian union was born at the
end of World War I as the result of the dissolution of the
Austro-Hungarian Monarchy and the coming into existence of
the Austrian state (Deutschösterreich). The German Electoral
Law of November 30, 1918 (actually a decree of the Council of
the People's Commissars), provided for membership of Austrian
representatives in the German National Assembly if Austria, in

accordance with her wish, were to be admitted to the German Reich. Article 61, paragraph 2 of the Weimar Constitution of August 11, 1919, stipulated that Austria "after her union (*Anschluss*) with the German Reich shall have the right to participate in the Federal Council (*Reichsrat*)." Until such time representatives of Austria were to act in a consultative capacity. Implementation of these provisions would have meant that Germany, in accordance with the wish of the Austrian people, would have emerged from the war with increased territory. This was contrary to the intentions of the Allied governments. Hence the prohibitive clauses in the Treaty of St.-Germain and subsequent international agreements.

France submitted the case of the Austro-German customs union to the Council of the League of Nations. The Council, for its part, requested an advisory opinion from the Permanent Court of International Justice at The Hague. The Court offered the governments concerned an opportunity to present their respective legal views in oral proceedings.

At the beginning of June in 1931, Professor Bruns was named as the representative of the German government in the proceedings at The Hague. Professor Erich Kaufmann, a leading authority on international law and one of the scientific advisors of the institute, undertook to represent the Austrian government. Months of intense work and hectic activity at the institute followed. Written submissions by the two governments had to be prepared; documentary material and excerpts from literary sources, often under pressure of deadlines, had to be collected and made available to rebut arguments advanced by the other side in the course of oral proceedings; individual problems had to be studied, for example the concept of the independence of states as it had developed in the diplomatic practice of the nineteenth and the beginning of the twentieth century, a task which had been assigned to me.

We were convinced that the projected customs union in no way jeopardized the independence of Austria. Germany and Austria had done only what is customary in international relations. By agreeing on a customs union the two states had, in fact, manifested their independence. Agreements on economic matters, such as a customs union, or any restrictions on its liberty of action which a state may agree to, do not affect its independence.

The court did not agree with these arguments. In its Advisory Opinion of September 5, 1931, by a vote of eight to seven, it ruled in favor of the French thesis. The majority held that "the régime established on the basis of the Austro-German Protocol of March 19, 1931, would not be compatible with the Geneva Protocol of October 4, 1922," while the dissenting judges took the position that "the proposed Customs Union was not incompatible either with Article 88 of the Treaty of St.-Germain or with the Geneva Protocol." Even before the advisory opinion was handed down, Germany abandoned the project on September 3.

International jurists severely criticized the ruling of the court. There could be no doubt that the decision had been influenced by political considerations rather than by legal arguments. It reflected the political climate which at the time was dominated by French concepts. Supported by her position of continental leadership, France resisted changes in the existing European system, even such a relatively minor modification as the Austro-German customs union.

Although his four-day argument before the court was a recognized masterpiece of forensic advocacy, Professor Bruns was not surprised at the outcome of the case. I remember that he once told us that in the French view the prevention of a German-Austrian union was an indispensable element of the postwar order and that the French would consider any move to establish such a union an attack upon the foundations of the Paris peace settlement which France was committed to uphold.

France's unyielding attitude had fateful consequences. As a result of its foreign policy failure the authority of the Brüning government suffered irreparable harm. Moderate elements in Germany were disappointed. The course of German domestic policy was forced into a direction which eventually led to Hitler's seizure of power. This opinion is shared by so neutral an observer as the previously mentioned Carl J. Burckhardt: "It would have been in the interest of the victorious powers," he wrote, "to give Brüning tangible satisfaction."

Evidence of the world-wide reputation enjoyed by the institute was a visit, in 1931, by an Indian prince, the Gaekwar of Baroda, who had asked Professor Bruns for an advisory opinion on questions regarding a federal constitution. The prince planned the incorporation of his state into the province of Bombay, which eventually materialized in 1948-49. He intended entering into a federal union with the neighboring state. I still remember the visit of the Indian potentate when we all gathered in the conference room of the institute to be greeted with a handshake and a gentle look from dark eyes in a deeply bronzed face.

Assigning members of the institute abroad in order that they might become acquainted with foreign legal systems constituted another means of keeping the institute in touch with the outside world. I profited from this policy. The institute had a special relationship with a French lawyer in Paris, Maître Jean-Paul Coulon, *avocat à la Cour*, who represented German firms before French courts and was retained as a consultant by the German state representation at the Mixed Arbitral Tribunals in suits by the German Reich. In October of 1929, I was sent for several months to Paris to work in the *cabinet* of Maître Coulon. I was to assist Coulon with suits of German firms pending before French courts, and to familiarize myself with French law.

For his law practice Coulon used his apartment in the stately Rue de l'Université. After passing the porter's lodge, a visitor ascended broad winding stairs to the first floor, rang the bell and was received by a maid who showed him to the "office" of the Maître, an elegant drawing room equipped with period furniture, precious rugs and original paintings. No filing cabinets were in evidence; files were kept hidden from sight in a huge oaken closet. There were no bookcases. A few books lay on the frail looking rococo desk. They had been ordered for the case at hand from Sirey, the largest purveyor of legal literature in Paris. The lack of a private law library was in keeping with Coulon's method of work. He would analyze the legal problems involved in a case and determine the pertinent literature from a catalogue of law books. He then rented the required books from Sirey to be returned after use.

In the serene, cultivated atmosphere of the elegant parlor, legal problems could be discussed, as Coulon once remarked, *philosophiquement*, without haste.   No annoying rattle of typewriters interfered with the conversation.   The *dactylo*, Coulon's secretary, was installed in the adjoining drawing room of the lady of the house; she would discreetly withdraw when the lady received visitors.   No one would suspect that this was the work-room of a busy lawyer.

The relatively small amount of written work a French lawyer has to perform is, as Coulon explained to me, the result of the French system of court proceedings.   A lawsuit is conducted primarily by oral pleadings before the judge.   A lawyer's brief contains no more than what is expected to be presented to the judge at the hearing.   This system differs widely from the custom in Germany. A German lawyer will put a full discussion of the case into his brief with all possible arguments and counterarguments, including quotations from court decisions and the legal literature. This often verbose and laborious composition is meant for thorough study by the judge.   The elaborate preparation of a case is reflected in the pleadings of German lawyers. Here, too, as Coulon learned from his own observations, the rule is an "abundance" of learned discussion with no regard to the attention span of the judge or his personal interest in the case.   In this connection Coulon told me of his experience with Professor Partsch, my teacher from Berlin with whom Coulon had appeared in a number of lawsuits before French courts.   Coulon admired Partsch's enormous vitality, his prodigious memory. Partsch pleaded in fluent French. Sometimes he knew French law better than his adversaries. He could plead for hours without a trace of fatigue. But he spoke, Coulon remarked, as if he were alone.   Out of pure love of legal analysis, he could recite court decisions for half an hour, adding critical comments.   Coulon thought that his pleadings might have been more effective had they been shorter and better adapted to the receptiveness of the judge.

Coulon enjoyed a special trust among Russian emigrants possibly because of his international connections.   Their cases were among the most interesting ones of his law practice.   One case concerned the widow of a Russian industrialist from Kiev. During the First World War her husband, fearing the collapse of the currency, had converted his fortune of several millions into jewelry. When fleeing from the Bolshevik revolution, he had left the greater part of the jewels with a jeweler friend in Kiev. After years of perilous wanderings through Europe, the two friends met by accident in Paris. It turned out that the Kiev jeweler had established a jewelry business in Paris with the jewels that had been entrusted to him. When asked to return the jewels, he refused. The district attorney shrugged his shoulders. The crime—breach of trust and embezzlement—had not been committed on French territory and was thus of no concern to the French state. The case was now pending before a civil judge who had been requested to settle the question of ownership. Coulon, after patiently listening to the plea of the widow and secretly convinced of the hopelessness of her case, recommended that she get in touch with Alexandre Millerand, president of the French Republic from 1922-24. He was at that time a practicing attorney and, as Coulon advised the lady, had the reputation of being "honest, careful, but not cheap."

Another case concerned the Russian inventor of a diesel-type engine. He claimed that a partner had cheated him of the fruits of his invention. His relatives held a veritable council of war in Coulon's office to plan the tactics to be employed against the crooked partner: the sister, lively and impetuous, wanted aggressive action; her husband, former Chief of the Office of the President of the Republic, an elegant figure with white mustache and cultivated speech, the epitome of the high government official, counseled a conciliatory approach; the nephew, brash and crafty, did not think much of the negotiations; a fourth relative, the "spy," was to be sent out to gather confidential information about the family foe.

Apart from his private practice Coulon, as consultant and adviser for German parties, was involved in a number of lawsuits pending before the Franco-German Mixed Arbitral Tribunal. Among them was a "monstre" lawsuit conducted by the German Reich on behalf of German banks which jointly with the French bank of Dreyfuss had acquired large guano concessions in Peru in 1868. The banks now claimed part of the compensation which the International Court of Arbitration at The Hague had awarded the Dreyfuss heirs in 1921 for the loss of their guano concession as a result of the war between Chile and Peru. The object of the dispute had a value of 26 million gold francs. Another case involved the city of Strasbourg and a Frankfurt insurance company. The city had been ordered by a German court in 1918 and by a French court in 1922 to pay damages for accidents that had occurred in 1913 and 1915. The city then asked the insurance company with which it was insured against liability claims to pay the full gold value of the damages. The insurance company was willing to indemnify the city, however, only within the framework of the German revaluation legislation. The case raised complicated issues of French and German law and also involved the question of the jurisdiction of the Mixed Arbitral Tribunal.

Coulon was interested in scientific work. He asked me to translate into German a monograph which he had written with others on the taxation of foreign companies in France, Great Britain and the United States. "Un travail considérable," he remarked with some concern. The translation was eventually published.

Scenes of French life from the "City of Lights," the name given to Paris at that time because public buildings, church towers and fountains were floodlit at night, cross my mind like snapshots: the French way of enjoying food represented by diners sitting closely packed at tables along the walls and in the middle of the room in the Rôtisserie Périgourdine at the Place St.-Michel; the din of voices mixed with the clatter of dishes and plates; waiters with full-length white aprons deftly balancing hors d'oeuvre platters through the crowds; sizzling vapor from skillets in which cooks at individual tables prepared specialities. A fair on the square in front of the Versailles palace: among the crowd pressing around the booths priests in long cassocks with flat, broad-brimmed black hats, infantrymen in blue-gray, artillerymen in black uniforms with berets and capes, Algerian cavalrymen in long red coats, a white fez or a hood on their heads, the tall figures of black soldiers in khaki coats wearing their red fezzes and native jewelry. And finally the first "film parlant et sonore" (talkie) with Maurice Chevalier and "actualités parlantes" showing scenes from a session of the Assembly of the League of Nations featuring Briand and Stresemann.

During my stay in Paris I visited the World Exposition in Barcelona in 1929. The entrance of the German pavilion was flanked by two mighty flagpoles with two German flags atop; black-white-red and black-red-gold, vivid reminders of the fatal dispute about the German national flag which arose after the war.

The Weimar Constitution adopted as the flag of Germany the black, red and gold colors of the liberal and democratic unity movement of the first half of the nineteenth century while preserving the black, white, and red tricolor of imperial Germany as the "mercantile flag" in order to placate nationalistic emotions. "The conflict over the flag was to prove one of the worst divisive issues in the Weimar Republic." (Hajo Holborn, *A History of Modern Germany, 1840-1945*. Princeton, N.J. 1969, p.558.)

The Free City of Danzig, 1930-31

In October of 1930, the institute, at the suggestion of the *Senat* (government) of the Free City of Danzig, sent me to Danzig for several months to study conditions in the Free City and to act as counsel on questions of international law. I was to replace my colleague, Eduard von Schwartzkoppen, who had performed similar functions. During my stay I was assigned to the foreign affairs section in the office of the president of the *Senat*.

The Free City of Danzig was an artificial creation of the victors of World War I. They had promised the newly created state of Poland "free and secure access to the sea." To this end a strip of land along the Vistula River stretching to the Baltic sea, the so-called "Polish corridor" mentioned above, was carved out of German territory. The city of Danzig at the mouth of the Vistula river provided the only port on the Baltic seaboard suitable as an outlet to the sea. However, ninety-six percent of Danzig's population were German. Their incorporation into the Polish state would have been in flagrant violation of the principle of national self-determination proclaimed by President Wilson; there could be no doubt that the people of Danzig wished to stay within the German Reich. Furthermore, it had been agreed at Paris that Poland should receive only territories with an indisputably Polish population. Wilson therefore had in mind the creation of a free port within the area of the Danzig harbor. Similarly, the Versailles Treaty had granted Czechoslovakia a free port within the Hamburg harbor—supplemented by preferential railroad tariffs—to secure her access to the North Sea. This solution, however, did not satisfy the Poles. They demanded that the administration and development of the Danzig harbor should be managed by Poland. This would not be possible, they claimed, if Danzig were to remain under German sovereignty.

The Polish position was accepted by the Allies. Although Danzig was not annexed to Poland, the city was detached from Germany contrary to the wishes of its inhabitants. Together with three adjoining counties with a total population of 400,000 inhabitants, Danzig, under the designation of "Free City," received the status of an independent state and was placed under the protection of the League Nations, which also agreed to guarantee the Danzig constitution.

The sovereignty of the small state was considerably limited by a number of rights which the Versailles Treaty accorded to Poland. Thus Poland undertook the conduct of the foreign affairs of the Free City as well as the diplomatic protection of its citizens abroad. Poland controlled and administered the railroads within the territory of the Free City. A Harbor Commission composed of an equal number of Poles and Danzig representatives was in charge of the harbor, the Vistula river traffic, and the railroads leading to the harbor. The commission was headed by a president to be appointed by agreement between the governments of Poland and Danzig; lacking such agreement the president who in this had to be a Swiss citizen, was appointed by the Council of the League of Nations. Poland was entitled to establish within the harbor area a postal, telephone and telegraph service for direct communications with Poland. Poland and Danzig formed a unified customs territory where Polish customs legislation and Polish customs tariffs were in force.

From these few provisions it will have become abundantly clear that the international status of Danzig contained the seeds of inevitable future conflicts. The authors of the Danzig statute, the statesmen of the Allied Powers, were fully aware of its inherent weaknesses. In order to make the system work, it had to be under constant supervision by an independent authority enjoying international respect. According to the belief at the time, only the League of Nations possessed this qualification.

Thus a High Commissioner representing the League of Nations was installed in Danzig. His primary function was to resolve disputes between Danzig and Poland. His decisions were subject to an appeal by either party to the Council of the League of Nations. The Council, for its part, could submit the dispute to the Permanent Court of International Justice at The Hague.

While the basic provisions on the international status of the Free City were laid down in the Treaty of Versailles, additional details governing the relations between Poland and Danzig were set forth in a treaty between the two states signed in Paris on November 9, 1920. Because of the multitude of subjects dealt with in the treaty, and because of the often intentional imprecision of the text, the treaty gave rise to interminable quarrels in subsequent years. The last High Commissioner of the League, Professor Carl J. Burckhardt, has characterized the Danzig statute as "one of the most complicated creations that ever emanated from the theoretical thinking of improvising international lawyers," a "textbook example of abstract constructions." And Jósef Beck, the last Polish Foreign Minister before the outbreak of the Second World War, called the Free City of Danzig "undoubtedly the most bizarre and most complicated product of the Versailles Treaty."

According to German and Danzig opinion, the Free City enjoyed the status of a regular member of the community of nations with all the rights and duties pertaining to an independent, sovereign state. Poland, which had originally aimed at incorporating Danzig into the Polish state, never accepted this basic position. Instead, Poland considered Danzig to be merely an autonomous entity within the Polish state, comparable perhaps to the Hanseatic cities of the German Reich.

By treaty, Poland maintained a "diplomatic representation" in Danzig which was supposed "to serve as an intermediary between the Polish and the Danzig Governments"—a function perfectly compatible with the international law on diplomatic missions. The official title of the Polish representative, however, was "General Commissioner of the Republic of Poland at the Free City of Danzig." The title was designed to indicate that the Polish representative was by no means a diplomatic agent in the ordinary sense, but an official of the Polish government exercising supervisory functions vis-à-vis Danzig authorities similar to the High Commissioner of the League of Nations.

I had just taken up my duties in Danzig when the question of the legal position of the Polish diplomatic representative once again became a matter of dispute. On the occasion of a visit of a foreign warship, the Polish diplomat claimed to have the right to be the first one to welcome the ship. He justified his claim by alleging that a foreign warship is on Polish territory when it enters Danzig harbor. As the representative of the Polish president, the right to salute the ship on behalf of the

territorial sovereign therefore belonged to him. This view was
in sharp contrast to the thesis held by Danzig that the harbor
and the adjoining waters were subject to Danzig sovereignty
and that the *Senat* as the head of state under the Danzig
constitution took precedence over any other representative of
political organizations in the Free City. Danzig demanded that
the president of the *Senat* when coming aboard a foreign warship
receive the 21-gun salute customarily accorded heads of state.
The High Commissioner of the League of Nations, to whom the
dispute was submitted, decided in favor of Danzig: the president
of the *Senat*—if he visits a warship accompanied by a member of
the *Senat*—acts in the capacity of a head of state and is entitled to
all the honors customarily accorded the territorial sovereign.

What might appear to be absurd, trivial formalities or even
personal vanity, had serious political consequences for the legal
status of Danzig. In view of Polish efforts to deny Danzig the
status of a sovereign state, it was essential from the beginning to
resist granting concessions, even in the field of protocol, which
might be cited as precedents in support of the Polish thesis.

At the request of the *Senat* I prepared a memorandum
which was designed to settle all protocol questions in connection
with the visits of foreign warships once and for all. The
memorandum was to take into consideration the decisions of the
High Commissioner and of the Council of the League of Nations.

I began by establishing a list of participants in the ceremony
arranged according to their rank. First on the list was the *Senat*
as the head of the state and government of Danzig. The *Senat*
was followed by the consul of the country of the visiting ship,
the High Commissioner of the League of Nations, the Polish
representative in his capacity as diplomatic envoy, and by the
president of the Harbor Commission.

This order of precedence was to govern all ceremonial
functions on the occasion of visits by foreign warships. The
captain of the visiting vessel also had to adhere to it when making
his calls ashore.

The president of the *Senat*, accompanied by a member of his
government, was the first to go aboard. He was to be honored by a
21-gun salute and the setting of the flag of Danzig. Next in line
was the High Commissioner of the League of Nations: nineteen

guns, no flag. Then came the Polish representative: seventeen guns, Polish flag. The last one to go aboard was the president of the Harbor Commission: no guns, no flag.

Despite these efforts to guarantee to all participants a treatment commensurate with their constitutional and international positions, no visit went by without causing new difficulties. Professor Burckhardt once remarked that some of the participants "already felt insulted in advance." More serious for the political development in Danzig than indignant reactions of individuals was the use made by the Nazis of the protocol called "nonsensical" by Burckhardt (because of the system that had produced it). After the Nazis had achieved actual power in the Free City around the middle of the thirties, the protocol's intricacies served them as a means to unhinge the Danzig statute systematically, for example by failing to attend official functions so as to demonstrate their contempt for the office of the High Commissioner.

The foreign affairs section of the *Senat* was responsible for cases affecting the relations between Danzig and Poland, and for questions of international law. Examples from notes I kept illustrate the type of duties my work in the section entailed.

We had learned from newspaper reports that during an election rally a member of the Polish diplomatic mission had appealed to Danzig citizens of Polish nationality to vote for certain candidates. The action of the Polish representative was a clear violation of the principle of international law prohibiting a diplomat from interfering with the domestic affairs of the receiving state. The incident proved once more that the Polish minister was not prepared to observe the rules of the law of legation. As previously noted, he claimed a special position which had no basis in the treaties governing the status of Danzig and which, if left unchallenged, was apt to prejudice the interests of Danzig. In a note of protest the Danzig government denounced the act of the Polish diplomat as being contrary to international law and warned against its repetition.

When Danzig and Norway, by an exchange of notes between the two countries, abrogated the visa requirement, the Polish representative who had conducted the negotiations added his signature to the notes, even though Poland was not a party to the agreement. Poland was responsible for the "conduct" of the foreign affairs of Danzig by placing its diplomatic apparatus at the disposal of the Free City (Danzig because of its small size could not afford diplomatic representatives of its own). But party to international treaties which Poland negotiated on behalf of Danzig was Danzig and Danzig alone. The *Senat* in the case at hand reminded Poland of the legal situation and demanded withdrawal of the Polish signature.

The same tendency on the part of Poland to assert a substantive role as distinguished from mere assistance in matters affecting Danzig's external relations became evident when Poland demanded that a treaty between Danzig and the German Reich concerning legal assistance should have both a German and a Polish text. Danzig and Germany insisted that the language of the treaty could only be German. Adding a Polish text would mean that Poland would also be a party to the treaty which she was not, as the treaty established reciprocal rights and duties between Danzig and Germany. A note of the *Senat* rejected the Polish demand.

These cases, trivial as they may appear, demonstrated the need for constant vigilance and firm insistence on the legal situation in order to prevent the gradual erosion of the international status of the Free City by Polish "salami" tactics.

Even private individuals were occasionally caught in the web of tension that existed between Poland and Danzig. Thus a lady from Danzig who, during a railway trip from Danzig to Marienburg, had vehemently protested against a Polish fellow traveler smoking in a non-smoking compartment was arrested by Polish police after the train had left Danzig territory, was taken off the train and detained in a prison cell during the day and the following night, and was fined the next day by a Polish county court for creating a disturbance. The act had been committed on Danzig territory and should have been tried, if at all, by Danzig courts. Again, the Danzig government was forced to protest this encroachment upon its sovereign rights.

Between 1922 and 1933, one hundred and six disputes between Danzig and Poland were brought before the Council of the League of Nations. Some were even considered by the Permanent Court of International Justice at The Hague, among

Free City of Danzig

23. St. Mary's Cathedral (14th/15th century)

22. Three Landmarks (from left to right): Tower of the Town Hall, St. Mary's Cathedral, Crane Gate. View from the Vistula River.

24. Crane Gate (1443)

25. Armory (1605)

them the case of the "Polish Postal Service in Danzig." The object of the dispute were mailboxes—painted red with the white Polish eagle and Polish inscriptions—which Polish authorities had set up at various places in town for the apparent purpose of collecting mail destined for Poland. Under existing treaties, Poland was entitled to establish mailboxes only within the area of the harbor for direct postal service with Danzig. In the general picture of the city, the mailboxes looked like installations of the Polish postal service, i.e. a Polish governmental agency. Danzig demanded that the boxes be removed—to no avail. The court, however, limited the number of the boxes and determined the places where they could be located in order to be available for general use. Poland had won an important psychological victory since the mailboxes were highly visible signs of Poland's presence in town. More threatening was Poland's attempt to establish a berth for Polish war vessels in Danzig harbor because of the potential danger it presented to the existence of Danzig as an independent state. In long-drawn-out proceedings before the Permanent Court of International Justice, the court denied Polish war vessels the right of access to, or anchorage in, the port of Danzig. Had Poland succeeded, Danzig harbor would have become a Polish naval station; this would have been contrary to the intentions of the framers of the Danzig statute that the harbor was to be used exclusively for commercial purposes.

At the beginning of November 1930, the election campaign for the "People's Diet" (*Volkstag*), the Danzig parliament, was in full swing. After their decisive victory in September of 1930 in the German elections for the federal parliament (*Reichstag*), the Nazis made tremendous efforts to continue their triumphal advance. "Air Force Captain Hermann Göring" and "*Gauleiter* Albert Forster" were announced as speakers at an election rally on November 7 in the sports arena. I was curious to learn how the Nazis would deal with specific Danzig problems and went to the arena on the appointed day. As I approached the place I became aware that this was not like a regular rally devoted to the discussion of political issues; instead a carefully staged show intended to arouse expectations of extraordinary events was in progress. The scene on the street was dominated by brownshirted storm troopers acting like barkers in front of a circus, shouting

slogans and soliciting contributions for the party as they rattled
their tin cans. Under glaring lights young men and women were
crowding around the entrance, eager to get in, as though they
were expecting some sort of revivalist gathering. Inside the
hall the din of voices was drowned out by sharply accentuated
military music. The ubiquitous presence of uniforms, the strict
discipline enforced by party members wearing swastika armbands,
and the ceremonial entry of massed flags raised the excitement of
the packed audience to an emotional, frenzied pitch which did not
admit of rational thinking.

Forster's native Franconian accent seemed out of place in
this northern town. He spoke about the "shameful" Versailles
Treaty and of an imminent radical change. "In Germany
developments are moving forward with giant steps. Here
Bolshevism! Here National Socialism!" He said he had been at
the Obersalzberg (Hitler's mountain retreat) the day before and
had talked with the *Führer*. "Adolf Hitler is convinced that in
two years at the latest he will assume power in Germany." This
prediction seemed absurd to me at the time. It came within an ace
of being accurate; it failed by two months.

Göring, wearing a brown shirt, breeches and high boots
exclaimed that National Socialism was Germany's "last chance."
"We must be quite clear about this: If our movement does not
win, then the Soviet star will rise . . . . We shall exact vast
and heavy sacrifices from the German people. But the people will
know what they make sacrifices for: For Germany's freedom . . .
. We are revolutionaries. We are being told that we made tactical
mistakes in parliament. There are people who have nothing else
on their mind but parliamentarianism. We are against the system,
against everything that exists today. . . ." The rally closed with
the third verse of the national anthem, a cheer for Adolf Hitler
and a National Socialist battle hymn sung with the right arm
raised.

Denunciation of the Versailles Treaty and of the political
system in Germany which the Nazis claimed was the outcome of
Versailles was calculated to inflame the audience, to intensify
their resentment of the forced separation from Germany and to
strengthen their apprehension of a slow assimilation into Poland
or even of a "return to the Polish fatherland" which a member of

Free City of Danzig

26. Residence of the High Commissioner of the
League of Nations

27. A Polish Mailbox

the Polish diplomatic mission on Danzig had once proclaimed as the aim of Polish policy. From such sentiments and fears the Nazis drew their power. "If the official policy of demanding the revision of the Versailles Treaty does not succeed this will be the end of the political order in Germany as we know it today," I wrote in my diary under the impression of the election rally of November 7, 1930.

In 1927, under the designation of "National Socialist German Workers Party, Revaluation and People's Rights Party," the National Socialists had garnered just 1,482 votes. At the elections of November 16, 1930, they became the second largest party in the Danzig *Volkstag* with 31,500 votes after the Social Democrats. The conservative German Nationalist party was relegated from second place to fourth. Their losses (25,000 votes) were exceeded by the Social Democrats; although their votes were reduced from 61,700 to 48,000, they still retained their position as the strongest party. The Communist vote rose from 11,000 to 19,000; they ranked in the distribution of parliamentary seats just behind the German Nationalists. The Polish party likewise was able to improve its voting record greatly. The elections showed a clear trend towards radicalization and confrontation in the population as well as in the relations between Germans and Poles.

As a consequence of the elections, the president of the *Senat*, Dr. Heinrich Sahm, resigned. He was replaced by the German Nationalist Dr. Ernst Ziehm, president of the Danzig Supreme Administrative Court, a compromise candidate, since the National Socialists were not yet willing to assume governmental responsibilities. They were, however, prepared to tolerate a minority government led by the German Nationalist party. Dr. Sahm was soon thereafter chosen Lord Mayor of Berlin and, after losing that position when Hitler came to power, was the German Minister to Norway for a number of years.

During my stay in Danzig, the High Commissioner of the League of Nations was Count Manfredo Gravina, an Italian naval officer. His mother, Blandine Countess Gravina, was the second child of Hans von Bülow and Cosima, the daughter of Franz Liszt and later wife of Richard Wagner. I made the acquaintance of this "grand old lady" clad in matronly black at a luncheon in the house of Dr. Sahm. I had been introduced to her as a member of the

Mendelssohn-Bartholdy family which caused her to address some friendly remarks to me about the composer, my great-granduncle. Her resemblance to her mother Cosima, as one knows her from pictures, was striking.

"In Danzig one still senses the great days when Danzig was a member of the Hanseatic League," I wrote to my father in December of 1930. "The spirit of the Hanse survives in magnificent churches and stately secular buildings. Whoever has been exposed to the sight of the mighty brick-built St. Mary's Cathedral with its stump-like bell tower will keep a life-long memory of it. Danzig's burghers knew how to use the wealth they accumulated from trade with the Polish and Russian hinterland to beautify their city. Danzig's refined cuisine is a remnant from those days. In small crooked lanes off the main streets, one can find cozy taverns where the high art of preparing dishes worthy of the city's aldermen has been preserved to this day. . . . Today Danzig is the most endangered outpost of German culture and civilization in the East. The compulsion to resist efforts at 'Polonization' weighs heavily upon the inhabitants. The situation here resembles the Rhineland under French occupation. Inscriptions in two languages in the railroad station, Polish uniforms on the streets, the ominous mailboxes—all this strengthens the impression of a foreign occupation . . . . Adding to Danzig's woes is the construction of the harbor at Gdingen (now Gdynia); it poses a serious threat to the economic life of the Free City. With the aid of French capital, Poland has turned a small fishing village into a city of 40,000 inhabitants with a harbor which possesses the most modern installations and will soon rank among the great ports of the Baltic Sea. During a recent visit to Gdingen I could convince myself of the indeed imposing construction work, even though it is still unfinished in parts. The planning of the new harbor was not supported by economic reasons. The Danzig harbor in its present condition as well as after further expansion for which almost unlimited space was available, could have satisfied all of Poland's future trading needs. Statements to the contrary notwithstanding, the construction of the Gdingen harbor was motivated exclusively by political considerations. Danzig would have to compete with Gdingen, and that meant that the Poles could put pressure on Danzig and make it accept their demands. In addition to its economic role Gdingen was important for Poland also in the context of the corridor problem. A Polish harbor at the Baltic Sea would always need a Polish hinterland. . . ."

The independent existence of Danzig was eventually destroyed not by Poland but by the Nazi government in Berlin. From the mid-thirties Danzig, for all practical purposes, was governed from Berlin. *Gauleiter* Forster was the executive arm of the Berlin central government. In August of 1935, the National Socialist government of Danzig, in order to adapt the legal situation of the city to that of the Reich, by a decree that was the literal copy of a similar measure of the Reich government, abrogated the constitutionally guaranteed rights of inviolability of the person, freedom of movement, and freedom of speech. The Council of the League of Nations, as the guarantor of the Danzig constitution and supported by the still existing opposition in the Danzig parliament, protested this violation of the constitution. The Permanent Court of International Justice agreed with the Council and declared the Danzig decree to be unconstitutional. The Danzig *Senat* gave in and rescinded the decree. But neither the High Commissioner nor the Council of the League of Nations was able to prevent the introduction of the "Aryan clause" (discrimination against all persons of "non-Aryan blood") in Danzig. This constituted a flagrant violation of the constitutional principle of equality of treatment, and led to the subsequent persecution of the Jews. The office of the High Commissioner gradually became a farce. Its only usefulness, if any, was that it served for a while as a listening post. Despite its practical ineffectiveness as an instrument of control the High Commissioner did not relinquish his mission but held out in Danzig till the bitter end. In the early hours of September 1, 1939, the German battle cruiser *Schleswig-Holstein* while in Danzig harbor ostensibly on a "visit", began shelling the Polish ammunition depot on the peninsula at the entrance of the harbor called "Westerplatte" with heavy artillery. On the same morning at 8:00 a.m., *Gauleiter* Forster appeared at the residence of the High Commissioner and informed him that he had to leave Danzig territory within two hours. The war against Poland had begun. The Free City of Danzig had ceased to exist. Nobody knew it at the time, but with the end of the Free City, Hitler had forever gambled away Danzig's German character and its ancient affiliation with German history and civilization.

End of an Era

In February of 1931, I returned from Danzig and resumed my duties at the institute. My principal concern was to complete my study on territorial changes in Europe since the Congress of Vienna. I intended to use it as the basis of an academic career. My connection with the institute was limited in time by the leave of absence I had been granted by the Prussian government. The leave had been extended from year to year. I could, however, not be certain of further extensions in view of the shortage of civil servants in the higher administrative service.

Since the end of March, 1930, the Brüning government had been in office. Brüning, leader of the Catholic Center party, had been appointed chancellor by President von Hindenburg with the mandate to carry through financial reforms and, in particular, to seek relief for the farmers. The new government, a "presidential cabinet" clothed with the authority of the head of state, was to be independent of party-political support but should try to cooperate with the *Reichstag*.

In July of 1930, the government submitted to the *Reichstag* a drastic economy program providing for tax increases, budget cuts, and assistance to agriculture. The *Reichstag* rejected it, whereupon the president authorized the chancellor to enact the program by emergency decree pursuant to Article 48, paragraph 2 of the constitution.

Realizing that a democracy must be in a position to ward off extraordinary dangers threatening the existence of the state, the framers of the Weimar Constitution had entrusted the president with dictatorial powers authorizing him to rule by decree in an emergency situation.

When drafting the constitution it could hardly have been foreseen that the presidential emergency powers might be interpreted to include also measures in the economic field. The first president of the Republic, the Social Democrat Friedrich Ebert, had already been forced to use dictatorial powers to deal with economic emergencies. Up to 1924 he had issued more than one hundred emergency decrees on financial and economic matters. I never thought that this constituted a danger to the republic. On the contrary, we felt gratitude and relief that the government, with firmness and determination, had succeeded in leading us out of the chaos of inflation. My father received his salary in good money. This meant that the family could breathe a sigh of relief; we children could get new clothes and the meals could become more diversified.

On July 16, 1930, the emergency decree "to safeguard the economy and the finances," as authorized by the president, was issued by the Brüning government. Two days later the *Reichstag*, making use of its constitutional prerogatives, demanded the repeal of the decree. The demand was complied with. Although the *Reichstag* had acted within its constitutional rights, it was dissolved by the president. Elections were scheduled for September 14. On July 26 a new decree was issued "to redress financial, economic, and social emergencies." It was more exacting than the decree of July 16, which the *Reichstag* had rejected.

On September 14 the new *Reichstag* was elected. In the evening of election day, I went to Wittenbergplatz in the western part of Berlin. On large billboards just north of the Metro station, election results were posted as they came in from the precincts. What I saw happening before my eyes was like the eruption of a volcano, the coming to light of elemental forces that I never suspected might exist. Hourly increasing figures blazoned forth the triumphant march to victory of the Nazi party, a rise from 12 to 107 deputies in the *Reichstag*.

I had never concerned myself to any appreciable degree with the brownshirts. Off and on uniformed troopers could be seen in the streets or crowds of people gathering around assembly places displaying Nazi symbols. I found the Nazi press, Goebbel's boulevard sheet *Der Angriff* (*Attack*) and the *Völkischer Beobachter* (*The People's Observer*), the official organ of the Nazi movement, repulsive both in make-up and in language. It was a shattering experience for me to realize that disillusionment with the existing political order, despair at the deplorable economic situation and a feeling of being a despised underdog in the world and the victim of foreign oppression could find expression in a protest movement of such magnitude without my having been aware of it. I went home dazed. It seemed to me that I had been out of touch with the times for years.

I was not alone. Many were as surprised as I was. A contemporary report on that night in September "when everybody panicked," remarks: "The bourgeois parties seemed broken up . . . . Their leaders and followers with few exceptions looked paralyzed by the wave of radicalism. People either joined up or expected, trembling, the first shots of the apparently inevitable civil war. A jumble of advice was addressed to the chancellor: Resign! A Government of the Right! Return to the Grand Coalition! Form a Government with the Nazis! Directory!"

Nothing of that sort happened. In violation of the basic rules of parliamentary democracy, the Nazis, clear winners of the September elections, were not asked to form the government. The Brüning government remained in office. Its character, however, changed. Up until that time, the government had at least made an effort to obtain approval of a majority of the *Reichstag* for its program. From now on it would suffice that parliament "tolerate" it. Under the shock of the Nazi election victory, the Social Democratic group in the Reichstag had decided to forego active opposition. Their "standstill" position enabled Brüning to continue his necessary, though unpopular, economic policies. His government acted almost exclusively on the authority of the president. Like the parliament under Bismarck, the *Reichstag* was confined to the role of an observer; it had no influence on the formation or the policies of the government.

The primary aim of Germany's foreign policy was the peaceful revision of the Versailles Treaty. Like Stresemann before him, Brüning, trusting in the the justice of the German cause, endeavored to achieve liberation from the chains of the Versailles Treaty through tenacious, patient negotiations with Germany's former enemies. Germany was in no position to pursue power politics. In their struggle against the injustices of Versailles, the German people had to rely on the force of the law. What mattered was to obtain a fair hearing in the forum of international politics of the German position with respect to fields of particular importance to Germany such as reparations, interpretation and application of the peace treaties, disarmament, and in general the question of revision of the Versailles territorial system.

With due consideration to scientific objectivity, the Bruns Institute was committed to assisting the government through research and publications in the pursuit of these objectives. The case of the Austro-German customs union had taught us that defeat could not be avoided on this road. But there were also successes: Brüning was able to obtain concessions from the Western Powers with respect to the payment of reparations, and the question of German equality in armaments. There was increasing support for the German thesis of peaceful change of the most glaring injustices of the Versailles Treaty. Especially in Great Britain and the United States, the conviction grew that the Versailles Treaty was not suited to ensure the peaceful coexistence of the European states and in the long run to form the statute of Europe.

I was convinced that the cause of the German people in the world could have no better champion than Brüning. "Moral integrity, no empty talk but honesty, the will to be objective, passionate love of the country," these were, as I wrote in a diary note of August 1931, the qualities which led me to trust Brüning and his political leadership. Brüning, I continued, knew when to say "No" to intolerable demands. "He never makes promises he cannot keep, but he expects that promises made to him will be fulfilled. The objectivity and candor of the German chancellor will carry the day for him at international conferences. In pleading the German case he serves at the same time the cause of European survival."

I considered it the indispensable duty of the "national forces" on the right to support Brüning's policy of prudent advance and reconciliation with Germany's former enemies, and to collaborate with him in the great task of constitutional reform. In my view, only a forthright policy that shunned recklessness would open the way to freedom. I was persuaded that the turn of the German Nationalist party under the leadership of Hugenberg to uncompromising rejection of any type of conciliatory policies and to political radicalism would inevitably invite disaster.

Alfred Hugenberg, formerly a Krupp director and eventually director of a large newspaper and a movie corporation, had replaced the moderate Count Westarp as chairman after the defeat of the German Nationalist party in the election of 1928. Hugenberg represented the right wing of the party which promoted racist and Pan-German tendencies. In cooperation with Hitler, he supported, in 1929, the petition for a referendum against the Young Plan (an American-sponsored plan for the settlement of reparation payments). The call for a referendum was coupled with the draft of a so-called "Freedom Act" which rejected the war-guilt article of the Versailles Treaty and made it a crime to burden Germany with additional reparation payments. The Act provided that the chancellor, ministers, and other plenipotentiaries of the Reich would be liable to imprisonment with hard labor if they were to violate the Act (i.e. agree to further reparations). This penal clause on which Hitler insisted revealed with brutal clarity the demagogic extremism of the Nazis. Hugenberg's own party demanded the elimination of this infamous clause, but Hugenberg yielded to Hitler's dictate. As a consequence, the moderate wing split from the party and founded the Conservative People's Union under Treviranus.

I placed high hopes in the new party as a rallying point for a moderate right committed to upholding the constitutional order and to opposing radical, destructive elements of the Hugenberg type. I was deeply disappointed when the party suffered a crushing defeat at the general elections in November of 1932.

The referendum against the Young Plan failed. And so did a plebiscite inaugurated in February, 1931, by the *Stahlhelm* (Steel Helmet), a rightist veteran's association. The plebiscite was meant to force the dissolution of the Prussian diet in which the parties of the co-called Weimar coalition of Centrists, left-wing Liberals, and Social Democrats still held the majority of the seats.

Instead of the expected 40 or more percent, only about 37 percent of the electorate voted on August 9 in favor of new elections in Prussia. I regretted the outcome at the time, not because the plebiscite had failed; there had never been a chance that a majority might demand the dissolution of the Prussian diet. Yet a more impressive result, I thought, might have convinced the world of the seriousness of the "national opposition" which stood behind the plebiscite and might have strengthened the bargaining position of the Brüning government with the foreign powers. The vote had been influenced primarily by domestic policy considerations. The danger existed, I felt, that it might be misinterpreted abroad as a defeat of the forces which were striving with increased belligerence against everything connected with the Versailles system and might create a false sense of security. Comments in the foreign press bore me out. "France breathes a sigh of relief," "The world is relieved," I read in foreign newspapers. The conspicuous failure of the plebiscite gave fresh impetus to the militant activists of the radical right. They saw confirmed what they had been preaching with growing stridency, namely, that a change of existing conditions could not be attained within the present system.

After the joint walkout of the German Nationalists and National Socialists from the *Reichstag* in February 1931 and the plebiscite of February/August 1931, the next move of the parties of the "national opposition" was a huge assembly staged, in October 1931, in Harzburg, a little spa in the state of Brunswick. They were joined there by the *Stahlhelm*. As a consequence of the "Harzburg front", the German Nationalist party became entangled in Hitler's tow for good. In order to keep up with the Nazis, the party had to match their radical hostility to the Weimar system. Because of his obstinate opposition to everything that the Brüning government undertook, I felt that Hugenberg was becoming the "gravedigger of the republic." He was not interested in settling crisis situations but rather in using them, in association with Hitler, as a means to weaken democracy and to "destroy the system." This policy intensified the discontent of the masses and made millions of voters ready to accept radical solutions. However, it was not Hugenberg who attracted the masses; the winner was Hitler.

In the meantime, the economic situation worsened. When, in May of 1931, the Austrian *Creditanstalt* stopped payments (the French government, in retaliation against the plan for the Austro-German customs union, had withdrawn credits in Germany and Austria), a severe banking crisis also erupted in Germany. In the middle of July, two of Germany's major banks suspended payments, first the *Darmstädter und Nationalbank*, *Danatbank* for short, and soon thereafter the highly respected *Dresdner Bank*. Minor banks followed suit. The government declared bank holidays and limited foreign exchange operations. On trips abroad, travelers were not allowed to carry more than 100 marks with them. Civil servants were paid only half their salaries. A new inflation seemed imminent. I worried about my modest bank account. An atmosphere of gloom was spreading. On August 4, 1931, at 8:00 p.m., Brüning spoke to the nation on the radio "in a deadly serious, almost melancholic-somber voice that sounded as if he were about to announce the end of the world," I noted in my diary. I took down parts of the speech in shorthand. Here are some of the highlights; they give a picture of the economic situation and what the government did to cope with it:

> As of tomorrow, money will circulate once again in the form of cash and notes. Decrees will be issued to prevent the flight of capital and to control dealings in foreign currencies. The penalty provided in these decrees—imprisonment with hard labor—will demonstrate the determination of the government to counteract most decisively any special demands on the capital market which are harmful to the general good. Difficult times require harsh measures. They will not cause the economy to slow down.
>
> What the president and the government have done these last few weeks has nothing to do with inflation. We do not have too much money in circulation. There is no substance to the fears that the money might be in danger. On the contrary, it would be prudent not to withdraw money from the bank, because the measures and policies of the government will raise the purchasing power of the money.
>
> Emergency decrees and supplementary measures are merely technical means. It is up to an enlightened populace to make them work. It is a sign of nervousness to look for cash when it is not absolutely needed. It is wrong to withdraw cash before it is actually needed.

Tackling the problem of the major banks was our first priority. The special action we took in this case was clearly in the interest of middle-income people. The government cannot refrain from carrying out measures in the fields of credits and stocks that had been planned long in advance when the government, upon the urgent request of the persons concerned, had intervened in these matters.

The government is not infallible. It does not assert that it has succeeded on all counts. However, as far as the magnitude of the task and determination are concerned, there are only a few comparable examples in world history. Timely action is better than procrastination.

To sum up: We have reached our goal. As of tomorrow, conditions exist for the normal circulation of goods and money. It is necessary that confidence grows and endures. Everyone can do his part.

An indispensable prerequisite is freedom from disturbances on the domestic front. All forces must be welded together. Self-destructive internecine strife must be avoided. Through creative synthesis we shall overcome our differences.

After the resumption of all payment transactions on August 5, there was no run on the banks. Had a miracle occurred of which I had not been aware? How was it possible that confidence had returned so soon, a circumstance all the more surprising since all major measures to improve the economy—such as bringing in new funds from abroad—had failed? What was the reason for this absolute trust? "We see a government at work which tackles problems energetically, which is determined to do away with things that are not needed, which is willing to balance the budget and to collect the revenues aggressively. We will not succumb to threats of catastrophe. We have trust in the economic vigor of the German people and its will to live." With these thoughts written in my diary, I tried to explain to myself the change of mood that had taken place after we had been in the lowest of spirits only a few months earlier.

The situation had become stabilized to such a degree that I was able to take a short vacation cruise on the Dutch East-Indian liner *Baloeran,* in October of 1931, from Rotterdam to Marseilles. Among my fellow passengers were young officers of the Dutch-Indian Army who were returning from home leave to their units in Bandoeng and other places. The majority of the service personnel aboard were people from East India. They wore their native costumes—wide breeches and colorful head scarves. Sometimes one saw them squatting in a corner and softly conversing with each other. In their sandals they glided through the gangways at a measured pace, silently and gravely. In their dealings with the passengers they remained reserved and distant. A friendly greeting, a cheerful look did not evoke a similar response. There were no human contacts of the kind that customarily develop between passengers and the ship's personnel. Pride? Mistrust? Obedience to orders? On the railroad trip from Marseilles to Paris I shared the compartment with a Hindu. When he learned that I was German, his eyes lit up. "Oh, General Hitler." He had heard of him. India is still a "jewel in the British Crown," he said, "but Hitler will go to war with England and then India will be free."

In Paris I visited the *Exposition Coloniale* in Vincennes. The main attraction was the temple of Angkor Wat reconstructed to scale in papier-mâché. The temple had been excavated by French archaeologists in Cambodia, then a Kingdom under French protection, and is considered one of the proudest achievements of French colonial archaeology. (Angkor Wat was the ancient capital of Cambodia and was abandoned as the Khmer capital in the fifteenth century. The ruins were rediscovered by the French in 1861.)

The economic recovery, the result of Brüning's emergency measures, was of short duration. The campaign of hatred conducted relentlessly by Hugenberg and Hitler against the system aggravated tensions on the domestic front. The "national opposition" was determined to deny Brüning the success of his policies at all costs. Economic recovery and undisturbed evolution of domestic politics would have enabled a return from presidential dictatorship to parliamentary democracy as had happened in the early days of the republic under the presidency of

Ebert. However, this was not what Hitler and Hugenberg had in mind. In his last speech before the *Reichstag* on May 12, 1932, Brüning had beseeched its members to "hold fast during these last few minutes . . . . not to give up at the last hundred meters before the goal." Brüning did not know it; but at this very moment he and his cabinet were being overthrown, not, however, by his radical opponents, but by a clique of "advisers" around President von Hindenburg. Under its leader, General von Schleicher, this group had been waiting in the wings and now hoped, by taking advantage of the growing pressure from the extreme right, to realize their concept of a new form of authoritarian government.

Brüning's "presidential government" had been tolerated by parliament. At least the appearance of a government in accordance with the principles of the constitution had been preserved. Brüning's successor, Franz von Papen—a little known deputy of the Catholic Center party in the Prussian diet whom Schleicher had picked as his candidate for chancellor—openly broke with the parliamentary system. His "cabinet of the barons" (the majority of the ministers came from noble families) could count on the support of only about ten percent of the members of the *Reichstag*, essentially the German Nationalist party. "Hindenburg's chancellor" based his authority exclusively on the trust of the aged president.

The overthrow of Brüning, it seemed to me, had shaken the constitutional order to its very foundations. I did not trust the new political leadership. With this type of government, which had no firm constitutional basis and lacked popular support, one could never be sure that it might not embark upon an adventurous course. For the first time in my life I was overwhelmed by a sense of pessimism and despair. Where would all this end? I felt in need of a firm footing in my personal life, a guiding star.

Friends had told me about Johannes Müller and his Alpine castle, the "Elmau." There, I was told, worldly wisdom was taught. There I would be able to find myself and undoubtedly would be freed from the unrest which had seized and paralyzed me in the face of the desperate political situation.

Already before World War I, Johannes Müller, a religious philosopher, had made a name for himself far beyond Germany's frontiers through unorthodox writings which had brought him into conflict with the Protestant Church. In lectures and books he propagated an "unspoiled" art of living based on Christian foundations, as it was practiced at Elmau.

In June of 1932, I spent three weeks at Elmau. The advice of Johannes Müller—not to burden oneself with too many thoughts, rather "to let things grow," to do what is on hand and to wait and see what will happen—was, given the circumstances, undeniably of genuine help. The beautiful Alpine scenery greatly contributed to the recovery.

The "castle" looked more like a sanitarium—square, several stories high, and crowned with a tower. It was situated in a broad valley of the Wetterstein mountain range at the foot of the Wetterstein cliff in perfect seclusion and tranquillity, "like a remote paradise" with wholesome mountain air which was free from smoke and dust. In those days no motor cars were allowed in the vicinity of the castle. The railroad station for Elmau was the village of Klais, on the line from Garmisch to Mittenwald. Either one followed an easy footpath for three-quarters of an hour to reach the castle or one was met at the station by a horse-drawn vehicle. Luggage was brought once a day from the station to the castle.

A further element in the process of achieving mental and emotional balance was superb music. During my stay the Stuttgart Wendling Quartet, one of the leading quartets of the time, gave nightly concerts for a whole week. On specific occasions the world-famous pianist Wilhelm Kempf or clarinet, viola, or violoncello artists performed. The programs consisted of chamber music by Bach, Beethoven, Mozart, Haydn, Schubert, Brahms, and Chopin. Applause was "discouraged." On other evenings there were dances in the large meeting hall. The music was provided by the artists in residence, and the waltzes were not by Johann Strauss, but by Chopin, Schubert, and Brahms.

Elmau's "regulars" affected a slightly sectarian attitude of "intimacy, naturalness, humaneness." Despite Müller's objection, a guest called it the "Elmau mannerism." As a newcomer, this behavior was at first hard for me to bear. I had, however, no choice but to adapt myself to it since this "Home for Physical and Mental Rest," in the words of the prospectus, was primarily designed for readers of Müller's writings. Prior to my visit, I had known hardly anything about Johannes Müller (I remember that our teacher of religion at the Neuwied *Gymnasium* had mentioned him approvingly). I had read none of his writings. Guests like me who had never before stayed at Elmau were not accepted for less than one week. That much time was needed, Johannes Müller insisted, "so one will experience the vital force and the mental climate" of Elmau and be able "to participate in the creative development of one's nature as a human being and in the behavior resulting from it." The daily change of the seating order at the dinner table was meant to acquaint people with each other in a free and easy way. The ritual was administered with friendliness, yet firmness by Miss Krause, a dignified elderly lady from the Baltic provinces; her decisions brooked no protest, although they sometimes rather rudely cut off personal relationships that were developing in the course of table conversations.

The family character of the guest community was enhanced by the absence of hired personnel. The necessary services were rendered by "female assistants," young ladies between twenty and thirty years of age from "good families." Once accepted for service at Elmau, they were permitted to pay fifty marks per month for this privilege. In return, they were expected to "make up at least eight rooms in the morning, to serve at the table, to do the dishes, to clean vegetables and perform other household chores." After having their breakfast at 6:30 a.m. in the company of Johannes Müller, the girls were on their feet from 7 o'clock in the morning until 8 o'clock at night. There were rest periods at noon and at teatime. Only hardy and healthy persons were able to stand the strain of these services. As compensation, they were allowed to dance with the guests at night—until 10 o' clock, their bedtime.

The last day of my stay at Elmau was overshadowed by the news that one of the girls—I believe she worked in the administration—was missing. She had not returned from a hike. I had made her acquaintance eight days before she vanished. She told me on one of our walks that she had experienced a grave disappointment the year before. I tried to comfort her, but her gloomy mood persisted. Neither time nor the healing power of Elmau, so often proven effective, had helped her. Shortly after my departure she was found. She had fallen from a cliff 3,000 feet to her death.

At the beginning of July 1932, I returned from Elmau to Berlin. On July 20, when I went out for lunch with some colleagues to the *Franziskaner* on Friedrichstrasse, I noticed at a newsstand papers with the headline: "State of Siege." What had happened? In the morning, at ten o'clock, Chancellor von Papen, acting pursuant to a decree issued by the president of the Reich for the specific purpose of "restoring public order and safety in the territory of the State of Prussia," had ousted the legally constituted Prussian government with military force. The decree appointed the chancellor "Reich Commissioner for Prussia" and authorized him to replace the Prussian ministers with Reich commissioners. Executive power in Berlin and the province of Brandenburg passed to General Gerd von Rundstedt, commander of the Third Military District. The coup, referred to as a "Reich Enforcement Action Against Prussia," was justified by the allegation that "high Prussian officials" were "making common cause with Communists." In a radio address on the evening of July 20, Papen hinted that the action had averted "the danger of Bolshevism at the last moment."

In the streets there was little evidence that the coup of the Papen government was, in the words of Secretary of State Lammers, "the trumpet call of bigger things to come." Returning from the palace at about 7 o'clock in the evening, I walked along the boulevard Unter den Linden to the Brandenburg Gate. The day had been cloudy, but now the sun shone brightly. Many people were outside enjoying the balmy evening air. At the corner of Friedrichstrasse small groups had gathered. Some mounted police were on patrol; a police squad car slowly cruised the street. A double police sentry armed with rifles was posted in front of the Prussian Ministry of the Interior. No military forces could be seen. In the Wilhelmstrasse, seat of the Reich chancellery and other Reich ministries, pedestrian and car traffic proceeded on its normal course. When a police officer's car entered Unter den Linden from Wilhelmstrasse, the sharp sound of a whistle could be heard. This was the only "demonstration" I observed. Groups of young people bearing the emblems of opposing parties—the National Socialist swastika or the three silver arrows of the Iron

Front, the paramilitary organization of the Social Democratic party and the trade unions—passed each other peacefully. The transfer of power to the military had taken place behind the scenes, as it were, and practically unnoticed.

In response to the act of force perpetrated against it, the Prussian government filed a suit before the Reich Supreme Court, which was charged with settling disputes between the Reich and one of its constituent states. In its brief, the Prussian government denied the allegation by the Reich government that Prussia had violated its duties vis-à-vis the Reich by failing to combat effectively Communist subversion. It concluded that the facts needed to justify an enforcement action by the Reich against Prussia were lacking and that the decree of the Reich president of July 20 was unconstitutional and therefore null and void.

In its decision of October 25, 1931, the Supreme Court recognized that a violation of the duties of the Prussian state vis-à-vis the Reich had not been proven and that an enforcement action of the Reich against Prussia was not justified. The court, however, drew a sharp line between an enforcement action pursuant to Article 48, paragraph 1, and the dictatorial powers of the Reich president pursuant to Article 48, paragraph 2 of the constitution. The prerequisites for the exercise of these powers, the court ruled, did exist. In the view of the court, it was obvious that the presidential decree had been issued at a time of serious disturbances of public safety and order.

"Great political parties are facing each other in bitter enmity and are ready for combat. Hostilities erupt almost daily in bloody confrontations which claim many lives. There exists the danger that political tensions may increase to the point where they threaten the very foundations of the constitutional order. The prerequisites for action pursuant to paragraph 2 of article 48 undoubtedly existed."

In this situation the court considered the president to be authorized "to combine in one hand the instruments of power of the Reich and of the largest state by installing a Reich commissioner empowered to act in specified fields within the jurisdiction of the Prussian government." Under no circumstances was it permissible, the court continued, "to put the Reich commissioner even temporarily in the place of the Prussian state government or to remove the constitutionally appointed Prussian ministers from their posts." Under this ruling the Prussian government remained in office with all its rights and duties but was obligated to come to some kind of an agreement with the Reich commissioner on the "partition" of governmental functions in Prussia.

This grotesque situation was bound to lead to endless friction between the Reich commissioner and the Prussian government. Heinrich Triepel, the Nestor of German constitutional lawyers (who has been mentioned earlier) sharply criticized the decision. He compared it with the judgment of Portia in the *Merchant of Venice*: Take your pound of flesh but spill not a drop of blood. "The reader may test his ingenuity by asking who will play the role of the duped Shylock, the Reich commissioner or the Prussian government. What the court has allotted to the parties is of no use to them, i.e. none of the two will actually be able to govern."

The new masters thought that their powers extended also to the realm of morals. This was demonstrated by an affair which at the time was much ridiculed, but which also aroused anger and indignation because it showed incredible tactlessness and an intolerably patronizing attitude. Certain groups in the government had apparently taken offense at the current fashion of both male and female bathing apparel. According to their way of thinking, it left too little to the imagination. The Reich commissioner for the Prussian Minister of the Interior, Bracht, in the exercise of his power "to restore public order and safety" issued a decree"—facetiously nicknamed by the public "the gusset decree"—which provided that ladies be admitted to public beaches only if they wore "swimsuits which completely cover breasts and the upper part of the body, fit tightly underneath the arms and are provided with cut-off hose and a gusset." Also, gentlemen were enjoined not to appear for bathing in public unless they wore at least swimming trunks "with cut-off hose and a gusset." Absurdities such as these were on the list of priorities of an official who had been put into office by military force allegedly to restore public safety and order in a civil war situation.

Upon the dismissal of Brüning and the installation of the Papen government, the *Reichstag* had been dissolved and elections had been scheduled for July 31. On election day, the streets were inundated with flags, most of them bearing swastikas. The sensational advance of the Nazis continued.

Having gained 230 seats, the Nazis became the strongest party. According to the rules of parliamentary democracy, the leader of the strongest party had a legitimate claim to be nominated chancellor and to form a new government. On August 13, Papen and Hitler went to see the Reich president. Hitler demanded the "absolute leadership of the government." In his language this meant that he should be vested with totalitarian rule, a power to the exclusion of all other constitutional organs. Hindenburg declined; he was prepared to grant Hitler participation in the government, but not full powers. Now it was Hitler's turn to decline. With his demand for total power of the state he was, as I noted in my diary of August 13, "the prisoner of his own radicalism. Politics for Hitler is not the art of the possible. His inability to act within the scope of a given situation proves his lack of statesmanship."

At the beginning of September the new *Reichstag* assembled. Hermann Göring was elected Speaker of the House. The first working meeting took place on September 12; the only item on the agenda was the presentation of a governmental declaration. Before Göring was able to give the chancellor the floor, the Communists brought in a motion of nonconfidence in the government. Göring immediately put the Communist motion up for vote without first giving the chancellor an opportunity to deliver his speech. Highly agitated, Papen took from his briefcase a presidential order he had prepared for the dissolution of the *Reichstag*. Göring refused to accept it. Thereupon Papen left the order on the speaker's desk and departed with his cabinet.

Papen's action led to lively discussions among lawyers. In order for the message to become effective, was acknowledgment of receipt by the person to whom it was addressed necessary, or did it suffice that it was left to be picked up, as Papen's gesture had implied?

The question was moot. The *Reichstag*, by an overwhelming vote of 512 to 41, accepted the Communist motion. Never before had a German government suffered a parliamentary defeat of such proportions; nor had it ever occurred that a government was not allowed to make a declaration from the floor. The constitutional order was disintegrating fast. New elections were set for November 6. In these elections the Nazis, for the first time since they had embarked upon their victorious advance, sustained considerable losses. The myth of their invincibility had been broken, and their forward movement had been stopped. Yet they still emerged as the strongest party.

Shortly before the elections, we experienced a wildcat strike of the public transportation system in Berlin conducted jointly by the Communists and the Nazis—mortal enemies who nevertheless made common cause in attacks upon democracy and the republic. Whenever the occasion arose to strike a blow at the common enemy, neither of the two wished to come out second best. Storm troopers and members of the Communist Red Front-Line-Fighters' Union picketed the entrances to subway stations together. They rattled their collection boxes; the Communists for the strike fund of the Revolutionary Trade Union Organization, the Nazis for the National Socialist Organization of Factory Cells. The tactical alliance of these radical groups revealed how serious the totalitarian threat to German democracy had become.

On December 6, the new *Reichstag* assembled and on December 9, voted to adjourn temporarily. The next weeks were replete with attempts to settle the political crisis by changing chancellors. It had become all too obvious that the people were in no mood to tolerate the cabinet of the barons any longer. Papen was replaced by General von Schleicher. An attempt by the new chancellor, through an opening to the left, to gain the support of the trade unions and of a social splinter wing of the Nazi party under Gregor Strasser, failed. Schleicher, because he was suspected of wanting to return to parliamentary democracy, lost the confidence of Hindenburg. Papen, Hugenberg, and Hitler revived the "Harzburg front." On January 28, Schleicher resigned. Now Hindenburg appointed Hitler to the post of chancellor since he was "the strongest man in the coalition of the national forces." A new government of National Socialists and conservative bureaucrats and politicians was formed; it took office on January 30, 1933, under the chancellorship of Hitler.

On the evening of that day, while listening to the radio, I learned that a giant demonstration was being formed in the

center of the city. Out of curiosity, I went by metropolitan train
from Westend to Friedrichstrasse station and from there walked
along Unter den Linden to Paris Square. The Brandenburg Gate
and the buildings surrounding the square were illuminated by
the light of innumerable torches. People were streaming into
the square from all sides, most of them in storm trooper or SS
(*Schutzstaffeln*, security units) uniforms. Mixed together were
members of the *Stahlhelm* and ordinary citizens, groups with
standards, music bands, and drum and bugle corps. I was caught
up in the wake of the procession as it moved along. It wound its
way from Brandenburg Gate through the Wilhelmstrasse, between
densely packed crowds, passing by the Reich chancellery for many
hours until far into the night. At an illuminated window in the
northern wing of the chancellor's palace, Hindenburg could be
seen in civilian clothes, standing (or sitting) behind a transparent
curtain. It seemed as if he hardly noticed the acclamations of
the passing throngs. His face was rigid; he just stared at the
procession. At an open window of the new chancellery, a wing
attached to the old chancellor's palace, Hitler and Göring were
standing, both wearing civilian clothes. In the room behind the
two leaders other members of the new government had assembled.
Hitler greeted the wildly cheering masses with his right arm
raised, turning occasionally for a brief remark to Göring.

The light and smoke of the burning torches, the pressing,
shoving crowds, the loud cheers, the martial music, all this
created an atmosphere in which I felt I was witnessing a fateful
moment in history. The torchlight procession had been intended
by its organizers as an ovation to the "Day of National Uprising,"
as homage to the new political leadership, and to symbolize the
setting out of the German people into the National Socialist
future. I remember that I remarked to an acquaintance of mine,
who had come with me from Westend to the inner city and had
joined the procession, that we should meet ten years from now at
the same spot. Only then would we be able to judge what this hour
had meant.

After the procession had disbanded, restaurants both large
and small in the vicinity of Potsdamer Platz were overcrowded.
Masses of people gathered around street car and bus stops,

disappeared into subway stations or marched home in formation to their respective districts.

The Third Reich Breaks Out

At the beginning of January of 1933, my leave of absence from the administrative service expired. I left the institute and was assigned to the district government in Potsdam. Attached to the district government was an administrative court which became my workplace for the immediate future.

One morning there was a knock at the door of my office. An elderly gentleman entered and introduced himself as governmental counselor (*Regierungsrat*) H. He said that he had hardly trusted his eyes when he saw the sign on the door of my office: "Dr. von Elbe, *Regierungsassessor*." He remembered seeing the same sign on the same office door many years ago. At that time it referred to my father who, in 1902, had been transferred from the county government in Hamm to the district government in Potsdam and, like me, had been assigned to the administrative court. Mr. H. had known my father quite well. Since he had a house in Potsdam which he did not want to give up, he had declined promotions and had stayed at his post. Thus, time had passed him by.

On February 27, the world was shaken by the news that the *Reichstag* building had been set on fire. There were reports that a similar attempt had been made at the imperial palace the previous day. In one of the institute's offices in the attic of the palace, a fire had been discovered in time and had been put out at once.

Communists were suspected of having been the perpetrators in both instances. In view of the strict fire watch which was enforced around the clock in the attic of the palace, it was inconceivable to me how anybody could have made his way into the attic unnoticed, and entered an office of the institute to set a fire. The report seemed highly improbable.

In this connection I remembered a strange incident. After I had left the institute, I continued to work regularly on Saturday afternoons to complete a study for the *Journal* of the institute. I still had a key to the main door of the palace, but not to the elevator or the door of the institute. I had arranged with the janitor, who lived with his family in rooms adjacent to the institute, that he would leave the entrance door of the institute at the head of the stairs ajar for me. I could also ring the bell since there would always be a member of the family to let me in. This procedure had worked well for weeks.

On Saturday, February 25, 1933, as was my custom, I arrived from Potsdam at the palace between five and six p.m., opened the main door, and ascended the stairs to the institute. To my surprise, the door of the institute was closed. I rang the bell repeatedly—to no avail. I heard footsteps inside coming towards the door. There was a window draped with a curtain that overlooked the staircase. Although I stood with my back to the window, I had the impression that the curtain was moved ever so gently. I vigorously rang the bell again and also knocked on the door. Nothing happened. The muffled steps inside receded into the interior. I could not understand why the person whose footsteps I had heard had failed to respond to my entreaties. Finally I gave up, descended the stairs, locked the main entrance door and left the palace through the Eosander portal. Obviously, visitors to the institute were not welcome that afternoon.

That very evening the fire, which the newspapers reported two days later, was set. All I saw of the fire on my next visit to the institute was a scorched window frame in the office of Ernst Schmitz. He had been in the United States since January. Only someone familiar with the institute could have known this. This strengthened my suspicion that the arson attempt must have been committed, or at least tolerated, by someone who had an intimate knowledge of the activities of the institute. Later on, it was said that there had been a Nationalist Socialist cell among the service personnel of the institute. The janitor died in 1934; it was the year of the so-called Röhm *Putsch* and of many mysterious deaths among Nazi partisans who were assumed to have been implicated in the *Reichstag* fire.

According to the historical record, the arson attempt in the palace and the *Reichstag* fire were connected, and the same persons were responsible for both acts. The Dutchman van der Lubbe, whom the Leipzig Supreme Court sentenced to death as the *Reichstag* arsonist, confessed during the trial that he had also committed the crime in the palace. On the evening of February 25, according to his testimony, in spite of his poor eyesight he

Berlin: January 30, 1933

28. The Torchlight Procession forms at the Brandenburg Gate

29. Hitler and Göring at a window of the Reich Chancellery acknowledging the cheers of the passing crowds

"The Day of Potsdam": March 21, 1933

30. Hitler and his Cabinet on the way to the Garrison Church

31. Inside the Garrison Church: Hitler speaks before Reich President von Hindenburg, his cabinet and the *Reichstag* Deputies

had climbed a scaffold erected next to the Eosander portal, had gone to the roof, and had thrown a burning coal lighter into an open ventilation shaft. How was it possible that a window frame in Schmitz's office could catch fire and become scorched through the action described by van der Lubbe when the frame could be reached only from the outside or from the inside of the office? Van der Lubbe said he had then descended the scaffold. Criminologists who investigated the incident were baffled by the story. They could not believe that the arsonist had come over the roof.

Dissatisfied with the progress of their election campaign, the Nazis had been casting about to find a pretext that would enable them to eliminate their adversaries. The *Reichstag* fire provided it. Van der Lubbe's alleged connections with the Communist party were cited as evidence that the *Reichstag* fire was meant to signal a general uprising of the Communists in Germany. On the day after the fire an emergency decree "for the defense against Communist acts of violence endangering the state" was issued pursuant to Article 48 of the constitution. The decree suspended basic constitutional rights, such as freedom of speech, of assembly, the inviolability of property, and habeas corpus, thus paving the way for the Nazis to assume total power.

On March 5, a new *Reichstag* was elected. Despite the government's use of the emergency decree of February 28—arrests of political leaders, prohibition of newspapers—to interfere with the election campaign of the opposition parties, and despite a surge of Nazi propaganda of hitherto unknown dimensions unleashed by the new Nazi Minister of Propaganda, Dr. Goebbels, the Nazis failed to attain an absolute majority of the votes. They needed the support of Hugenberg's "Black-White-Red Fighting Front" to gain a slim common majority of 52 percent. Specifically, they lacked the two-thirds majority required for constitutional amendments. But this did not disturb those who were newly established in power. I remember the National Socialist Minister of the Interior, Frick, dismissing the importance of the election by declaring, "Never mind its outcome; we shall stay in power!"

The opening of the new *Reichstag* was scheduled to take place on March 21, 1933, at the tomb of Frederick the Great in the Garrison Church in Potsdam. The ceremony, it was reported, would be attended by President von Hindenburg and the entire cabinet headed by Chancellor Hitler. The area around the church was declared a security zone. Access was by invitation only. The district government had received a limited number of admission tickets which were distributed among the members of the government by lot. One of the lots fell to me. I was thus an eyewitness to the "Day of Potsdam," a superbly staged spectacle that was designed to advertise the claim, soon to be proved fraudulent, that the new political leadership was grounded upon the venerable traditions of old Prussia.

It was a glorious spring day. The area in front of the Garrison Church—a parade ground of Prussian guard regiments since the days of the "Soldier King" Frederick William I—was bustling with a motley crowd of uniforms, including those of the old imperial army, brownshirts, and members of the elite SS. Civilians were in festive dress; the gentlemen were wearing tophats (as had also been prescribed for me). A detachment of the *Stahlhelm* was lined up in field gray. I happened to pass by when the commander was about to chastise his men with a bellowing voice in the vilest terms imaginable for what seemed to have been a minor infraction. The great moment had gone to his head, and with his outburst he apparently wished to demonstrate his concept of Prussian soldiering to the crowd. I noticed in the front row the portly figure of Prince Eitel-Friedrich, one of the sons of the former Kaiser. Standing at attention he had to endure, together with his comrades, the torrent of abuse hurled at them by their raging commander.

Members of the *Reichstag* and the new cabinet made their appearance. As in the days of the Prussian kings, the chimes the Garrison Church intoned the melody which admonishes people to "stay faithful and honest until they go to their cool graves." Suddenly, the crowd began to stir. President von Hindenburg, in the uniform of a Prussian field marshal, a marshal's baton in hand, drove up to the church. Hitler, wearing a black coat, and holding his tophat, greeted the president at the foot of the stairs and bowed slightly as Hindenburg took his hand. (What a sight: The private first class of World War I meeting his former commander-in-chief on equal footing.) Both disappeared into the interior of the church. Hindenburg read a declaration reminding the deputies of the Prussian virtue of devotion to duty, and appealing to them to support the new government. Then Hitler made his usual speech accusing the November revolution and the Weimar Republic of having brought about the decline of Germany; praising the union between the old and the new forces; and announcing a program of national rebirth.

The ceremony was broadcast by radio throughout the Reich. In many cities and villages the broadcast was accompanied by church services. In the evening an endless torchlight procession passed through the festively illuminated Brandenburg Gate among throngs of people in a holiday mood.

"Mongrel of the Second Degree"

One evening in April when I returned on the metropolitan train from Potsdam to Berlin, I read in the evening paper that the *Reichstag* had enacted a law aimed at eliminating Jewish elements from the civil service. A hitherto unknown test, the so-called "Aryan clause," was to determine who qualified as a Jew. All persons of "non-Aryan blood" were to be excluded from public service. The brief report failed to clarify whether my relationship with the Mendelssohn family of well-known Jewish origin might have a bearing on the law's applicability to me. My grandmother on my mother's side was born a Mendelssohn-Bartholdy. Her father Paul had been the brother of the composer Felix Mendelssohn-Bartholdy. We discussed the matter in the family circle and agreed that any thought of my falling within the purview of the law was utterly absurd, all the more so since my grandmother had been baptized in the Christian faith soon after her birth.

I procured a full text of the law. It was entitled "Law to Restore the Professional Civil Service" and was dated April 7, 1933. Among the charges of the Nazi propaganda against the Weimar system was the contention that the traditional public service had been corrupted by admitting non-professional outsiders, either on the strength of their affiliation with one of the ruling (leftist) political parties or because they were Jewish. The Nazis promised that once they had achieved power they would restore the time-honored principle of professionalism coupled with removing alien and unworthy elements from the public service.

The provision which I had read in the brief newspaper account stated: "Civil servants who are of non-Aryan extraction shall be retired" (provided, of course, the non-Aryan person had accumulated an appropriate number of service years towards retirement; someone not so entitled faced outright dismissal). An implementing regulation defined as "non-Aryan" a person "who is descended from non-Aryan, in particular Jewish, parents or grandparents. It suffices that one of the parents or grandparents is non-Aryan."

Every civil servant received a questionnaire with questions about his descent. In the column "Grandparents" I entered the maiden name of my grandmother on my mother's side: "Fanny Mendelssohn-Bartholdy."

Some of my colleagues who learned of my relationship with the Mendelssohn family voiced concern. In July, I was requested to submit the birth and baptism certificates of my "ominous" grandmother. I considered this a favorable sign. Perhaps the Christian baptism was pertinent after all. I added some data from the family history to the certificates which showed that the Mendelssohns had been loyal citizens of the Prussian state, and which called attention to their prominent rôle in the cultural and economic life of Germany.

A few weeks later the chief of personnel of the district government summoned me to his office for an interview. These were his remarks taken from notes which I wrote in shorthand immediately after the interview:

> You can imagine how disagreeable this matter is for me just as it must be for you. I am talking about your questionnaire. People in the Ministry of the Interior are extremely tough in these matters. They tell us: Everybody knows that the Mendelssohns are a Jewish family. Your case, they say, is therefore absolutely clear. Now someone who wants to help you has asked that the following additional questions be answered: Was the family of the great-grandmother Christian? Were grandmother Elbe and grandfather Richthofen cousins, or brother and sister? This would be favorable, we are told. I have never done racial research. But this is supposed to be favorable. Merits of any type are of no importance whatever. Decisive alone is race. The Mendelssohns belong to the oldest, best known Jewish families. What once was a matter of pride may now be bad luck. Further statements, I believe, are of no use because, as I said before, all that matters is race.

The factors thought to be "extenuating circumstances" did not apply. Nothing was known about the family of my great-grandmother except the name. Even if her family had been

The "Aryan Clause"

33. Eugen Freiherr von Richthofen

32. Fanny Freifrau von Richthofen
née Mendelssohn-Bartholdy
The "Non-Aryan" Grandmother

New Haven, Connecticut

34. 244 Edwards Street: The House of "Mrs. B."

35. June 22, 1938: LL.B. Yale Law School

Christian it would have made no difference as far as the question of race was concerned. In the eyes of the Nazis, conversion of Jews to Christianity was but a ruse to conceal their Jewish origin. "Religion is unimportant. Race alone decides whether a person is Jewish or not."

My father, who had grown up in the traditions of Prussian officialdom and who in his own career had lived up to these traditions in an exemplary manner, found the statements of the Potsdam official both incomprehensible and appalling. Although I thought it useless, I could not prevent him from submitting a petition to the Prussian minister president (the post was filled at the time by Hermann Göring) asking that in examining my questionnaire and determining whether I was qualified to be a public servant, consideration be given to the loyal and meritorious service several of my ancestors had rendered to Prussia and Germany as army officers and public officials. The petition reads like a short history of modern Prussia and Germany. Reference is made to the Franco-Prussian War of 1870-71 in which both grandfathers participated as Prussian officers. The story is told of the feat of bravery of my grandfather Richthofen, husband of Fanny Mendelssohn-Bartholdy, in the war of Austria and Prussia against Denmark of 1864 when, as the commander of a battery in an artillery regiment, he was the first to reach the top of the Düppel entrenchments with his battery; he later fought in the battle of Königsgrätz, also known as the battle of Sadowa, in the war between the German states of 1866, one of the most decisive battles in European history. Mention is made of his elder brother Ferdinand von Richthofen who achieved international fame as a geographer. Particular emphasis is placed on the life of my great-grandfather Richthofen, who was the first Prussian minister to Mexico in 1851 and later served with distinction at international conferences and in other diplomatic posts. On the list of relatives who had won public acclaim the name of Manfred von Richthofen, the famous flying ace of World War I, also appears. During his years as a cadet in Berlin he had been a frequent guest of "Aunt Anna," my grandmother Elbe, who was born a Richthofen. As a final touch, my father added that I belonged to the fifth generation of family members who had served at the Potsdam district government.

My father sent his petition to the chief of personnel at the Ministry of the Interior for transmittal to the minister president. Dr. Sch. was known to my father from the time when my father was a county executive. Ten days later the answer arrived. Dr. Sch. wrote that to his regret there was no possibility of avoiding the application of Section 3, paragraph 1 of the Law of April 7, 1933, (the Aryan clause) to my case. I was advised to resign from the service "if I wished to avoid being dismissed." This "backdoor" method of leaving the service was obviously meant as a concession which the old bureaucracy was willing to grant to my father and me. For my father, at any rate, a dismissal from the service without a valid cause was unthinkable, even a disgrace.

I was urged by the Potsdam officials to act on the ministry's suggestion at once. Perhaps they feared that the new watchdogs at the district government might learn about my action, and, considering it an evasion of the law, might try to stop it with unpleasant consequences for all concerned. For my father's sake, to whom my imminent forced departure was a heavy blow, I did what I was told and submitted my resignation. The letter from the ministry made it abundantly clear that I acted under the compulsion of the Aryan clause which had stripped me of my qualification as a civil servant and of all the rights pertaining thereto. I also complied with my father's wish to go to the lion's den and throw myself upon "the mercy of the court," that is, to make a last minute appeal in person to the all-powerful chief of personnel. While I was waiting in the outer office to be called into the inner sanctum, I overheard some of the talk among my fellow "antechambrists," all of them senior bureaucrats who had come to give vent to grievances over injustices which they thought had been inflicted upon them. One of them complained that he had been transferred from Wiesbaden to Aachen "without a promotion." The president of a district government in the Rhineland and a governmental counselor were discussing whether it would be a good idea to pin the Nazi party badge on now (obviously it was of recent vintage). Possibly they had been fulminating for years against those "party book officials" who had degraded the professional civil service. Now they worried about the best way to ensure that they were recognized as members of the party.

My worries were of a different kind. The secretary in the outer office asked me whether I wasn't there by mistake, whether I really wanted to see *Herr Ministerialdirektor*. According to his experience, the mighty chief was not likely to receive lowly characters like me. Finally I was called in and told what I already knew. I thought that it would make my father feel better if I could tell him that Dr. Sch. had verbally confirmed what he had written in his letter. Everything humanly possible had been done to reverse the course of events. The decision was irrevocable.

When I returned from my conversation to the outer office, I noticed that those waiting had a frightened look on their faces. One of them knew my father, and had heard my name when I was called in to see the chief. He later told my father that my face had been white as a sheet.

On October 6, 1933, I received a letter from the president of the district government of Potsdam stating that the "dismissal I had requested" (sic) from the Prussian civil service had been granted. The discharge certificate of September 23, 1933, was signed by the Prussian minister of the interior "on behalf of the Prussian minister president." With one stroke of the pen I had been deprived of everything I had worked for after years of study, exams, and faithful service. Occupational prohibitions for "non-Aryans" also applied to nonprofit private-law organizations, such as the Bruns Institute.

The German propensity for thoroughness and perfection soon took hold of the Aryan clause with a vengeance. A whole system of categories and subcategories was developed. "Jews" were divided into "Jews, Half-Jews and Quarter-Jews." Half- and Quarter-Jews were called "Jewish Mongrels." A Jewish mongrel with two full-blooded Jewish grandparents was a "Mongrel of the First Degree," while a Jewish mongrel with only one full-blooded Jewish grandparent was a "Mongrel of the Second Degree." Nazi Minister of the Interior Frick, who was responsible for all matters connected with the law on public servants, added the following comments:

> The concept of the Jewish mongrel has been defined and is valid in every respect. . . . According to this definition mongrels are all those persons who are

descended from either one or two racially full-blooded
Jewish grandparents. . . . Mongrels are subject to special
treatment. . . . Since they are not Germans they cannot
be put on an equal footing with Germans. . . . Mongrels
are a mixed race and stand between the races. For this
reason care must be taken that they disappear as soon as
possible.

In response to complaints that the Aryan clause had been
interpreted too extensively since "Half- and Quarter Aryans" had
been brought within its purview, Frick stated in a speech that
"infiltration of foreign elements into the ranks of public officials,
lawyers, doctors participating in a health-insurance plan and
others" had reached such proportions that "young Germans hardly
had a chance of entering these professions. . . ." Purging the
professional civil service of alien elements could be accomplished
only through a "deep incision. . . . The Law to Restore the
Professional Civil Service has ignited the sacred flame of racial
consciousness not only among public officials but among Germans
in general. . . . In this sense the battle-cry: 'First a German,
then a civil servant,' takes on a new meaning. It has provided
for one profession what will be the common doctrine of the whole
German nation: a Germany for the people of German blood."
Carl Schmitt, at the time the most prominent of a new generation
of constitutional lawyers and later the chief legal counsel of the
Third Reich, summarized Frick's thoughts with these words: "The
importance of the Law to Restore the Professional Civil Service
lies in the fact that it eliminates alien elements from the civil
service. By this action, the fundamental tenet of the National
Socialist ideology of racial uniformity has been put into effect in
one of the most important stations of public life."
The situation of Jewish mongrels in the body politic
of the German people, indeed their very "capacity of being
Germans," was discussed in some detail in a commentary on
German Racial Legislation (published by Beck in Munich) by
Dr. Wilhelm Stuckart, State Secretary, and Dr. Hans Globke,
Senior Governmental Counselor, both in the Reich and Prussian
Ministry of the Interior. They wrote: "Assigning the mongrels
purely and simply to the Jews would have been a viable legal

solution. However, it would have been at variance with the biological facts and would have precluded what the legislation is aiming at, namely, making this mongrel race disappear. Assigning mongrels to the Germans likewise would have disregarded the biological facts and would have presented a not inconsiderable danger to the purity of the German blood. . . . The legal treatment of mongrels is based on the realization that mongrels are racially compatible neither with Jews nor with Germans."

At one point during a walk along Unter den Linden in the days following my dismissal—I would still be able to find the place had the Linden preserved their appearance (they were completely changed under Hitler)—I was suddenly overpowered by a feeling that Germany was being enveloped by a black cloud of collective insanity.

My colleagues at the Potsdam government with whom I had formed bonds of genuine friendship despite the brevity of my service, were profoundly shocked by my dismissal. At the risk of arousing the suspicion of disloyalty to the new regime some of them tried to intervene with higher authorities to allow me to stay on "in the interests of the administration." I received letters which expressed sympathy with my plight and dismay that I was forced to give up a cherished occupation. My immediate superior Dr. Zaun, President of the Administrative Court, of his own volition and in an effort to be helpful, gave me an "efficiency report" in which he attributed to me "profound knowledge in all fields of legislation and jurisprudence," "clear and well-balanced presentation" and "skillfulness in dealing with people." I mention these statements merely to show that my colleagues, despite official policy, did not consider me an "alien element" which had to be purged from the civil service. They realized that a doctrine which the highest authorities of the state had adopted as a guiding principle led to nonsensical results.

I became increasingly convinced that I could no longer stay in Germany. A compromise with the Nazi racial ideology was out of the question. The circumstances surrounding my removal from the service had stigmatized me as a second-class citizen. Even my "capacity of being a German" was being questioned. In the Third Reich I was a "Quarter-Jew," a "Jewish mongrel," a "non-Aryan." Occasionally I noticed that not all of my acquaintances were

as understanding and generous as my Potsdam colleagues. At
accidental encounters I was met with an embarrassed turning
aside, or with outright avoidance. From the behavior of some of
these "friends" who were eager to climb on the new bandwagon,
I learned what it meant to be socially ostracized. No human
relations worthy of the name would be possible in the poisoned
atmosphere of the Third Reich. Whatever I were to undertake,
I would be subject to "special treatment" on the part of the
authorities. As a former civil servant who had been dismissed
for racial reasons, I would always meet aloofness and mistrust.
As an outsider in a racially "pure" society, under suspicion as
"politically unreliable," I had to reckon with being observed,
spied on, and even seized without recourse at any moment. There
was no escape from the fear of persecution.

Since 1930 a younger brother of mine had lived in the United
States. Together with fellow American students he had done
research in chemistry at the University of Berlin. In order to
continue their common projects, he had accompanied them to the
States, first as a student and later as an immigrant. Considering
my situation, he urged me to follow his example and join him in
the States. By that time he was employed by the Coal Research
Institute in Pittsburgh, and offered to share his salary with me for
as long as I needed assistance.

I could not immediately make up my mind to accept his offer.
I felt it was prudent to explore at first possibilities for obtaining a
fellowship at an American university. I thought that I might be
able to secure some kind of academic employment. My case had
also been registered with the London-based Academic Assistance
Council (later called the Society for the Protection of Science and
Learning). The Council endeavored to place scholars who had
been expelled from their homes, in particular Germans who had
lost their positions for political or racial reasons, with universities
in the British Empire.

My brother conducted a veritable campaign with numerous
academic institutions in the States. While I was waiting I
prepared a part of my study on *Territorial Changes in Europe since
the Congress of Vienna* for publication, and tried to improve my
English.

The National Socialist Revolution

While my fate hung in the balance, I experienced the onset of Hitler's rule.

The seizure of power by the Nazis was not simply a change of government as in previous years, when a leftist government was replaced by a government of the right or vice versa, an event that took place at the government level and did not affect the people. This time the change of government signaled a total break with existing conditions. It aroused pent-up, primitive emotions, an almost religious fervor. Supported by its newly achieved political power, the "brown ideology" penetrated all spheres of life like a river overflowing its banks.

From my own experience I knew that Nazi slogans such as "public need before private greed," because it expressed individual willingness to sacrifice private interests for the good of the community, as well as Nazi emphasis on comradeship and love for the country, appealed to many outside the Nationalist Socialist movement proper. These were the "idealists", the "believers" of whom Carl Zuckmayer in his *Memoirs* writes: "They imagined this allegedly 'popular' movement (in reality it was cunningly contrived) to be something decent, ethically superior, positive. . . . a genuine and true revival, in the realm of morals as well, the return to clean, stable forms of social and private life."

One of the strangest phenomena which I encountered after the new government had come to power, a sight which perturbed me very much, was the expression of blissful contentment on the faces of many people. While I felt that the ground underneath my feet was shaking, that one thread after another was being torn out of the fabric that held Germany together, these people, after years of confusion, felt secure. A strong government was in power. They were relieved, once and for all, of the worries about the well-being of the country. The *Führer* would do what was right for the country. He was one of them. He expressed their innermost feelings. He needed no "checks and balances." The Nazis had a word for this almost mystical harmony between the leader and his followers: Hitler and the men around him were "pure Aryans"; thus their thinking was *arteigen* (true to type)—it automatically proceeded along the lines of thought of every other pure-blooded German.   There was, then, absolute certainty that everything that these men did was right and in the best interests of the country. They simply could not do otherwise. The law-abiding citizen could go back to work. Germany and the nation were safe.

Among the reasons why so many accepted the new government without much question was the fact that it had come into power by legal means within the framework of the constitutional order.

Ever since the abortive beerhall *Putsch* of 1923, when his attempt to seize power by violent means had been defeated by the superior military might of the republic, Hitler had taken pains to assert the "legality" of his movement.   True, his lieutenants continued to promise "mines, machine guns, and hand grenades" and the "night of the long knives" as instruments in the struggle for power in order to maintain the trust of the radical activists among the masses.   Yet Hitler who claimed dictatorial authority over the party, when called to the witness stand in 1930 to testify before Germany's Supreme Court in the trial of young army officers accused of subversive activities in the army, declared under oath on behalf of the Nazi party that he insisted on "strictly legal means" in the pursuit of his aims.   A previous statement that "heads will roll" was explained as having meant that he would "execute traitors to Germany" after they had been "legally convicted by a Nazi Supreme Court" upon his assumption of power.   Through this pious protestation of strict legality in achieving his aims, he at once appealed to the German infatuation with "orderly" government and managed to lull the conscience of the powers that be; they became convinced that nothing untoward would happen if the Nazis were allowed to proceed within the legal bounds of the constitution.   It became respectable to support openly the rising star of Nazism. Many a man and woman who sympathized with the movement "for idealistic reasons" succumbed to the spell of legality and orderliness. Revolution under the law was accepted as the magic formula that would cure Germany's ills. Closing their eyes to the hateful aspects of the movement, such as the coarseness of the propaganda, the alien flags and uniforms, and the violence of Nazi tactics, solid citizens, who secretly endorsed the party's policy of resurrecting Germany's military and political power, hailed the young movement as the spearhead of Germany's advance toward a better future.

This euphoric mood, this enthusiasm for the "National Revolution," a term used to make the Nazi seizure of power palatable to the people, at times bordered the sphere of mysticism and religion. In 1934, I came across a pamphlet by Johannes Müller entitled *The Making of a Nation*. Ever since my visit to Elmau I was interested in everything that bore Müller's imprint. In this pamphlet I found sentences like these:

> At this turn of an era, Adolf Hitler is the organ and instrument of God, the leader empowered by God to save the German people from extinction and secure its existence. . . . the National Socialist upswing. . . . is objective deed and creative act by the living God who sent Adolf Hitler as the voice of His word into the German desert. . . . Hitler is nothing but the organ of a higher authority. This elevates him. . . . into the direct rule by God and into the acting of His will through him. . . . It is this living will of God which is active in the present crisis of salvation of our people and which speaks through Adolf Hitler.

In his book *Annotations to Hitler* Sebastian Haffner writes: "In the days of the most intense faith in the leader, Adolf Hitler was a 'miracle,' a 'messenger of God' to the Germans. . . . For the Germans, Hitler always came from far away, at first. . . . for a while from the heavens, later from the deepest jaws of hell."

I was convinced—without wishing to attribute a particular degree of foresight to myself—that National Socialism would inevitably lead to war and chaos. In the few notes which I have preserved from these days, I find, dated April 29, 1933, these remarks: "In the meantime, people are being prepared for war through war movies and the din of battle that these films emit. The German people do not deserve to be led to slaughter through criminal madness." On February 22, 1934, I noted: "In the view of the Nazis, chaos will be the consequence if National Socialism is not successful. It is true, the Nazis do everything to create a situation which can only lead to chaos."

Because of its turgid language, interminable, often obscure sentences, exaggerations, half-truths, queer concepts and muddled thoughts, Hitler's book *Mein Kampf* struck me as repulsive. I was loath to read it and could stand only a few pages at a time. But I learned Hitler's concept of history from it: that nations are eternally engaged in a power struggle for world domination and living space, and that Hitler was determined to secure living space for the German people through conquests in Russia and Eastern Europe. What convinced me, however, that Hitler's policy was directed toward war were not his statements, but his deeds and the mood they induced, or what one may call the atmospherics.

The government lost no time in re-educating the German people from belief in democracy and prosperity to the glorification of war and conquest. Through movies dealing with patriotic subjects from the military history of Prussia, the people were openly admonished to brace themselves for the inevitable clash. Through "one-dish-dinners" (*Eintopfgerichte*), the government started a campaign of austerity, sacrifice, and communal feeding. Brass bands, military parades, an abundance of uniforms—everything was designed to create an atmosphere of war, reminiscent of the years from 1914-1918. Columns of soldiers marching through town singing martial songs, appeals to youth—all these were signs of a growing militarization.

Consistent with this mood of awakening, of departing for new shores after Hitler's assumption of power, was the report of an acquaintance of mine that on her estate the women gathered in the evening to sew and knit "for our soldiers, just as in 1813," (the year the "War of Liberation" against Napoleon broke out).

My view that Hitler's foreign policy sooner or later would lead to armed conflict was shared—I did not know it, of course, at the time—by Sir Horace Rumbold, the British ambassador in Berlin. He had tried to convince his government that Hitler's future policy "would be—with almost inescapable certainty—a policy of expansion and war." Karl Dietrich Bracher, the Bonn historian, in his book *Germany Between Democracy and Dictatorship* writes that Hitler's expansionist foreign policy began "deeply and decisively" to influence all spheres of life immediately after his seizure of power. Modern research, he says, has explicitly refuted the opinion still held by some that Hitler developed destructive tendencies only in later years.

The fact that Hitler did not shout his intentions from the housetops but that he loudly proclaimed his love for peace, was prompted by the necessity to prevent the Great Powers from taking countermeasures before his preparations for war had been completed. In November of 1938, in a speech to the the chief editors of domestic newspapers, Hitler voiced concern lest the peace propaganda he had conducted for years lead to the false conclusion that the present regime "is identical with the determination and the will to maintain peace in all circumstances." This might create a "mood of defeatism" among Germans, he complained. In an aside, he added that protestations of his desire for peace had enabled him to provide Germany "with the armament necessary for the next step."

To me, Hitler and his coterie were the eternal "soldiers from the front" of World War I, who abhorred civilian life and who had never accepted the fact that Germany had suffered a military defeat. Their aim—besides eliminating the Versailles Treaty—was to accomplish Germany's military rehabilitation and to restore respect for the German army. Now they had the power to mold the German people into a military state as an instrument for achieving German might and greatness which had eluded them in 1914-1918.

Among the destructive measures of the National Socialists which I observed from the outset, was their fight against Christianity. My knowledge, however, was marginal. What I knew I learned from foreign newspapers, in particular the London *Times* which I read on occasional visits to the Bruns Institute. The first Nazi attack was aimed at the organization of the Evangelical Church. The Protestant churches of the various German states (*Landeskirchen*) were to be unified in a national Protestant Church under a Reich bishop in conformity with the slogan: One Nation, One *Führer*, One Church. The unification plan was supported by a new religious movement called "German Christians." They advocated a "Germanized" church doctrine based on Nazi ideology that was apt to erode "the foundations of the Evangelic creed." "In Hitler the time has come to its fulfillment for the German people. Through Hitler, Christ, the God Helper and Redeemer, has become mighty among us," the German Christians proclaimed clearly in analogy to Galatians 4:4. They demanded that the church be guided in the spirit of Adolf Hitler and that the Bible and liturgy be "Germanized." The emblem of the German Christians was a cross with swastika in the center.

As was to be expected, it did not take long for the Aryan clause to be introduced into the life of the church. It was first applied to the clergy and later to the members of the church, in order that "German Christians" could be segregated from "Judeo-Christians."

I have kept a few notes which I took down when the Nazis began making the church subservient to Nazi ideology. I quote a few of them; they may serve as incidental information on this process.

January 13, 1934. "Tonight on the radio news there was an item which must have been incomprehensible, surprising, and alarming to the masses of listeners and newspaper readers. It was announced that 'in view of imminent fundamental decisions' the declaration of the 'emergency federation of ministers' on the subject of the ordinance of the Reich bishop will not be read from the pulpit tomorrow, Sunday, January 14. It was stated further that discussions on church policy will be postponed until January 17. Like a bolt of lightning this news threw light on the situation of the church—something that the government did not wish newspaper readers to know about—namely that 6,000 members of the emergency federation (an association formed spontaneously by Protestant ministers opposing the new Nazi church regime) in a message read the preceding Sunday from several hundred pulpits had declared the ordinance of the Reich bishop to be illegal. This ordinance dealt with the introduction of the Aryan clause into the church and prohibited, under threat of disciplinary penalties, any criticism of measures the Reich bishop might take. The federation had also refused the Reich bishop further obedience. I had more or less kept up with the controversies within the Evangelical Church through reports in the *Times*. The emergency federation of ministers had been founded, among other things, for the purpose of waging a defensive struggle and of preventing the application of the 'Law to Restore the Professional Civil Service' (including the Aryan clause) which had been enacted by the General Synod. The federation also sought to ensure that the institution of the Reich bishop did not lead to the creation of an un-Evangelic *Führer* concept, and that coercion disappear from the life of the church."

In a letter to the *Times*, Bishop Bell of Chichester had warned the German government against intervention by force in the ecclesiastic controversy since it concerned matters of conscience. If the Evangelical Church in Germany were to be placed under constraint by the state, no community with the Protestant churches in the rest of the world would be possible. He quoted the words of the Declaration of the Ministers that the Aryan clause violated the essence of baptism, of ordination, and indeed of the church itself and that it threatened to disrupt the community of the German church with the whole of Christianity.

The struggle of the Nazis against Christianity also included the demand that the Old Testament be removed from church services and religious education. According to Nazi concepts, a Christian doctrine which kept adhering to the writings of the Old Testament was a "Jewish religion" and consequently incompatible with the "ethical and moral feeling of the Germanic race."

In his Advent sermons in December of 1933 in St. Michael's Church in Munich, considered sensational at the time, Cardinal Faulhaber had pondered the significance of the writings of the Old Testament for Christianity, and had admonished the German people to adhere to the teachings of the Old Testament. "Don't let anybody take the precious heritage of the sacred writings away from you, and do not tolerate that biblical education be eliminated from Christian schools." On the other hand, high members of the Protestant clergy, at a mass rally in the Berlin Sports Arena, had kept silent in the face of attacks on the Old Testament.

In his New Year's Eve sermon of 1933, in the same Munich church, Cardinal Faulhaber warned against efforts to establish, in addition to the two Christian creeds, a "Nordic-Germanic" religion, and to grant it the constitutional rights enjoyed by the established religions. We know that such plans were fully in accordance with Hitler's ultimate goal of destroying Christian faith and the churches. Faced with the threat posed by the Nazis to the very survival of Christianity in Germany, the Cardinal was moved to exclaim: "The German people will either be Christian or will not exist at all. The repudiation of Christianity, a backsliding into paganism would be the beginning of the end of the German people."

The sermons of the cardinal were available in bookstores. I purchased them. I was heartened by this genuine, impressive voice of resistance against the expanding madness of Nazi ideology.

On *February 6,1934*, I noted that *The Myth of the Twentieth Century* by Alfred Rosenberg, Hitler's plenipotentiary for the spiritual and philosophical education of the Nazi party, "had been placed on the Index of the Catholic church. The manner in which the *Völkischer Beobachter* criticized this action by heaping contempt on ecclesiastical institutions was no different from the atheist propaganda of the Communists."

The cancerous growth of the Aryan clause metastasized throughout the body politic of the German people. After the church, the army became infected. On *March 12, 1934*, I noted: "It was just announced on the radio that the Reich president acting on a suggestion by the minister of defense has ordered the application of the Law to Restore the Professional Civil Service [Aryan clause] to the army. This is a stab right into the heart of soldierly comradeship. Now this last bulwark of Prussian tradition has been destroyed." On *April 12, 1934*: "The minister of defense today announced that the 'Aryan clause' had been fully implemented. Affected were a total of. . . . [I did not note the exact figure]. Even if only one of its members had been affected, the moral defeat of the army would have been no less severe. How can this action against loyal comrades be justified from the point of view of military honor? What does the song of the 'Good Comrade' mean to forces which are no longer based on comradeship but on racial uniformity? 'He marched by my side in step,' the song proclaims, but not, 'of equal blood. . . .' The Askaris [the black native soldiers in the German colonial forces in East Africa] under General von Lettow-Vorbeck together with their white comrades faced a British-Indian army for four years and never gave up. Were they less genuine German soldiers because they were black? Their example demonstrates that the virtues of German soldiers are not dependent on race."

I first became aware that the rule of law was collapsing under the new regime when I learned by hearsay—I was still with the district government in Potsdam—that concentration camps had been established; one of the camps was said to be located in Oranienburg in the district of the Potsdam government. The camps allegedly were not run by the regular police but on behalf of the secret state police. The *Gestapo*—its acronym soon became a dreaded byword—had first been set up in Prussia and from there had been extended over the whole of Germany. Under the pretext that they were being held in protective custody, political opponents of the regime, so the rumors went, were detained in these camps without court orders.

There was no legal basis for detaining a person for political reasons. True, a Prussian law of 1850 provided for protective custody, but only if urgently required in the interest of the detainee or in order "to maintain public morals, safety and order." According to this law which, of course, was still in force, the prisoner had to be released as quickly as possible, at the latest on the day after his apprehension. Under no circumstances was it permissible to detain him for weeks, let alone for months. Furthermore, the law provided for legal remedies against the order of detention, first a complaint, followed by a suit filed before an administrative court. Why then this total disregard of a law still on the books? In the first place, any resistance against the illegality of the concentration camps was crushed by the brutal force of Nazi commandos (storm troopers, SS-men recently integrated with the police). Insofar as the applicable law was concerned, I found the answer in a Nazi party journal. A lawyer who, no doubt, possessed impeccable Nazi credentials wrote: "It does not matter what the written law prescribes. All that matters is the living law that resides in the hearts of our German compatriots. According to the precepts of this law, the inmates of concentration camps, enemies of the people, are neither entitled to court orders nor to legal remedies."

The concentration camps were subject to no control, either by the legally constituted law enforcement agencies or by the courts. With the unlimited detention of political opponents and the denial of legal protection, Germany had already ceased to be a state governed by the rule of law. On *January 15, 1934*, I wrote in my diary with regard to the remark of the Nazi lawyer quoted above: "It becomes more and more evident that the National Socialist uprising has brought about a state of spiritual collapse. A German lawyer no longer has the strength to hold on to the fundamentals of the established legal order. The tide of the 'sound popular instinct' (the doctrine introduced by the Nazis into German criminal law that an act may deserve punishment because 'the people's sound sense of justice' demands it) sweeps him off his position and into the sea of vacillation where he will perish together with the state."

The same trend toward undermining law and justice became apparent in a lecture by the secretary in the Ministry of Justice at the time, Roland Freisler, who in later years became president of the notorious "People's Court" and in that capacity was guilty of numerous judicial murders. On *January 17, 1934*, I noted: "According to newspaper reports, State Secretary Freisler in a lecture last night before the Academy of Administrative Science and Practice spoke about the imminent introduction of a new criminal law. Should this project ever be realized, arbitrariness will become the rule. The mere manifestation of criminal intent is supposed to suffice to render a person subject to punishment. Nothing is said as to which acts constitute criminal intent, and in the future no legal norms shall be required to define the types of offenses. The door will be opened to endless persecution and denunciation."

Among Nazi perversions of the law, the frequently cited Law to Restore the Professional Civil Service takes a prominent place. The title itself is fraudulent. The professional civil service was not "restored." On the contrary, its provisions authorizing dismissals from the service on racial, ideological or political grounds in disregard of vested rights crushed the very heart of the system. In fact, the law became an instrument in the hands of the Nazi autocrats to blackmail the civil service into submission. "What the Nazis called the restoration of the professional civil service was, in reality, its demise" (Schoeps).

In July of 1933, the trial of the *Reichstag* arsonists opened before the Leipzig Supreme Court. Indicted were: the Dutchman Martinus van der Lubbe; Torgler, chairman of the Communist parliamentary group in the *Reichstag* since 1929; the Bulgarians Dimitroff, member of the Executive Committee of the Communist International in Moscow, Popoff and Taneff, both members of the Central Committee of the Bulgarian Communist party. Martinus van der Lubbe had been a member of a Communist splinter group in Holland. He had been seized at the time of the fire in the *Reichstag* with incendiary material in his hands. The other defendants had been arrested merely because they were Communists. The *Reichstag* had been set on fire, so the Nazi propaganda proclaimed, by Communist conspirators with the aim of creating chaos in Germany, and of using the ensuing turmoil for the establishment of Bolshevist rule. Adolf Hitler had saved the German people from this mortal danger at the last minute, Goebbel's propaganda proclaimed. The proceedings before the Leipzig court were intended to affirm this assertion.

Even at that time rumors were rife that National Socialists had been the real perpetrators. Possibly to counter these rumors, the government promised that the trial would be conducted in full view of the public. Everybody would be admitted, yet because of limited space, by ticket only. No special qualifications were needed for obtaining tickets. Furthermore, parts of the trial would be broadcast daily on the radio.

I was skeptical. Would the general public really be allowed to watch the proceedings closely enough to be able to form its own judgment? Any deviation from the promised course of full publicity would be a sign, I thought, that there was something to hide.

And so it happened. The general public was not admitted to the trial. Tickets, it was said, were available only to specified groups of interested people (journalists, officials, etc.). The nightly broadcasts of the proceedings on the radio were short and were limited to testimony which corroborated the official theory of Communist involvement in the fire. Goebbels and Göring were heard as witnesses. Their statements were aimed primarily at depicting the Communist threat in lurid colors. The possibility that the fire might have been caused by other circumstances or that suspects other than the accused might be involved were not discussed. Göring appeared in riding attire, complete with horsewhip. He behaved rudely and violently, calling Dimitroff a scoundrel who should have been sent to the gallows long ago. The intellectual superiority that Dimitroff demonstrated in his defense so excited Göring, that he attacked him bodily during an exchange of words. Newspapers and magazines showed pictures of van der Lubbe as he was conducted into court, in prison clothing, his head drooping and hardly able to walk. He gave the impression of a person under the influence of drugs. This impression was intensified when one heard him talk on the radio. He could hardly be understood. I remember him saying during an interrogation that he had been the "victim of mystification."

Sentence was pronounced on December 23, 1933. The four Communist functionaries were acquitted. Van der Lubbe because he had been caught *in flagranti* was sentenced to death for high treason in conjunction with arson committed with the intention of provoking fear and terror in the population and attempted simple arson. He was executed on January 10, 1934.

The outcome of the trial was a defeat for the government. After the acquittal of the four Communists there was only one arsonist left, Martinus van der Lubbe. Was it at all plausible that this clumsy man with poor eyesight had been capable of turning the huge *Reichstag* building into a sea of flames with a few matches within so short a time? The first few uncensored news reports during the night of the fire disclosed the discovery of a number of fires which had been skillfully distributed throughout the building, especially in the large chambers.

Many people gave the Supreme Court credit for having had the courage to destroy the myth that the *Reichstag* fire had been the work of Communist conspirators. As was carefully explained in the opinion, no evidence had been adduced to show that the accused Communists had had any part in starting the fire. The court, however, went no further. It failed to investigate or even raise the question of who, besides the unfortunate van der Lubbe, might have been the real culprits. Still, the Communist arson trial was a setback for the government; the idea of a Communist conspiracy had vanished into thin air. The court did not succumb to political pressure; it refused to lend its prestige to bestowing upon Hitler the nimbus of Germany's savior from Bolshevist chaos.

Hitler flew into a rage. He accused the judges of "being as international as the criminals but not as skillful." For Hitler and his accomplices, Communists were criminals who had to be punished irrespective of whether they had been found guilty of a crime or not. In Hitler's eyes, courts were instruments of power designed to be used by the government to annihilate the enemies of National Socialism. Searching for truth and justice under law were outmoded concepts for him.

That this was his basic belief had become evident from his notorious telegram in the Potempa case. In the Upper-Silesian village of Potempa, five Nazi storm troopers had broken into the house of a Communist functionary at night, and had savagely murdered him before his mother's eyes. On August 22, 1932, a court in Beuthen had sentenced the storm troopers to death. In a telegram to the condemned men, Hitler heaped abuse on the "courts of Mr. von Papen" and their scandalous decision. He called the murderers his "comrades" and assured them of his "unlimited loyalty."

"The courts of Mr. von Papen!" These words have remained in my memory as the expression of a total contempt for the established legal order and the independence of the judiciary. Hitler's infamous Potempa telegram was a subject we in the Bruns Institute discussed with utter disgust.

As a consequence of the *Reichstag* fire trial the "unreliable" Supreme Court was stripped of its jurisdiction in treason cases. In April 1934, a new court was established, the so-called "People's Court" with exclusive jurisdiction over political crimes. This court, indeed, was nothing but a political tool in the hands of Hitler "to annihilate the enemies of National Socialism." In later years, it discharged this function under Freisler in the most brutal manner.

Despite their acquittal, Dimitroff and his co-defendants were not immediately released—they were, after all, "criminals" in the eyes of Germany's new leaders. They were transferred to Berlin and handed over to the secret police. Dimitroff's mother tried in vain to learn the whereabouts of her son. The acquittal, as stated in an editorial in the *Times*, had restored Germany's reputation abroad and trust in the German courts. Yet the illegal detention of Dimitroff was apt to wipe out the respect which Germany had regained and to do more harm than any political agitation which Dimitroff might have carried on abroad had he been released. (Dimitroff and the two Bulgarians were later deported to Bulgaria; Torgler was liberated from a concentration camp at the end of World War II.)

There were early signs of spiritual resistance to the spread of Nazi barbarism. On January 22, 1934, during a walk in Berlin, I noticed the name of Felix Mendelssohn-Bartholdy in an announcement for a concert to be given by the Berlin Philharmonic Orchestra. The program listed three pieces from Mendelssohn's incidental music to Shakespeare's *Midsummer Night's Dream.* The concert was billed as homage to Mendelssohn's 125th anniversary. I could hardly believe my eyes. "'Jewish music" presented to a "German" public by one of the most prominent orchestras in Germany under the direction of "Councilor of State" (a new Nazi title) Furtwängler? A review of the concert in the weekly *Deutsche Zukunft* of February 18, 1934, stated that the performance of Mendelssohn's music had been more than just a means to remember the composer's 125th anniversary. It signified the refutation of "certain doubts" as to Mendelssohn's right to claim Germany as his artistic home. After the orchestra had finished playing Mendelssohn's music, "there was no end to the applause." A report on the concert in the *Deutsche Allgemeine Zeitung* of February 13, 1934, begins with this sentence: "With the music of Weber, Mendelssohn, and Schumann the program of the Philharmonic concert offered works . . . . in which the spirit of German Romanticism manifested itself in ways specific to each of the [three] masters." (Note that Mendelssohn, together with the other two composers, is characterized as representative of *German* Romanticism, an appellation the Nazis, of course, vehemently denied. To them the "Jew" Mendelssohn was incapable of composing "German music.") At the end of his report, the reviewer (Oboussier) wrote: "The applause which lasted several minutes after the *Midsummer Night's Dream* music was a spontaneous tribute to the memory of Mendelssohn." The Nazi *Völkischer Beobachter* of February 14, 1934, also published a review of the concert.

Not a word, however, that the concert had been dedicated to the memory of Mendelssohn. And, likewise, complete silence about Mendelssohn's music, even though it had aroused enthusiastic applause, as was reported in the other two reviews. For the Nazi racial fanatics, Mendelssohn was just a "Jewish composer" whose name and work had to be obliterated.

It had indeed taken some courage to stand up for Mendelssohn the way Furtwängler had done. On May 19, 1933, members of the German Student Union publicly burned Mendelssohn's music. Records of his music were smashed, monuments of Mendelssohn were removed, memorial plaques vandalized.

In the history of music, it is an undisputed fact that the rediscovery of the *Passion according to St. Matthew* by Johann Sebastian Bach is due to Felix Mendelssohn. After it had been long forgotten, the *Passion* was performed again in 1829 under the direction of Mendelssohn in the Berlin *Singakademie*. Because of the great popularity of the work in Germany and its special place in German cultural life, this deed by Felix Mendelssohn has always caused pain and embarrassment to Nazi cultural functionaries. On the occasion of the jubilee of Zelter's *Liedertafel* in 1934, a Nazi speaker called Mendelssohn's accomplishment "a legend which it seems impossible to eradicate." In a letter to the editor of the *Deutsche Allgemeine Zeitung* of March 11, 1934, Mrs. Helene d'Alton-Rauch, in response to this statement and with a view to "clarifying the situation," merely quoted from the *Memoirs* of Therese Devrient, wife of Eduard Devrient, who, together with Felix Mendelssohn had brought about the performance of the *Passion* in the *Singakademie*. The quotation read: "It was on an evening in October that a small company had gathered at the Mendelssohns. They had been invited to become acquainted with some of Sebastian Bach's *Passion* music for the first time. This marvel had lain hidden for just one hundred years. Felix had discovered it in Zelter's, or rather the *Singakademie*'s rich treasure of music, and had brought it to light." She then related how Felix and his friend Devrient had succeeded in prompting Zelter to agree to a performance of the *Passion*.

On the morning of June 20, 1934, a female acquaintance of ours from the neighborhood appeared at our house in a state of great excitement. She brought a hectographic copy of a speech which Vice-Chancellor von Papen had given on June 17 in the *auditorium maximum* of the University of Marburg. She asked us to read the speech as quickly as possible since she was pressed for time and had to pass the copy on without undue delay.

I quickly jotted down some of the highlights of the speech. The speech sharply criticized Nazi ideology and the conduct of the new political leadership. Those who had witnessed the beginnings of the Nazi regime easily recognized the conditions and events which were the targets of Papen's attack. The speaker denounced Nazi tyranny, the legal insecurity, the oppression of "defenseless sections of the populace" (he obviously meant the Jews), the brutality of the "little Hitlers," their lack of education, the deification of Hitler, the mendacity of Goebbels' propaganda. The speech also voiced disappointment felt by Christian and conservative elements which had supported Hitler in the hope that decency in public life would be restored. The speaker referred to the loss of confidence which the government had suffered within a short time on account of the persecution of the Jews, the hostility to Christianity, the terror of the concentration camps, and other injustices and acts of violence.

The speech had been drafted in large part by Edgar E. Jung, a Munich lawyer and unofficial associate of Papen. Jung had become known as the author of a book entitled *The Rule of the Inferiors*, a critical appraisal of the existing social order. He advocated "rule by a superior élite" based on a conservative, romantically idealized image of the German national character.

In his *Memoirs*, Papen speaks of "tumultuous applause" at the conclusion of the speech. It had drowned out, he claimed, expressions of disapproval by a few party bosses among the audience. It had been agreed that the speech would be broadcast on the radio that same evening. Goebbels, however, immediately had the speech suppressed. The press was ordered not to print a single word of it. Through his connections with the Catholic *Germania* printing house in Berlin, Papen succeeded in having several thousand copies printed. However, anyone caught distributing the speech ran the risk of being arrested and put into a concentration camp. Even the possession of a copy sufficed to mark the holder an enemy of the state.

The fact that the vice-chancellor had spoken was of no importance to those in the government who possessed the real power. For me, however, this speech, the "first trumpet call of open resistance" (Ritter), was a tremendous relief and an encouragement. From the midst of the government a voice had been heard calling for a change of conditions that had become unbearable. This seemed to herald a turn for the better, I thought.

Nothing could have been further from the truth. Dramatic events were soon to prove that my hopes had been utterly unfounded.

Saturday, June 30, 1934, was a clear, sunny summer day. Coming at noon from the palace where I had been working in the library of the institute, I took a streetcar down Leipziger Strasse and crossed Leipziger Platz. In the gateway of the *Preussenhaus*, formerly the Prussian House of Representatives, I saw units of state police with steel helmets and carbines. The iron-barred gates of the office building of the Prussian minister president were closed. Behind the gates stood state police in battle dress. Numerous policemen were posted around the square. The unexpected presence of large police forces made me aware of the deep chasm that had developed between the people and the government since the Nazis had seized power. While the citizen peaceably went about his day-to-day chores, things happened in the political world of which he had no inkling, to which only those in power were privy. I felt that I was being unwittingly exposed to unknown, sinister forces.

In the afternoon, a cousin of mine, Wolfgang von Richthofen, a lieutenant in the air force, brought the news that Röhm, chief of staff of the storm troopers, had been arrested. He told me that during the day he had flown, "on behalf of the secret police," to various cities, among them Stettin, Breslau and Dresden. That was all he could tell me; he knew nothing about the purpose or the content of his mission. He had an appointment with friends at Marquardt, a former estate on the outskirts of Berlin which had been turned into a restaurant, and took me along in his small car. There we enjoyed the peaceful rural scenery until a rumor reached us that Röhm had been dismissed and that a relatively unknown storm trooper, Lutze, had been named his successor.

This then had been the reason for the extraordinary show of police which I had observed at noon in the city. On the way back to town we passed columns of army vehicles moving in the direction of the city. At home, the radio was crammed with news: Grave irregularities among the storm troopers; a quagmire of immorality uncovered; several high officers of the storm troopers, among them such well-known names as Heines, von Heydebreck, and Count Spreti had been shot. In the evening an acquaintance from the neighborhood called and asked whether we had heard that General von Schleicher and his wife had been murdered. The news left us stunned. The next day kiosks were covered with red-rimmed posters describing in lurid detail the foul deeds of the storm troopers and their leaders.

What had happened in Berlin and other German cities on June 30, 1934, and the two following days is history and need not be told here. However, what needs to be remembered is that in those days an untold number of people in public life were murdered on Hitler's order, either in their homes, like General von Schleicher and his wife; or at the desk of their office, like Dr. Erich Klausener, Section Chief in the Ministry of Transportation. He had been chairman of the Catholic Action, and only a few days earlier, on June 24 at a Berlin "Catholic Day," had protested against political oppression, the racial policy, and national arrogance. Also dead was the dismissed Chief of Staff of the storm troopers, Röhm. Hitler's other victims included: Gregor Strasser, who had been one of Hitler's earliest followers, and who, in December of 1932, without Hitler's consent had dared to negotiate with Chancellor von Schleicher about joining the government; the former Bavarian Minister President von Kahr who had crushed Hitler's *Putsch* of November 9, 1923; and E. Jung, co-author of Papen's speech at Marburg—he was murdered in the basement of the *Gestapo* prison in the Prinz Albrecht Strasse. Another of Papen's co-workers, Senior Governmental Counselor von Bose, was shot by SS-men in Papen's office when he tried to resist the intruders.

None of the victims had been indicted for alleged crimes against the regime, such as high treason, and put before a court, although the People's Court had been established to deal with just such crimes.

In a speech before the *Reichstag* on July 13, Hitler himself addressed the question as to why he had not called upon the courts to proceed against suspected enemies of the state. The explanation he gave for his failure was an incredible mockery of constitutional government. He claimed that at that hour he alone was responsible for the fate of the German nation and consequently he had been "the supreme court of justice of the German people." Here then was the chief of the executive branch who arrogated to himself the judicial power as well and, in the exercise of this supreme power, condemned whomever he chose to death, and had the death sentences carried out by hired killers. This was the end of the constitutional order. The concentration of power in Hitler's person had become total and ever more menacing. There were no longer any restraints.

On July 3, the Reich government enacted a "law" signed by Hitler and Minister of Justice Gürtner. Its sole Article read: "The measures taken on June 30, July 1 and 2 for the purpose of suppressing treasonable attacks are acts of national self-defense and for that reason are lawful."

This "law" was evidence of the cynical contempt for law by those in power. The murderer became judge of his own case and at the same time the legislator of his deed.

Names of the victims in addition to those which Hitler mentioned in his speech of July 13, such as General von Schleicher and his wife, eventually became known through the grapevine. I asked myself how the murder of old Mr. von Kahr, of Dr. Klausener, of Edgar Jung and Mr. von Bose could have been "acts of national self-defense." None of them had been accused of, nor did they ever harbor seditious intentions. No. What had been done on June 30 and the following two days was murder in the sense of criminal law; the murderous deeds were acts of personal revenge on former adversaries or blows against possible future rivals.

In my judgment, the events of June 30 and their aftermath signified the final collapse of the rule of law, or rather, its total eradication. Germany, so I confided in my notes, was in the hands of a criminal regime which was headed for chaos. There was no protection anymore against arbitrary actions by the state. There were rumors about lists which allegedly had served as basis for the selection of the victims of June 30. Anyone who might appear to be opposed to the regime—and I had been officially classified as a non-Aryan and thus "undesirable" in the national community—could not help but feel threatened. I realized that Germany was no longer my homeland, if homeland is not just a geographical concept but has spiritual meaning. I could remain in Germany no longer.

I endeavored more energetically than heretofore to prepare for my emigration. The efforts of my brother to obtain a fellowship for me at American academic institutions had been unsuccessful. He had collected a voluminous file of laudatory comments and just as many refusals. I could wait no longer. I decided to leave for the States to try my luck there in person.

Emigration

A severe illness caused perhaps by physical and mental exhaustion delayed my departure for several months. Eventually, in September of 1934, I was able to start the emigration procedure. I applied for an immigration visa at the American Consulate General in Berlin. I was informed, first of all, that industry and agriculture in the United States were in a state of severe depression and that there was widespread unemployment. Considering the poor economic conditions, many applications for visas had been denied. My case could only be considered if I was able to prove that someone would support me after my arrival in the States. But even if the evidence were sufficient, the final decision of the consul, I was told, would depend on the situation and the capabilities of the applicant.

There were no problems when I presented myself in person at the consulate. I was interviewed about the reasons for my emigration, my occupation and my plans in the States. I signed the declaration that, among other things, I was not an anarchist and had no intention of changing the Constitution of the United States by force or of murdering the president. I passed my physical examination. My brother's affidavit that he was willing and able to support me dispelled whatever misgivings the consul might have had about my becoming a public charge. At the end of October I received a "Quota-Visa" for immigration to the United States, together with the green card of the Department of Labor permitting me to seek employment there.

A big black box with my personal papers, notes, and most of my books remained in the cellar of my parents' apartment in Berlin. I owe it to the preserving care of my mother that the box survived several moves, Allied bombing attacks on Berlin during World War II, and the first few months of the Allied occupation of Berlin. After many years the box followed me to the United States.

When I took leave of some of my former colleagues in the institute, they assured me that the excesses and abuses which were responsible for my present plight and which all people of good will deplored, would soon be overcome. They expected me back in two years.

My parents had taken out a bank loan to cover the costs of my passage on the Hamburg-Amerika liner *New York*, a double-screw turbine steamer of 22,000 tons. The sailing date was November 29, 1934. I went to Hamburg the previous day to meet my oldest brother and his wife. They had promised to see me off at the pier. We went to a movie the night before my departure. I have forgotten which film we saw, but what happened to me in the darkness of the movie house is something I can still feel when I remember that night. Reflecting upon my imminent departure from my family, my friends, and country, pondering the leap into the unknown, I suddenly felt as if I had lost my footing, the connection with my surroundings, and that I was literally being lifted up into the air. A psychic trauma, the shock of becoming uprooted, had transformed itself into the physical sensation of floating in space. This feeling of suspension lasted for several frightening minutes. I recall that I could not quite recover from it. During the preparations for my departure with its many troublesome chores, I had had little time or inclination to think about the forthcoming event, with all its attendant losses, and the utter uncertainty of my condition. In the darkness of the room these thoughts and fears crept up from my subconscious and took hold of me.

The place of embarkation had been changed at short notice from Hamburg to Bremerhaven. During the ride on the boat train, passengers were requested to show the money that they were carrying with them. The maximum allowed was ten marks. I had some small change in my pocket above the permitted amount which I gave to my brother. "I see you have more money with you than is permitted," the inspector said in a threatening tone of voice. He asked me to open my luggage, which he searched thoroughly. I knew there was no "contraband" in it, but I could not know what he might consider as such if he were out to "get me." Eventually he gave up, possibly because of the ridiculously small excess amount of money. The incident was a tremendous shock. I had been entirely in the hands of the inspector, very likely an ardent Nazi. A small gesture on his part and my departure might have foundered at the last minute.

I stood at the stern as the ship weighed anchor. At the pier some storm troopers watched the maneuvers. Tugboats slowly moved the ship out of the harbor. The distance to shore increased. The last of Hitler's representatives eventually disappeared from sight.

I had little contact with my fellow passengers. The passenger list revealed that many among them were sharing my fate. I noticed the name of Arnold Brecht, *Ministerialdirektor* (ret.). From 1921-1927, Brecht had been chief of the constitutional law section in the Reich Ministry of the Interior. He had also been plenipotentiary of Prussia in the Federal Council and, in 1932, represented the Prussian government in the suit described above before the Supreme Court concerning the appointment of a Reich commissioner for Prussia. Brecht had been removed from his position by the Nazis because of his close association with the Weimar regime. He followed a call to the New School for Social Research in New York.

Shortly before we reached the coast of America we encountered one of the winter storms which frequently occur in those latitudes. Captain Kruse, who had invited me to the bridge along with other passengers, told us that he had seldom experienced a storm of such fierceness. The storm had still not abated when the *New York*, after her stay in New York, left on her return voyage to Hamburg. She had hardly reached the high seas when she picked up distress signals from the Norwegian freighter *Sisto*. In an unprecedented rescue action in the middle of the night, volunteers from the *New York* succeeded in taking the sixteen crew members of the *Sisto* aboard their ship. The *Sisto* drifted in the stormy sea, a helpless wreck. The heroic deeds of the German rescue team aroused respect and admiration throughout the world.

We arrived in New York on December 7. My brother had cabled $75.00 to the ship which I had to present as "landing money" to the immigration inspector. Surely, the ten marks which I had been allowed to take out of Germany would hardly have opened the gates of the New World to me. My brother appeared on the ship as soon as it had docked in New York harbor in order to assist me with the immigration formalities. A few questions, a cursory glance at my luggage, a friendly word of welcome—and I stood on American soil.

Many years later I came across an issue of the German illustrated magazine *Berliner Illustrirte* (sic) *Zeitung*, at one time a leading German magazine and highly respected until 1933, when it was nazified. The issue was from 1939. It showed the photograph of a Jewish immigrant from Germany who upon arrival in New York, kisses the soil of America. The caption read; "One for the photographer's benefit. A revolting pose contrived for the American yellow press." How utterly wrong! There was no need for artifice. Everyone who came from Hitler's Reich felt like the man in the picture when he stepped onto American soil.

I stayed in New York for a few weeks. My brother had arranged for me to visit some of his friends and acquaintances who had expressed interest in my case. I also needed to learn at least the rudiments of American life before venturing forth in search of employment. I moved from the hotel where I had stayed with my brother to a club house which someone had recommended to me. The manager, a former German, had preserved very little of his native tongue. He pronounced German words with an American accent even though he had come to the States as an adult. This baffled me. Might this also happen to me? I was keen to observe everything which related to immigration. I later realized that the manager belonged to a type of person geared to speak only one language, the language of his environment, and apt to forget his native tongue once he became thoroughly immersed in his new habitat.

I was deaf and dumb during those first few weeks; I could neither understand others nor make myself understood. In order to familiarize myself with the day-to-day language and accustom my ear to the way American was spoken, I watched movies (in those days double-billed) and remained in the theater during the intermission for the repeat performance of the whole program. As I watched the same movies for the second or third time the percentage of my comprehension increased. I noted the figures of speech used in certain situations of daily life as they appeared in the movies and wrote them down in a notebook I carried with me. I read newspapers and magazines. The terse headlines, often in slang, presented stumbling blocks that at times exasperated me.

Signs on shops which I studied during my peregrinations through the city, and the menus in restaurants were also valuable sources for augmenting my vocabulary.

One morning when I looked out of my window I saw a window washer on the huge, flat wall of a skyscraper opposite me. He was hanging in his straps above the abyss of the street below like a small black fly. Was my situation not similar to his? Was I not dangling between a crash and a hazy future which stretched like the open sky above the building? What prevented me from plunging to the ground? A thin belt like the window washer's strap kept me from falling for the moment. Would it last? Everything was strange. The gigantic towerlike buildings seemed to be beyond the range of eye and mind to grasp. I wandered through the streets. A sharp, icy wind swept around the corners of the broad avenues with a force I had never experienced. Would I ever be able to adapt to the rhythm of life in this country? What had I brought with me from my former existence that I could use to build on?

At Christmas, I went to see my brother in Pittsburgh. He had written that I should take the Greyhound bus. The fare for the round-trip at holiday prices would be $15. The bus left New York at 9:00 p.m. From my window seat I saw small green, red, blue, and yellow lights in the darkness outside. They came from Christmas decorations on trees in front of houses, a color scheme new to me like the blue lights on top of passing trucks and buses. There were stops on the way. The driver announced the name of the town and the duration of the stop. Before continuing the journey, he would count the number of passengers to make sure no one was left behind. I shuddered at the thought that I might get lost in one of those places deep in the Appalachian mountains. I did not venture outside the bus.

Around noon on the following day, we approached Pittsburgh from the surrounding hills. The city was covered by a thick, dingy-brown layer of smog. Only the tops of a few tall buildings were visible. The smog was the result of the smoke from steel mills and innumerable soft coal burning stoves. All that has changed now. The air has been cleaned. In the course of a campaign for urban renewal, the "Golden Triangle," the area at the confluence of the Monongahela and Allegheny rivers, has been turned into a park where the remains of Fort Pitt have been preserved in an open-air museum. The fort was a British bastion from the time of the French and Indian War (1756-63). Bridges dating from the turn of the twentieth century have been replaced by modern structures. After the nerve-racking hustle and bustle of New York, Pittsburgh was the first city in the United States where I felt welcome. My brother introduced me to his circle of friends. They all received me with warm friendliness. Since that time I have kept a soft spot for Pittsburgh in my heart. Its modernization and beautification has increased the city's attraction for me.

Student at the Yale Law School

Time was passing. I had to decide what to do next and take the initiative. In the middle of December I met Professor Edwin Borchard in New Haven, an authority on constitutional and international law at the Yale Law School.

For years Professor Borchard had been on friendly terms with Professor Bruns, my former chief in Berlin. Bruns had asked me to assist with questions on the legal status of the Free City of Danzig during one of his visits to the institute in 1931. Professor Borchard had been thus one of my contacts in the States even before my emigration. I had exchanged letters with him, without achieving tangible results. At lunch with Professor Borchard we were joined by Professor Arnold Wolfers. A Swiss citizen, he had been Director of the Academy of Political Science in Berlin and had left his post after Hitler had come to power. Without knowing that we would meet, he had borrowed a copy of my article, *The Congress of Vienna and the Restoration of the European Balance of Power* from the library the day before my visit. In the course of the conversation we discussed some preliminary plans for joint research projects. As a result of these talks I left New York at the beginning of January and moved to New Haven.

For a few days I was the guest of Professor Wolfers, Master of Pierson College, one of the residential colleges where students live and have their meals. I then took a room in the home of a Yale professor.

There I experienced, possibly as an after-effect of the trauma of emigration, what I believe was an attack of persecution mania.

One weekend I was alone in the house with a maid. The professor and his wife had gone away on a trip. Late at night someone rang the doorbell. I thought that it was a gentleman with a hat and a briefcase. Unable to think rationally, I was convinced that the nocturnal visit was aimed at me, and that I was to be kidnaped. Terrified, I hid in the house until dawn and then called the police who promptly came and, of course, found nothing. I was very confused. Shocked back into sanity, I could hardly conceal my embarrassment. I wonder how the police reported the incident in their logbook.

I was fortunate to find a boarding house, where I could settle down. It became my home for many years. Mrs. B. (short for Boykin—that was what her tenants called her) came from one of those New England families which are rooted in the traditions of the English "motherland." In her youth she had taken part in educational tours through Europe. Her marriage to a plantation owner in the South had been a failure. Her active Yankee character had not adapted to the lifestyle of the Southern gentry—superficial, interested mainly in social events, insensible to arts and letters, somewhat boorish and partial to liquor. She moved back to New England with her small daughter and opened a boarding house in a residential district of New Haven where lovely houses abound. As the zoning laws did not permit commercial enterprises in this area, Mrs. B.'s establishment was sponsored by the university as a sort of guest house for transient scholars. In reality, however, it was run like a boarding house. The neighbors were kind enough not to take offense. She also served dinner at night for lonely hearts, mostly lady teachers who lived in the neighborhood. Her tenants came from many countries. Not only did she find contact with foreign customs and manners stimulating, she also liked to introduce newcomers like myself to the American way of life. She was always ready to listen, showed a warmhearted concern for everybody's problems, was untiring in her efforts to make everyone feel at home, and was always helpful, patient, and kind. It was part of her generous nature to take everyone as he or she was (a quality, incidentally, one finds particularly often with Americans). She was never adverse to suggestions for a little party on whatever grounds, whether a fancy dress party or an "art exhibition" to which everyone contributed works of his or her own. It was a house from which sadness was banned and cheerful fellowship was the rule.

I was not the only one of Mrs. B.'s tenants who found a safe haven in her home. Soon after the Nazis' aerial bombardment of England began, Mrs. B. took in the wife and three small children of an English professor from Oxford. Apparently afraid that the German bombardments might wipe out whole sections of the population, or wishing to spare their children the terrifying experience of witnessing death and destruction in their own country, British and American universities had started an action to evacuate children of British academic families to Canada and to the United States for "safekeeping," as it were. The action, we learned, was less than popular in England since it benefited only a select group of people. Later on, young Germans and Austrians who had succeeded in escaping from Hitler's clutches found temporary refuge at Mrs. B.'s.

The most prominent guest for some time was Professor Steiner-Prag, a renowned book designer, graphic artist, illustrator, and author. New Haven was Steiner-Prag's third station on a long and arduous journey. He was Jewish and in 1933 had been removed by the Nazis from his position as teacher of a master class at the Leipzig Academy of Graphic Arts. The loss of his livelihood in Germany forced him to return to his native Prague where the foundation of the *Officina Pragensis*, a graphic arts school, provided him with a new basis for teaching and artistic production. Shortly before the German occupation of Czechoslovakia in 1938, Swedish friends offered to establish a school similar to the *Officina Pragensis* in Stockholm and succeeded in getting Steiner-Prag out of Czechoslovakia just before the German occupation. But even in Stockholm Steiner-Prag did not feel safe after the Nazis had overrun the European continent. After an adventurous journey that took him to Finland, Russia, Japan, and across the Pacific Ocean, Steiner-Prag and his young German wife whom he had married in Sweden arrived in the States in 1941. New York University offered him a position in the Division of Graphic Arts. Before he was prepared to accept the appointment, he and his wife needed time to adjust to life in the United States. In Mrs. B.'s boarding house, the couple found the seclusion and anonymity they desired.

In 1916, Steiner-Prag's lithographs for Gustav Meyrink's novel *Der Golem* had made him world-famous. (In Jewish mysticism and folklore, a golem is an artificial human being built from clay by religious masters, in particular the "High Rabbi" Löw from Prague, in the sixteenth century and brought to life by being infused with verses of Scripture and the name of God.) The number of Steiner-Prag's book designs and book illustrations is legion. In his drawings, demoniac, mystical themes predominate, often represented in chiaroscuro hue. He was a master of creating pictorial images of mysterious and legendary subjects. Yet he was also successful, "as though emerging from the *Biedermeier* time or a second Rococo, in creating winsome, elegant, amorous drawings and ornaments" (Ernst Schremmer).

While Steiner-Prag—we called him "the Professor"—had an air of distinction and intellectual superiority about him, we were not aware of his international fame. His modesty did not admit of enlightening us on his achievements. Far from publicity, in the quiet of Mrs. B.'s house and its family atmosphere, he was content to let the novelty of his surroundings and of his life in the States sink in. Like those of us who shared his fate, he had to make a fresh start and establish a new order in his life. We helped as much as we could to acquaint him with American customs and manners. At the time when the Steiner-Prags joined Mrs. B.'s household, I owned a little car which allowed us—the Steiner-Prags and myself—to explore the scenic beauty of Connecticut. Sketches and watercolors by the Professor were the fruits of these excursions.

Among Steiner-Prag's last creations were illustrations for an English translation of E. T. A. Hoffmann's works for the Limited Edition Club, a collection of valuable reprints issued in limited numbers.

E. T. A. Hoffmann (1776-1822), one of the master novelists of German Romanticism, was Steiner-Prag's favorite author. Some of his tales that deal with the cryptic, the uncanny, and the gruesome are similar to stories by Edgar Allen Poe. Offenbach's opera *The Tales of Hoffmann* is based on novels by the German poet. During my years in school I had become enamored of Hoffmann's works which were among the first books of my student library. After my school years Hoffmann had vanished from my mental horizon. When I met Steiner-Prag, the literary idol of my youth came to life again—on American soil. As a parting gift, Steiner-Prag gave me a copy of his famous lithograph of Hoffmann which had been used in many editions of Hoffmann's works. It shows the poet wearing an old-fashioned, broad-brimmed high hat, his face marked by an angular nose and piercing eyes. In 1943, Steiner-Prag moved to New York. He died there in 1945 at the age of 65.

Through the good offices of Professor Borchard, I was given a place to work in the Yale Law School. From time to time Professor Borchard would ask me to prepare a study on some question of international law. In November of 1935, I received an invitation from Lawrence Preuss, Professor of Political Science at the University of Michigan, to participate in a meeting of the American Political Science Association to be held on December 27 and 28 in Atlanta, Georgia. Professor Preuss was going to lead a discussion on "The United States and Neutrality," and asked me to contribute a report on "Germany's Policy of Neutrality Since the War." I felt that my English was sufficiently advanced to permit me to take on this task, and I accepted. Furthermore, I had been told that meetings of this kind were a sort of "talent fair" where I might make connections which could possibly lead to a position at an academic institution.

The prospect of escaping the severity of the eastern winter in the sunny South caused my brother to suggest that we travel to Atlanta by car and continue from there to Florida. (My brother owned an old two-passenger coupe, and gasoline was still cheap in those days.) In the mountains of Tennessee we were caught by a blizzard and had to seek refuge in a small town where we were lucky to get a hotel room. The next day we found ourselves in the midst of an ice storm. We were fascinated by the fairy tale scenery of trees, shrubs and grass which were transformed into gleaming crystals. The driving was hazardous, and in order to make sure that I would arrive for the meeting on time, my brother had me take the train from Chattanooga while he struggled to make it to Atlanta by car.

Atlanta also felt the destructive force of the ice storm. In the evening, from the window of my hotel room, I saw what looked like fireworks. They were actually sparks from a fiery electrical discharge that was generated every time the overhead cable of a streetcar broke under the weight of the ice and hit the ground.

I did arrive in Atlanta on time and was able to deliver my speech, meet people, and make new friends. This, no doubt, was a welcome gain, but otherwise there were no results.

Although spring had eluded us in Atlanta, we met it in northern Florida and encountered summertime in Miami. On New Year's Eve we took a swim in the ocean. For the first time I realized the enormous expanse of America, which has different seasons at the same time of the year within the frontiers of the same country. On the way to Miami we had passed through the Everglades, a swampy wilderness and home of the Seminole Indians. They wore native costumes and offered their wares—handmade ornaments and woodcuts—at trading posts along the highway. We noted that the tribesmen we met hardly spoke a word of English.

I soon realized that the small niche Professor Borchard had provided for me at the Law School could last only for a transitional period until I had adjusted to life in the States. What I lacked in order to start a professional career in the States, especially a career in law, was an American background, the proof that I possessed the knowledge required of an American in this field. My German legal education was of no practical use. It could at best serve to show that I had been exposed to law, that I knew its basic elements, had a legal turn of mind and had been successful in pursuing a legal career under the continental system. However, without studying American law, I had no chance of ever reentering my chosen profession.

Yet I still faced a difficult decision. I had to ask myself if I were capable of sustaining, over a number of years, the strain of studying a field of law which was entirely new to me. Could I in good conscience take the risk, not knowing what the outcome would be? Should I not rather look for something else which might afford me a chance to earn my livelihood? I did not know what this "something else" might be. My experience in legal matters was the only capital I had saved when my lifeline had been cut by the Nazis and I was set adrift. The talent that was given to me was for the legal profession. I felt that I was incapable of deviating from the road I had traveled in life thus far—I did not know which other way to turn. I discussed the matter with my brother who generously promised to help.

I also spoke with Professor Borchard. After consultation with the dean it was decided that in view of my previous experience in law I would be permitted to enter the Law School as a student "with advanced standing" i.e., as a second-year student, provided that, through successful examinations, I earn credit for at least 48 units by the end of my course of studies. What appeared to be a privilege was, in fact, a mixed blessing. I had to achieve in two years what my American fellow students had three years to accomplish; they also possessed the added advantage of having studied at a U.S. college for four years. Two other German refugees from Hitler's Germany were admitted to the Yale Law School on the same basis—a successful lawyer from Berlin and the son of a well-known Jewish author. After all the preliminaries had been settled, I applied to the Registrar of the Yale Law School for admission as a second-year student for the winter semester of 1936.

I knew nothing about the study techniques at an American university, including the "point" system(the need to accumulate a prescribed number of units over the years in order to stay in school), examinations at the end of each course, and other such requirements. I had been told that first-year students at Harvard Law School are greeted by the Dean at their first session with these words: "Look closely at your neighbors on your right and on your left. One of them will not be here next year." Yale boasted that the Legal Aptitude Test, which applicants had to take before being admitted to the School, had sharply reduced the number of dropouts. However, even Yale was not immune to this type of defection, and the word dropout, incidentally a concept entirely new to me, had an ugly sound.

For a lawyer trained in the continental legal system, the study of American law requires a new approach, a re-orientation of the process of legal thinking. The German jurist looks for a provision in a statute that fits the facts of his case and that tells him how to decide. This method has been in use in Germany since the the fifteenth and sixteenth centuries when Roman law was "received" as in other continental European countries. It was in force in Germany until the adoption of the Civil Code in 1900. Since that time German lawyers are accustomed to equate law with statutory law, and to think in abstract terms. This approach differs from the empirical procedure of Anglo-Saxon law which is based on the concept that law originates from what happens in daily life. The legal principles evolved by courts in individual

cases are law, and, together with statutes, form the legal order of
the state. The essence of the concept of Anglo-Saxon law has
been stated with incisive brevity in a motto inscribed in stone
letters above a doorway at Yale Law School that law is a living
growth, not a changeless code.

From the "case law" method, it follows that the legal
principles governing a case are cited by the names of the parties
to the suit, for example the principle that the Supreme Court
has the power to declare a Congressional act unconstitutional is
referred to by the names of "Marbury v. Madison," the two
parties whose dispute gave rise to the famous ruling by the
Supreme Court. On the other hand, a continental lawyer cites the
law which governs his case by the number of the provision in a
statute.

As the method of citation varies in the two legal systems,
so does the teaching material. The law books of the American
student, and the principal literary products of an American law
professor, are annotated collections of court decisions such as
Cases on American Constitutional Law, *Cases on Taxation*, *Cases
on Labor Law*.

The German law student receives his education, insofar as
books are concerned, from systematic textbooks on specified
subjects such as *The Law of Obligations*, *The Law of Property*, etc.
Since Anglo-Saxon law relates directly to day-to-day occurrences,
it is more lively than the abstract norms of continental law. It is
also more stimulating for a student to analyze cases than to learn
by heart, or at least to become familiar with, a thousand or more
provisions of the Civil Code or other basic statutes.

In addition to learning a new vocabulary of legal terms, the
method of instruction at the Law School was also new to me. For
each day, lessons were assigned and announced on the bulletin
board. The professor would call upon a student by name to recite,
standing up, the assigned case and answer questions. Some of the
more argumentative students would use this opportunity to engage
the professor in protracted discussions which could be instructive
and sometimes amusing, but were also time-consuming.

The system of preparing lessons, of being called upon in
class, of answering questions reminded me, at first, of my days
in high school. In Germany a law student is more or less free

to arrange his course of study. He attends, or fails to attend without prejudice, courses, takes notes home for study or review, participates in exercises and seminars to collect the required number of certificates. As he nears the end of the time usually allotted for the study of law (seven semesters), the student finds out that he still lacks the comprehensive knowledge of the law that must be present in his mind when he takes the final written and oral examinations. In this situation he turns to the *Repetitor* (as related earlier in this book). Under the tutelage of the *Repetitor*, the student gains the necessary overall view of the law. He acquires the ability to focus on the particular field of law that the examiner may choose for the test. He also learns the technique of the written examination.

The American method has the advantage of keeping the student "on the ball" at all times, and of forcing him to learn. If the student keeps up with this pace, if he follows the prescribed procedures, he is practically assured of advancing to the next higher class and of eventually graduating. There is no sudden awakening to the realization that he may not be qualified to face the final examinations. There is no room for a *Repetitor*. With the successful completion of his last course, the American law student has arrived and has earned his degree.

Approximately fifteen years after graduating from the *Gymnasium* and after many years of professional life, I was at school once again. I did my homework, filled reams and reams of paper with lecture notes and case analyses, was called upon in class, felt the pressure of examinations, wrote papers (one of them on *The Evolution of the Concept of the Just War in International Law* was published in the *American Journal of International Law* and received an award). After two years, in May of 1938, I had collected the prescribed 48 points and was ready to receive the degree of Bachelor of Laws.

Commencement Day was June 22, 1938. It was an overwhelming experience for me that, my parents could be present on that day in addition to my brother. When I first learned about their plan, I was both skeptical and perturbed. Would they be allowed to travel to the United States? Just at that time it was Hitler's policy to make it appear that there was no need to be concerned about the political situation, that people could travel (the liner *Bremen* had recently been launched) in order that the world might believe his protestations of peace and be lulled into a sense of security. My parents had long hoped for a reunion with my brother and me, and, in the end, this overcame all of our doubts.

The Commencement began on a beautiful warm and sunny summer day with the traditional procession of the members of all the faculties in their colorful academic robes and of the candidates for the various degrees in black gowns with mortarboards. It started at the center of the campus and wound its way across the Green to Wolsey Hall. The procession entered the hall to the strains of the overture to Richard Wagner's *Meistersinger*. After the customary speeches and hymns, each candidate mounted the platform in order to receive the certificate of his or her degree, along with a handshake from the President of the University.

My feelings at that solemn moment were mixed. Should I be proud? Was this a "commencement" for me as well? I knew all too well that the future still lay hidden behind an impenetrable veil.

At the same ceremony several honorary degrees were awarded. Among the recipients were the world-famous German novelist Thomas Mann, who at that time had already been stripped of his German citizenship by the Nazis; Lord Tweedsmuir, Governor-General of Canada; Serge Koussevitzky, the conductor of the Boston Symphony Orchestra; and Walt Disney, creator of "Mickey Mouse," who received an honorary M.A. degree. In his citation, Professor William L. Phelps, inspired by the Horation verse *Parturiunt montes, nascetur ridiculus mus*, called Walt Disney the man who labored like a mountain and brought forth a mouse with which he conquered the world.

In his citation for Thomas Mann, Professor Phelps called the author a steadfast descendent of the free citizens of Germany's seashore on whom Providence had bestowed the gift to recognize the hidden movements of the human soul and who through his own efforts developed an artistic mastery to reveal those movements in great literature.

I had seen and heard Thomas Mann at the beginning of March 1938 when he gave a speech at Yale. He spoke in halting

English with a heavy German accent. The subject of his speech was *The Role of the Artist in the Struggle for Democracy.* He said that in the near future he would talk about democracy in many cities, universities and city halls. This, he said, was an eminently human concern. Deviating from his proper calling to fight for the good in life the artist, as a human being, is called upon to raise his voice against "the terrible, monstrous and inhuman totalitarian claim of the state." The final words of his speech were, "I shall proclaim my faith in the future triumph of democracy."

Naturalization

Most of my fellow students after graduating either joined a law firm, put out their own shingle, or became law clerks for a while, preferably of a Supreme Court justice in Washington, D.C. I stayed in New Haven to work on a research project in international law together with Professor Borchard and received the rank of an instructor at the Yale Law School.

In December of 1939, I had lived in the United States continuously for five years and was thus entitled to present myself for naturalization. Immediately after the expiration of the five-year waiting period, I submitted to the immigration authorities an application to be naturalized as a citizen of the United States. Organizational changes delayed action on my application for several months. By January of 1941, the necessary paper work had been completed. I was summoned to appear before the United States Court for the Second District in the New Haven Post Office, together with two witnesses who could testify about my conduct and residence during the past five years (Mrs. B. and a friend from the Law School). I was then examined by representatives of the Justice and Labor Departments about my knowledge of the basic principles of the American Constitution. The questioning went like this: What is the Constitution of the United States? (The right answer is: "The supreme law of the land." When a simple-minded candidate once answered "The President," he was advised to study some more before trying again.) What type of government do we have? What is the procedure for amending the Constitution? What are the functions of the Supreme Court? How old must a person be to be eligible for Senator, for Representative? What is the legal status of aliens? After I had passed the test to the satisfaction of the examiners, I was told that I had to wait another ninety days before I would be summoned to take the citizenship oath.

On April 24, 1941, along with about one hundred other candidates for citizenship I appeared in the great hall of the United States District Court before Federal Judge Hincks. The judge, tall, white-haired, his dignified bearing enhanced by a black robe, stood at the judge's bench; behind him was a large flag of the United States. In a solemn voice he recited the words of the Oath of Allegiance. We all raised our right hands and repeated the words after him. The taking of the oath in open court was the culminating event in the procedure of naturalization. We were now legally accepted into the community of citizens of the United States. The Daughters of the American Revolution welcomed us and distributed small flags. It was a warmhearted gesture; it was meant, I thought, to make us feel that we belonged to the great American family from now on. My separation from Germany, from Hitler's Third Reich, had become final. I had reached the point of no return. Concepts like "Quarter Jew," "Three-Quarter Aryan," and "Mongrel of the Second Degree" were things of the past. At this decisive turn of my life, Lincoln's words in his Gettysburg Address went through my mind: "Under God a new birth of freedom."

The legal change from German to American citizen had been accomplished. I had undergone a spiritual transformation during the past several years almost without my realizing it. When I decided to emigrate, I had no idea of what it might take, of what I had to go through in order that this adaptation might occur. I was a German and a European by tradition, education, and life experience. Would it be possible for me to undergo the process of transformation without "suffering harm to my soul?" I was not a visitor. Having escaped an unworthy, hopeless existence, I wanted to take root in this country and find a new home. In order to achieve this goal, I had to get rid of the shell of an emigrant as quickly as possible. I never hesitated to tell anyone who wanted to know, the reasons for my emigration, truthfully, without bitterness or complaints. *Res ipsa loquitur*, as the jurist would say. The facts should speak for themselves; I left it up to the listener to draw his or her own conclusions as to the conditions in Germany. I never thought of trying to ingratiate myself with my new countrymen by condemning Germany and the German people as a whole. I noticed that Americans fully understood that being an exile did not mean that one had to forsake one's cultural heritage from the "old country" for good. In conversations and occasional talks before church groups and other organizations I endeavored to make people understand—news and reports about

Nazi Germany notwithstanding—that there was another, a decent Germany, in fact the only Germany I knew.

Among my fellow refugees there were some who, through their manner of speech and behavior, tried to pose as native Americans. I considered this attitude affected, lacking in credibility, and even embarrassing. I had to face the fact that I would never be able to disguise my foreign origin. What mattered to me was to behave the way people acted toward me: openly, trustingly, without prejudice, in a positive and straightforward manner. The kindness and friendliness Americans show to newcomers, their willingness to make them feel that they are welcome, that America lies open before them, made me lose the inhibitions that at first hampered my relations with people. When I adopted the custom, which at first was somewhat strange, of calling new acquaintances by their first names, it demonstrated that I had gone a long way in shedding my initial reserve.

Knowing the history of the United States and American political thought and institutions is of paramount importance to anyone who wants to become adjusted to the life and the customs in the States, who is keen about understanding the American people and communicating with them intelligently. My brother had lived in Virginia during his first few years in America and had become a "Civil War buff." He knew everything about the lives and the characters of the statesmen and generals on both sides, could describe in minute detail the great battles of the war, and during visits to historical sites, depicted the episodes and events both tragic and stirring in vivid terms. Lincoln's Gettysburg Address, because of its content and language, had made a profound impression on me, so much so, it became fixed in my mind when I first read it. The same was true with the most striking phrases of the Declaration of Independence. In later years, during my military service, when these two great documents were discussed in instruction periods, I volunteered to quote passages from them by heart for the benefit of my comrades.

War

At the beginning of September 1939, Hitler attacked Poland. The Second World War had started. Nobody had threatened Germany. The revision of the Versailles Treaty had been accomplished beyond all expectations. Its discriminatory clauses had been eliminated, Germany's grievances had been removed—with the consent of Germany's former enemies. Without firing one shot, German power had reached a pinnacle unparalleled in history. Hitler had launched the war out of pure lust for conquest, to obtain the *Lebensraum* in which to build the "Germanic Empire" of a thousand years.

Although I had declared my intention to become an American citizen, I was still an alien in the legal sense, and subject to registration. This was, for the time being, the only consequence of the outbreak of the war for me personally. My naturalization in April of 1941, eight months before Hitler declared war on the United States, saved me from being declared an "enemy alien."

After the outbreak of the war, I wrote to my brother: "In this war principles are at stake which transcend national interests. Through tradition and education our place is on the side of freedom. Hitler will be conquered as conquered he must be." When I left Germany in November of 1934, I was convinced, as I have related earlier, that the government of the Third Reich was a war government from its inception, that Hitler's policies were directed toward war and that this war would eventually engulf the United States. We thought of our family in Germany. Postal communications were still functioning. There was even an airmail service to Europe, the so-called "Clipper Service." Postage for ordinary letters was thirty cents. Letters from Germany to the United States passed through British censorship, as handwritten numbers and discreet stamp marks revealed. German agencies might also have been involved. I studied the departure and arrival times of ships in the *New York Times* for available postal connections with Germany. Sometimes there was an Italian, sometimes a Dutch liner. A letter to my sister in Germany in December of 1941 was returned "to sender" with the stamp: "Service suspended."

December 7, 1941, was a Sunday. I had gone with friends into town for lunch. When we returned home in the early afternoon, Mrs. B. received us with the news of the Japanese attack on Pearl Harbor. Instead of being shocked, I had the definite feeling that this event marked a decisive turn in my life. All day long there were newscasts. The next day I listened on the radio to the speech in which President Roosevelt asked Congress to declare war on Japan. His famous words that December 7, 1941, "will live in infamy" are still as vivid in my mind as on the day they were spoken.

On December 11, Italy and Germany declared war on the United States. "This is the crowning and . . . . utterly unexplainable mistake whereby Hitler, in 1941, dug his own grave. . . . Still today there is no rationally convincing explanation of this, one is tempted to call it, insane act of Hitler. Consider: The declaration of war was, for all practical purposes, an invitation to America, for its part, to make war on Germany" (Sebastian Haffner). The American historian Gordon Craig, in his *German History 1866-1945*, expresses the opinion that Hitler might have thought that the declaration of war on the United States was the least he owed to his Japanese ally, and that he was not troubled by any thought of harmful consequences for Germany, since the energies of the United States would be fully absorbed by the Pacific conflict while he was disposing of the Russians; and that after having dealt with Russia, he would be strong enough to resist any nation that might challenge him. In his essay on *The German Declaration of War on the United States 1941* (in the *Festschrift* for Wilhelm G. Grewe), which also utilizes Japanese documents, Bernard Jäckel concludes that Hitler set the greatest store by Japan's participation in the war and for this reason was prepared to pay a price, namely, the declaration of war on the United States. Thus, from Hitler's point of view, his action was not unreasonable even though "this was . . . . madness. But there was method in the madness."

On December 14, 1941, I wrote to my brother in Pittsburgh: "The feeling of being utterly stunned is gradually being replaced by a clear appreciation of the situation and the growing resolve to master it. We are at war. The same ruthless power which uprooted us once before again threatens our life, has dared to reach out for our country. Everything we do, all our thoughts from this time forth stand under the shadow of this threat. . . . For this year Hitler had promised the German people their greatest victory in history. Instead, he offers them war with the United States as a Christmas present."

America was ill prepared for war. During all my years in the States I had seen very few military uniforms. It proves the enormous strength of this country that within the shortest possible time a highly trained army was created consisting of more than a million men equipped with the most modern war materials; it eventually struck across the Atlantic and Pacific oceans at the very heart of the enemy.

On December 15, four days after Hitler's declaration of war and the declaration of war by the United States against Germany, compulsory military service was introduced. Men from twenty to forty-four years of age were subject to conscription. This also applied to me.

It did not take long before I was caught in the wheels of the selective service system. My first duty was to register for service.

On February 16, 1942, the registration day, facilities were provided in the Law School to enable faculty members and employees to comply with the presidential proclamation. I noticed an acquaintance of mine among the clerks and proceeded to her table. The formalities of the registration were soon completed. I was issued my "Registration Certificate," signed my name to it, and left. I had become a "Registrant." My name had officially been entered among those available for military service.

Evidence of the inexorable workings of the drafting machine was soon forthcoming. On September 4, 1942, I was notified by my local board to appear for physical examination at the New Haven Hospital-Medical Clinic prior to final classification. Hundreds of other registrants had received identical notifications.

One evening in September we assembled in a large, amphitheatrical lecture hall of the New Haven Hospital, a bunch of bewildered, uneasy men. After the noise and chatter had quieted down, a roll call was taken by an energetic looking woman clerk for whom all this was routine, and we were sent off in groups to the examination ward. Here we were initiated into a procedure which was to be re-enacted frequently in later army life: the taking of blood to be tested, and the inevitable passing-out of a muscular, strapping youth at the sight of his own blood; the hasty, confused undressing and subsequent procession through adjoining rooms where we were looked over by tired, impersonal doctors; the peremptory question: "Anything wrong with you?" to be answered with a cheerful "No, Sir." After getting dressed, everybody departed on his own, an individual and civilian still, but somehow conscious of an impending change and feeling none too elated.

A few days later, I was informed that I had been classified 1A and that I had been given an order number in the national lottery of selectees. My friends began asking me about my status in the draft. I felt that the turning point was fast approaching.

While I was waiting, I began contributing to the war effort in the capacity of an "Air Raid Warden." Simultaneously with the build-up of the armed forces a Civil Defense Organization was established to assist the population in the event of an enemy air raid. Whether the government actually reckoned with air attacks by the Nazis seems very doubtful. Hitler had no long-range bombers with which to inflict even minimal damage on the States. However, German U-boats prowling along the North American coast presented a real danger. The lights of coastal cities that lit up the night sky were used by U-boats to pinpoint their positions. The U-boats whose mission was the sinking of shipping, were also able to catch their prey at night as it was silhouetted against the bright lights ashore. "On a single night, March 18, 1942, five ships went down off Cape Hatteras." For this reason "brown-outs" (partial dimming of lights) and "black-outs" (total extinction of lights) were ordered for cities on the East coast, including New Haven.

Members of the Civil Defense Organization were all volunteers. We had been trained in first-aid and were assigned certain districts, usually within our immediate neighborhood. We wore white helmets, an armband with the letter "CD," and a whistle around our necks. We patrolled the streets of our districts to ensure that brown-outs and black-outs were being complied with, and would blow our whistles if we noticed a suspicious glimmer of light. Air-raid exercises were held from time to time and were announced by sirens. Upon hearing a siren, everyone had to go immediately inside a house or seek shelter elsewhere. No one was supposed to stay on the street. It was the duty of the air-raid wardens to make sure that everyone got off the street. At times it truly was a duty. There were those who doubted that their presence on the street would hurt the war effort. I believe the exercises were held primarily for psychological reasons, and served, along with the rationing of gasoline and the confiscation of spare tires, to remind us that America was at war.

I had postponed my vacation that year until my brother was free to join me on a trip through Connecticut; we used gas coupons which I had saved during the summer months. One misty morning in September we started off on our journey. It was to take us through the hills and forests in the northwestern corner of the state, across the rolling midlands, then south again to the shores along the ocean and the Sound where we hoped for an after-season swim. Sunny, warm weather favored us most of the time. The leaves had started to change color, casting a deep purple hue over the hillsides or, along the highways, forming patterns of bright red and yellow, occasionally mixed with green, under a blue sky. Driving in my little car through the changing scenery of this blessed country, I felt happy again, as I had so often before, in my warm affection for this land of Connecticut, with its white, elm-shaded farmhouses, its sturdy red barns, its forested hills and cool, clear streams, its brown rocks and winding rivers, its meadows and tobacco fields, the white sand of its beaches, glistening in the hot sun, and the foam-rimmed rocks of its coastline.

A Call to Arms

In late September my brother and I returned from our trip. September 30 was a regular working day. When I went down to breakfast, I noticed a letter at my place on the table. The upper left-hand corner of the envelope was marked "Selective Service." I opened it hastily and with some trepidation. My foreboding was confirmed—it was the well-known letter, the "Order to Report for Induction." It bore the greeting of the President and informed me that, having submitted to a local board composed of my neighbors for the purpose of determining my "availability for training and service in the armed forces of the United States," I had been selected for training and service in the Army. I was ordered to report to the Union Railroad Station at 6 a.m. on October 12, 1942, to be taken to the Induction Center in Hartford, Connecticut.

Walking to the railroad station on that morning in October through the dimly lit, deserted streets—there were no buses or streetcars running at that early hour—the only people I met were boys on delivery errands or men heading silently, like myself, in the same direction.

Where would the road end that had started here in New Haven, in the darkness of an October morning? I thought of my relatives in Germany. I had the distinct feeling that the road led in their direction. I was so certain of it that from that time on I carried with me the letter to my sister which had been returned after the outbreak of the war because mail service to Europe had been discontinued. I intended to deliver it to the addressee one day in person.

After arriving at the station, I saw a crowd milling in a far corner of the large reception hall. I joined them near a sign which bore the number of my draft board. After roll call, we walked to a waiting train. As we pulled out of the station, the sun began to rise. It had taken nearly two hours to get us started. I looked around for a familiar face and saw a former classmate of mine from the Law School. We made the trip together, but then parted ways. He failed to pass the physical examinations, was rejected and returned to his wife.

At the Hartford station, we were met by soldiers who marched us in a column of twos—our first military formation—to an office building opposite the station located on, of all things, Asylum Street. In a large room with chairs and benches—not enough for all to go around—we were greeted by an officer who briefly explained the purpose of our visit and the induction procedure. Soon, the wheels of the induction mill began to grind. My turn came after hours of waiting. The girl who took down my personal data at station No. 1 was shocked when I told her that I did not know where my parents were living or whether they were still alive. This information was required in order to determine who would be the beneficiary of a sum of money payable upon my death. My parents, of course, were enemy aliens and under no circumstances entitled to receive anything from the United States Government. The incident made me realize that my case did not fit the normal routine, and that I was a marked man even in the utter anonymity of army life. Fortunately, this feeling later disappeared when I became more accustomed to my new existence.

The physical examination, next in line on the induction program, followed a well-established procedure. Guided through a maze of examination stations by numbers, signs, and arrows painted on the floor, a steady stream of men in various stages of undress passed in front of the searching eyes of the examining physicians. While the most intimate details of one's physical and mental condition were scrutinized and tabulated, perhaps more thoroughly than the family doctor would have done, one remained conscious of the fact that this process merely served to determine the characteristics and comparative values of physical specimens which were to be stamped and delivered to another processing mill. There could be no show of personal interest beyond a matter-of-fact appraisal of each individual as a potential cog in a vast, impersonal machine, except on the part of the neurologist who had to concern himself with the mental and emotional health of the inductee. His probing questions touched upon the psychological complexities of his client ever so lightly, merely in order to classify him according to established norms. However, during that brief interview one regained for a moment the status of a distinct personality that was otherwise obliterated in the process of being tabulated. In the midst of the emotional turmoil which resulted from the impending transformation into a new life, the brief talk about past experiences, craving recognition, was somehow comforting and soothing.

A band formed by patriotic citizens of Hartford played for our benefit, while we were waiting for the decision in the reception room, and a sergeant gave us a demonstration of army humor by telling time-honored stories about the traveling salesman and the farmer's daughter. A community sing-along relieved some of the strain of waiting. Late in the afternoon, the verdict "Accepted" or "Rejected" was announced, together with the classification for each individual. I was found to be in perfect shape and kept my 1A pre-induction rating. I had passed the test and felt justly proud of it. Nothing at that moment would have grieved me more than to be rejected on physical grounds. I had already advanced so far in burying the past and adjusting myself to the thought of military life that I could not conceive of returning to my old ways. I was glad that I had been accepted into the community of men called to active duty for the defense of their country. I pitied those who, like my classmate from the Law School, had been weighed in the balance and been found wanting.

The day's climax came when we took the oath in front of a large American flag. We were lined up in two ranks according to height. The commanding officer of the induction station read the oath. Raising our hands, we pledged before God and our fellow men "to bear true faith and allegiance to the United States, to serve them honestly and faithfully against their enemies and to obey the orders of the President and those appointed by him." After the brief ceremony, each man received a copy of the mimeographed order transferring him to the Enlisted Reserve Corps and automatically granting him a fourteen-day furlough. After its expiration on October 26, 1942, we were to report to the New Haven railroad station once again to be taken to the Recruit Reception Center, Fort Devens, Massachusetts. Failure to comply with this order was punishable under the Articles of War.

I had become a member of the armed forces of the United States.

On the return trip from Hartford to New Haven that same evening, I had time to reflect upon the profound change which had occurred in my life since the moment I had taken the oath placing me under the military law of the United States. I became aware that an unbridgeable gulf not yet visible to others separated me from those who continued their normal existence. Like millions of others, I had ceased to be the master of my life. Freedom was replaced by obedience to orders—and every move was dictated by duties of which I had no clear perception.

For years I had not lived a "normal" life the way I had planned it. The many changes, the confrontations with unprecedented situations had taught me to accept what fate had ordained, to do what the moment required, to move ahead step by step. At my confirmation in April of 1916, the Reverend Merten, our beloved pastor, had selected for me as my life's motto the passage from Isiah 43, verse 1: "Fear not, for I have redeemed you; I have called you by name, you are mine." I have always considered the choice of this text as particularly felicitous. Its words have given me strength at many turns in my life; they were again a source of trust and hope.

In my case, a full comprehension of the new situation was especially urgent; I keenly felt the need of understanding all its consequences. The enemies whom I had sworn to fight against with my life included members of my immediate family. True to my oath, I would have to take their lives just as they were pledged to take mine. I would have to invade the country of my birth as an enemy. Could there be a conflict of conscience so crushing that it would break me?

My new oath was nothing but the implementation of an oath I had taken a year earlier when I had become a United States citizen. At that time, I had sworn to support and defend the Constitution and the laws of the United States of America against all enemies, foreign and domestic. Hitler had declared war on the United States. In other words, he had announced his intention of imposing his will on the American people by force of arms. This meant the destruction of the very foundations of my new existence. To fight him, in terms of personal interests, was a matter of self-defense. It was "either him or me." It was that simple.

Was the moral law equally clear-cut? I reviewed once again the events which had led me to leave Germany. I had experienced the beginnings of the Hitler regime; I had been profoundly shocked by the collapse of the rule of law. I had been exposed to the mendacity of the Nazi government and had become aware of the fact that it was capable of committing heinous crimes.

Germany, like other European countries, had been overwhelmed by alien forces diametrically opposed to a social and political order based on the principles of Christianity. The forces which had conquered Germany had exterminated all means of resistance. Delivery for the German people as well as for other Nazi-dominated countries could come only from those who were still masters of their destiny, the Anglo-Saxon nations. The fight for the return of the German people to the fold of Western civilization had to continue. I remembered the day in March of 1933 when, standing in front of the government building in Potsdam, I saw the swastika flag hoisted amidst a celebration by a small group of officials who secretly had been members of the Nazi party. Storm troopers, symbols of conquest, were posted as sentries at the main entrance. In their ugly, outlandish uniforms they appeared to me as soldiers of foreign occupation forces. I later learned about the friends who lost their lives in the vain attempt of July 20, 1944, to set Germany free from Nazi tyranny, and of the monstrous crimes committed by the Nazis in Germany and in conquered countries behind the fronts of the *Wehrmacht*. In retrospect, I need only to conjure up in my mind the bloodthirsty Freisler raging at his victims in his "People's Court" or the image of one of the transports of Jews to concentration camps and all the subsequent horror to feel satisfaction that I had been destined to do my part in bringing the guilty ones to justice and in overcoming the madness of the Hitler ideology. What had been done to me personally was of no consequence. I was not out to avenge myself. It is not for us to seek revenge; that is the Lord's prerogative. What was at stake was the defense of the values which are enshrined in the words of the Declaration of Independence: Life, Liberty and the Pursuit of Happiness. I was pledged as a citizen of the United States to uphold these values. They had once been valid in Germany as well. That these values would be defended where they were threatened and restored where they had been lost, was the promise America gave as "the last best hope of mankind."

On October 26, my two-week leave as a member of the "Enlisted Reserve Corps" had expired. According to the orders which I had received after my induction, I was now called to "active duty" and ordered "to proceed from New Haven to Recruit Reception Center, Fort Devens, Mass." The night before my departure, my friends at Mrs. B.'s house gave me a farewell party which lasted until the early hours of the morning. There was much good cheer but also some secret doubts as to my ability to withstand life in the army. I was surprised when Mrs. B. stated that what I needed most in the army was a sense of humor. She proved to be so right.

It was damp and cold, and a light rain was falling when I marched, together with a trainload of fellow "rookies," through the gate of Fort Devens—from civilian into military life. The first station in the transformation process from civilian to soldier, was a barracks close to the gate where the "intelligence test" was given. Rows of school benches had been set up. The room was soon filled with a noisy, restless crowd. Directions were transmitted through a poorly functioning public address system. In the general confusion I was shoved onto a seat in the last row. There the directions were hardly audible, let alone comprehensible; they did not penetrate the din of excited voices. Then forms and pencils were distributed. The forms contained questions on the meaning of words, small mathematical problems and drawings of differently arranged boxes which had to be counted. After one hour, the forms were collected. Fatigue, the unaccustomed surroundings, the initial shock of the sudden change in my existence made me understand only half of what was happening. The results of the test were less than satisfactory, in fact, they were devastating. According to the test, I did not even reach the minimum of points prescribed for officer candidates. I wrote to my brother about my experience. He told me I should not feel too bad about it. He recently had heard that a psychologist had flunked the intelligence test he himself had devised. Later on I was given the opportunity to retake the test and was able to improve my score.

Everything else was routine (as in all armies the world over), injections, "chow," making beds, receiving equipment and learning the military ground rule: There are three ways of doing things—the right way, the wrong way and the army way.

My first military assignment was to paint a fence around the barracks with white paint. It still felt strange to be wearing a uniform. During this transitional stage between civilian and soldier, I pictured myself being whirled around like a top: under the impact of the centrifugal force my lightweight civilian elements would fly away. What remained would be the hard core, the only part of me, if there was such a thing, suited for soldiering. "I am still rotating," I wrote to my brother.

After a waiting period of about ten days, I was assigned to the Medical Corps and was shipped to Camp Pickett in Virginia, where I received my basic training. The camp was named after the Southern general whose murderous charge at Gettysburg won him fame. The camp was located in an area of about 100 square miles and could accommodate 100,000 men. The space for the camp had only recently been cut out of the Virginia woods, and construction of the camp was still not completed when I arrived in early November. The continuous stream of new recruits had to be put up temporarily in a huge tent camp. In addition to the housing and administrative barracks, the camp possessed five large movie theaters, numerous kitchens, and several service clubs for rest and recreation.

Basic training was half infantry training, complete with hikes, obstacle course, tent pitching, and bivouacs, and half theoretical instruction with elementary courses in anatomy and medical assistance. The learning by heart of concepts and rules as part of the training was a painful experience for many of my younger comrades. The prospect of the monthly inspections caused apprehension among officers and men, since reciting from the "Medical Soldier's Handbook" was part of the inspection procedure. At one of these inspections, a case of beer was promised to the squad that achieved the best results. Our squad had done quite well with tent pitching and displaying of equipment. The theoretical part, however, had revealed considerable weaknesses.

I was sitting in the rear of the barracks on my field chest when the eye of the inspecting officer caught me. "What is a compound fracture? You there, in the rear." The finger of the officer pointed squarely in my direction. I jumped up, stood at attention and promptly recited the precise definition from the Handbook. (In case the reader does not know: "A compound fracture is one in which the wound extends from the broken bone through the skin and therefore is exposed to the danger of infection from the outside.") The officer seemed to be startled, then looked at me in wonderment. "This is the first time that this inspecting officer has gotten the right answer," he exclaimed. The comprehension span of the medical recruit could usually handle the concept of a simple fracture but could not be stretched to encompass such an outlandish notion as a compound fracture. The surprise effect of my performance decided the contest in favor of our squad. The case of beer was duly awarded to us and "Pop" (my nickname) became a hero.

A trip to Richmond for an interview on the radio was an unexpected disruption of my daily routine. On the evening program I was asked, together with other GI's, about my life. All of us had been selected for this program because of the extraordinary nature of our life stories. The program was meant to make the listeners aware of the circuitous roads that certain members of the U.S. forces had traveled in order to reach their common destiny, namely, joining the army to defend America.

One morning loudspeakers were set up in the barrack streets to broadcast an announcement from headquarters requesting that soldiers with a knowledge of foreign languages report to their commanding officer. They would then be sent to headquarters for a proficiency test in the language or languages which they claimed to know. I had indicated knowledge of German and French.

The soldier who tested me was a Jewish immigrant from Prague. In 1941, he had succeeded in escaping from Nazi-occupied Czechoslovakia to the United States via France and Portugal. His sister had not been so lucky. She perished in the extermination camp at Auschwitz.

We had a pleasant talk, both in German and in French. He found that I possessed sufficient knowledge in both languages. As a result, I was assigned for special training—I did not know at the time what that meant—to Camp Ritchie in Maryland.

However, before the assignment was to become effective, all of us who had been selected were required to prove our physical fitness by running the obstacle course while equipped with steel helmet and full field pack. I only made it halfway. My comrades far outdistanced me. Eventually, my knowledge of languages was rated higher than my ability, or inability, to jump and climb, and the assignment remained.

For a few days while awaiting my transfer, I acted as the examiner at headquarters who selected candidates for Camp Ritchie. One of them was a former lawyer from Berlin who had left Germany for racial reasons. After that first meeting in Camp Pickett, our paths crossed many times in the service of American military and civilian authorities, and we became friends for life. The same is true for the examiner from Czechoslovakia who helped me later on decisively in my army career. Both have passed away. I keep the fondest memories of both of them.

Camp Ritchie is beautifully situated on a lake high in the Blue Ridge Mountains. In peacetime it served as a training camp for the Maryland National Guard. After its takeover by the U.S. Army its facilities needed to be greatly expanded. The barracks were only half ready when one late evening in the middle of December of 1942, I arrived at the camp with a detachment of comrades who like me had been withdrawn from their original units to be assigned to Camp Ritchie. Melting snow had turned the unfinished camp streets into soft, brownish mud which stuck to our boots. Yet the barracks had be be kept clean.

Camp Ritchie was the Military Intelligence Training Center. Assignment to Ritchie meant immediate promotion from Private to Corporal. Life at Ritchie started with "KP." We reported to the mess sergeant at 6:00 a.m. and, on many occasions, left the kitchen after fourteen hours of work. Camp veterans told us that everyone had to go through this routine which was meant as an endurance test. Only those who passed it could reckon with being admitted to the much coveted training course. The story might have been a trick to spur us on to do our very best. It did work, however. In fact, we performed so well that the mess sergeant, a friendly Italian by descent, did not want us to leave when we were called to start the course. We had been the best team he had ever had, he told us. He thought we should stay with him, since we wouldn't pass the course anyway. He promised to keep us in his kitchen "for the duration of the war."

On Christmas Day we donned white jackets and served our comrades the traditional turkey dinner with all the trimmings. During the dinner, the Colonel appeared in person to commend the "kitchen boys." We received thunderous applause. I had the next day off and went to Hagerstown to stay at the Hotel Alexander. It later became my stamping ground where I spent "Ban-day," the free day named after Colonel Banfill, the camp commander. He had introduced the system of making every tenth day the day off at the camp.

I was sitting in the lobby reading a paper when the manager approached me. A family in town, he said, had told him that they wanted to invite a soldier who was alone to have Christmas dinner with them. He had seen me in the lobby and wondered whether I wished to accept the invitation. I gladly accepted after I had overcome certain doubts as to whether I was the sort of person my prospective hosts had had in mind when tendering the invitation. They might have been thinking of a genuine "American boy," a regular GI like their son who, as they later told me, was in camp awaiting his assignment and whose emotional state away from home at Christmas they could easily imagine. Instead they had as their guest a stranger from another world, as it were, with a life story quite unlike anything they had ever heard. They showed full understanding of my situation and a slight initial uneasiness disappeared as the dinner proceeded in the relaxed atmosphere of family Christmas cheer.

Our training course lasted two months. The program was taught in a high school manner with short written tests indicating how much or how little we had learned. Such testing was necessary in view of the great number of subjects. To master them within the short time allotted to each subject required close attention, but even the most attentive student had difficulties keeping up with the pace. We were taught map reading and the drawing of military situation maps. Other subjects were the fundamentals of the Morse telegraphy and the organization of the American and British armies. We were given general staff problems which involved estimates of the situation based on evaluated messages. The centerpiece of the course was the German army, its organization, German military terms and military maps, and the treatment of German prisoners of war with practical exercises in prisoner interrogation. The objects of these interrogations were German-speaking American soldiers in German army uniforms. The masquerade was designed to enhance the realism of the situation. We were told to act as if this were "the real thing" and not to refrain from invectives if we thought that our opposites merited rough handling because of their behavior (which had to resemble that of German prisoners of war). German subjects were taught in German. The weekly quizzes were graded, with "excellent" for the best results. Among our fellow students was an elderly Austrian who had great difficulties absorbing the subjects of instruction. His laborious but ineffectual efforts were reflected in the results of his tests. "Again no excellent," he was heard to complain when, returning to the barracks, he stretched out on his bunk exhausted and discouraged.

Besides theoretical instruction there were practical field exercises, notably the so-called "night problems" with which we were confronted in the second week of our course. A night problem started with a truck ride into an unknown area where we were dropped off in pairs at various places along the truck route. Our first problem was to establish our location by means of maps, but using a minimum of light. We then had to walk cross-country within a specified time to a point marked on the map where trucks were stationed to take us back to the camp. Whoever lost his way or did not make it in time had to march back on foot through the night. I was lucky to have had an Austrian mountain guide, an experienced pathfinder, as my companion. We were told that we should not stop at fences on our cross-country walks, although it could happen when climbing a fence that we might be mistaken for prowlers whom farmers in this area were known to shoot at. In such cases we were to shout: "Soldiers on patrol."

The "Ritchie Boys" came from a variety of nations: they included Germans, Swiss, Austrians, Czechs, Yugoslavs. Among the Germans was a black man who spoke German with a pure Cologne accent. He was an occupation child of the First World

War. The native American element was represented, in particular, by members of Indian tribes. Their capacity for scouting and patrolling, a subject taught at Ritchie, far exceeded our own feeble attempts. Even within the camp they moved noiselessly as if they were stalking the enemy.

One of my comrades with whom I "GI-ed the barracks" (as scrubbing the barracks floor was called before one could go to town on "Ban-day") was Private First Class Bourbon. His name had nothing to do with Bourbon whiskey. His full name (not used in the States) was Gaëtan Prince of Bourbon-Parma. He was the youngest brother of the former Austrian Empress Zita. He had somehow been involved in the Spanish Civil War, and had emigrated to the States. When we relaxed together over a steak dinner at the Dutch Kitchen in Hagerstown, we would talk about European history. He once mentioned in passing that his great-great-grandfather had been King of Etruria. The kingdom had been created by Napoleon I and had lasted only seven years, from 1801 to 1808. After this royal interlude, his ancestor had once again become the Duke of Parma.

One day I was talking to a newcomer who occupied the bunk next to me. He came from Germany. To my surprise, it turned out that his home town in Germany had been Neuwied-on-the-Rhine. His father had been the owner of a well-known ladies' garment store. The family was Jewish and had succeeded in escaping from Nazi persecution. Although he was younger than I, we still had a great number of common acquaintances. He spoke in particular about a "stately lady" who bought the most expensive items, a "really well-to-do customer who always paid cash." When he mentioned her name, I realized that he had been talking about my old "flame" from high school. Her father was the owner of a nail factory. Later I learned that she and her husband had been victims of the fighting around Neuwied when the American army, after crossing the Rhine at Remagen, had moved south along the right bank of the river. The unit of my barracks companion had been involved in the fighting.

Our training ended at the beginning of March 1943 with an eight-day field problem. Everything we had been taught, from the drawing of maps to the interrogation of prisoners of war, was tested one more time. We received a certificate upon the successful completion (called "graduation") of the "Fourth Course at the Military Intelligence Training Center, Camp Ritchie, Maryland," and awaited further orders.

Overseas Service

In 1942, the American army had come under fire for the first time in Northern Africa, and had passed the crucial test. The Americans, together with the British, had defeated the German Africa Corps under the legendary Field Marshal Rommel. After the destruction of the German forces on African soil, the next move was the landing of the Allies in Sicily. In the East, the German offensive had been stopped. With the capitulation of the German Sixth Army at Stalingrad at the end of January 1943, the large-scale Russian counter-offensive started on its inexorable advance toward the West.

In March of 1943, the German war at sea had reached its climax. As a result of improved Allied defensive tactics against U-boats, the number of ships sunk by U-boats had decreased while the number of American convoys that safely crossed the Atlantic had increased. In the Pacific, American superiority had been restored. In the South Pacific, a major Allied offensive was in the offing. In the European theater of war, Stalin urgently demanded the opening of a second front. Some of my fellow trainees of the fourth course at Ritchie had left the camp without much commotion, almost furtively. It was said that they had gone to England.

A nerve-wracking waiting period began for me. It lasted for almost a year and was filled with close-order drills, hikes, clerical work, and other useful occupations which armies all over the world have invented for troop therapy, such as sorting out two-by-fours from a pile of wood and throwing the selected pieces onto another pile, or digging trenches and filling them up again. Attempts which I made with the help of friends in Washington to find work more in keeping with my knowledge, skills, and expertise failed because the army did not want to lose a body who had received the special Ritchie training.

One morning, in February of 1944, a long train of railroad coaches arrived on one of the camp's siding tracks. We had been alerted in the middle of the night and had been ordered to pack our duffel bags and prepare for being "shipped out." After boarding the train and waiting many hours, the train began to move. We were not told where we were going. To the East? To the West? The direction in which we were riding would be an indication. According to the war situation at the time, going east would mean that we were heading for Italy or England.

At night we arrived at Fort Hamilton, an old fortress at the entrance of New York harbor which had been converted into modern barracks. It was now clear that we would be going to Europe. Yet our final destination was still secret. We were warned not to reveal our present location in letters to family or friends or in any other manner.

Three weeks went by when one day we spotted a new ship in the harbor. That evening we were told to get our things together—field packs, steel helmets, duffel bags, and gas masks. Under cover of darkness a convoy of trucks brought us to the harbor. As we alighted from the trucks the large hulk of a ship loomed ahead of us—a black monster moored alongside a shed. We were formed into single file, reported to the control officer at the foot of the floodlit gangway, called out our names and serial numbers, were given a slip of paper with the number of our bunk, climbed with our heavy equipment up the steep incline, and disappeared into the bowels of the ship to find our bunks.

We were aboard a Liberty ship. It displaced about 7,100 tons and had a maximum speed of eleven knots.

In an incredible surge of national productivity almost 3,000 of these ships were mass-produced in eighteen American shipyards, the largest number of ships ever built from a single design. To speed their construction, the ships were welded and not riveted together, which gave them a tendency to break apart during storms. Liberty ships carried troops, planes, guns, and bombs to battlefields around the world. They were the backbone of America's sea force that helped crush the Nazi and Japanese war machines. However, more than 200 Liberty ships were sunk by storms or enemy torpedoes, many with heavy loss of life. Only a few days before our embarkation in New York the newspapers reported the sinking of an American troop transport in the North Atlantic. (Of the entire fleet of Liberty ships, only one authentic ship remains—the *Jeremiah O'Brien*. She now lies below the Golden Gate Bridge in San Francisco, a relic of history.)

War. Going Overseas

36. "Onward, Christian Soldiers"

A Peaceful Interlude at Ste. Mère Église (Normandy) September 1944

37. The Liberated and the Liberators

38. The Family with the Offspring who came down with the Parachutists

The entire hold of the ship was filled with iron frames to support five layers of hammocks. Miraculously, everybody found his assigned place. This would be our living space for the next twelve days, we were told. One could only use it lying down. The space between the hammocks was so narrow that one's nose touched the bunk above and one's posterior the one below. This space had to accommodate one's person as well as the entire equipment. It required apelike agility to move about in this jungle of iron bars.

When I got to my bunk, I found lying on the hammock a letter in a white envelope with the imprint: "The White House, Washington, D.C." The letter was signed "Franklin D. Roosevelt" and was addressed "To the Members of the United States Expeditionary Forces." It read:

You are a soldier of the United States Army. You have embarked for distant places where the war is being fought. Upon the outcome depends the freedom of your lives: the freedom of the lives of those you love—your fellow-citizens—your people.

Never were the enemies of freedom more tyrannical, more arrogant, more brutal.

Yours is a God-fearing, proud, courageous people, which, throughout its history, has put its freedom under God before all other purposes.

We who stay at home have our duties to perform—duties owed in many parts to you. You will be supported by the whole force and power of this Nation. The victory you win will be a victory of all the people—common to them all.

You bear with you the hope, the confidence, the gratitude and the prayers of your family, your fellow-citizens, and your President.

In the emotional turmoil of the first few moments aboard ship, in view of the uncertainty of what lay ahead, this reminder of our mission (although only a form letter), this firm faith in victory which the President, the Commander-in-Chief, expressed to each of us in warm, human terms of classic simplicity was soothing and profoundly reassuring.

When we went back on deck the next morning—there was standing room only—we saw that we were part of a convoy of about twenty ships.   We were positioned outside right at the southeast edge of a rectangular position. The center was occupied by the former Italian luxury liner *Vulcan*. Some claimed to know that its entire contingent were members of the Women's Army Corps. This, of course, excited the imagination and gave rise to suggestions such as: Let's swim over there! Small cruisers were constantly circling the convoy like shepherds' dogs guard a herd of sheep. There were no lights of any sort during the night and, of course, no smoking on deck. We moved in total darkness. Only from the position of the stars did we learn that we were traveling on a zig-zag course.

We never got out of our uniforms; nor were we ever allowed to take off our life jackets. Occasionally we had the opportunity of taking a shower with cold sea water and a specially adapted soap. Since there was no rush to form lines in front of the shower room, I was always able to take advantage of this much needed and most refreshing convenience.

In the mess hall below, as on deck, there was standing room only. The place was crammed at "chow" time. One somehow managed to gulp down what was offered. Fortunately, the sea was calm most of the time.

We had been given a small pamphlet, *What to Do Aboard the Transport*, to acquaint us with the things which were worth knowing on a sea voyage. There were no duties to perform except throwing garbage into the sea or attending brief instruction sessions.

One morning we found ourselves alone on the wide ocean. The convoy had been disbanded during the night. In the evening we reached shore. We did not know that we had arrived at Belfast, capital of Northern Ireland.   The fact that we had crossed the ocean without mishap was, I thought, proof that Hitler had lost the war.   His U-boats were no longer in a position to prevent the build-up of invasion forces from overseas.   No one had the slightest doubt that the invasion would succeed.

Belfast was completely blacked out.   Buses with dimmed lights brought us from the harbor to the railroad station. After we had stowed our equipment in the railroad compartments, the bell-like voice of a young lady could be heard in the darkness. With a Bostonian accent she offered coffee and doughnuts, the standard snack of the American soldier the world over. The offer came from a USO (United Service Organizations) lady. It was like a welcome from home. We could not thank her enough.

For two weeks we lived in Nissen huts on the estate of Lord Londonderry near Belfast. These huts, the field barracks of the British army, were prefabricated metal shelters shaped like a half cylinder resting on its flat surface. A part of the estate had been turned into a military camp. Under the influence of a side arm of the Gulf Stream, tropical and subtropical plants and trees grew in the park. Parrots flew about or sat on branches of trees enhancing the exotic character of this Irish landscape. Off and on one could see His Lordship tending shrubs and flowers with the assistance of a gardener. He invited us to visit his castle. While he was in residence a flag with his family crest flew from the roof of the castle.

The next stage on our way to the European continent was a camp near Liverpool. On a small sea voyage across the Irish Sea we passed the Isle of Man. Marching through Liverpool in full battle dress we were cheered by people lining the streets. They looked upon us as harbingers of great things to come.

Aboard ship and in the camps in England, I belonged to the "unassigned, unattached" category of soldiers, a position at the bottom rung of the military ladder. A private of a cadre running a camp could give orders to an unassigned, unattached master sergeant, a situation considered by many to be a disgrace. It turned out to be advantageous in my case as I was free for someone to grab me. One morning at reveille I was called out and ordered to pack my things. To my utter surprise, I learned that I had been assigned to Supreme Headquarters Allied Expeditionary Forces (SHAEF). I was put on a train to London and was ordered to report to the Transportation Officer at Victoria Station for further orders. They directed me to Bushy Park near London where SHAEF was located.

My assignment to SHAEF was due to my comrade who had tested my language abilities at Camp Pickett. He had in the meantime advanced to the rank of master sergeant, and had been given the task of organizing a section for the analysis and evaluation of German military documents within the G-2 Division (military intelligence) of SHAEF. He had remembered our meeting; I was the type of person he needed for his organization. He succeeded in locating me at my last station and obtaining an order for my transfer—a remarkable feat considering the sometimes mysterious ways in which army records were handled.

The section was organized, as was all of SHAEF, as an integrated American-British unit. It was headed by a British lieutenant colonel. His deputy was an American major. The staff was also partly British, partly American. The only Canadian in the unit fitted both categories. Knowledge of German was, of course, obligatory regardless of whether it originated from Germany, Austria, Switzerland, Czechoslovakia, or Hungary.

I had to walk the last few hundred yards from Bushy park station to the gate at SHAEF. I wore all the gear in strict accordance with army regulations. When I arrived at the gate, the military police guard looked at me. "Here comes a real soldier," he commented approvingly.

The "G-2 Document Section," its official designation, had office space on the top floor of an apartment building on Hyde Park Gate, one of the most fashionable residential districts in London. All the building's inhabitants had been evacuated. Only an old janitor remained. He would ring an ancient bell when an air raid was imminent. Usually sirens had already warned us.

At the beginning of June 1944, shortly after the Allied invasion of the continent had started, I reported for duty to the document section. Our function was to examine German army records captured in the field during military operations in France and papers taken off prisoners of war, to extract from them information of military significance, to classify documents for circulation to specialized units, to write reports and summaries for the daily intelligence reports of SHAEF which were then distributed to lower headquarters. Our work sometimes required the skill of a detective. Everything was new; there were no set rules to go by in our work. We had to invent our own methods. The immensity of the task may be judged by the fact that during the first five weeks of the invasion 48,000 Germans had been captured. Every piece of paper they carried with them—letters, notes, photographs—was scrutinized. On one single day 6,000 paybooks had to be examined. Trucks with boxes and bags, among them inventories of entire offices with files, registers, and books unloaded their cargo at our door. Going through this massive amount of material without missing important information was truly a gigantic task.

The necessity of paying attention to even a tiny scrap of paper was brought home to me by an incident that gained our section recognition from no less a person than the Commander-in-Chief of the German armies of the West. We learned about this highly implausible interrelation between ourselves and one of Germany's top soldiers through a chain of incredible coincidences. While sifting through the personal papers of a colonel, aide-de-camp to a corps commander, I suddenly held in my hand a page covered with figures and shorthand scribbles which had been torn out of a small notebook. I was about to discard it when I took another look. What I discovered almost knocked me off my feet.

In front of me I had a complete tabulation of officer losses sustained by the German army since the beginning of the war, listed by services, from lieutenant to general, including present vacancies. Explanatory comments were added in an out-of-date shorthand system I happened to know. The material was the essence of a report a representative of the German War Ministry had given at a conference of high-ranking aides-de-camp, aimed at showing difficulties in replacing officer losses and stressing the need to speed up the training of officer candidates. In view of the highly sensitive nature of these figures, the participants at the meeting had been warned not to take down notes. For this reason, the colonel who had violated the order had not kept his notes together with other classified information, but rather among his personal papers where they were forgotten.

Our discovery created a minor sensation at Supreme Headquarters. It was included in the daily SHAEF intelligence report with a note stating that the figures brought into sharp focus the German problem of finding officers suited for units and formations of the field army, and that they gave a comprehensive picture of officer losses and the expected need for replacements.

We thought we could not trust our eyes a few months later when we discovered in the files of a German divisional headquarters an "Order of the Day" signed by Field Marshal von Rundstedt, Commander-in-Chief West, dated November 30, 1944, which dealt with our report on German officer losses. The report had been distributed by Supreme Headquarters to subordinate corps headquarters and, in circumstances not described further, had fallen into German hands. The document was obviously considered important enough to be called to the attention of the field marshal. People at his headquarters were impressed by the extent of our knowledge. The field marshal even found words of commendation for our work. The material, he conceded, had been carefully and clearly evaluated. Our comment on the significance of the figures—and this had at first caught our eye—was quoted in the order verbatim in translation. Rundstedt's order of the day was designed to put the entire German Army of the West on notice of the consequences that might follow from noncompliance with orders. Only a few months before, instructions had been issued to troop commanders down to company level on measures to be taken to protect secret material against enemy capture. These orders, the field marshal warned, had been disregarded in this case, with the result that the enemy had gained valuable information on the shortage of commissioned officers and the critical replacement situation. We could not resist the temptation of publishing the Rundstedt order in our daily summary under the headline "Field Marshal von Rundstedt gives the Document Section a Pat on the Back."

It was raining and the sky was covered with low hanging clouds when, on June 15, 1944, we returned from our office on Hyde Park Gate to our quarters on Cadogan Place in the heart of London. Suddenly sirens started to wail all over town. We had not expected an air raid alarm but, considering it was ten days after the invasion, such an event could not be deemed extraordinary. Experience had taught us that the alarms would last for one to two hours. Instead of going into the cellar, we put on our steel helmets and went out into the street. Soon there was an unusually heavy detonation. We thought that a bomb must have hit close by. Then something surprising happened that had nothing to do with bombs as we knew them. We heard a strong, rhythmic noise that sounded like the engine of a heavy truck. Illuminated by numerous searchlights, the source of the noise soon came into view. Flying low over the roofs of the city was a black, stumpy object with short rectangular wings, an aircraft of unknown, strangely puzzling design, followed by furious flak. From the distance came the sound of a tremendous explosion. So it went on all night. Explosion followed explosion. After ten hours came the all-clear signal. Yet almost immediately thereafter: a new alarm, flak, and explosions.

The next day the secret of the night attack was revealed: Hitler's miracle weapon, the "V-1," *Vergeltungswaffe* (Retaliation Weapon), a flying bomb whose existence had become known from aerial photographs of the production site at Peenemünde and of launching pads on the Atlantic coast, had been sent on its mission of destruction.

The flying bomb was what its name implies: a bomb with wings. It was driven by a small jet engine mounted on its back. The British soon called it the "doodlebug." At first the bomb did considerable damage in London and terrified the people because one could never be sure where the bomb would hit. The attacks continued day and night and did not allow an all-clear signal. People sought shelter in the deep underground subway stations where they slept on mattresses and cots. Trenches were also dug in Hyde Park to provide shelter when one heard the noise of an approaching flying bomb. I once experienced a hit in my immediate vicinity. I had gone to one of the service clubs where one could have a good meal and a comfortable bed on one's day off. The thunderous sputter of an engine woke me. "A doodlebug is approaching," I thought, and quickly crawled under the bed. When the bomb was quite near, the engine abruptly shut off. A short hissing noise followed as if compressed air was escaping. Then came silence, and a second or so later a tremendous bang. The bomb had hit a neighboring building. It had obviously stopped above our house and had then veered off before coming in for the hit.

During the last few weeks of June 1944, about 1,000 flying bombs reached London. Various defensive measures were tested. In Hyde Park wires were suspended on barrage balloons to catch the bombs and force them down. After only a few days antiaircraft guns were moved to the coast since flak in the city was much more dangerous than the bombs themselves.

The use of fast fighter planes to shoot down the bombs near the coast turned the tide. More than half of the bombs were destroyed in flight. Still, between thirty and sixty bombs reached London per day where they destroyed houses, churches, and hospitals and killed civilians. I once saw a bus whose upper deck had been totally torn to pieces, undoubtedly while en route.

The danger ceased only after the launching pads on the European coast had been conquered and destroyed. (Up to that time—September 1944—about 8,000 V-1 bombs had been aimed at London. Twenty-nine percent reached their destination. See *War Diary of the German Supreme Command*, vol. IV, p. 971.)

Dr. Goebbels' propaganda had told the German people that the flying bombs would decide the war in Germany's favor. It was an utterly false claim. The bombs would hit military targets only by accident; they could not be aimed like a marksman's gun. The bombardment of ports where troops and war material for the invasion were concentrated was soon abandoned. Such small targets were outside the effective range of the bombs. Military transports continued to roll; only once was a railroad station blocked for an hour on account of a bomb. Only the huge target of the city of London offered a guarantee that bombs would fall upon built-up terrain.

There were no longer air raid alarms and all-clear signals. The attack was permanent. It was everyone for himself when the sputtering noise of a doodlebug approached. Despite this constant threat, the people of London kept calm and continued going about their daily business. They lined up at bus stops as in normal times and were courteous and considerate to each other. We laughed at reports in captured German newspapers that Hitler's secret weapon had caused the British to panic, that food had become scarce, that half of London had been reduced to rubble. Hitler had expected that the bombardment of London would force the British to sue for peace. "London under retaliatory fire." "The attack on London by retaliatory fire continues." "Heavy V-fire on Greater London." Reports like these appeared in the German press up until February of 1945. The German Supreme Command tried to delude the German people into thinking that the V-weapons were effective. In fact, the bombardment was counterproductive. It completely failed to demoralize the British people. Rather then compelling them to give in, the senseless destruction strengthened their resolve to hold out until victory was won.

Hitler committed the same error of judgment when he activated his second "Retaliation Weapon," the V-2, although the weapon was more deadly than the V-1. It was a guided rocket with a warhead that was shot high into the atmosphere and descended steeply upon its target. Unlike the V-1 which announced its arrival noisily and could be seen, the V-2 rocket was invisible and inaudible until it hit the ground. There was no chance to take cover.

I still remember the day when the first V-2 reached London: It was on September 8, 1944, at 7:00 p.m. that we heard a sharp, extremely loud explosion from our office in Hyde Park Gate. We immediately sensed that it was not a flying bomb. It sounded like the sharp crack of a pistol rather than the muffled bang of a bomb. It was loud enough to make us believe that the detonation had occurred in our immediate neighborhood. The next morning newspapers reported that on the evening before a gasworks had exploded. The news was intentionally misleading. The government was not sure how people would react to this new threat. The Allies had known about the rocket for some time. A total of 1,115 V-2's hit England; as stated in the *War Diary of the German Supreme Command*, their effect was like "pinpricks." Another 2,050 rockets were fired upon Antwerp, Brussels, and Liège up until April 5, 1945. Hitler had miscalculated again. People took his latest miracle weapon in their stride.

Allied military operations were not affected. When the launching pads of the V-2's were either destroyed or captured, Hitler's last attempt to achieve the final victory by means of a new war technology had come to naught.

Around the middle of September, SHAEF was moved to France where the Allied invasion armies had rapidly advanced. This meant that we, too, had to leave England. On a warm sunny day in September a landing craft took us across the Channel from Southampton to "Utah Beach," the westernmost Allied bridgehead on the coast of the Cotentin Peninsula. This part of Normandy had been the American army's point of departure on its victorious march through Europe.

We spent the first night on French soil in a farmer's barn near Ste. Mère Église. During the invasion in early June an American airborne division had occupied the area. The farmer's wife told us, gesticulating vividly, how soldiers had suddenly "fallen from the sky," while she was giving birth to a child. For her numerous progeny we too, with chocolate and chewing gum, were messengers from another world.

The hedged-in meadows and fields of Normandy reminded me of *Knicks* in the countryside of Schleswig-Holstein which I had known during my student years in Kiel. That was as far as the similarity went, however. Huge depots of war materials dotted the landscape, and vestiges of the bitter fighting that had taken place only a few months ago still remained. Villages and cities which we passed on our way to Paris were nothing but heaps of rubble. Caën offered the picture of a large city totally in ruins. The wreckage made me realize for the first time what had become of the old continent in the relatively short span of ten years since my departure. This was just the beginning. I did not know it then, but I was to be confronted with much worse destruction in the months ahead.

The roads we traveled were lined with battered German tanks, assault guns, and trucks. From time to time, one still saw German road signs at intersections.

People in front of their gutted houses waved at us as we passed, and at brief stops offered us apples and nuts.

Our first quarters in Paris were known to me. It was the Rothschild palace on the Cours Albert 1er, once seat of the International Chamber of Commerce where I had worked for a short time in 1929. I also succeeded in locating Me Coulon. He no longer resided at the Rue de l'Université 11; he lived in an apartment on the Rue de la Faisanerie near the Étoile. He was surprised and at first incredulous as I presented myself in an American uniform. Only a few weeks earlier, his youngest son had been shot as a member of the *Résistance* by the retreating Germans. Coulon himself was about to leave Paris. He had been appointed President of the Cour d'Appel in Orléans. It seemed that the administration of justice in France was still, or was again, functioning.

War

40. "Haras de Bel-Ebas"—Headquarters of G-2 Document Section near Paris

39. The Author (left) with two comrades of SHAEF, G-2 Document Section (London)

War

41. Victory Won - Home Again

Paris had been liberated only a few weeks before we resumed our work there on a provisional basis. A German tank still stood on the Place de la Concorde at the entrance to the Tuileries, silent reminder of the profound change in the fortunes of war.

After the initial enthusiasm created by the entry of French and American troops had subsided, Paris relapsed into a state of exhaustion. There were hardly any pedestrians on the streets. Restaurants and cafés were closed. Traffic on the streets was limited to military vehicles and ricksha-like cabs, driven, in contrast to their original Asiatic model, by cyclists, not runners.

The city's churches, bridges, and historical buildings had escaped destruction. General Dietrich von Choltitz, the last German commandant of Greater Paris, had disobeyed Hitler's monstrous order to "defend Paris to the last, destroy all bridges over the Seine and devastate the city." After the war, the general lived in Baden-Baden, seat of the headquarters of the French occupation forces, as an honored guest. I met the general there—he was a distant relative—at a family gathering.

After September of 1944, SHAEF was located in Versailles. The document section moved into a luxurious villa near La Celle-St. Cloud, a suburb about twenty kilometers west of Paris. The villa was surrounded by a spacious park and included large dining room, an electrical kitchen, a living room with a grand piano, and several bathrooms. It belonged to the owner of a racing stable and was named "Haras de Bel-Ebas" after one of his successful horses. Only a month before our arrival the villa had been occupied by German officers. The plush quarters had apparently been evacuated in great haste. At some distance from SHAEF we could work in our villa relatively undisturbed—until December of 1944, when the Allies were surprised by Hitler's last offensive in the West.

SHAEF believed that as a result of the rapid advance of the Allied invasion armies, the German *Wehrmacht* was on the point of collapse and incapable of staging major offensive operations. Yet on December 16, 1944, fourteen German infantry divisions supported by armored divisions advanced before daybreak in the area between Monschau and Echternach through the fog-bound forests of the Eifel mountains against the thinly-manned main American battle line and forced a breakthrough. Thus began the Ardennes offensive, called in American military history the "Battle of the Bulge" after the wedge-like German salient.

Among the German documents captured during the operation and sent to the document section was the letter of a lieutenant of the Hitler Youth Division to his fiancée. The letter is filled with enthusiasm over the imminent offensive. We shall drive the enemy from our homeland, "a sacred duty," he writes. "We are advancing, we are marching again, we are marching," the letter concludes. We published the letter in our daily summary as evidence of the spirit of patriotic exaltation which still animated at least some of Germany's youth. The letter could have found its place among war letters written by German students in August of 1914.

The initial success of the German offensive made the situation appear so grave that people in France feared the Germans might be back in Paris by Christmas time. Reinforcing the embattled front line troops as fast as possible was a major task of the Allied High Command. Our younger comrades were pulled out of the section to form a battle reserve together with non-combatant SHAEF personnel. We seniors stayed at our posts, but for the first time since the days of training, were issued arms.

Agitation at headquarters was intensified by rumors that the Germans had dropped parachutists in American uniforms to assassinate the Supreme Commander, General Eisenhower. The leader of the supposed operation was SS-Lieutenant-Colonel Skorzeny who had become famous through his daring rescue of Mussolini from a retreat in the Abruzzi mountains. The rumor contained a kernel of truth. Among the attack units of the Ardennes offensive was the so-called "Trojan Horse Brigade." It was composed of English-speaking German soldiers wearing American uniforms and equipped with captured American army vehicles and tanks under the command of Skorzeny. The mission of the brigade was to spearhead a break through the American lines. The deception was partly successful.

The fear that bogus GI's might infiltrate Allied lines near the headquarters at Versailles had some strange side-effects. Military police were ordered to stop suspicious-looking GI's and test their authenticity with questions about American customs, events, and colloquialisms which only someone thoroughly familiar with life in the United States would be able to answer. They would ask, for example, what "two bits" were, or for the first lines of a current song popular among American soldiers, or for the scores of major American sporting events.

One evening, as some of my comrades and I were walking from the railroad station of Bougival to our quarters conversing loudly with one another, after having spent a free day in Paris, we were stopped by a military police patrol. They had been following us for a while, obviously noting that we all spoke English with an accent. "These guys must be Skorzeny people," they happily concluded. Here was an opportunity of making a good catch and of earning honor and rewards. In the beam of flashlights, our papers were thoroughly scrutinized. Some of the trick questions we answered correctly, to the surprise of our interrogators. Eventually they let us go, disappointed and visibly disgusted. "Ah, that crazy outfit down the road," was their parting comment.

After a few weeks the Ardennes offensive came to a halt and turned into a hasty retreat. In view of Allied superiority, especially in war material, the offensive could never have succeeded. The German armored divisions were short of gas and oil. They had to rely on capturing Allied fuel dumps, which they failed to do. The improvement of the weather made the Allied air force the uncontested ruler of the skies once again. For some time, the Germans had not had the equipment with which they might even begin to match the power of the Allies on land, on sea, and in the air.

As a result of the scare caused by the Ardennes offensive, all outlying units of SHAEF were concentrated at the headquarters in Versailles. The document section was moved into the Grande Écurie located on the square facing the palace. It was here that we learned about the Allied victory and the demise of the Third Reich.

I received an idea of the size of the coming German catastrophe while I was working on a report from captured German documents relating to so-called "ARLZ" measures. The acronym stood for Hitler's orders for the progressive preparation and execution of a "scorched earth" policy. I do not recall the details of the orders to "evacuate, paralyze, and destroy," but the documents clearly show that the object of the orders was to create a desert.   During their advance into Germany, the Allies were to encounter a totally devastated land.   What was to happen to the population was of no concern to Hitler.   That would be the responsibility of the Allies.   Hitler wanted the German people to perish in the chaos of the collapse which he had caused, because "it had proven itself weak and unworthy of his greatness and of National Socialism."   (The "scorched earth" decrees were eventually countermanded by Albert Speer, the German Minister for Armaments and War Production.)

Shortly before the final triumph of the Allies we were shocked by the death of President Roosevelt on April 12, 1945, and experienced the swearing-in of his successor, Harry S. Truman. ("Who is Truman?" French people would ask us, and we could hardly give a proper answer ourselves.) We listened to the last speech that Goebbels made on the radio at the command of Hitler who had himself long ceased to speak in public. On April 30, "Lord Haw-Haw" made his exit with an utterly confused radio talk. His real name was William Joyce, an Englishman who had broadcast Nazi propaganda during the war—directed especially at British soldiers—and was arrested after the war by the British, convicted as a traitor and hanged. Apparently he was drunk at his last performance. His final words "It is all over" were spoken with a definite slur.

On May 7, 1945, Colonel-General Jodl and Admiral von Friedensburg signed in Reims the document calling for the unconditional surrender of the German armed forces.   In Versailles people danced in the streets. During the day groups of demonstrators marched through the town. They carried gallows with a dummy and shouted: *Pétain au poteau!* (Pétain to the gallows.)

With the cessation of hostilities our intelligence mission had come to and end, but not our work with documents. Ahead of us lay the immense task of collecting, sorting and examining files and records of the German armed forces, the German government, and the Nazi party.

The End of the Line

As the occupation of Germany by the Allied forces progressed, SHAEF was moved to Frankfurt am Main. Its seat was the modernistic high-rise building of *IG-Farben*, a combine of German chemical companies which had been founded in 1925. It was even said that it had intentionally been spared Allied bombing because of its potential as the seat of Allied authorities after Germany's defeat.

The document section had found temporary quarters in the Belgian resort town of Spa, recently headquarters of the American First Army. On May 21, 1945, a small party under the command of a lieutenant set out from Spa to Marburg. Its mission was to locate archives of the German Foreign Office which had been evacuated to Marburg, and, if need be, to seize whatever required immediate attention, such as personnel records.

I was a member of the party, thanks to the kindness of my commanding officer, Colonel Hans Helm. My sister lived in Marburg. I had heard of her and her family twice during the war through the Red Cross which had merely reported that she and her family were alive. The last time I had seen her was shortly before my emigration in 1934. I hoped that in Marburg I would be able to learn of her whereabouts. Both she and her husband were "non-Aryans." What had been their fate in Nazi Germany?

It was a sunny spring day when we left Spa early in the morning. At Aachen we crossed the frontier into Germany. After twelve years I was on German soil again. Yet what an appalling sight! The city was almost totally demolished; in its place stood nothing but mounds of rubble. Only the cathedral with the Carolingian octagon stood upright like a ship in a sea of ruins. The situation was the same in Düren: a few isolated house walls, empty shells in the midst of general devastation. We passed through the outskirts of Bonn where we saw the first undamaged houses and trees along the streets in the green of spring. We crossed the Rhine at Godesberg on a pontoon bridge built by the American army. Access to the bridge was provided by a wide passageway which had been cut through the park of a huge villa dating from the late nineteenth century when wealthy Rhenish industrialists indulged their taste for stately residences in Gothic castles with turrets and balconies. The passageway is visible to this day, but is overgrown. People no longer remember its origin. Where the bridge touched the river bank there now stands a street lamp surrounded by a circular flower bed. Many years later as I was walking past this spot recalling the day in 1945 when I had crossed the Rhine here, by a strange coincidence I met Mrs. Steiner-Prag from the New Haven days at Mrs. B's. She was one of the heirs who owned the villa, and had come to Godesberg to meet with her co-heirs in an effort to dispose of this enormously valuable property.

Nothing motor-driven moved on the roads except our personnel carrier and other military vehicles. There were people, alone or in groups, plodding along on their arduous journey from nowhere to homes that might no longer exist, their few belongings on their backs or in handcarts which they pulled, tired to death. Some greeted us as we passed. Despite the glorious spring, we sensed that the dogs of war were still present. What we saw was the picture of a totally vanquished nation. In the evening we reached Marburg. The way to our quarters in a fraternity house led through the street where I knew my sister lived. I had never seen the house since she had moved to Marburg after my emigration.

The first house on the street lay in ruins. Yet as we rode on I saw that the house with my sister's number was undamaged. It looked somewhat run-down. There were no curtains in the windows. I wondered whether it was still occupied. Then, as we passed, I saw a young girl at the garden fence. She looked at us. I recognized a family resemblance and knew that it was my sister's oldest daughter. When I had seen her last, she had been a small child; now she was in her teens. She gave me the hoped-for assurance that the family still lived in the house, but I could not make myself known at that moment.

The next morning the lieutenant and I went to the house. We rang the bell. Nobody answered. Then I saw my sister. She was in the garden and slowly came to the steps which led to the door of the house. I hardly recognized her. She had a terribly sad look on her face and squinted nearsightedly to see who the strangers were who had appeared so suddenly at the door. As I learned later, when she saw two uniformed figures, she was afraid that the house might be seized again. Belgian soldiers has left just a few days before. Had she been forced to leave, there would have been no place in town for her and her six-member family, including a baby. I told her who I was, and asked her not to be afraid. She just stood there, unable to move, not saying a word, her right hand on her forehead. Then she had to sit down on the steps. I went over toward her. I was afraid the suddenness of the encounter might have been too much for her. After a few moments, she regained her composure and called out to her husband who was working in the garden. He came running up the garden path with his son. The tension gave way to unrestrained joy.

My sister had known nothing about me. During the war, when she thought of me and my brother, she was certain, as she told me later, that because of our age we would not have to go to war.

The change wrought by my appearance, and the feelings of delivery and relief were almost beyond my sister's capacity to comprehend. Only a few weeks before an agent of the *Gestapo* had come to see her and had asked menacing questions. Since that day she had lived in fear that Hitler's henchmen might come at any moment to take her away. The arrival of the American troops had removed an intolerable strain.

I stayed with the family during the day. I finally delivered to my sister the letter which had been returned to me at the beginning of the war and which I had been carrying with me since that morning in New Haven when I began my long march back to Germany. With the help of an understanding lieutenant of the local American military government, I was able to protect my sister's home from possible seizure or other future intrusions.

The news about the reunion soon spread in my sister's circle of friends. For all of them it was like an appearance from a different world, deliverance from isolation, a ray of hope. Some wept, I was later told.

The next morning we started for Thuringia which at that time was occupied by American troops. We went as far as Weimar. I don't recall what our mission was. People asked us whether it was true that the Americans would soon leave and that the Soviets would occupy Thuringia. They couldn't believe it. We were not quite sure ourselves, and could only give evasive answers.

Upon my return to Spa, a new mission awaited me. On May 26, I was ordered, together with a few comrades, "to proceed to Flensburg/Germany for temporary duty with the SHAEF Control Commission at OKW (North)." The Control Commission was an interallied agency of 500 British and American officers and enlisted men set up at the headquarters of *Oberkommando der Wehrmacht* (OKW), or the Supreme Command of the German armed forces, for the purpose of supervising the execution of the surrender terms. A document section was attached to the commission.

The last days of the Third Reich in Flensburg are described in a *Chronology of Events* compiled by State Secretary Wegener, chief of staff of Dönitz, which we discovered among the Flensburg documents. The following remarks are based on notes I took from Wegener's account.

Since May 2, 1945, Flensburg (in the province of Schleswig-Holstein in northern Germany) had been the headquarters of Grand Admiral Karl Dönitz, Commander-in-Chief of the Navy. On April 10, Hitler had given orders that in the event that land communications were interrupted between northern and southern Germany, a commander-in-chief would exercise unlimited power of command in the area where he, Hitler, was not present. This would be Field Marshal Kesselring in the south and Grand Admiral Dönitz in the north.   On April 22, Dönitz, with Hitler's approval, had departed for the northern area and had at first established his headquarters in Plön (Schleswig-Holstein). During the night of April 21 to April 22, most of the Reich ministers, among them Count Schwerin-Krosigk, Himmler, Rosenberg, Speer, Thierack, and Rust, had left Berlin to join Dönitz and continue functioning as the government of the Reich.   To add to the confusion, Field Marshal Keitel and General-Colonel Jodl also appeared in the same area and laid claim to the supreme military command while Dönitz insisted that he alone had been vested with supreme power in the north and that he alone was authorized to give orders to all military, civilian, and party organizations.

On April 29, Dönitz learned from Hitler's Secretary Bormann that that he had been appointed as Hitler's successor. In the afternoon of the following day, Dönitz received a radio message signed by Goebbels and Bormann stating that "the *Führer*, at 15:30 hours yesterday, had passed away" (*sei verschieden*). Actually Hitler had shot himself. The message added that "in his last will" of April 29, the *Führer* had appointed Dönitz as president of the Reich. Goebbels was to be Reich chancellor, Bormann party minister, and Seyss-Inquardt (at the time *Gauleiter* in the Netherlands) minister of foreign affairs. The message was already outdated when it reached Dönitz. Shortly after it had been sent, Goebbels, following Hitler's example, committed suicide after poisoning his family.

On May 2, Dönitz moved his headquarters to Flensburg. On the same day, he appointed Count Schwerin-Krosigk, then finance minister, as minister of foreign affairs. On May 5, "dispensing with formal procedures of forming a government and appointing ministers," he set up a "cabinet of experts" under the overall direction of Count Schwerin-Krosigk as minister of foreign affairs and finance minister. Other cabinet members were the former State Secretary in the Ministry of the Interior Stuckart (Interior and Culture), Speer (Economy and Production), Backe (Food and Agriculture), Seldte (Labor), and Dr. Dorpmüller (Transportation and the Postal Service). The following day Himmler, Rosenberg, Thierack and Rust were formally "dismissed." The seat of the "caretaker government," as Count Schwerin-Krosigk called his team, was the Naval Academy at Flensburg-Mürwick.

The Dönitz government, as the assembly of former Nazis was later called, was politically a continuation of the government of the Third Reich. It was anathema for the Allies just as its predecessor had been. A government headed by resistance fighters might have made a difference although at no time during the war did the Western Allies formally declare that they were willing to make peace with a non-Nazi government.

That Dönitz was still loyal to Hitler despite the devastation of Germany and the horror the German people had suffered at the hands of Hitler is demonstrated by two remarks. In an "Appeal to the German People" on May 1, 1945, he called Hitler's demise "a hero's death" although he knew from Goebbels' and Bormann's radio message only that Hitler had "passed away." He translated this to read that Hitler "had fallen in battle." And in an "Order of the Day to the Armed Forces" of the same day, he called Hitler "one of the greatest heroes in German history."

Until May 6, one of Dönitz' colleagues was Himmler, the architect of the Nazi death camps.   In his memoirs, Count Schwerin asserts that Dönitz had no knowledge of the Holocaust. Dönitz, he writes, "exemplifies how uninformed even high-placed people were."   On the other hand, Walter Lüdde-Neurath, aide-de-camp to Dönitz since September 1944, reports in his book *The Doenitz Government.   The Last Days of the Third Reich*, that rumors about extermination camps sometimes reached Dönitz. Nobody believed them, he writes, because "their sources were in most cases foreign news services."   Yet, was Dönitz "unsuspecting," as Schwerin-Krosigk wants us to believe?   He might have suspected something, but nothing was further from his mind or that of his entourage than to follow up on these rumors. According to Lüdde-Neurath, the relationship between Dönitz and Himmler was based on a clear understanding of their respective competencies and "on mutual respect."

The ignorance of millions of Germans must be distinguished from the alleged ignorance of high functionaries of the Third Reich.   Despite deceptions and concealments, they were in a position to find out if they had wanted to. Or was the reason for their indifference a sentiment I once heard expressed—it might have been in 1933 or 1934—by an army officer: "Germany will not perish by what may happen to the Jews." The men of the Resistance knew. They paid with their lives for the consequences they drew from their knowledge.

The Allies treated the Dönitz government at first as an institution they could use.   On May 23, the government was dissolved.   Simultaneously, the Allies arrested the group of functionaries of the Third Reich who had hoped to survive the collapse of the regime as the caretaker government of the German Reich.

Our journey to Flensburg on May 26 met with obstacles. We lacked adequate road maps. Impassable roads and destroyed bridges forced us to make detours. The sight of the destruction in the Ruhr district, the industrial heart of Germany, was ghastly. The Krupp works, once Germany's armory, were a tangled maze of steel and iron bars.

Upon our arrival in Flensburg, we reported to the British town commander to be assigned quarters. The sergeant on duty wrote on our orders: *S.S. Patria.* We should go to the harbor, he said. There we would find a ship which would be our quarters.

The liner *Patria* had once belonged to the Hamburg-Amerika Line and was used for cruises in peacetime. During the war when officer quarters in Flensburg became scarce because the Naval Academy in Mürwick was filled to capacity, the *Patria* was transferred to Flensburg with its entire service personnel and turned into officer's barracks. The ship's cooks prepared the meals and stewards took care of everything else. One of the first actions of the SHAEF Control Commission in Flensburg was to seize the *Patria* for its use. She served, as before, as quarters, and her social rooms were used for meetings and parties. Our quarters were staterooms in the tourist class. Meals were served in the large dining room.

Flensburg was overcrowded with refugees from the East. The streets were one big mass of people. We could hardly move among the dense crowds. Their faces had an empty, impassive look. One felt that these people were utterly exhausted, helpless, and aimless, and used the streets just for escape.

At the time the Control Commission arrived in Flensburg there were about 30,000 German troops, officers, and men in the area, some still armed, remnants of the German occupation forces from Norway and Denmark. On occasional trips into the country we saw them moving about rather freely and unconcerned, as if preparing for another campaign. A number of officers, in particular members of the German Supreme Command, were held in Flensburg as prisoners of war. One day, passing the prisoner-of-war compounds, I noticed German generals with double red piping on their pants and golden oak leaves on the uniform collars confined behind barbed wire fences. Truly a sight to behold.

In town, our small group were the only military personnel among the pressing, shoving crowds. We carried handguns—less for protection than as symbols of our prerogative to carry arms.

Although we were a tiny minority among the masses of refugees, nobody would have dared to be disrespectful, let alone use violence against Americans.

One morning at breakfast we were startled by an enormous bang. Windows broke all over. The first explosion was followed by several others of equal force. It soon became known that an ammunition depot on the outskirts of Flensburg was exploding out of control. The ship was hastily evacuated. We sought refuge in an air raid shelter, actually a cave dug into one of the hills surrounding the Flensburg Bay. There were no lights; it was as dark as Erebus. The din of a thousand voices coming from the depths of the cave indicated to us that the place was overcrowded. We thought it prudent to stay at the entrance.

The Flensburg Naval Academy had become the repository of the records of the German Supreme Command. They had to be registered and catalogued before being sent to Allied archives for further study. This preparatory work was assigned to our group. Among the many papers that passed through my hands there was a small note scribbled hastily on a piece of paper by Field Marshal Keitel informing his wife of his imminent arrest. "I have always been simply the loyal servant of my *Führer*," the note concluded.

The most important documents we discovered were the originals of the directives signed by Hitler for the major campaigns of the war. We were first among the Allies to see these top secret documents of the highest historical significance.

The campaigns bore code names, for instance, "Operation Sea Lion," the less than imaginative designation for the planned invasion of England; "Operation Barbarossa," for the attack on Russia; "Operation Felix," for the conquest of Gibraltar. The directives filled many pages and were typed in oversized letters, capitals 1/2 cm, lower case 3 mm. Members of the German equivalent of the Women's Auxiliary Corps who had remained at headquarters and who helped us with our work told us that the large letters came from *Führer* typewriters. They were used for all Hitler's written work. Hitler had eye trouble, they said, but did not wish to wear glasses; he could read the large type without glasses. A few of these *Führer* typewriters were still usable. It gave us great pleasure to regale friends and relatives with letters typed on one of these machines.

"War Directive No. 16," the directive for "Operation Sea Lion" of July 16, 1940, after the victory over France, began with these words: "As England in spite of her hopeless military position has so far shown herself unwilling to come to any compromise, I have decided to begin preparations for and, if necessary, to carry out the invasion of England." The code name "Barbarossa" (the epithet given to the German Emperor Frederick I [1122-1190] who perished on a crusade) for the attack on Russia was obviously designed, by evoking the memory of the emperor, to characterize the operation as a crusade. The introduction of "Directive No. 21. Operation Barbarossa" of December 18, 1940, reads: "The German armed forces must be prepared, even before the end of the war against England, *to overthrow Soviet Russia in a rapid campaign*" (emphasis in the original).

Operation "Sea Lion" was never started because the Germans had been unable to eliminate the British air force. "Felix" was abandoned in December of 1941; Franco had misgivings. What happened to "Barbarossa" is well known.

During our work we occasionally were visited by two Russian colonels. They were interested in what we did. We treated them with all the respect and courtesy due to their rank—but that was all. Only our superiors were entitled to know the nature and results of our work.

We used duty-free hours for trips into neighboring Denmark. For members of the United States forces there were no state boundaries in Europe. We were the liberators everywhere. The Danish border guards just stood aside and lifted the barrier when our jeep arrived. On the road, school children stopped us and asked for autographs to put in their exercise books. A family in a small town invited us for coffee and cake. The sons proudly displayed photographs which showed them as "resistance fighters" wearing some imaginative uniforms.

At the beginning of June, an American lieutenant appeared at the Naval Academy with a jeep and a truck to take the records of the German Supreme Command—all registered and catalogued—to SHAEF in Frankfurt. The jeep had an oil leak which apparently could not be fixed. I had the dubious honor of driving the vehicle while the lieutenant by my side, oil can in hand, added more oil whenever needed. On our trip south we encountered more scenes of appalling devastation. What once had been the city of Kassel was now a heap of rubble. We could hardly recognize streets. The *Autobahn* bridge across the Werra, a marvel of construction, had been blown up. Wedged in a long line of army trucks, we had to descend with our ailing jeep on a temporary road into the deep valley and up again on the other side under equally trying conditions. We eventually reached Frankfurt late at night.

The documents we had collected and seized in Flensburg were once more thoroughly examined, packed, and shipped to the appropriate authorities in Washington. They eventually reached the National Archives where they were available for research. Documents of general interest, such as the directives for operations "Sea Lion" and "Barbarossa" were put on public display. They have since been returned to Germany.

In April of 1945, the War Department notified the commanding generals in Europe that every enlisted man forty-two years of age or over was eligible for discharge, provided additional requirements were fulfilled, such as a certain number of points earned after a specified duration of overseas service. I qualified. I "voluntarily applied in writing" to my commanding officer for a discharge. The application was granted. On June 23, I found myself, together with other soldiers of similar age, on a temporary airfield near Frankfurt. In the pale light of the early morning an army transport plane arrived. We had seen it flying low over the crest of the Taunus mountains. It took us to a "Reinforcement Depot" in Le Havre. We sat on bucket seats along the walls of the plane. It was the first flight of my life. The sight of the Reims cathedral from above still lives in my memory.

In Le Havre we waited in a tent camp for the ship which would return us to the States. After two weeks it arrived. It was more spacious than the Liberty ship which had taken me in March of 1944 on my fateful journey to Europe. We slept on army cots and could move around on deck. There were even movies and a mimeographed ship's paper called "Garbage Can." The title aptly described its contents.

In New York harbor we were given a "hero's welcome." A ship which carried playing bands and waving girls, and a large sign proclaiming "Welcome Home" met us at the entrance of the harbor. Fountains of water were hurled into the air by a ship of the Harbor Fire Brigade.

The discharge formalities proceeded with precision and without unnecessary delays. In the staging camp after landing, we were served what every GI allegedly dreams about when he thinks of home: a dinner, on a compartment tray, of steak, mashed potatoes, fresh vegetables, butter and rolls, and ice cream. The latter had become steak sauce before one got to it. I received my discharge papers at Fort Devens where almost three years earlier I had undergone the transformation from a civilian to a member of the armed forces.

By one of those strange coincidences which had been a recurring experience in my army life, I was put in the same barracks where I had learned how to make a bed in the proper army fashion; where I had scrubbed the floor and had waited for the moment when I would hear my name called out on the loudspeaker with the order to report to the orderly room to learn about my assignment. Listening to the public address system required special attention. It was by no means certain that one would be able to catch one's name when it came over the loudspeaker in a strident voice mixed with the background noises of the orderly room and, if the name was foreign, as in my case, was pronounced in some peculiar fashion. The fence was still there which had been the object of my first military duty. Had the white paint come from my brush? It showed numerous cracks, signs of considerable age. I looked at my probable handiwork not without a touch of affection in memory of bygone days.

On July 20, all formalities had been completed. It was a warm summer day when I strode through the gate of Fort Devens to return to civilian life. It was the same gate through which I had passed on a damp, rainy day in the fall of 1942, in the opposite direction, tired and bewildered, to face an uncertain future.

I had time to reflect on what had happened between these two dates. America was still at war in the Pacific, but for me the war was over. The "city had been freed from the tyrant." To reach this goal, I had worn the uniform of my new country for almost three years. I had crossed into Germany as a member of the victorious army. What a feeling to be a victor! It did not express itself in arrogance or superiority toward the vanquished; its main ingredient was freedom of movement. And there were no longer SA and SS uniforms on the streets, a sight which had formerly sickened me.

My uniform did not symbolize new oppression. True, "Germany will not be occupied for the purpose of liberation but as a defeated enemy nation." This was one of the basic principles governing the treatment of Germany in the initial post-defeat period, as stated in the Directive of April 1945 by the Joint Chiefs of Staff to the Commander-in-Chief of the United States Forces of Occupation. Yet it was equally true that through the Allied victory Germany had been liberated from the scourge of Nazism, which the German people had not been able to stamp out by themselves and which had brought about the most ruinous catastrophe in German history. I had met at least a part of my family. They would never again be menaced by sinister forces, such as the *Gestapo* and the SS.

I had seen inconceivable devastation and the misery of the survivors. The guilty ones—"a clique of megalomaniac, brutal and unscrupulous criminals"—were dead, captured or scattered to the four winds. This was the main thing. The material damage could be repaired, the shattered order restored. To help in this endeavor and at the same time promote German-American understanding was among the goals I had set myself when on October 12, 1942, I walked through the dark, deserted streets of New Haven to be inducted into the armed forces of the United States. I had done my part to the best of my abilities; I had started at the bottom. "Shoes well shined, bed well made," I saw one day posted on the company bulletin board with my name. At the end of my military service, my commanding officer, a British lieutenant colonel, of his own volition, wrote a "Report of Record" which contained these sentences: "Von Elbe contributed vital intelligence to Supreme Headquarters. His work was frequently given wide circulation throughout the Theater. He showed exceptional application to his work, set an excellent example to his fellow men and won the admiration of all those he served with for his generous attitude and patient cooperation."

In the Service of the American Military Government for Germany

Soon after my discharge from military service, I began looking for a position with the American occupation authorities in Germany. My instructorship at Yale Law School had lapsed in the meantime. Professor Borchard kindly offered to have me work with him on other projects of international law. Lacking other means of support, I at first accepted the offer. After the experiences of the last few years, however, scholarly work in Yale's ivory tower had lost all attraction for me. How would I be able, as a research assistant at best, to contribute to what I considered the most pressing task for me, to help restore the German legal order?

The thought of Germany haunted me. What will happen? *Vae victis*? Vengeance? Punishment? The plan submitted by Secretary of the Treasury Morgenthau for the treatment of defeated Germany provided for the destruction of Germany's industrial potential and "pastoralization," i.e. Germany would be turned into a predominantly agricultural country to prevent her from ever again becoming a threat to the world. Help for Germany? "The Germans have themselves to blame if the world gets back at them. Their misery deserves no compassion," was a sentiment shared by many. Private individuals, politicians, and representatives of churches warned against this attitude; it would not lead to a solution.

Added to this were voices which could not be suspected of harboring undeserved sympathy for Germany: enemies and victims of Nazism who had found refuge and a new life in America. They urgently appealed to the American people and government to reconsider American policy in Central Europe. "The spreading of spiritual and physical degeneration in Central Europe threatens to demoralize the whole world. Unemployment, hunger, and despair, and the hatred they generate. . . . are no foundations upon which to build peaceful democratic societies." Immediate relief action was necessary to stave off mass starvation. "We believe that a policy of indifference is neither desirable from a practical point of view nor compatible with the moral principles for which this war was fought." The appeal was signed by Thomas Mann; the pacifist writer Leonard Frank; the publisher Kurt Wolff (since 1961 editor of the Helen and Kurt Wolff Books at Harcourt, Brace and Jovanowitch); and many German scholars and scientists, historians, mathematicians, and jurists who had emigrated to America.

The United States, by virtue of its preponderant might, was primarily responsible for developments in Germany. I was convinced that my knowledge of German legal and administrative institutions and my familiarity with the German scene would be useful to the American occupation authorities in their task of governing postwar Germany. An added advantage, I thought, would be the fact that, having studied American law, I would be in a position to explain to my American colleagues in terms familiar to them the unknown world of German legal concepts and social conditions with which they would be confronted in their daily work as trustees of German governmental affairs.

I therefore applied for a position with the American Military Government for Germany. At the end of July 1946, after a seemingly endless wait, I was notified that I had been appointed a member of the Legal Division of the Office of Military Government for Germany (U.S.) (OMGUS) in Berlin, thanks—I knew—to the vigorous and indefatigable efforts of friends (in particular of the highly esteemed Professor Karl Löwenstein who had been a lawyer and well-known authority on constitutional law in Munich prior to his emigration to the United States and since 1945 was employed by OMGUS). The telegram from the War Department with the news of my appointment is one of the most cherished documents of my life. It signified the ascent from the valley for me. The annual salary of $8,000 which the position paid, appeared to me, after more than a decade of a rather light purse, as inconceivably high.

On August 5, 1946, I boarded the army transport *President Tyler* in New York. There were 550 passengers, including 197 children, for the most part family members of army personnel traveling to Germany. The 15,000-ton ship had been built in 1920 and had been used for cruises prior to the war. During the war it served as a hospital ship and as a troop transport.

Single male passengers were accommodated in a large, barracks-like room on the lower deck of the ship. The room was equipped with army cots, chairs, and tables. In the middle of the ocean—fortunately as smooth as glass at that moment—the engine broke down. A rumor circulated that the condition of the ship did not permit continuation of the voyage, and that we would have to be towed back to New York. The crew, however, managed to get the engine started again. On August 17, we arrived in Bremerhaven without further incident. It was the same port from which I had left Germany for the United States twelve years ago.

A train was waiting for our trip to Berlin. It was made up from wagons of the former *Rheingold* train. The *Rheingold* was the first German train that had its own name and had run between Hoek van Holland and Basel since 1929. It belonged to the luxury class and, as far as being on time was concerned, had no equal among European trains. One could have meals and refreshments served at one's seat. I rode the train once in the early thirties on a trip from Cologne to Basel. The wagons were now part of the rolling stock of the Transportation Corps of the American army.

During a brief stop in the half-destroyed station of Hannover, I observed furtive figures dart among stopped freight trains to fill bags with coal or potatoes and quickly disappear, a picture of the dire need that gripped Germany and a terrifying sight for someone like me who had come from a safe and sound America. When passing Potsdam I noticed the ruined garrison church which had been the center of the "Day of Potsdam" in March 1933.

In the past, the first stop in Berlin for long-distance trains from the West had been Charlottenburg, now situated in the British sector and not available for American military trains. After we had endured a great deal of crunching and squeaking, noises due to the newly installed tracks and switches, the train came to a halt at the suburban station of Wannsee in the American sector. A military band had taken up position to welcome us with popular tunes. One of my travel companions whom I had told that I had once lived in Berlin, pointed at the band and remarked to me: "Local boy made good."

A few days after my arrival in Berlin a miracle happened: I was reunited with my parents. A German friend in the States had once told me that we could not expect to see our parents alive again. Old people would not be able to survive the war.

My parents, both in their seventies, were in good health. During the last few years of the war they had stayed on a small farm in Pomerania with my eldest brother who had managed, with his family of five, to keep a low profile and thus escape difficulties with the regime. After Germany's surrender, Pomerania was occupied by Soviet troops, but the family managed—miraculously—to weather the storm. My parents were able to return to Berlin where they found their apartment still in habitable condition.

The first sign that they were alive was a letter I had received in New Haven in August 1945 from France. The envelope contained a slip of paper with a line saying: "We are still alive, healthy and in our house but have gone through trying times." The paper was dated July 31, 1945, and was signed by my parents and all members of my brother's family.

It was after many months that I learned how this message got to France and from there to my address in the States. A French prisoner of war had worked since February 1941 as a barber in the small town near my brother's farm. A doctor and his wife—she was Jewish—had looked after the man. The couple were close friends of my brother's family. After being liberated by the Russians, the barber was able to return to France. Informed by the doctor's wife of the imminent departure of their French friend, my brother quickly penned the message which the barber, at the request of his German benefactors, took along to France with the promise to forward it to my address in the States. This he did. As he had indicated his address on the envelope, I immediately got in touch with him in the hope of learning further details. He answered that he could unfortunately give me no further news. After his liberation, he wrote, he had stayed in the Soviet-occupied zone for three more months. "My dear Sir," he continued, "I do not wish to cause you worry, but conditions in the Soviet zone are wretched. Many things are inhuman, especially as far as women are concerned. The Russians, although I was their ally, treated me like an enemy and took everything from me." I was dismayed and worried. Fortunately, my worst fears later proved unfounded.

Since my return to the United States, Germany had been the center of momentous events in the aftermath of the Allied victory. The physical destruction of Germany had been accompanied by a total breakdown of Germany's legal and constitutional order. As the governmental power during the Nazi regime had increasingly been concentrated in Hitler's person, his suicide on April 30, 1945, created a political and constitutional vacuum. This vacuum was filled by the victorious Allies by an act unprecedented in history. In the absence of a "central Government or authority in Germany capable of accepting responsibility for the maintenance of order, the administration of the country and compliance with the requirements of the victorious Powers," the Governments of the United States, the Soviet Union, Great Britain, and the Provisional Government of France, by Declaration of June 5, 1945, assumed

. . . . supreme authority with respect to Germany, including all the powers possessed by the German Government, the High Command and any state, municipal, or local government or authority.

Germany "within her frontiers as they were on 31st December, 1937," was occupied by the Allies, and for the stationing of their respective forces was divided into four zones, one to be allotted to each of the occupying powers.

For the purpose of exercising supreme authority, governmental affairs were divided into categories. Matters requiring central direction, or, in the terms the "Statement on Control Machinery in Germany," of June 5, 1945, "matters affecting Germany as a whole," were the responsibility of a "Control Council" consisting of the four commanders-in-chief. With regard to all other matters, supreme authority was exercised, on instructions from their governments, by the commanders-in-chief "each in his own zone of occupation."

The seat of the Control Council was Berlin, capital of Germany. As a result, the city of Berlin within its boundaries as defined by a Prussian law of April 27, 1920, was not included in any of the four zones (especially the Soviet zone), but was constituted as a separate area to be administered by an inter-allied governing authority, the so-called "Allied

Kommandantura," which consisted of the commanders of the Allied forces stationed in Berlin. Each of the four powers occupied a specified sector of the city.

A map attached to the "Protocol on the Zones of Occupation in Germany and the Administration of Greater Berlin," signed in London on September 12, 1944, by representatives of the United States, Great Britain and the Soviet Union, clearly demonstrates the separation of the Berlin area from the surrounding Soviet zone. The boundary of the Berlin area is marked by a red line; the same marking is used on the map for the boundaries of the four occupation zones.

In addition to the Control Council as the central governing body of the Allies, the four occupying powers set up their own machinery for the government of their individual zones.

The American zone—it included the states (*Länder*) of Bavaria, Württemberg-Baden (its designation was later changed to Baden-Württemberg), Greater Hesse and Bremen—was administered by OMGUS. Occupation authorities below OMGUS were in the capital of each state a Land Office of Military Government and in each city (*Stadtkreis*) and county (*Landkreis*) a Liaison and Security Detachment, the agency of the Military Government closest to the population on the local level.

OMGUS was housed in the former headquarters of the Central Regional Command of the German air force in Dahlem, a suburb of Berlin which had survived the war practically unscathed. The two-story, white-washed building comprising a large central and projecting wings was undamaged. In the high-ceilinged, dimly lit entrance hall, the visitor was greeted by a life-size bronze statue of an American infantryman.

In August of 1946, when I took up my duties with the Legal Division of OMGUS, the Military Government in the U.S. zone was headed by General Lucius D. Clay, a three-star general at the time. He earned his fourth star by fulfilling his mission in a way that made history.

OMGUS was divided into functional divisions which were responsible for various administrative fields: an economic division dealing with production, reparations, control of German industry, the industrial disarmament of Germany, food and agriculture, trade and commerce, restitution of looted property, decartelization; a finance division to supervise the public and private financial structure of Germany; a transport division to control the operation of railroads, inland waterways, ports, coastal shipping and road transport; a manpower division to allocate German labor supply and to supervise working conditions, wages, hours and social insurance; an internal affairs and communications division for postal matters, education and religion, public health and welfare, and for the reconstruction, decentralization and control of German governmental agencies including the German civil service, and public safety.

The legal division was responsible for legal advice, legislation, prisons, administration of justice and the apprehension, trial and punishment of war criminals. The director of the division also had charge of the widely distributed network of Military Government courts; in particular, he had to review death sentences and submit recommendations to the military governor.

I was attached to the legislative branch which dealt with Military Government and German legislation. The branch was headed by an elderly lawyer from New York. After World War I, he had become interested in questions affecting the seizure of German property in the States during the war. He knew Germany from his many trips, and liked the country. Although he was Jewish, I never heard him speak a harsh word against the German people. He was a model of serene composure and guided his co-workers with a deft hand, a quality that was particularly useful for an operation in which no one was experienced, where temperaments sometimes clashed, and the atmosphere tended to become hectic. As a result of his attitude, morale in his branch was very high. He used to say that with his small group of dedicated lawyers, he would be able to run the whole legal division single-handedly. He gave me and others who knew something about German law and German institutions free rein, and was proud of the accomplishments of his branch.

Although I had not engaged in any form of legal thinking during my military service, let alone legal drafting, I was able to resume legal work in the shortest possible time. It was either sink or swim; there was no grace period. I had the satisfaction that some of my first opinions were included among the *Selected Opinions* published by the legal division at regular intervals.

The majority of my colleagues were lawyers trained in American law who either sought a new field of activity in legal problems arising from the occupation, or who had joined the Military Government out of patriotism in order to help the United States government reconstruct Germany along the lines of American concepts of law and democracy. There were, however, others, opportunists, even adventurers who were out for personal gain, to whom the unsettled conditions in Germany seemed to offer opportunities for an easy life and lucrative dealings, similar to the carpetbaggers who invaded the vanquished South after the Civil War. In the early days of the occupation it did happen that unworthy elements took advantage of recruiting difficulties and found jobs in the occupation administration for which they were neither professionally nor morally qualified. Such mistakes caused Frau Louise Schroeder, Mayor of Berlin, to implore her American interlocutors—I overhead a conversation at a party in Berlin—to send "only the best" to Germany lest the trust that the German people, recently freed from Nazism, had in the integrity of the United States should be jeopardized.

I was billeted in a villa on a quiet, tree-lined street in the Berlin suburb of Dahlem. To judge by the books I found in the library, the former resident must have been a loyal follower of Hitler. This might have been the reason for his departure from Berlin and why his villa had been seized by the occupation authorities to house occupation personnel.

Situated near the American headquarters building was the so-called *Harnackhaus*, formerly a guest house and meeting place for public functions of the Kaiser Wilhelm Society for the Advancement of Sciences, the holding company, as mentioned earlier, of scientific institutes, including the Bruns Institute. It had been commandeered by the American authorities for use as an officers' mess. As a member of the Bruns Institute, I had often gone to the *Harnackhaus*, had attended many festivities there, and was present, in 1932, when Lise Meitner, assistant to Professor Otto Hahn, the Nobel laureate, delivered her famous lecture which gave a first glimpse into the secret of nuclear fission. I gladly concede that the lecture went largely over my head. That

Berlin

Prewar Years

42. Cathedral, Armory, Memorial Shrine,
Boulevard "Unter den Linden"

43. Brandenburg Gate (1788-1791)

Berlin

44. The Elevated

45. A Suburban Track

it was an important event, however, had been made clear to us by a letter from the president of the Society urging us to attend. I still recall the circumstances: the overcrowded lecture hall, the petite figure of the lecturer, her modest ways, the tension among the audience who felt that they were witnessing the beginning of a new epoch in the history of mankind. Lise Meitner, like Einstein, left Germany because of her Jewish race to escape persecution after the Nazis had come into power.

The image which Berlin had presented in those days remains in my memory: the radiant metropolis pulsating with life, crowded streets, the yellow cars of the subway, a feature of urban life which never ceased to fascinate me, and the colorful, continuously changing neon signs at night.

Berlin in the twenties and early thirties was the cultural and economic capital of Central Europe. External evidence of its tradition as a capital city were its palaces, grandiose government buildings, museums, monuments and statues, a sight familiar to me since my early childhood. During my absence, whenever I tried to visualize Berlin, the sights which first came to my mind were the *Tiergarten*, the Central Park of Berlin, with its lawns, grand old trees and artificial lakes, and the splendid boulevard Unter den Linden, stretching from the imperial palace to the Brandenburg Gate. How often had I seen this the heart of Berlin, the same way that Heinrich Heine describes it standing near the palace during a visit to the city in 1822: "Truly I know of no more imposing sight than looking towards the 'Linden.' To the right, the magnificent armory, the new guard house, the university and the academy. To the left the royal palace, the opera, the library; here stately edifices abound."

Soon after my arrival in August of 1946 I rode the subway from Dahlem to Wittenbergplatz. The trains still consisted of the same yellow cars I had known from innumerable trips. I stood, as had been my custom for many years, in the corner next to the door to make sure it was closed when the train started to move. The station building at Wittenbergplatz where several lines merged had preserved its original face; not a stone had changed since it was built in 1912. In contrast, the nearby *Kaufhaus des Westens*, one of the largest and most renowned department stores in Berlin, was a roofless and windowless ruin. Of the Emperor

William Memorial Church at the end of Tauentzien Street only
the tower, cracked and looking like a decayed tooth, was still
standing. In place of rows of apartment houses, stores and hotels,
were mere heaps of rubble. In the desert of stones, here and
there, I found a sign naming a street well known to me; the street
itself was recognizable only by its curb. A burnt-out, battered
streetcar stood where it had come to its last stop, on tracks that
led nowhere. Between ruins and wrecked cars was a tank riddled
with bullets—an iron gravestone, reminder of the battle of Berlin.

In this environment of general devastation, it was almost
unreal to see a single house that was still standing. The
Tiergartenviertel, once Berlin's most fashionable residential
district, had disappeared; not even the ruin of a house could
be seen. Potsdam square and Potsdam station, formerly the
focal points of dense, metropolitan traffic, were utterly deserted.
In their midst had stood the *Haus Vaterland*, once a famous
amusement center for Berliners and visitors from all over the
world. Under one roof it had combined: a beer garden on the
Eibsee lake in the Bavarian Alps with hourly rainstorms, thunder
and lightning; a Turkish coffeehouse at the Bosporus; a Japanese
tea house; a garden terrace in Grinzing near Vienna with a view
of St. Stephen's Cathedral where *Heuriger*, Austrian wine of the
latest vintage, was served; and a saloon from America's Wild
West—now a black, roofless skeleton, in its grotesque shape a
caricature of its former self. In the *Tiergarten*, not a tree,
not a shrub was left. The area was wasteland as far as the
eye could see, with a few wretched wooden shacks on isolated
patches where vegetables were grown. The noble oaks and
beeches had long since been consumed by the fire of innumerable
stoves. Alone in the wilderness, at its original site, stood the the
bronze statue of the "Amazon on horseback," once surrounded
by meadows, trees and shrubs, a deathless monument to man's
creative will and a preserver of beauty and dignity in the midst
of a vast, derelict void. Nothing made me realize the dimension
of the German catastrophe more poignantly than the sight of this
desolate expanse, at one time the peaceful habitat of plants and
animals where I had strolled often under shady trees in search of
recreation and peace.

Berlin

Prewar Years

46. Potsdamer Platz (Potsdam Square) 1926

47. "Haus Vaterland" 1930

48. Bismarck's Chancellery

49. Hitler's Chancellery

I continued through the ruined Brandenburg Gate, passing the wrecked facade of the Adlon, once Berlin's most elegant hotel—the name in ornate letters above the entrance was still legible—into Wilhelmstrasse, or what was left of it, the street of the torchlight procession of January 30, 1933. I thought of the remark I had made that evening to an acquaintance of mine: that we should meet at this place ten years from now—only then would we be able to judge what all this had meant.

The Reich chancellery, Bismarck's residence where the Congress of Berlin had been held in 1878, was gone. The new chancellery where Hitler had stood with Göring on a balcony to watch and salute the frenzied crowds, was largely a ruin, yet sufficiently preserved to permit one to enter the building from Voss-Strasse over still passable stairs. Nobody was there to stop me, no SS guard sought to prevent me from proceeding to what had been the most guarded, the most inaccessible inner sanctum of Nazi power. As I made my way through debris lying on the floor, I suddenly found myself in a high-ceilinged hall, the room where Hitler's desk had once stood. Shreds of curtains hung in the glassless windows, moving gently in the wind. The floor was covered with dust; here and there lay small pieces of marble from the wall paneling. What scenes this room had seen! Here Hitler had received foreign diplomats and potentates, the highest dignitaries of the realm, field marshals and generals to award them batons and medals. Here the Third Reich had celebrated its triumphs before it was reduced to ruins. And here my long march back to Germany came to an end. For the first time since victory had been won, it was at this point that I was seized with a feeling of personal gratification.

I wiped the dust of Hitler's workroom off my shoes. I stepped down a flight of stairs and went outside into the garden. Hamlet's words crossed my mind: ". . . . 'tis an unweeded garden that grows to seed, things rank and gross in nature possess it merely." I walked over to Hitler's bunker, the subterranean, multilevel structure that after January of 1945 had been Hitler's headquarters in Berlin where he had withdrawn to seek protection from Allied bombs and defend the Third Reich "to the end."

The entrance to the bunker was encased in a huge concrete block; next to it lay the ventilation system. There was nothing to bar me from entering. A German civilian seemed to be posted there as a guard, but it was not clear on whose orders. He offered to be my guide. As I had no flashlight, I accepted his offer. We went down several flights of stairs to the ground floor. There was a hallway and several rooms around it. In the center of the hallway stood a switchboard. Someone was carrying a piece of furniture upstairs. Otherwise there was nothing but empty rooms. I stood in the room where Hitler and Eva Braun had been married only hours before they both perished there in a suicide pact. I looked into other rooms without knowing their purpose. In one of them Goebbels, his wife, and children might have died. The stillness of the damp, dark rooms, the scene of Hitler's last days, was oppressive. I slowly ascended the stairs. In front of the entrance was a still visible hollow in the grass. It was here that the bodies of Hitler and his wife had been incinerated.

I went back to the bunker several times thereafter. As a former Berliner, I was asked by the director of the legal division to serve as a guide whenever we received prominent visitors from the States. The bunker was one of the sights included in my program. When I went there for the last time, it was completely inundated with groundwater. No traces of the bunker are left. It is said that the Soviets blew it up to prevent it from ever becoming an object of sightseeing or, worse, a memorial. All the other ruins around the bunker have also been leveled. What had once been the seat of Nazi government has disappeared from the face of the earth. Those who still retain a visual memory of what the old Wilhelmstrasse looked like will notice a small mound of earth if they stand on the platform at "Potsdamer Platz" near the Berlin Wall and look toward the Soviet sector. The mound marks the spot of the chancellery and the bunker. The Wilhelmstrasse, with its rows of magnificent buildings, the Foreign Office, the Presidential Palace—symbols of German governance like 1066 Pennsylvania Avenue in the States, No. 10 Downing Street in Great Britain, and the Elysée Palace in France—no longer exist. Their place has been taken by the broad death strip that reaches up to the Berlin Wall and separates East Berlin from the western part of the city.

Like his colleagues of the other occupying powers, the American commander-in-chief performed a double function. He was a member of the Allied Control Council and the Military Governor of the American zone of occupation.

This dual role was reflected in the tasks of his administrative staff. As a member of the Legal Division of OMGUS, I dealt with matters within the jurisdiction of the Allied Control Council as well as with those pertaining to the American zonal government.

As mentioned earlier, the Control Council was responsible for "matters affecting Germany as a whole." During the three years of the Council's activity, it was never clearly defined what these matters were. In general, it may be said that acting as the central government of Germany—in addition to implementing basic objectives of the occupation such as demilitarization or denazification—the Control Council took over fields which under the former German constitution had been handled by the federal government.

The Control Council enacted tax laws, established administrative courts, and fixed a standard time for Germany. It even enacted a "marriage law" which is in force to this day. The need for this law arose from the fact that the German marriage law was tainted with Nazi ideology, in particular with racist elements. As people persisted in getting married, desperate conditions notwithstanding, a law purged of Nazi ideology was urgently needed. Control Council Law No. 16 on Marriage was enacted on February 20, 1946. Actions such as these, which intrude upon the private life of individuals are generally not within the purview of occupation authorities under international law. They were, nevertheless, taken by the Control Council in the absence of a German governmental organization capable of dealing with these matters.

Without going into detail about the somewhat complicated organization of the Control Council, it may suffice here to say that the preparatory work for the Control Council's actions passed through a layer of committees, sub-committees and working parties.

Shortly after my arrival in Berlin, I became the American member of the Committee on the Reform of German Law. Its function was to identify Nazi provisions in German legislation and to prepare for their repeal through Control Council legislation.

Headquarters of the Allied Control Council and its committees was the building of the former Prussian Supreme Court, the *Kammergericht*, in the American sector of Berlin. At the entrance the flags of the four occupying powers were hoisted on huge poles. As the chairmanship of the Control Council and its committees passed to a different nation each month, so the guards changed in front of the building. Even the order of the flags was rearranged in accordance with the rotation of the chairmanship.

The building was not unfamiliar to me. In one of its rooms I had taken the written tests and the oral examination as a candidate for the judicial and higher administrative service in January 1924. When I started my duties with the Control Council committee I looked for the room where I had undergone this ordeal and found it. Here I was, twenty-two years later, an American citizen in an American uniform, member of an occupation force. Not by the wildest stretch of the imagination would I have been able to visualize myself in this role.

The discussions in the committee were conducted in the languages of the occupying powers. Likewise, all documents had to be prepared in three languages. We were surrounded by interpreters and translators. The subject of our deliberations, German law, had to be produced in English, French and Russian. Every word of a delegate had to be translated into each of the other two languages, an incredibly cumbersome procedure which made real progress impossible. We found the only reasonable solution: we agreed—without informing our superiors—that we would communicate exclusively in German which we all understood. The Russian representative had studied German law; the British delegate had been a lawyer in Berlin; the French member was a judge from Alsace-Lorraine who used German in his court; and my knowledge of German had not deteriorated.

The committee met twice a week, hardly enough time to cope with the amount of work that seemed to grow rather than diminish as time went by. There were the large codes that had to be scrutinized, such as the codes of civil and criminal procedures. In addition, we had to prepare legislation on matters which urgently required attention by the Control Council, such as citizenship for Jews and other victims of Nazi persecution who wished to return to Germany as well as for the millions of people

Berlin

From Prewar Years to World War II

50. Residence of the President of the Reich

51. The same Building 1945

52. Berliners amidst their ruined city

53. Coming Home

who because of their German origin had been expelled after the war from Poland, Czechoslovakia, and Hungary (the so-called "expellees").

Only a fraction of our work saw the light of day in the *Official Gazette*. The Council's decisions required unanimity. It became increasingly difficult to arrive at unanimous decisions, in particular in the economic field. Under the Potsdam Declaration of August 2, 1945, on postwar policies, Germany was to be treated as a single economic unit. France refused to cooperate for fear of a united Germany, and Western economic concepts were irreconcilable with a Soviet-style economy.

The Soviet blockade of Berlin in June of 1948 in the wake of the currency reform in the Western zones (more about it later) brought about the demise of the Control Council. It ceased to function after the Soviets walked out. Although never officially dissolved, the Control Council has remained inactive to this day while the Allied Kommandantura—minus the Soviet representative—continues to govern the Western sectors of Berlin.

A few military missions in Berlin are relics of the time when the Control Council was the central government of Germany. A Canadian and a Netherland Military Mission are the lone survivors of the many missions which had been accredited to the Control Council as diplomatic representatives of their respective countries immediately after the war (there even had been a Chinese Military Mission).

Some remnants of quadripartite cooperation have survived the breakdown of the four-power administration, notably the Berlin Air Safety Center (it still meets in the old Prussian court building) established in 1946 by quadripartite resolution "with the object of ensuring safety of flight for all aircraft in the Berlin area." The War Criminal Prison in Berlin-Spandau, with Rudolf Hess as its sole inmate, was in operation until August 1987 when Hess died at the age of 93, an apparent suicide.

In 1969 I saw Rudolf Hess in his Spandau prison cell during a routine inspection of the prison by the American general. The old man with the deepset eyes, who had once been at the epicenter of power in Germany, presented a pathetic sight in his shabby brown suit. Upon being asked by the general about his well-being, he stood at attention and answered with a soft voice that he had no complaints. As we departed, the door of his tiny cell was locked again. Only a few wardens remained in the high-ceilinged hall around which lay the cells.

More than forty years have passed since the first war criminals were incarcerated in Spandau. The routine of life at the prison remained the same from its inception until the day of Hess' death. Military patrols, armed with rifles, made their rounds twenty-four hours a day on top of the brick wall surrounding the prison. The guards rotated monthly among the four occupying powers. The changing of the guard was performed with all the trappings of a solemn military ceremony in the presence of military and civilian guests. The parade was followed by a banquet in the prison's officers mess given by the outgoing power in a style customary of the host nation. The banquet offered an opportunity for regular contacts, a forum for talks, in particular, between Western and Soviet officials—a useful by-product of the Spandau prison routine. But what a macabre background!

Hess' detention became a problem. According to Anglo-Saxon concepts of retributive justice, Hess should have been eligible for parole many years before his death. However, any act of clemency required the unanimous approval of all four powers. The Soviets steadfastly refused to agree. A Soviet officer once told me that Hitler's attack had cost the Russians twenty million dead. "It would be an intolerable imposition upon the Russian people to grant Hitler's deputy an act of clemency such as a premature release from prison."

Hess' guilt may have been less than that of some of the concentration camp murderers who got away with prison sentences of a few years. Hess paid the price for his position in the Nazi hierarchy. Hitler's deputy took the place of his master even in the punishment for his crimes.

Despite the best intentions on our part, the experiment of a four-power administration of Germany with the Control Council as the supreme governing body was doomed to failure. The Soviets, from the moment of their entrance into Germany, considered themselves as conquerors in the most primitive sense of the word. Industry, agriculture and labor in the territory

Berlin

Under Allied Occupation

54. American Headquarters Building on Clay Allee

55. Spandau War Criminal Prison: Changing of the Guards between the Americans and the Soviets

56. "Villa Reitzenstein" (Stuttgart). Seat of the *Länderrat*, U.S. Zone of Occupation

57. The Author as Military Government Officer

they occupied were considered spoils of war and objects of exploitation for the benefit of the U.S.S.R. They imposed upon the conquered people a political order modeled along the lines of their own system, namely dictatorship and one-party rule—a system, incidentally, which the German people when granted a free choice have consistently rejected as alien to their tradition, their mentality and their concept of a life worth living.

The Western Allies, on the other hand, were bent on assisting the German people in reconstructing their political order on principles of democracy and freedom. The Germans themselves were to develop institutions of popular self-government. As stated in the directive of the Joint Chiefs of Staff of July 11, 1947, to the Commander-in-Chief of the American occupation forces: "Your Government does not wish to impose its own historically developed forms of democracy and social organization on Germany and believes equally firmly that no other external forms should be imposed." The final goal of the Western Allies was the reintegration of the German people into the community of free nations as an independent member with equal rights.

The political differences between the Soviets and the Western Allies engendered mistrust. We never succeeded in establishing personal contacts with our Russian colleagues in the Control Council committee.

At quadripartite parties prescribed by the protocol, the Russians appeared in groups. They remained isolated, stayed together the entire time, and left after only a brief stay. Invitations to share meals in our mess hall or to watch American movies were routinely declined, courteously but firmly. Did they fear ideological contagion from close association with our way of life?

Because of its inherent contradictions aggravated by Soviet obstructionism and French intransigence, the Control Council was incapable of moving toward the reconstruction of Germany's political and economic order. As a result, the practical administration of Germany shifted from the central authority to the zone commanders.

In the American zone the process of political reconstruction started with the formation of administrative areas called states or, according to German usage, *Länder*. They included Bavaria,

practically unchanged from its pre-war existence as one of the
federal states of the Weimar Republic; Württemberg-Baden, a
combination of parts of the two former states; and Greater Hesse,
composed of Prussian territories and the former state of Hesse.
In January of 1947, the city of Bremen was separated from the
British zone and included in the American zone. Proclamation
No. 2 of September 19, 1945, defined the legal status of these
areas as "states exercising, subject to the authority of Military
Government, full legislative, judicial and executive powers." The
nucleus of a new form of German self-government had been
created in the American zone only a few months after Germany's
collapse.

The next step on the agenda of the American Military
Government was the establishment of state governments
composed of representatives of political parties which the
occupation authorities had allowed to be formed, largely from
those that had existed in 1933, with the obvious omission
of the Nazi party. Established parties which returned after
having been outlawed by the Nazis were the Social Democratic
party of Germany (SPD) and the Communist party (KPD).
Members of the old Catholic Center party and Protestant elements
rallied round Christian politicians of both persuasions to form
the Christian Democratic Union (CDU); Bavarian Christians
remained a separate group under the name of Christian Social
Union (CSU). Liberal-democratic elements joined together to
establish parties which were named differently in the various
states (in Württenberg the German Popular party, in Bavaria
the Free Democratic party). Marginal parties were banned
or persuaded by the Military Government to work within the
established parties.

The state governments were headed by ministers-president.
Pending the adoption of constitutions which would regulate
legislative procedures, the ministers-president were authorized
by the Military Government to enact laws. "For the validity
of state laws," Proclamation No. 2 provided, "it suffices that
they have been approved by the ministers-president and have
been published." It was the policy of the American Military
Government to abstain from legislating for the Germans.
Legislation should be a German responsibility, and laws should

be German laws even though they derived their binding force from the supreme authority of the occupying power. Under this system, each minister-president was in theory free to enact whatever law in whatever field he deemed appropriate and useful for his state. The unlimited exercise of this power was bound to lead to administrative disorder and fragmentation where uniformity was imperative, especially in fields for which the early quadripartite agreements had planned central agencies, such as finance, postal services, communications, transportation, foreign trade, and agriculture. In order to avoid legal and economic disruption, coordination of the actions of the ministers-president was required. This was achieved, upon the suggestion of the Military Government, by the creation of a coordinating agency called the *Länderrat* (Council of States) in November of 1945.

The function of the *Länderrat* was, "within the framework of the political guidelines of the occupying power, to settle by joint deliberations all questions transcending the territory of one state, to eliminate difficulties in the relations among the states and to assure uniformity of development in the political, economic, social and cultural life." The *Länderrat* consisted of the ministers-president of the states of the American zone. The chairmanship rotated among the ministers-president at a three-month interval. All decisions had to be unanimous and were made by the ministers-president personally. The site of the monthly meetings of the *Länderrat* was a palatial villa on the hills overlooking Stuttgart, capital of Württenberg.

The *Länderrat* was not a legislative body. The ministers-president were authorized to enact laws as before. The function of the *Länderrat* in the legislative process was limited to preparing and coordinating the texts of those laws which required zonal uniformity. Ultimate decision rested with the Military Government; its approval was required before a law could be enacted and promulgated.

In no other zone had the drive for the establishment of responsible self-government made such rapid progress as in the American zone. "Clay's policy was certainly superior to that of his counterparts in the other zones where self-government was delayed for months," and, generally, "proceeded in a leisurely pace." (Edward N. Peterson, *The American Occupation of*

Germany. Retreat to Victory. Detroit 1977, p. 175.) Military
Government in the British zone was based, it has been said, on
British experience in dealing with subject peoples. It assumed
semi-colonial character as a huge corps of British officials
descended upon the British zone assisted on the German side by
technical advisers rather than politicians. In the French zone,
states with their own constitution were created only in 1947;
they were not even allowed to communicate with one another.
The French considered their zone (which, incidentally, had been
carved out of territories originally assigned to the British and
American zones) primarily an object for economic exploitation.
They administered their zone as an area virtually independent
from the rest of Germany. The Soviet zone was ruled, in the
words of the late Secretary of State George Marshall, by a regime
that "exercised a monopolistic stranglehold over the economic and
political life of the zone which made that region little more than a
dependent province of the Soviet Union."

I had been assigned responsibility for all matters connected
with the *Länderrat*. I made it a habit to attend the monthly
meetings of its legal committee as an observer. This meant that I
could inform OMGUS of legislative proposals in advance and thus
enable OMGUS to raise possible objections before the *Länderrat*
took action. Furthermore, I could answer on the spot questions as
to whether a proposed law might conflict with occupation policies.
I was thereby able to speed up procedures and to contribute to
a better understanding between the Germans and the occupation
authorities.

The chairmanship of the committee rotated in the early days
among the ministers of justice of the states until a permanent
chairman was agreed upon. The first chairman was Dr. Zinn,
Hesse Minister of Justice. During the last two years of
its existence the chairmanship of the *Länderrat* was held by
Dr. Joseph Beyerle, Minister of Justice of Württemberg-Baden.

Members of the committee were, among others, Dr. Arndt,
a prominent constitutional lawyer and in later years legal adviser
to the Social Democratic group in the federal parliament; the
Stuttgart lawyer Dr. Küster, an expert on matters relating to
reparation for victims of Nazi persecution; and Dr. Martens,
deputy president of the Court of Appeals in Karlsruhe. Secretary

of the committee was Dr. von Arnim who rose to a high position in the future federal Ministry of Justice.

As can be seen from this brief survey, the members of the legal committee were jurists of outstanding caliber. Their professional competence was reflected in the level of their discussions. My own experience confirmed the judgment of a German observer on the committee's performance: "Exceptional knowledge, a gift for brilliant formulations, a critical mind that came both from intelligence and from the heart—this created an atmosphere which evoked the highest degree of responsibility" (H. Klein). I was, in particular, impressed by Dr. Beyerle's summations of the discussions, his ability to get all essential points recorded in the minutes in concise language. This group was indeed well qualified to restore German law to the high standard it possessed before it fell into the abyss of Nazi lawlessness; the legal philosophy of its members had proven impervious to the corruptive influence of the Nazi era. The Military Government could rest assured that the committee's work would be guided by the principles of a democratic legal order.

At the end of 1946 (in Bremen in 1947) the states of the American zone adopted democratic constitutions. With the entry into force of constitutions, legislation became the responsibility of the state parliaments. Furthermore, the ministers-president and their cabinets were from now on dependent upon the confidence of the elected parliaments in the conduct of their offices.

The Military Government had expected that the state parliaments would be willing to take over laws approved by the *Länderrat* for uniform application in the zone. This, however, proved to be wrong. The parliaments refused to adopt laws in whose preparation they had not participated. The Military Government was faced again with the danger of diversified state legislation and a resulting chaos which the institution of the *Länderrat* had been designed to avert. The difficulty was overcome by a simple expedient: With respect to all laws which required zonal uniformity, the power of the chief executives of the states to legislate was maintained. In all other matters, the parliaments were free to act.

"Legislation by decree" under the special authority granted to the ministers-president, a residue from the pre-constitutional period, confronted the Military Government with a dilemma: the procedure suffered from the opprobrium of being authoritarian, undemocratic.   Its use as a regular way to legislate for any length of time was bound to cause irreparable harm to the newly adopted constitutions. On the one hand, the legislative power of the ministers-president could not be dispensed with for the sake of zonal uniformity.   On the other hand, the state parliaments had to be brought into the legislative process. This requirement was met by expanding the *Länderrat* in March 1947 to include a Parliamentary Council composed of twenty-four representatives elected by the state parliaments.   Although the Council had only advisory functions, the ministers-president never adopted legislation without the Council's approval.

The *Länderrat* existed for almost three years.   Not only was its establishment a significant advance toward German self-government; its work contributed a major share to the reconstruction and development of Germany's economy and her legal order. Thus, the *Länderrat* started a program of land reform by setting aside areas for settlement.   The irregular flow of millions of expellees from the East was brought under control and was directed into proper channels.

An important part of the work of the *Länderrat* was the elimination of remnants of the Nazi tyranny.   A "Law for Liberation from National Socialism and Militarism" of March 5, 1946 (drafted mostly upon direction of the Military Government) defined four classes of former Nazis (major offenders, offenders, lesser offenders, and followers) who were subject to various penalties.   It established special tribunals to provide a judicial hearing for each person affected by the law.   A comprehensive "Law on Redress of National Socialist Wrongs" assured adequate financial compensation to victims of Nazi persecution. Furthermore, names that had been forced upon Jews could be stricken from the record. Nazi persecutees who had been denied a civil marriage for political or racial reasons under National Socialist legislation were given a chance to have their liaison turned into a legal marriage by merely applying to the appropriate minister of justice.

The *Länderrat* has the reputation of having been the most successful experiment of American occupation policy. After a decade of dictatorship, it practiced the art of political compromise in addition to its extensive legislative work. In June of 1948, General Lucius D. Clay, in his farewell speech before the *Länderrat*, confirmed that it had stood the test as a democratic institution.

In March of 1948, I was transferred from Berlin to Frankfurt am Main to the Legal Group of the Bipartite Control Office. (Its organization will be described later.)

When I arrived, the old part of Frankfurt was still a heap of rubble—the opera house a burnt-out shell, and the Rothschild park a weedy wilderness. It was a scene of total devastation such as I had found everywhere I went in Germany since my return.

After a brief interval in a bank, the legal group moved into offices in the IG-Farben building, the headquarters of American military units and occupation authorities since April 1945. The entire area around the building—whole city blocks between Miquel Allee in the north, Fürstenbergstrasse in the south, Siesmayerstrasse in the west and Öder Weg and Eckenheimerstrasse in the east—was surrounded by a high barbed-wire fence. Situated at a distance from the center of the town, the area was the only part of the town which had survived the war practically undamaged. All houses in the area had been seized, and their residents evacuated to accommodate military and civilian personnel of the occupying power.

We lived in a "forbidden city," in total isolation from the rest of Frankfurt. Entry into this vast compound was through a few checkpoints by special authorization. The only Germans allowed inside were employees of the military administration, janitors, maids, cleaning personnel, mechanics. The fence was not always as secure as it should have been. Attempts were occasionally made to "smuggle in" unauthorized persons. In this supposedly protected zone I suffered the only major burglary of my life. One evening, when I came home from the office I found my wardrobe wide open. All my clothes were gone. At that time clothing was a particularly sought-after item on the black market. The perpetrators were never apprehended. Military police were powerless, and accidents like these were just "occupational hazards."

During the Soviet blockade of Berlin from June 1948 to May of 1949, Frankfurt's military airfield was the southern pier of an "air bridge" to Berlin. I often stood on the road leading to the air field to watch the planes as they arrived and left in a continuous procession. It was a fascinating spectacle and a demonstration of the power and firm resolve of the United States to meet Soviet aggression together with the courageous people of Berlin.

The details of this "most unexpected and least likely Western triumph in the history of postwar Soviet-American confrontation" have been described in a masterly summary by Daniel F. Harrington in his contribution to *American History Illustrated* (vol. 16, February 1982) titled "Against All Odds." A few facts are worth recalling in the present context.

General Clay is reported to have feared the worst when, on June 15, 1948, he ordered an airlift of food and supplies into the city of Berlin which had been suddenly blockaded the day before by the Soviet army. Asked by a friend whether he thought an airlift could defeat the blockade, Clay was "emphatically negative." "I wouldn't give you t-h-a-t," he said, snapping his fingers, "for our chances." The London *Times* described the effort as a "brave but futile gesture."

Before the blockade, some 13,500 tons of food, coal, and other necessities had come into Berlin each day by road and rail. When the airlift began, Clay had about one hundred aging twin-engine planes at his disposal built to carry passengers, not cargo. With seats removed, they could haul two and a half tons at a time. When Clay asked his air force commander, Lieutenant General Curtis E. LeMay, whether he had planes that could carry coal, the General at first thought he had not heard correctly. Upon repeated questioning, he replied that the air force could deliver anything.

Reinforcement of Clay's tiny air force was imperative. The airlift was bound to fail without it. The U.S. air force possessed a few hundred four-engine transport planes to move men and equipment. Clay asked President Truman to commit virtually the entire air cargo fleet to the airlift. But was it prudent to deprive the United States defense system of this element of critical importance in the event of war and to concentrate the planes on a handful of bases close to Soviet forces? Truman took the risk and sent the planes to Germany. They came from Panama, Alaska, Hawaii, from Montana, Texas, and Japan. Also British planes flew in from around the world—Australia and Canada, India and Singapore. By August 4, the daily average of food and coal delivered to Berlin was over 4,000 tons. A vast network of supply depots and maintenance for the airlift fleet was established, stretching across two continents. Repairs were handled on British and American air bases as far away as the West Coast of the United States. Aviation fuel was brought in from everywhere to satisfy the unprecedented demand. A fleet of ships and planes was continuously hauling spare parts and rebuilt equipment. Reservists were called to active duty to be trained in Montana for airlift duty under conditions parallel to those in Germany.

The Allied air corridors to Berlin were turned into one-way airlanes. Planes flew at different altitudes and were spaced exactly three minutes apart. Flight plans and loading and unloading times were coordinated down to the smallest detail so that in the end a "steady, even rhythm was produced with hundreds of planes doing exactly the same thing every hour, day and night, at the same persistent beat."

Eventually there were too many planes flying to Berlin. Tempelhof airbase almost broke down under the pounding of landings and takeoffs. A new airport had to be built. This was the beginning of Tegel airfield. It was constructed of rubble left from wartime British and American air raids and became the longest runway in Europe.

I could gauge what "Operation Vittles"—the name Americans gave the airlift—demanded of the young pilots when I saw their pale, worn-out faces at breakfast in the officers mess of the IG-Farben building. They came from overcrowded bases where two or three of them often had to share the same bed. They were lucky to get five hours of sleep a day. Defying the worst weather conditions, they flew in rain and snow and even in dense fog, at the risk of their lives. Accidents did happen. Men who had been enemies only three years before, sacrificed their lives for the Berliners. The airlift monument at Tempelhof airfield is dedicated to their memory. The inscription reads: "They gave their lives for the freedom of Berlin in the service of the airlift 1948-49."

On April 16, 1949, the amount of supplies flown into Berlin reached over 12,900 tons. The Russians gave up. On May 12, the blockade was lifted and free access to Berlin by road, rail, and water was restored.

Besides having served as the southern pier of the Berlin air bridge, Frankfurt, the old coronation city of German kings and emperors became, in 1949, the administrative center of the greater part of West Germany.

On December 2, 1946, the governments of the United States and the United Kingdom had signed a Memorandum of Agreement on Economic Fusion of Their Respective Zones of Occupation in Germany; it was to take effect on January 1, 1947. The two governments had taken this step out of dire economic necessity. Soviet and French obstruction in the Control Council had frustrated all efforts on the part of the two Anglo-Saxon powers to treat Germany as an economic unit in accordance with the Potsdam Agreement of August 2, 1945, and to establish central agencies for the administration of specified economic fields. Both the French and Soviet zones were being administered without regard to the other zones. None of the zones were, in fact, self-supporting. The American taxpayer spent $200 million a year for food to save the people in the American zone from starvation. As a result of this "administration by compartments," Germany was threatened with economic paralysis. In the view of the American and British governments, an attempt should at least be made to treat the U.S. and British zones as an economic unit "as the first step towards the achievement of the economic unity of Germany as a whole if the policy agreed to in Potsdam could not be put into effect." In the words of Secretary of State Marshall, "Certainly some progress towards economic unity in Germany is better than none."

The merger of the U.S. and British zones for the purpose of a joint administration of the bizonal economy was accompanied by the establishment of a German governmental organization; it was a measure of decisive importance for the evolution of the political and economic reconstruction of Germany. Since 1946, the organization had developed in stages by trial and error. It had achieved its final form when I came to Frankfurt in March of 1948.

The Bizonal Economic Administration (*Die Verwaltung des Vereinigten Wirtschaftsgebietes*) had its seat in Frankfurt. It had come onto existence by fiat of the occupation authorities (Proclamation No. 7 of February 9, 1948) and was a mixture of Anglo-Saxon and German constitutional principles: strict separation of powers combined with traditions of German federalism and parliamentary democracy.

Legislative power resided in the Economic Council (*Wirtschaftsrat*). Its 144 members were elected by the state parliaments. While the Economic Council represented the people of "Bizonia" (the name popularly given to the combined U.S. and British zones), the constituent states were represented in the Council of States (*Länderrat*, not to be confused with the Stuttgart *Länderrat*, which had ceased operations on September 2, 1948). The members of the Council of States—two for each state after the model of the U.S. Senate—were appointed by their respective state governments. Enactment of laws called ordinances (*Verordnungen*) required consensus between the Economic Council and the Council of States. The Speaker of the Economic Council was Dr. Erich Köhler, a member of the Hesse Christian Democratic Union (CDU). He later became the first speaker of the Parliament of the Federal Republic of Germany.

Executive power was exercised by the Administrative Council (*Verwaltungsrat*) which functioned as the government of the bizonal area. It was composed of the directors of six functional offices dealing with economic affairs; agriculture and forestry; transportation; postal services and telecommunication; finance; and labor. The directors formed a cabinet presided over by a Coordinating Chairman (*Vorsitzender des Verwaltungsrats* or *Oberdirektor* for short). He and the directors were elected by the Economic Council to whom they were responsible and which could dismiss them by vote of nonconfidence.

The coordinating chairman was Dr. Herman Pünder. In the days of the Weimar Republic he had been state secretary in the Reich chancellery and, like all other members of the bizonal government, belonged to the CDU.

The judicial power of the Bizonal Area was vested in the German High Court for the Combined Economic Area (*Deutsches Obergericht für das Vereingte Wirtschaftsgebiet*), which was set up by Allied Proclamation No. 8, dated February 9, 1948. The court had its seat in Cologne. As stated in its statutes, the function of the court was "to facilitate the uniform application, interpretation and execution of laws enacted by the Economic Council." Disputes in connection with Economic Council laws could arise between the Economic Council and individual states or between the states, and in civil and criminal proceedings. The German High Court acted in the dual capacity of a constitutional tribunal and a court of last resort. Its functions were similar to those of the United States Supreme Court; it was a novelty in the German court system. Also originating from Anglo-Saxon legal concepts was the provision that decisions of the High Court on questions of law should have "binding effect." To that end, the operative part of a decision was published in the *Legal Gazette* of the Economic Council (later, for a short time, in the *Federal Legal Gazette*).

In its capacity as a parliament with speeches and debates and as the source of a flood of laws which affected everyone's daily life, the Economic Council was very much in the public eye. The German High Court, on the other hand, acted in almost total seclusion. E. Krumme, a former member of the court and later a federal justice, attributed ignorance of its significance to the fact that it was a "foreign element" and not rooted in German legal tradition. Furthermore, recourse to the court could be had only after legal remedies in the lower courts had been exhausted. It took considerable time before decisions of the German High Court were made public.

President of the court was Dr. Herbert Ruscheweyh, also President of the Court of Appeals and of the Supreme Administrative Court in Hamburg. Vice President was Dr. Hans Lukaschek, former provincial governor in Upper Silesia and minister for expellee matters in the first cabinet of Chancellor Adenauer. To my great surprise, one of the members of the court was Dr. Werner Zachariae. As ministerial counselor in the Prussian ministry of finance in 1928, he had graded and accepted my study on the *Reform of the Prussian Administration* which I had prepared in Gumbinnen as the required thesis for my final examination when my tour of duty in East Prussia had ended.

The jurisprudence of the court fills only a single volume. This might appear at first sight as somewhat embarrassing, but Justice Krumme has fully explained it: "The German High Court was established to last only for a transitional period in which to lay the groundwork for legal unity in the state now being formed [a reference to the Federal Republic of Germany]. As a consequence, the number of its decisions may appear small. The cases, however, which were submitted to the court presented immense difficulties owing to the profusion of bizonal regulations pertinent to the cases. . . . The often highly complicated opinions of the court prove: Implementation of the judicial function assigned to the court was by no means a sinecure."

Attached to the court was a Solicitor General (*Generalanwalt*), likewise a novelty in the German judicial system and a brainchild of OMGUS lawyers who had drafted the court statute in the image of Anglo-Saxon legal institutions. The solicitor general had the function "to represent the public interest" in litigations before the High Court, which meant primarily that he had to ensure that legal uniformity was preserved within the Bizonal Economic Area.

To this end he was authorized to intervene in cases pending before lower courts when laws of the Economic Council were in dispute. He was thus able to bring the case before the High Court even against the wishes of the parties. The court was given a chance to interpret the law with binding force for the whole Bizonal Economic Area.

The solicitor general depended upon the cooperation of the German courts for the discharge of his duties. Only from them could he learn whether a case required his intervention. The Military Government was fully aware of the fact that German courts would not act on their own initiative in this matter since they had no previous experience with the functions of a solicitor general. There were no directives, no prescribed procedures, no forms. In order to make the system work, the Military Government, by a "Regulation under Proclamation No. 8" of April 4, 1949, ordered the presidents of German state courts of last resort to inform the solicitor general of all proceedings involving legal questions which were within the jurisdiction of the High Court. At his frequent visits to the legal group Dr. Quambusch, the Solicitor General, bitterly complained about the lack of cooperation between his office and the German courts. He once spoke of a "wall of silence" surrounding the High Court. The German courts, he added, had neglected "in an absolutely outrageous manner" their legal duty to inform him of proceedings relevant to his office.

One of the reasons for the indifference of the courts to his office, Dr. Quambusch suggested, might have been their mistrust of the High Court as a creation of the occupation authorities. In any case, the institution of the solicitor general was something unaccustomed and far removed from their experience. Time and a certain amount of good will were required before the courts would report relevant cases to the solicitor general as a matter of bureaucratic routine. Furthermore, at the very time when cases had passed through lower courts and were ready for submission to the High Court, the Federal Republic was about to come into existence and replace the bizonal governmental organization. On December 27, 1951, the court was dissolved. Its functions were taken over by the Constitutional Court of the Federal Republic of Germany.

The German bizonal administration was a creation of the Military Government which was, at the same time, its controlling agency. A vast new machinery was set up to exercise this function.

At the apex of the control structure stood the Bipartite Board in Berlin. It consisted of the two Military Governors, General Clay acting for the United States and General Sir Brian Robertson for Great Britain, and a staff of advisers. At the regional level and in close contact with the German agencies was the Bipartite Control Office (BICO) with its seat in Frankfurt. Joint chairmen were Major General Clarence L. Adcock for the United States and Lieutenant General Sir Gordon McReady for the British side. Their staff was divided into bipartite panels called "groups" to deal with the various fields of administration corresponding to the directorates of the German Bizonal Administration. They were integrated U.S./British units; if the chairman was an American, his deputy was British, and vice versa. A decision required unanimity of the chairman and his deputy.

Ordinances of the Economic Council were subject to approval by the Bipartite Board. The BICO legal group had the function of reviewing proposed legislation to ensure that it conformed with "international, multi-partite and Military Government laws as well as existing German law" before it was submitted to the Bipartite Board. Again, knowledge of German legal terminology and legislative practice was essential for a speedy and effective review. There were translations, but they were no substitutes for the original German text.

In the legal group, I was in charge of reviewing Economic Council legislation for the American side. My British colleague, Bernhard Wolff, was, like me, well versed in German law. He had been a lawyer in Berlin. Together with his brother Ernst who had been president of the Berlin Lawyers Association, he had emigrated to England in 1938 because of "non-Aryan" descent. The grandfather of the two brothers was Eduard von Simson, the speaker of the Frankfurt National Assembly of 1848, later the speaker of the German parliament of the 1871 Constitution, and, from 1879-1891, the first president of the German Supreme Court at Leipzig.

Both brothers had returned to Germany after the war. Ernst became President of the Supreme Court for the British Zone of Occupation in Cologne; Bernard took a position with the Military Government in the British zone before being transferred to the Bipartite Control Office in Frankfurt. After the dissolution of BICO and the founding of the Federal Republic of Germany, he started a new career in Germany when he was appointed justice at the Federal Constitutional Court in Karlsruhe.

Out of a total of 171 Economic Council ordinances, the Military Government vetoed only eight. Two were turned down on the ground that they delegated legislative authority to administrative agencies. This was a common flaw in German laws and of particular concern to the occupation authorities because it violated the constitutional principle of the separation of powers. In another case, the Economic Council had exceeded its legislative authority. Several laws suffered from technical defects or were incompatible with objectives of the occupation.

The relative calm on the legislative front was due primarily to the close cooperation between occupation and German authorities. However, things did not always run smoothly. Major, protracted conflicts between the Military Government and the Bizonal Administration arose, in particular, with respect to legislative proposals dealing with the freedom of trade and the civil service. Military Government considered German institutions in these fields undemocratic and in need of reform. It was believed that "authoritarianism" in traditional German institutions was partly responsible for the rise of Nazism. In order to make victory meaningful, it was an objective of the occupation to reconstruct German institutions which, in the view of the Military Government, were defective in this regard.

Under the Nazis, freedom of trade had, for all practical purposes, been abolished.

After Germany's collapse and in the absence of a central government, the states tried to take remedial action. The results were laws that differed widely from one state to another, causing economic disruption.

In view of this chaotic situation, the Economic Council considered it one of its most urgent tasks to establish uniform legislation in this field.

The proposed Economic Council legislation was based on the time-honored principle that anyone wishing to enter a trade or profession needed a license. The license could be denied if the applicant either lacked the necessary skills or professional knowledge or if facts existed which indicated that the applicant was unreliable.

Professor Ludwig Erhard, Director of the Office of Economic Affairs, and initiator of the proposal, justified the licensing requirement by arguing that the public needed to be protected. "The test of professional and personal, and, if you wish, also moral qualifications must be maintained," he declared when he introduced the draft legislation into the Economic Council.

Erhard's philosophy of trade licensing was in stark contrast to the policy of the American Military Government. The licensing of activities of individuals and corporations in trades and the professions was considered undemocratic. Licensing could be tolerated only if required for reasons of public safety, health, and welfare. Under no circumstances should an inquiry into the reliability or the moral character of a person be allowed. Furthermore, in the estimation of the Military Government, the licensing practice of the states, had impeded productivity and had proved to be an obstacle to economic recovery. Millions of refugees and expellees from the East had met with insuperable difficulties when confronted with the necessity of obtaining a license when they tried to establish themselves in business.

The licensing law of the Economic Council accordingly was disapproved. The Bipartite Board, however, did not base its disapproval on the grounds advanced by the Military Government. Owing to the reluctance of the Allies to discuss the issue with the Germans on its merits, the Board used a rather far-fetched, if not disingenuous, argument. Allowing the Economic Council—a kind of federal legislative body above the individual states—to legislate in the fields of trade licensing might prejudice the distribution of legislative competencies between a future federal government and its constituent states then under discussion in Bonn. A long list of counter-arguments by the Economic Council was curtly dismissed. The Bipartite Board merely replied that after examining the Council's request for reconsideration the Board's decision was "reaffirmed."

An incident I still vividly recall demonstrated how much the fronts had hardened between the Military Government which was trying to create a free, democratic society entailing in the economic field unfettered freedom of trade and healthy competition, and the German authorities defending a traditional position. In a last attempt to overcome the resistance of the Military Government, the Economic Council submitted a new licensing law which they thought was in conformity with the restrictive licensing policy of the Military Government.

It still contained a clause on "personal reliability" by providing that a person might be excluded from a trade or profession if convicted for a criminal act which showed the person to be unfit for the trade or profession in question.

One morning I received a call from the American chairman of the group in charge of trade licensing. I was asked on short notice to act as interpreter at a meeting between the chairman and Professor Erhard. The subject of the conversation was the new

Economic Council licensing law. Erhard was sharply reminded
that the proposed law with its "reliability clause" violated the
express directives of the Military Government. He was informed
that General Clay had been outraged. The chairman also charged
Erhard with knowing exactly what the Military Government had
in mind. In spite of this, Erhard was told, he had failed to have the
new law amended; nor had he prevented submission of the draft to
the Economic Council. Erhard was accused of obstructionism and
disobedience to the Military Government.

The conversation lasted only a few minutes. Erhard was
hardly given a chance of replying. He left the meeting visibly
shaken. It should be noted that Erhard, as the creator of the
"Social Market Economy," already then enjoyed an international
reputation.

The Germans became convinced that there was no chance
of reconciling Allied and German views on trade licensing. As
stated in the final report of Dr. Köhler on the legislation of the
Economic Council, they simply dropped the matter.

Still, the question of freedom to engage in a trade or
profession remained an issue between the German government
and the Allies until the very end of the occupation. Eventually,
agreement was reached that on the question of trade licensing,
"the Basic Law of the Federal Republic of Germany was alone
decisive, and that the Federal Constitutional Court should have
the exclusive right to make binding decisions on the interpretation
of said Basic Law." The agreement was included in an exchange
of letters between the Federal Chancellor and the Allies of May
26, 1952; it was attached to the Paris Protocol on the Termination
of the Occupation Regime in the Federal Republic of October 23,
1954 and thereby was binding under international law.

Another subject high on the Allied reform agenda was the
German civil service. According to Allied concepts, the German
civil service was undemocratic, authoritarian and imbued with a
spirit of caste. In the view of the Allies, the only effective means
of eliminating these vital defects was a complete overhaul of the
German system using American and British experience in this
field as a model.

Initially the Allies tried to have the Germans work out the
reforms with the assistance of Allied experts. The resulting

legislation, the Allies declared, should be "German in its character and origin so far as it is consistent with the basic principles of the reform" as laid down in Allied directives. Endless discussions ensued between German representatives holding fast to entrenched positions and their Allied counterparts, pleading, cajoling, threatening. Deadlines were set, but not kept. Eventually, a draft Civil Service Act to govern the service relationship of bizonal employees emerged. It was scheduled to be considered by the Economic Council, after passage through various committees, on February 18, 1949, i.e. more than three months after the date set by the Military Government for submission to BICO.

It did not come to that. Irritated and feeling frustrated by the seemingly endless parliamentary proceedings, the two Military Governors ended the "creeping crisis" with a thunderclap. On February 15, they enacted, in the exercise of their supreme authority, identical texts of Military Government Law No. 15 on Bizonal Public Servants. By their lightning action only three days before parliamentary proceedings were to resume, the Military Governors demonstrated that they suspected the Germans of ill will if not outright attempt at sabotage.

The most radical innovation which Law No. 15 introduced into the German civil service system was what the Military Governors considered the very heart of the reform: the elimination of the traditional distinction between officials appointed for life and exercising "sovereign" functions (*Beamte*), and contractual employees (*Angestellte*) entrusted with less important tasks. This "two-track caste system," in the view of the occupation authorities, was the fundamental evil, the source of the authoritarian, undemocratic attitude of the German civil servant; his penchant for arrogance, his class consciousness and his self-complacency. The provision breaking with this long-established practice was curt and blunt: "All public servants are either officials or wage-earners."

The Military Government demanded that by May 15, 1949, all contract employees be converted to officials. This timetable was unrealistic and self-defeating. The financial consequences of establishing an untold number of civil service positions could not even be calculated approximately in the short time allowed.

It was illusory to think that 60,000 contract employees of the Bizonal Administration could be converted to officials within the same period of time.   Consequently, attempts by the bizonal authorities to comply with the directive of the Military Government failed completely.

The curtailment of political activities of public officials was another innovation of Military Government law No. 15 and likewise of primary concern to the Allies. Both in the days of the Empire and under the Weimar Republic there had never been any restraints on the political activities of public servants. They were free to campaign for political parties or programs and to be candidates for elective office. As a result, the percentage of public officials who were members of German parliaments had always been disproportionately high when compared with the general population. This overrepresentation of members of the executive branch in the legislatures was, in the view of the Military Government, incompatible with the principle of the separation of powers and the political neutrality of civil servants. Law No. 15 accordingly prescribed that an official could not be a candidate for elective office or engage in political activities in support of a particular party or political program. If the official was still interested in politics, he would have to resign his employment before accepting nomination as a candidate for election to a legislative body.

It was recognized by many inside and outside the service that the German civil service system needed reforming after the war. Its defects, however, could not be remedied "within a few months or years by means of external measures" (Brecht) or by the autocratic, hasty action of the Military Governors (Peterson). Alfred Weber, Nestor of the German Social Science, wrote that Law No. 15, "issued evidently in a fit of anger," had been "thrust into this situation [the German reform efforts] from the outside like a giant pole and had thrown everything into disarray. . . ."

Law No. 15 did not survive the Bizonal Administration for whose employees it was originally designed. It became ineffective simultaneously with the demise of *Bizonia*. Later Allied efforts to have the law extended to the civil servants of the Federal Republic of Germany failed, as did Allied attempts to have a say in the drafting of the planned federal civil service act. Was it really appropriate for the Allies to demand, as they did in a memorandum of January 1950 addressed to the federal chancellor on "Principles to Govern the Law on Public Servants," that "education for the higher German administrative service must be based on a comprehensive study of all fields of importance to modern administration and must not be limited to the study of law?" Could this be an objective of the occupation?

Efforts to introduce a new civil service system came at a time when German receptiveness to Allied reforms was on the wane. ". . . . the day for lecturing and preaching and for minor interferences in German domestic affairs has passed," George F. Kennan warned in a memorandum to the secretary of state of September 6, 1951, concerning the future relationship between the Germans and the occupation authorities.

> . . . . it is important that we recognize that the trappings and atmosphere of colonialism have not only lost their usefulness but stand in the way of progress in our dealings with the Germans. . . . Such things as the continuous fussing about decartelization and restitution and many of the elements of the pressure for reform and democratization, which still seem to occupy the time of our people in Germany, seem trivial anachronisms and caprices compared with the issues really at stake in the development of German affairs during the next two of three years. . . . I think we are in great danger. . . . of continuing measures of interference and control to the point where they are much more irritating to the Germans than useful to us.

I did not participate in the Allied-German negotiations since civil service reform was not one of the responsibilities of the legal group. However, as an interested observer, I gained the impression that some Allied representatives lacked the necessary understanding of the German institution which they were trying to reform. The German public service had developed over centuries to become a profession based on a specialized education and training toward a lifetime career dedicated to promoting the public good. It had evolved its own ethic. According to its precepts, the official is bound to the state by a particular relationship "requiring a higher degree of loyalty to permeate his entire life, public and private, than that expected of ordinary citizens."

History shows that attempts to transplant institutions from their native soil to foreign surroundings are doomed to failure. The Allies eventually recognized that the reform of the German civil service was solely a German responsibility.

The Federal Republic of Germany Under Allied Control

In the states of the western zones of occupation and on a higher level in the bizonal area, a form of democratic self-government had developed which was suited to serve as a model for an all-German constitution.

The decisive impetus toward progress in the political organization of Germany was provided by a conference held intermittently in London from February 23 until June 2, 1948, of representatives of the United States, Great Britain, France and the three Benelux countries on Germany.

The conference had been convened because the Council of Foreign Ministers of the four occupying powers in Moscow and London in 1947 had failed to reach quadripartite agreement on the treatment of Germany as an economic unit and a future German constitution. The Soviet government and the Western Allies were at odds, in particular, as to the form of a German government. The Soviet Union favored a strong central government. The United States and Great Britain were opposed because they thought that such a government could be easily converted into a regime similar to that of the Nazis. Consequently, it was agreed that the future German constitution instead of establishing a central government adapted to the seizure of absolute control should set up a "federal form of government which adequately protects the rights of the respective states, and which at the same time provides for adequate central authority and which guarantees the rights and freedoms of the individual."

As a first step in the process of rebuilding an all-German political structure, the conference agreed that the ministers-president of the states of the western zones should be authorized by the Military Governors to convene a "Constituent Assembly" to prepare a constitution of a democratic government on a federal basis for approval by the Allies. The constitution should "essentially be one of German devising and acceptance and should provide a basis and starting point for ultimate German unity." The conference realized that a fledgling German government would remain weak if exposed to the unlimited power of the occupation authorities. It was agreed that the Allies would exercise their supreme authority only in fields specifically reserved for them in an "Occupation Statute" while otherwise granting to the German government "broad executive, legislative and judicial power." The Statute would constitute "the legal basis for actions either by the occupation authorities or the German federal and state governments."

The political reconstruction was accompanied by the economic rehabilitation of Germany. One of the most serious obstacles to economic recovery, besides food shortage, the breakdown of the transport system, and the stagnation of industrial production, was the collapse of the currency. Monetary reform, long overdue, had been delayed as a result of the refusal of the Soviets in the Control Council to cooperate in a four-zone plan. It devolved upon the Military Governments in the western zones to take the necessary action. On June 20, 1948, people in the western zone were suddenly confronted with the introduction of a new currency. It hit them like a bolt of lightning. The plan had been the best kept secret of the occupation. It was the second such experience in my life, although this time I was not affected personally by it. In 1924, the return to a stable currency was like awakening from a nightmare. The shiny copper penny was again worth something. I was surprised to see how differently people reacted this time. They felt as though they had been impoverished overnight and put into the poorhouse. All the money they possessed was nothing but a heap of grimy paper. They were reduced to forty marks of the new currency which everybody received as a "quota per capita" (*Kopfbetrag*). On the other hand, the appearance of the new *Deutsche Mark* worked like a spring rain on plant life. Merchandise which had been kept hidden away suddenly appeared from nowhere. I remember a store on Friedrich-Ebert-Strasse in Frankfurt. A day after currency reform, it overflowed with watches and clocks of every description. In the evening the store was illuminated with glaring lights like a booth on a fairground where people are captivated by wondrous things. At the time, I could hardly have imagined that many years later I would live to see the day when, during a crisis on the foreign exchange market, German banks would coolly refuse to exchange my U.S. travelers' checks into *Deutsche Mark* (which, of course, we, the Americans, had created). On the same day I noticed on the front page of a German newspaper a cartoon, showing Uncle Sam with a pouch full of dollar bills being thrown out of a bank. "We don't need your dollars," the caption read. The rough treatment had caused some of the bills to fall out of the pouch onto the street.

The currency reform brought about one the severest postwar crises in the relations of the Allies with the Soviet Union. Because of its quadripartite status the inclusion of Berlin in the currency reform process required an understanding with the Soviets. The Allies had suggested retaining the old *Reichsmark* in Berlin provided the issuance of the currency would be controlled jointly by the four occupying powers. When the Soviets refused, the three Western Allies went ahead and introduced the *Deutsche Mark* into the western sectors of Berlin. This gave the Soviets a pretext for cutting Berlin off from all land and water connections with the western zones. Their aim was to dislodge the Western Powers from Berlin and starve the Berliners into submission and thus force the political and economic integration of the city into the Communist bloc. As described earlier, the Soviet blockade was ultimately defeated by General Clay's courageous and effective airlift.

In May 1949, work on the German federal constitution had been completed after a constitutional convention of representatives of the states had dealt with a draft from August 10 to 23, 1948, in a castle of the former Bavarian kings on Herrenchiemsee island. Subsequently a Parliamentary Council of delegates elected by the parliaments of the states with its seat in the Pedagogical Academy in Bonn adopted the final draft on May 8, 1949. Because its application was limited to the western occupation zones, and for this reason was considered provisional, the document was not given the designation of "Constitution," but was called the "Basic Law of the Federal Republic of Germany." On May 12, 1949, the Basic Law was approved by the three Military Governors and after ratification by the parliaments of the constituent states became effective on May 23, 1949.

Greater Berlin was listed among the states in which the Basic Law was to apply. This was incompatible with the status of Berlin as a territory outside the four occupation zones, and under quadripartite occupation. In order to safeguard that status, the Military Governors included in their Letter of Approval certain "reservations with respect to the participation of Greater Berlin in the Federation," in particular a statement that Berlin "may not be governed by the Federation." This had the effect that the power of the federal legislature did not extend to Berlin and that consequently federal laws did not *eo ipso* apply there. However, in order to preserve legal uniformity with the Federal Republic, a practice developed whereby federal laws are "taken over" by Berlin. They are enacted as Berlin legislation by means of a so-called "covering law." Furthermore, while Berlin was authorized to send delegates to the Federal Parliament (*Bundestag*) and the Federal Council (*Bundesrat*), the Military Governors directed that they should have no voting rights but would attend meetings of the federal legislative bodies in a consultative capacity.

On August 14, 1949, the German people in the three western zones elected the parliament of the Federal Republic. Apart from previous regional elections, this was the first free election on a national level in Germany since 1932.

With the establishment of the federal government by September 21, 1949, the organization of the Federal Republic was completed. This date marks its birthday.

The Federal Republic of Germany derives its legitimacy from the will of the German people. Its constitution embodies the rule of law, judicial guarantee of basic human rights, a federal system and democratic procedures in the best of pre-Hitler German traditions. The coming into existence of the Federal Republic, however, did not result in the transfer of the supreme governmental power which the Allies had assumed upon the defeat of Germany to the new organization. During an initial period the German federal government remained under Allied control.

Yet, military control was replaced by a civilian administration. (The other change, the issuance of an Occupation Statute in accordance with the decision of the London Six-Power Conference of 1948 will be discussed later.)

Allied prerogatives were exercised by the Allied High Commission composed of High Commissioners of the Three Powers. Each of the high commissioners had his own office with a large staff. The Office of the United States High Commissioner for Germany, soon known by its acronym HICOG, was organized simultaneously with the dissolution of OMGUS in Berlin in October 1949.

Geographical proximity of the Allied headquarters and the German government was essential for establishing close liaison between the two agencies. The seat of the Allied High Commission and eventually also of the offices of the three high commissioners was therefore determined by the selection of Bonn as the capital of the Federal Republic.

A strong case for selecting Bonn in preference to other candidates, notably Frankfurt, Karlsruhe and Hamburg had been made when, in 1949, the Parliamentary Council met in Bonn. Frankfurt, however, was not prepared to throw in the towel. From my vantage point in Frankfurt, I was able to watch how the struggle for the place of honor among German cities took on an almost dramatic aspect.

A new building for the Pedagogical Academy in Frankfurt in the area between the main cemetery and Eschersheimer Landstrasse was under construction at that time. The plans called for a large central rotunda which would be ideally suited to serve as a meeting place for the federal parliament. The Academy promised to become a most impressive structure far superior to anything Bonn's public buildings had to offer. Holding this trump card, Frankfurt was convinced it could win. The construction became a race against time. At night the floodlit site looked like a busy anthill as work proceeded around the clock. My apartment was close by. The noise of the cranes, the hammers and saws kept me awake.

On election day the building was finished, but the efforts were in vain. The *Bundestag* voted in favor of Bonn as the capital of the Federal Republic. Chancellor Adenauer's house in Rhöndorf near Bonn, where he tended his roses, carried the day. Furthermore, the political climate of Frankfurt in Socialist-dominated Hesse frightened the conservative majority of the *Bundestag* away from Frankfurt.

In October 1949, I was transferred from BICO's legal group to the Office of General Counsel of HICOG. From September to November 1951, HICOG moved from Frankfurt to Bad Godesberg, which was at the time still an independent municipality but now is incorporated into the city of Bonn. What HICOG needed was an office building and living accommodations for its 2,000 American employees, many with families, and about its numerous local employees. There were no buildings capable of housing this huge influx into the tranquil town. Bad Godesberg consisted mainly of elegant villas on tree-lined streets and of large parks, and was a favorite retreat, it was said, of retired mayors. Nearby Bonn was hopelessly overcrowded, and the office space and living accommodations that were available had already been taken over by the federal government. The American government had no choice but to provide for its needs through constructions of its own.

Since 1949, General George Hays, Deputy High Commissioner, had his headquarters in the Deichmanns Aue castle, formerly the residence of the Cologne banker, Baron von Deichmann. In 1950-51, in the record time of little less than one year, an office building seven stories high, with several four-story wings, was attached to the castle. The castle itself became the headquarters of the high commissioner.

At the same time, a housing project for HICOG employees was built on land used mainly for orchards and owned by the lord of another manor, Herr von Carstanjen, who had made a fortune in the chemical industry. The land was situated along the left bank of the Rhine between Bonn and Bad Godesberg and was purchased by the United States government for three million of the new German currency. The manor house was not included in the sale; it is now the home of the federal ministry of finance.

The project provided more than just housing. It was a self-contained community with a shopping center, a church built in New England colonial style, to this date an attraction for sightseers, a club with recreational facilities such as a swimming pool and tennis courts, a movie house and service station, a school and a guest house and a central heating plant.

Similar housing projects were built for the local employees of HICOG in Bonn and Bad Godesberg. For many Germans these modern apartments with kitchen and bath were an unheard-of luxury after the deprivations of the war and its aftermath which had affected everyone.

"Little America," as the project was soon called, had been a joint venture of American and German architects. The well-ordered, spacious layout of the simply-styled, yet appealing modern white-washed houses made the project look like a jewel in the still war-ravaged German landscape.

Firms from all over Germany had contributed their services and products. For many of them participation in this enterprise so soon after currency reform had been a promising new start. Completion of the constructions in record time had been a triumph of the revitalized German economy.

Many called the project a "gilded ghetto" because it insulated the Americans from the German population. While this is true, it was by the force of circumstances, not by design on the part of the American authorities, that the American employees of HICOG were left to live by themselves. Seizure of German housing on a large scale was, of course, out of the question. The construction of individual houses in built-up locations would have been disproportionately costly quite apart from the fact that building sites were difficult to obtain. American authorities themselves regretted that for these reasons no solution was possible other than to build housing for HICOG personnel with the inevitable consequence that the Americans had no German neighbors.

The meeting place of the Allied High Commission was a roomy hotel on top of the Petersberg near Königswinter on the right bank of the Rhine almost opposite to the HICOG office building. The hotel was owned by the Mülhens family, makers of the world-renowned "4711" Eau de Cologne. During the first few years of the occupation it served the Belgian army as a recreation center and officers' club. The building was taken over by the federal government for use by the High Commission. It became the permanent headquarters of the secretariat of the High Commission and was the place where the high commissioners and the committees and subcommittees of the High Commission held their regular meetings. Since the meetings usually lasted the whole day, restaurant facilities were provided on the spot. The restaurant was managed by the British like the dining room of a luxury hotel. The numerous waiters, dressed according to their rank in the service hierarchy, performed their duties under the watchful eye of an elderly dignified maître d'hôtel. He had been the headwaiter at the Adlon, the top hotel on Unter den Linden in Berlin and wore his tails with the *grandezza* of a duke.

At the high commissioners' table close to the window, I occasionally saw Chancellor Adenauer when he was invited by the high commissioners for talks at the Petersberg. The hotel gave its name to the "Protocol of Agreements Between the Allied High Commissioners and the Chancellor of the Federal Republic of Germany, of November 22, 1949."

The Petersberg Protocol was a contractual instrument whereby the German government entered the arena of Allied-German relations as an equal partner for the first time since the war. Among its major provisions were the cessation of dismantling steel, synthetic oil and rubber plants; the admission of the Federal Republic to the International Authority for the Ruhr; and the re-establishment of German consular representation abroad. All these provisions signaled important progress toward German sovereignty.

From the height of the Petersberg one's eyes could wander over the Rhine river deep below to the ranges of the Eifel mountains. On clear days, the spires of Cologne Cathedral could be seen. This indeed provided a lofty spot where one could transact the business which brought us here, detached and unemotional. Occasionally dense fog would drift up from the valley below enveloping the Petersberg in an eerie light and creating an atmosphere of the unreal, similar to the mood that sometimes overcame us on this misty mountain top.

The first United States high commissioner was the respected New York lawyer and banker John J. McCloy. He brought to his new post a varied experience in law, government, finance, and European affairs. For a few months, from July to September 1949 when the Allied High Commission was being established, he held the position of the United States Military Governor before he assumed his position of United States High Commissioner for Germany.

This was not Mr. McCloy's first official involvement with German affairs. As mentioned earlier, he had been on the staff of the American Third Army during the occupation of German territory on the left bank of the Rhine in 1918 and for a while had been stationed in Trier and Koblenz.

During the Second World War, Mr. McCloy became known to the Germans as the preserver of one of the most precious pieces of Germany's cultural heritage. During a wartime inspection tour as Assistant Secretary of War to the United States forces in Germany, he came one day upon troops who had taken up fortified positions opposite the city of Rothenburg ob der Tauber. They were about to shell the city to put down enemy fire which had impeded their advance. At the sight of the city, McCloy later related, he remembered from family conversations the significance of Rothenburg as a city which had preserved the appearance of its medieval past unchanged up to the present. He was able, he said, to persuade the commanding officer to stop the cannonade which had already started. This allowed the mayor to surrender the city to the Americans without bloodshed and destruction. As a token of its gratitude, the city in later years awarded McCloy the dignity of an "Honorary Protector" (*Ehrenschirmherr*) of Rothenburg.

Mr. McCloy very likely learned about Rothenburg through his family connections with Germany.

In 1862, two sons of Wilhelm Zinsser, a teacher in the Upper Hesse town of Grünberg, emigrated to the United States. The older brother established a factory for chemical products in New York. His granddaughter, Ellen Zinsser, married John J. McCloy. The younger brother became a medical doctor in New York, but later returned to Germany and practiced medicine in Cologne. His granddaughter, Auguste Zinsser, married Konrad Adenauer, the first chancellor of the Federal Republic of Germany. (She died in 1949.) Thus, the wives of Adenauer and McCloy had a common great-grandfather.

On December 18, 1949, at the suggestion of the mayor of Grünberg, two children of Chancellor Adenauer, Lotte and Georg, met with Mrs. Ellen McCloy and Ludwig Zinsser, a 79-year-old master-coachmaker in Grünberg. The reunion was entirely a family affair; it had no political connotation. Citizens of Grünberg gathered with the Zinsser relatives in a hotel over coffee and cake. Subsequently, children of the town were regaled with gifts at a Christmas party. In its issue of February 11, 1950, the *Münchner Illustrierte* published a picture story of the meeting under the headline "Kinship Adenauer-McCloy."

The change-over from military government to civilian control marked a significant easing of the occupation regime. This change was not limited to the replacement of military uniforms with pin-striped business suits, but had substantive consequences as well. The agreements of the London Six Powers Conference on Germany in 1949 were now implemented. An "Occupation Statute" limited the exercise of the supreme authority of the Allies to specified fields and established procedural rules. In other words, the relations between the occupying powers and the German people were from now on governed by the rule of law.

The Occupation Statute dated April 10, 1949, entered into force simultaneously with the coming into existence of the Federal Republic on September 21, 1949. The fields reserved for Allied action concerned basic purposes of the occupation. Among them were disarmament and demilitarization, foreign affairs, respect for the Basic Law (amendments required express approval of the occupation authorities) and the state constitutions, control of the care and treatment of persons sentenced by occupation courts in German prisons, and other matters. Otherwise the Federal Republic and its constituent states were given "full legislative, executive and judicial powers in accordance with the Basic Law and with their respective constitutions."

This sounded all-inclusive, but there was a catch to it. All federal and state legislation remained subject to examination by the Allied High Commission. Every law could be "disapproved provisionally or finally" within twenty-one days after official receipt by the occupation authorities if, in the opinion of the occupation authorities, the law was "inconsistent with the Basic Law, a Land constitution, legislation or other directives of the occupation authorities themselves or the provisions of this Instrument" or "constituted a grave threat to the basic purposes of the occupation."

The full text of the provisions of the Occupation Statute defining the right of the occupation authorities to intervene in the legislative process of the Federal Republic and the states had to be quoted here in order to demonstrate the magnitude of the task that lay ahead.

The review of German legislation involved not only safeguarding the basic objectives of the occupation as recorded in the legislation of the Control Council, the Military Government and the Allied High Commission. In addition, the Allies undertook the role of guardians of the German constitutions. This required exact knowledge of the constitutions as well as familiarity with the whole spectrum of the occupation legislation which still took precedence over German law.

As in the days of the *Länderrat* and BICO, the proper discharge of the reviewing responsibility demanded personnel versed in German legislative procedures and in German legal language. A further requirement was the ability to present to the superiors who made the decisions the results of their review coupled with recommendations for action—and all this under pressure of time. As already mentioned, the examination of legislation had to be completed within twenty-one days of submission of the law to the Allied High Commission, certainly a reasonable requirement. In the absence of a time limit, the entire legislative process would have been thrown out of order.

It was by accident that a handful of Americans were available who like me, had become "double-barreled" lawyers, as our colleagues called us. We were knowledgeable in both German and American law, and were also prepared to contribute the special skills we had acquired to the reconstruction of Germany.

For the review of German legislation, the High Commission established a special "Review Committee." It consisted of the political and legal advisers of the Three Powers or their representatives. As chief of the federal legislation section in the Office of the General Counsel, I participated regularly in the deliberations of the review committee. The federal government was required to submit to the Secretary General of the Allied High Commission fifty-five copies of every piece of legislation after it had passed parliament together with English and French translations (which, of course, were of little use to us as we never could dispense with studying the original German text). Before each meeting of the review committee, the political and legal advisers of HICOG were supposed to agree on United States policy with regard to the legislation under review. In practice, this procedure was rarely followed. There simply was no time. The review committee had to reach its conclusions usually within fifteen days to enable the high commissioners to take action if necessary. Sometimes a train ride offered an opportunity to confer with our colleagues of the political division. However, most of the time we went by car to the Petersberg, and consultations prior to the meeting were dispensed with.

During our stay in Frankfurt, we usually arrived at the Petersberg for the weekly meetings of the review committee between nine and ten in the morning. The first item on the agenda was a teacart rolled into the room by a waiter in tails offering a variety of refreshments. The meetings lasted the whole day interrupted by a sumptuous lunch and, according to British custom, by tea in the afternoon.

From the time of its first meeting on October 7, 1949, through March 6, 1951, when it was dissolved following a revision of the Occupation Statute, the review committee considered 1,682 federal and state laws and regulations. This number does not signify an unhealthy surfeit of legislation. Rather, it attests to an amazing accomplishment in the process of reconstructing Germany's social and economic life. There had been no central government since the collapse of the Third Reich; the new federal authority needed new organs and institutions to become fully operative, particularly in the field of the administration of justice. A number of federal courts at the apex of the judicial system were created: The Federal Supreme Court for Civil and Criminal Matters; the Federal Tax Court; the Federal Constitutional Court as court of last resort for the interpretation of the Basic Law; and agencies of importance for the security of the Federal Republic such as the Federal Office for the Protection of the Constitution, the Federal Office of Criminal Investigation, and the Federal Border Police.

As a consequence of the partition of Germany into zones of occupation, legal uniformity had to a large extent been lost. After the three western zones were combined to form a single political entity, the time had come to eliminate many divergences that had developed. The federal "Law to Restore Legal Uniformity in the Fields of the Constitution of Law Courts, Civil Jurisdiction, Criminal Procedure and Court Costs" was a first step in clearing up a confusing situation.

In addition to organizational matters, the federal government dealt with a number of economic and social problems which required immediate attention, for instance, the problem of "equalization of burdens" or just distribution of the financial and property losses arising from the war and its aftermath between the "haves" and "have-nots" and the integration of millions of refugees and expellees into the social and political life of the German people.

In only four cases on the federal level did the High Commission make use of its veto power. The disapproval, however, was only provisional and was canceled after the federal government had given assurances that it would comply with Allied requirements.

Of state laws, eight were disapproved with final effect. Among them were some budget laws, a Schleswig-Holstein "Law on the Establishment of Doctors' and Dentists' Offices," a North Rhine Westphalia "Law Relating to Jewish Communities," and a Bavarian Ordinance on Import Restrictions. In eight cases, provisional disapprovals were withdrawn after appropriate amendments were made (for instance, in the case of a Württemberg-Baden electoral law which was provisionally disapproved because it failed to provide that civil servants must resign their positions before running for elective office). Six ordinances were annulled in parts; a Hamburg Senate Resolution on tax exemption for cinemas was declared invalid in its entirety.

As this brief survey shows, Allied interference with German domestic affairs was moderate. The fact that the German legislators acted under the watchful eye of the High Commission might have exerted a restraining influence. In any event, the Allied review power was of comparatively short duration. It was abrogated with the entry into force of the "Instrument of Revision of the Occupation Statute" on March 7, 1951. Laws of the federal and state governments became effective upon the completion of the legislative process in accordance with the requirements of their respective constitutions without prior review by the Allies.

Some vestiges, however, of Allied prerogatives remained. The right reserved by the Allies to ensure respect for the Basic Law, in particular to uphold the civil rights of the individual as defined in the Basic Law, was relinquished only in October of 1951 when the Federal Constitutional Court had been established. Furthermore, state constitutions, amendments thereof, and all federal and state legislation could subsequently be repealed or annulled, either in entirety or in part, by the occupation authorities, essentially for the same reasons for which a law could have been disapproved under the original Occupation Statute. The High Commission has invoked this right in two cases: it annulled a federal law which abrogated provisions of a Control Council law without the prescribed authorization by the Allies, and another federal law which affected the legal status of Berlin.

The restoration of German legislative autonomy was the consequence of a policy aimed at enabling the democratically constituted Federal Republic of Germany to re-enter the community of the free peoples of Europe on a footing of equality. Since legal equality and occupation were incompatible, the occupation had to be phased out if equality was to be achieved.

This policy had been expressed in general terms in a Declaration issued in London by the Foreign Ministers of the United States, the United Kingdom and France on May 14, 1950. It was given substance in a communiqué issued in Washington on September 19, 1950, by the foreign ministers of the three Western Allies at the conclusion of a conference held to "review the situation in Germany and Allied relations with the Federal Republic." In this communiqué, the governments reaffirmed their desire to integrate the Federal Republic into the community of free nations. They spoke of the "spirit of the new relationship which they wish to establish with the Federal Republic" and of a "new phase in the relations between the Allies and the Federal Republic" which "will be marked by major extensions of the authority of the Federal Government." This would be made possible, the Allies declared, by amending the Occupation Statute.

Finally, the communiqué contained a statement of fundamental importance for Allied policy toward Germany in subsequent years. The three Governments declared that "pending the unification of Germany," they "consider the Government of the Federal Republic as the only German Government freely and legitimately constituted and therefore entitled to speak for Germany as the representative of the German people in international affairs."

The Federal Republic of Germany: Sovereign and Equal

If it is ever justified to speak of "Years of Decision" in the history of a nation, in Germany these were the years from 1950 to 1955. A country which had been totally vanquished and devastated, wholly occupied by the forces of the victorious powers, shorn of its sovereignty, governed dictatorially by the victors and rent by economic chaos, rose to become within the short space of five years a sovereign state endowed with full legislative, executive and judicial power and a free democratic constitution, economically healthy and an equal partner of its former enemies. I was present in Bonn, seat of the occupation authorities, when this happened—an event, no doubt, without precedent in recorded history. I propose to recapitulate briefly the principal stages of this development and to explain how the regeneration of Germany was accomplished.

After the Communist coup in Czechoslovakia in February 1948, which drove Ian Masaryk to suicide, and the Soviet blockade of Berlin in June 1948, which resulted in the collapse of the quadripartite administration of Germany, there existed a heightened danger of armed conflict in Europe. The Communist invasion of South Korea in the summer of 1950 increased the fear that a similar Communist surprise attack, a "Second Korea," might happen in Western Europe.

The growing threat to the security of the free world posed by Soviet expansionism had a profound effect on the mission of the forces of the three Western Allies in Germany. Up to that time, their presence guaranteed the implementation of the objectives of the occupation. In the changed world political situation, there was a chance that the Allied forces might be called upon to defend the West against attacks from the East. This was made clear in the communiqué of September 19, 1950, mentioned earlier. The Allied governments considered their forces in Germany to have "in addition to their occupation duties also the important role of acting as security forces for the protection and defense of the free world, including the German Federal Republic and the Western sectors of Berlin." They added that they would "treat any attack against the Federal Republic or Berlin from any quarter as an attack upon themselves."

With the mission of the occupation troops changed to a defense force of Western Europe, the strategic thinking of the Allies turned to Germany. A defense without Germany was unrealistic. The plan was born to make the Federal Republic a partner in this defense effort. In his governmental declaration before the *Bundestag* on September 8, 1950, Chancellor Adenauer for the first time publicly broached the question of including Germany in the Western defense system. Prior to the declaration, Adenauer had given assurances to the American high commissioner that the Federal Republic was ready to contribute a German contingent in the event that a Western integrated defense force was created.

The foreign ministers of the three Western Allies were aware of these statements when, in their communiqué of September 19, 1950, they referred to "sentiments recently expressed in Germany and elsewhere in favor of German participation in an integrated force for the defense of European freedom." The Council of the North Atlantic Treaty Organization (NATO), at a meeting held at the same time in New York, had considered the question of a German defense contribution submitted to it for examination by three foreign ministers and had declared itself in favor of "Germany being able to contribute to the setting-up of the defense of Western Europe."

Participation of the Federal Republic in Western defense was bound to have profound repercussions upon its legal status. As a partner in defense, it would be the equal of the other states. A Federal Republic subject to interference with its domestic and external affairs by the occupying powers would not be in a position to discharge its defense responsibilities. Thus the occupation had to end, not just in parts, but *in toto*.

The question naturally arose as to the method best suited to achieving this end. In a comment on the communiqué of September 19, 1950, Chancellor Adenauer stated that the relations between the Federal Republic and the Three Powers should no longer be determined by unilateral action, but should be placed as rapidly as possible on a contractual basis. At the beginning of December 1950, the Chancellor suggested to the three high commissioners that the Occupation Statute be replaced by a "Security Pact" between the Allied High Commission and the Federal Republic.

The plan advanced by the chancellor to use an agreement as instrument for abrogating the Occupation Statute was reflected in a directive of the three foreign ministers authorizing the high commissioners to negotiate a contractual relationship with Germany which would replace the Occupation Statute "as the logical consequence of a German defense contribution." The directive had been adopted at a meeting of the North Atlantic Council in Brussels and was publicly announced in a communiqué of December 19, 1950. The NATO Council again expressed itself in favor of including the Federal Republic in the common defense of Western Europe.

On February 22, 1951, the high commissioners transmitted a list of items to the federal government which would serve as a basis for the proposed negotiations. On May 10, 1951, exploratory talks of representatives of the High Commission with representatives of the federal government began in Bonn. Their aim was to formulate recommendations for establishing relations between the Three Powers and the Federal Republic on as broad a contractual basis as possible. On August 3, 1951, the first phase of negotiations between the Allies and the Federal Republic ended. A few days later, the high commissioners submitted to their respective governments a detailed negotiation package, already then called "Contractual Agreements," which were divided into five Chapters consisting of a number of separate agreements. Among the subjects for negotiations were: security questions in connection with Germany's role in the Western defense system; security and maintenance of Allied forces stationed in the Federal Republic; Allied policies regarding German domestic affairs; foreign affairs and treaties and the status of Berlin.

From September 10 to 14, 1951, the three foreign ministers met in Washington to consider a report of the high commissioners on the proposed program for negotiations with the Germans. As a result, the high commissioners received new instructions for their negotiations with the federal government, together with the draft of an agreement designed to "transform completely" German-Allied relations and to establish a new relationship between the Three Powers and the Federal Republic "with the aim of integrating the Federal Republic in the Western defense system on a basis of equality."

On November 17, the United States high commissioner transmitted to his government the draft prepared in Bonn of a "General Agreement" between the four governments. The draft was considered at a meeting in Paris on November 22, 1951, of the three Allied foreign ministers and Chancellor Adenauer in his capacity as federal minister of foreign affairs.

The meeting was a historical event. For the first time since the end of World War II, a German foreign minister sat at the same table negotiating with the foreign ministers of the victors as an equal among equals, "in itself a notable advance in the progressive association of the German Federal Republic with the West on the basis of equal partnership," as a statement to the press solemnly declared.

While approving the draft, the foreign ministers stated that it could "not be signed or published at present. . . . since it must be completed by a number of related conventions." The statement continued that with the entry into force of the General Agreement and related conventions, "the Occupation Statute with its powers of intervention in the domestic affairs of the Federal Republic will be revoked and the Allied High Commission will be abolished." In other words, the purpose of the contractual agreements was to restore German sovereignty.

In his report to President Truman of November 23 on the results of the Paris meeting, Secretary of State Dean Acheson expressed the hope that the negotiations with the Federal Republic could be completed and the agreements and conventions be ready for signing by the end of the year. This turned out to be impossible. Several months passed before May 26, 1952, could be fixed as the date for the signing of the agreements. Bonn was chosen as the place of signing.

The duration and climate of the negotiations were influenced by a number of factors. There were remnants of the "occupation mentality" in the attitude of the Allies: a tendency to hold onto the gains and a reluctance to relinquish the privileges they had enjoyed among a vanquished people who now had to be accepted as partners. The Germans, on the other hand, still had to get used to being treated as equals at the negotiating table. Knowing that the negotiations were, in the last analysis, aimed at restoring German sovereignty, they were unwilling to agree to compromises which they suspected might put this aim in jeopardy.

The Allied representatives were negotiating as a team; thus positions had to be coordinated between the various elements of the High Commission—this took time. New ideas and proposals which resulted from the negotiations often required consultations with governments. The German delegation sometimes experienced difficulties reconciling conflicting views of participating ministries.

However, the primary burden was the substance of the negotiations. Nothing had happened in modern history which could be compared to the situation in Germany: the capitulation in 1945; the subsequent occupation of the conquered country, and the government of the vanquished by the victors. The contractual agreements were designed to terminate the occupation regime and to settle matters arising out of the war and the occupation or, in other words, to obtain a binding commitment on the part of Germany that she would abide by the decisions which the Allies had reached as a result of their victory. The war aims of the Allies and the objectives of the occupation included, to name only a few, punishment of war criminals, compensation for victims of Nazi persecution, protection of foreign interests in Germany, reparations. Furthermore, the legal status of the foreign forces in the Federal Republic had to be redefined after their mission had changed from occupation duty to the defense of the West. What was the legal basis of their continued presence in the Federal Republic? Should their members be subject to German jurisdiction for crimes committed against Germans? To what extent should German tax laws apply to activities of the Allied forces? The questions which arose in this context were for the most part new and untested and of particular sensitivity to the Germans in the light of the promised restoration of sovereignty.

The Allies dealt with only a part of Germany. In matters affecting Germany as a whole, they were bound by agreements to which the Soviets were a party. The legislation of the Control Council was one area where the Western Allies had acted jointly with the Soviets in the exercise of their rights relating to

Germany as a whole. Control Council laws could not be repealed or amended without the consent of the Soviets; unilateral action on the part of the Western Powers would have been a violation of quadripartite agreements. Many Control Council measures, however, were either outdated, or incompatible with Allied High Commission legislation or inconsistent with German sovereignty. Since the Control Council was no longer functioning, and Soviet agreement to amending or repealing Control Council legislation could not be obtained, the Allies had recourse to an ingenious expedient to achieve the desired result. Conflicting or outdated Control Council laws were "deprived of effect." This meant that they remained on the books—thus avoiding formal repeal or amendment—but they lost binding force. As a consequence of the restoration of German sovereignty, the legislative authority of the Federal Republic extended to all legislation existing in the Federal Republic, including occupation legislation. With respect to Control Council legislation, however, the Federal Republic could have no more power than the Allies. It was agreed that the Federal Republic while entitled to deal with Control Council legislation could only "deprive a Control Council law of effect" after consultation in each case with the Allies who thereby maintained their continued quadripartite responsibilities. (It will be recalled that the German "Marriage Law" is a Control Council law; in the course of time it frequently needed amending.)

What remained entirely outside the legislative competence of the Federal Republic were provisions concerning organization and procedures of the Control Council. Although the Council had ceased to be active since 1948, the Allies wished to preserve this quadripartite institution, at least in theory, in the interest of Germany as a whole. In a letter to the federal chancellor which later became part of the contractual agreements, the foreign ministers of the Three Powers "required" that this legislation "not be deprived of effect in the federal territory by the Federal Republic."

One morning I received a somewhat desperate call from the legal adviser in the German foreign office. He was unable, he told me, to locate the Control Council legislation referred to in the letter of the foreign ministers to Chancellor Adenauer which the Federal Republic was enjoined not to touch. (The Control

Council, it is true, took at times a rather cavalier attitude toward its duty to publish its legislation; the legislation here involved was in that category.) The chancellor, he continued, would like to know precisely what his obligation was; not an unreasonable demand, the caller thought. Was I able to help? I did find the texts of the legislation in our archives. Copies were soon in the hands of the foreign office.

Of particular sensitivity in the Allied-German negotiations was the question of Allied emergency powers. The Allies were seeking to reserve the right, in the event of an emergency threatening the security of their forces stationed in the Federal Republic, to resume, in whole or in part, the exercise of the supreme authority which would lapse with the abrogation of the Occupation Statute. This the Germans considered to be a serious infringement upon their sovereignty. Both sides were interested in defining the scope of the emergency powers, in particular, the ways in which such powers are exercised. In this situation, Professor Robert Bowie, chief of the American delegation, urgently needed material on European emergency laws. I was requested, at short notice, to furnish a collection and an analysis of such laws. I remembered a study prepared in the Bruns Institute and published in the series *Contributions to Foreign Public Law and International Law*, which described emergency legislation in a number of European states and which would answer Professor Bowie's needs. Among the books I had taken along from Berlin to Frankfurt in 1948 was a copy of the study I had secured for myself when it was published in 1928. It put me in a position to comply with Professor Bowie's request on time—thanks to the preparatory work of my former colleagues in the Bruns Institute.

Another problem affecting the security of the Allied forces stationed in the Federal Republic resulted from the fact that Control Council Law No. 11 had repealed all German legislation dealing with offenses against the military. They included the betrayal of military secrets, sabotage of military installations, undermining the discipline of the forces. As long as the occupying powers exercised supreme authority, they were able to protect their security and the security of their forces by appropriate legislation or other measures. With the restoration of

German sovereignty the Allies lost this authority. In the future they would have to rely on German law for the protection of their troops; yet ever since Control Council Law No. 11 was passed, no such law existed. Thus, the absence of German criminal law in the field of military security presented a threat to the Allied forces—a consequence that could hardly have been foreseen when Control Council Law No. 11 was enacted. The legal vacuum had to be filled. This was done by inserting into the contractual agreements provisions on criminal liability for offenses against the security of the foreign forces in the Federal Republic. The negotiations in which I represented the American side proceeded smoothly. My British colleague had the same legal background as I; it greatly facilitated our task.

The negotiations were conducted at a time when Germany was still occupied territory and subject to the supreme authority of the Allies. This situation caused the French to raise the question as to "definition and status" of the contractual agreements. The American ambassador in Paris, David Bruce, reported to the secretary of state on April 23, 1951, that French governmental circles "viewed with horror a British proposal that reference be made to Article 59 of the Basic Law (foreign affairs, treaties) with respect to the legal background of the contemplated arrangements. This reference would place (them) in the category of treaties which in the French view they emphatically are not." The contractual agreements, the French maintained, were not "intergovernmental agreements but were concluded between the High Commission as the supreme authority in Germany on the one hand and the Federal Republic on the other." Nothing, the French insisted, must be done which would "detract from the principle of the continuing supreme authority" of the Allies. The French suggested that "a legal formula be found permitting the contractual arrangements to be ratified by the *Bundestag*." This, they admitted would present difficulties, but they thought that one might trust "the ingenuity of legal experts who will surely find a formula which is agreeable both to Germany and ourselves."

No appeal to the ingenuity of legal experts was needed. The French view regarding the legal nature of the agreements and the parties did not prevail. True, the negotiations on the Allied side were conducted by representatives of the High Commission, or to put it more clearly, of the high commissioners. Vis-à-vis the Germans, they acted as a single unit—a team—as pointed out earlier. Each national representative, however, received his instructions from his government, not from the High Commission. Parties to the agreements were on the one side the United States, Great Britain and France, referred to in the agreements as "The Three Powers," and on the other side the Federal Republic of Germany. The agreements were treaties under international law and binding in accordance with the constitutional procedures of the contracting parties.

The result of the negotiations was a set of agreements, the contractual agreements, later called the "Bonn Conventions" after the place of signing. The basic document attesting to the new relationship between the three Western Allies and Germany was the "Convention on Relations between the Three Powers and the Federal Republic of Germany," or "Germany Treaty" (*Deutschlandvertrag*) for short.

Article 1 proclaimed the termination of the occupation regime and the restoration of German sovereignty. The convention was supplemented by a number of related conventions. One of them dealt with the rights and obligations of foreign forces and their members in the Federal Republic of Germany (Forces Convention); it settled, among others, the hotly debated question of the jurisdiction of German courts over offenses committed by members of the Allied forces against Germans; it also preserved privileges dating from occupation days, such as the right of the forces to maintain their own shopping centers called post exchanges (PX's). A Finance Convention determined the financial contribution of the Federal Republic to the Western defense. The Convention on the Settlement of Matters Arising out of the War and the Occupation (Settlement Convention) was designed to "wind up in an orderly way" Allied war aims and occupation objectives.

Despite their wide range of topics, the Bonn Conventions were not a peace treaty. The conclusion of such a treaty would have required, on the one hand, the participation of all belligerent states which had been at war with Germany, and on the other hand a reunified Germany, which had been their common enemy. In the absence of a peace treaty, the state of war with Germany was terminated by unilateral declarations by each of the Allies, in the case of the United States, by the Proclamation of President Truman of October 24, 1951.

Simultaneously with the negotiations in Bonn on the termination of the occupation regime in the Federal Republic, a conference was held in Paris of a number of European governments, including the German federal government, to consider Western defense matters and the defense contribution of the Federal Republic.

On October 24, 1950, the French Premier René Pleven had submitted to the French parliament a plan for the formation of a European integrated army composed of contingents from each of the twelve member states of NATO. Germany was to participate, not with a national army which was still not acceptable to many of the Western nations, but with combat units of regimental or divisional strength to be combined with units of the other states to form a European defense force.

The Paris conference lasted for almost one year, from February to December 1951. The result was a treaty on the "Establishment of a European Defense Community" with common armed forces and common institutions (a commissariat as executive organ, an assembly, a council and a court). The Federal Republic was to contribute to the European army a contingent of the same type and strength as that of other member states with a population of equal size.

The Bonn Conventions were designed to restore German sovereignty; under the Paris Treaty Germany was to be admitted to the European defense community. Both documents were part of one single political master plan. The legal consequence was a linkage between these two agreements; the Bonn Conventions could enter into force only together with the Treaty on the European Defense Community.

May 26, 1952, was the date on which the foreign ministers of the United States, Great Britain and France were scheduled to meet with Chancellor Adenauer in Bonn to sign the contractual agreements. During the last few days before the arrival of the foreign ministers in Bonn, the negotiators, struggling against a tight deadline, experienced a state of indescribable frenzy. Many loose ends had to be tied up at the last minute. I got entangled in one of these operations. Roughly three weeks before the day of signing, I had been given the task, together with a British, French, and German colleague, to "harmonize" the texts of the Forces Convention. I had to make sure that the English, French, and German texts all had the same meaning since the three texts were to be equally authentic.

The negotiators knew the meaning of the texts in their own languages. This offered no guarantee that the meanings were identical, especially in the case of legal terms with which the negotiators, who had been trained in different fields, were not familiar. It frequently happened that we had to go back to the negotiators when we discovered discrepancies. This took time. Not only had the task of harmonizing the texts to be completed on the prescribed day; clean copies of the texts in three languages had to be typed on special treaty paper and sealed before they were ready to be submitted for signature.

The target date of May 26 could eventually be met only by staying together day and night in my office with brief intermissions.

It was May. As the sun rose the joyful chirping of birds from the nearby park would enliven the often tough discussions about the meaning of words and the construction of sentences. One of my colleagues tried to stay awake with a mixture of strong coffee and whiskey. Despite these efforts his head, in a fit of fatigue, would occasionally slump forward and hit the table with a dull thud. Edginess would also produce time-consuming incidents. Thus, one of our colleagues suddenly got up and left the room claiming that he had been insulted by another member's personal remark. Another colleague refused to consider the French text on the grounds that it had been submitted too late. As chairman, it was my responsibility to get the meeting going again. And the clock was advancing inexorably.

I also remember the critical situation which arose in the late afternoon on the day before the signing. Article 7, paragraph 3 of the Convention on Relations stipulated that a reunified Germany should be bound by commitments undertaken by the Federal Republic under the Bonn Conventions and the treaties establishing an integrated European community. The clause had been a bone of contention between the Germans and the

high commissioners for some time, and during the last phases
of the negotiations had been severely criticized by members of
the government coalition as a potential obstacle to a future
reunification of Germany. The leader of the parliamentary group
of the CDU, von Brentano, was sent in a hurry to Secretary of
State Dean Acheson who had already arrived in Bonn in an effort
to have the objectionable clause eliminated.   Failing this the
signing of the contractual agreements was in jeopardy. As a result
of von Brentano's intervention, the principal stumbling block,
namely, the automatic commitment of a future reunified Germany
to enter into the Western treaty system was removed.   In the
somewhat complicated language of the revised text, the Three
Powers agreed to extend to a unified Germany the rights which
the Federal Republic had under the Bonn Conventions.   They
also agreed that the rights under the treaties for the formation of
an integrated European community should be similarly extended
provided a unified Germany assumed the commitments which
the Federal Republic had undertaken vis-à-vis the Three Powers
under the aforementioned conventions and treaties. Briefly: the
Three Powers agreed to act in favor of a unified Germany if it
wished to obtain the benefits of these agreements in return for
assuming the obligations which they imposed.   The text of the
convention which was ready for signing had to be changed, the
three languages of the revised clause had to be harmonized, and
all this under the pressure of time. It was not so much the clause,
rather the feeling of uncertainty which made this incident such a
disturbing experience. It seemed that there would never be an end
to the negotiations. (The clause was deleted when the Convention
on Relations was revised in 1954. More about this later.)

During the night from May 25 to 26, we proofread the texts.
In the early morning hours of May 26, an official of the German
foreign office appeared with the paraphernalia for binding and
sealing the texts: candle, sealing wax, and red ribbon. Robert
Schumann, the French Foreign Minister, and Anthony Eden, the
British Foreign Secretary, were supposed to place their personal
seal next to their signatures, while the American consulate
provided an official seal for Secretary of State Dean Acheson.

A sudden crisis arose when the personal seals of Schumann
and Eden could not be found. Eden's secretary had the seal of his

chief so well hidden that it emerged only after a frantic search. For Schumann a suitable seal with the letters "R.S." was obtained in nearby Godesberg.

The signing of the Bonn Conventions took place punctually, as planned, on May 26, 1952, at 10:00 a.m. in the assembly hall of the Federal Council. Present were: the foreign ministers of the Three Powers, accompanied by the three high commissioners John J. McCloy, François-Poncet and Sir Ivone Kirkpatrick as well as members of their staffs. The German side was represented by Chancellor Adenauer in his capacity as foreign minister, the State Secretary of the Foreign Office, Professor Hallstein, and Federal Minister of Finance Schäffer. In his statement at the signing ceremony Dean Acheson spoke of the United Kingdom, France, and the United States, together with the other free nations "welcoming a new partner in their great effort to establish peace and security in the world." His concluding words were: "On behalf of the President of the United States and the American people, I welcome the Federal Republic on its return to the community of nations."

The next day the Treaty on the Establishment of the European Defense Community was signed in Paris.

What had to follow in order to bring the grand design to fruition was the ratification of the Bonn and Paris Agreements by the parliaments of the signatory states. This was by no means assured. Although the plan of a European defense community had been initiated by France, it was of all countries in France where voices of resistance against the scheme were raised.

In Bonn, a cloud suddenly appeared on the horizon, threatening to obscure the light so essential for the growth of the delicate plant of Germany's independence and her acceptance into the community of free nations. The cloud was a constitutional question. Did the Basic Law at all permit the Federal Republic to have armed forces which it could contribute to a European army? The framers of the Basic Law had deliberately omitted any reference to national defense. At the time the Basic Law was adopted nobody could even think of German rearmament. Germany was occupied by the forces of her former enemies. Demilitarization of Germany was one of the basic objectives of the occupation. In addition, popular sentiment in Germany was opposed to rearmament. The memory of the war with its horrors and devastations was still too vivid and painful. A military contribution by the Federal Republic to a European defense community would alter the very character of the new Germany as a state without an army.

The question, of course, troubled the Allies. Professor Bowie asked for my views. The answer was expected within hours. I took the position that without an amendment of the Basic Law the Federal Republic had no authority to contribute a military force to the defense of the West. My colleagues in the political section were greatly alarmed. Legal questions had been left more or less in limbo. An amendment of the Basic Law required a two-thirds majority in the federal legislature (*Bundestag* and *Bundesrat*). It was well known that the government did not have the necessary votes. Should legal objections stand in the way of realizing a plan that had been worked out with so much effort, and jeopardize the defense of the West? It was argued that among the basic rights of a state is the right of self-defense which includes the right to have armed forces. This argument, however, overlooked the fact that in a federal state such as the Federal Republic of Germany, the federal government is "a government of enumerated powers;" it has only those powers which the constitution expressly assigns to it. Without such express authorization, it can be doubtful whether the right to raise an army belongs to the federal government or to the constituent states. If the constitution is silent on this question, it must be clarified by an amendment.

The constitutional issue dominated German domestic politics for months. The *Bundestag*, the federal government, the federal president and the Federal Constitutional Court became involved in it.

As early as January 1952, several months prior to the signing of the Bonn Conventions and the Paris Treaty, 147 Social Democratic *Bundestag* representatives requested the Federal Constitutional Court to declare that "a federal law which deals with the membership of Germans in an armed force or which subjects Germans to compulsory military service is neither in form nor in substance consistent with the Basic Law unless the Basic Law has first been amended." The action was designed to prevent ratification of both the Bonn Conventions and the Paris

Treaty by the *Bundestag*. Plaintiffs and the government consulted experts from Germany and abroad; their opinions filled volumes.

No decision was reached. The court dismissed the petition as "not admissible at the present time" because the legislative bodies had not yet completed their deliberations.

A procedure initiated by Federal President Heuss before the Constitutional Court likewise failed to clarify the issue. Promulgation of federal legislation, including laws approving treaties, requires the signature of the president. Heuss wished to make sure that by signing the approval laws for the Bonn Conventions and the Paris Treaty he would not violate the Basic Law. He asked the court for an advisory opinion. When the court, by an intermediary decision of December 8, 1952, ruled that the two *Senate* (divisions) of the court in future litigation on this question would be bound by the advisory opinion, Heuss, on the urgent request of Chancellor Adenauer, who saw the president in the late hours of December 8, withdrew his petition the next day on the ground that the ruling of the court had altered the nature of the proceedings. A request for an advisory opinion had been turned into an action asking for a final decision which, the president contended, was contrary to his intentions.

In reality, Chancellor Adenauer was afraid that the court might come to an early decision, the outcome of which was highly doubtful. Hence his precipitate intervention with the president which scandalized the public as it appeared to undermine the authority of the president.

In the general elections for the *Bundestag* on September 6, 1953, the chancellor's party received an absolute majority of the votes. Together with its coalition partner, the Free Democratic party, a two-thirds majority needed to amend the Basic Law was now assured.

One of the first laws submitted to the *Bundestag* by the government and adopted with a two-thirds majority was a "Law to Amend the Basic Law" of March 26, 1954. "Defense, including compulsory military service" was added to the matters within the exclusive jurisdiction of the federation. The issue of the constitutionality of a German defense contribution was settled. If, as had been argued, the Federal Republic had been competent to act in the military field by virtue of a basic right, a constitutional amendment would not have been required.   I considered the constitutional amendment to be a vindication of the position I had taken when the issue first emerged.

While the whole world was waiting for the ratification of the Bonn Conventions and the Paris Treaty, the Federal Republic took another step on its road back into the family of nations. On February 27, 1953, twenty states signed in London the "Agreement on the Settlement of German External Debts."

The agreement deals with debts of the German Reich arising from the Dawes and Young loans granted to the Weimar Republic for the payment of reparations after the First World War.   It settled the payment of obligations arising from postwar economic assistance which the Federal Republic had assumed, and compensated foreign debtors for the damage which they had sustained when, under the foreign exchange regime of the Nazis, service of foreign debts was made through the so-called "Conversion Office" (*Konversionkasse*) in German, not foreign, currency and eventually was dispensed with altogether.

That the arduous and complex negotiations were successfully concluded was due for the most part to the efforts of the head of the German delegation, the banker Hermann Joseph Abs of the *Deutsche Bank*.   During several months in 1952 and 1953 when I was a member of the American delegation I had occasion to observe his superior negotiating style.   It was marked by a willingness to compromise and an astounding ability to react rapidly to unexpected problems with convincing proposals satisfactory to all concerned.   Serene, always sure of himself, patient with his colleagues—these were his most striking character traits which impressed themselves upon the conference; they created a relaxed atmosphere of general good will conducive to reaching mutual understanding.

The London Debt Agreement is the most comprehensive and unique settlement of financial relations of one country with its foreign creditors.   It has been hailed as one of the best international treaties ever concluded, in that a fair adjustment of the interests of all the parties had been achieved. The number of disputes that subsequently arose and were resolved by arbitration was minimal.

On August 30, 1954, the French parliament with the decisive vote of one hundred Communist members, cut off further debate on the Treaty on the Establishment of a European Defense Community. Although France had initiated the concept of an integrated European defense force, it was now the French who were concerned lest a joint supranational high command encroach upon their military sovereignty. The exit of France threatened the collapse of the European security system, fruit of laborious, long-drawn-out negotiations. The Bonn Conventions, because of their linkage with the entry of the Federal Republic into the European defense community, were in danger of losing their bearings. The prospect arose that the occupation regime which these conventions were designed to abolish might last for an indeterminate period.

There was, however, no turning back on the road to restoring German sovereignty and the participation of the Federal Republic in the Western defense system as an equal partner. How could this aim be attained despite the fiasco of the European defense community? The creative idea that rescued the grand design was conceived by a number of people, but it was eventually turned into reality by Anthony Eden, the British Foreign Secretary. The plan provided for a procedure in stages: It would start with transforming the Brussels Treaty of March 17, 1948, which had been concluded between England, France and the Benelux States to protect the contracting parties against German aggression, into a "Western European Union" to which the Federal Republic would be admitted as a full-fledged member. The newly won ally would then be brought into NATO with a defense force of its own. The program was accepted by a Nine-Power Conference (the seven members of the Western European Union plus the United States and Canada) held in London from September 28 to October 3, 1954. Considering the still lingering mistrust of Germany among Western European nations and their fear of a German defense contribution, the decisions of the London Conference were a diplomatic achievement of historical magnitude at a moment when, in the words of Dr. Conant, the United States High Commissioner for Germany, "the fate of the free world hung in the balance."

Next on the agenda was the task of converting the London decisions into treaties. This, the conference decided, was to be accomplished by adapting the Bonn Conventions to the new situation and attaching them to the treaties on the entry of the Federal Republic into the Western European Union and her accession to NATO. Revising the Bonn Conventions pursuant to the mandate of the London Conference involved deleting the numerous references to the European defense community and eliminating restrictions on German sovereignty which were incompatible with Germany's new position as an equal partner in the Alliance, especially provisions in the Settlement Convention which had originally been designed to preserve as much of the occupation policies as possible. Pending completion of these arrangements, the high commissioners were instructed by their governments, as stated in a "Declaration of Intent" issued at the conclusion of the London Conference, to act at once in the spirit of the new policy which was based on the recognition "that a great country can no longer be deprived of the rights properly belonging to a free and democratic people." The high commissioners were enjoined not to make use of occupation prerogatives which were to be abrogated, such as vetoing German legislation or measures of decartelization, except with the consent of the federal government. The declaration meant that for all practical purposes the exercise of Allied supreme authority was suspended even before the new agreements became effective.

When the London Conference adjourned on October 3, the conferees agreed to reconvene on October 20 in Paris to consider and sign the new agreements. In the meantime, many documents had to be drafted to implement the London decisions.

The task of "expurgating" the Bonn Conventions—in other words, to reach agreement on deletions and corrections and to draft new instruments for consideration and signature by the governments—had been assigned by the conference to the high commissioners in Bonn. The two weeks originally scheduled for this work from October 6 to 18, eventually shrank to one single week, insofar as actual work on the documents was concerned.

Thus began for us a time reminiscent of the hectic weeks preceding the signing of the Bonn Conventions in May of 1952. I was a member of the United States delegation.

We met with our British and French colleagues and German delegates in marathon sessions to hammer out the texts. The work was directed by Maurice Bathurst, legal advisor to the British high commissioner, with indefatigable energy and high efficiency. We could not afford long discussions; we had to focus on principal issues. Many a knotty problem was solved the way Alexander the Great handled the Gordian knot. Whole chapters of the Settlement Convention, such as decartelization and deconcentration, were deleted; individual articles were amended or redrafted. Eventually the results of the revisions of the Bonn Conventions were embodied in five "Schedules" and were annexed to a "Protocol on the Termination of the Occupation Regime in the Federal Republic of Germany." Added to the protocol were a great number of supplementary documents, such as the treaties on membership of the Federal Republic in the Western European Union and NATO, which also dealt with the German defense contribution; a "Convention on the Presence of Foreign Forces in the Federal Republic," whose status had changed from occupation troops to allied forces; and numerous governmental statements and letters exchanged between the contracting parties on special questions. The final result was "a massive collection of documents . . . . rather complicated because of the great many things that had been going on during this past ten-year period" (Secretary of State John Foster Dulles). It was the culmination of an evolutionary process which had turned the wreckage wrought by the collapse of Germany in 1945 into a new political order in Europe.

The fact that the documents were ready for signing on the prescribed date—an outcome at first thought entirely out of the question—has been explained in the *Memoirs* of Professor Wilhelm Grewe, leader of the German delegation, with these words: "That we succeeded was to a large measure due to the fact that all participants were convinced of the necessity that the task had to be accomplished and on time, and to the further no less important fact that the experts, namely the negotiators, approached their tasks with discipline and in a spirit of cooperation. . . . In these circumstances a working and negotiating style could develop such as I have never again experienced."

In the afternoon of October 21, 1954, the foreign ministers
of the Three Powers—Anthony Eden for Great Britain, John
Foster Dulles for the United States and Pierre Mendès-France
for France—and Chancellor Adenauer for the Federal Republic of
Germany met in the large conference hall *Des Pas Perdus* of the
Palais Chaillot in Paris to receive a report on the revision of the
Bonn Conventions. Mendès-France arrived at the last minute. I
saw him rushing up the broad stairs hastily throwing his coat to a
guard.

After a few words of greeting Eden, who was in the chair,
turned to Maurice Bathurst with the remark: "Our industrious
experts have taken a great load off our shoulders," and asked
him to explain what had been accomplished in Bonn. Bathurst
responded with a masterful presentation. While he spoke, we felt
once again the agony of the past few weeks. At the same time, we
were proud that the work entrusted to us had been delivered on
time.

In the afternoon of October 23, the leaders of the Atlantic
alliance assembled in the *Salle d'Orloges* of the French Ministry
of Foreign Affairs on the Quai d'Orsay to sign the documents
heralding the beginning of a new phase in the history of Europe.
Masses of papers were piled up at the seat of each of the
delegates.

In the morning, I had gone to the Quai d'Orsay to inspect,
together with representatives of the other contracting parties, the
"lay-out" of the papers. I had been charged by our delegation
to make sure that Mr. Dulles would find at his place only those
documents he was supposed to sign. It had happened, I was
told, at an international conference that Mr. Dulles, by mistake,
had signed papers meant for someone else. A repetition had to
be avoided. Despite the multitude and variety of the papers no
mishap occurred. What was signed in Paris on October 23, 1954,
has become known in diplomatic history as the Paris Agreements.

The entry into force of the agreements required ratification
by the parliaments of the contracting parties and the depositing
of the instruments of ratification at designated places. In April
of 1955, all ratification procedures had been completed. The
instruments of ratification had been deposited in the capitals as
provided in the agreements. No more hurdles had to be taken.

Federal Republic of Germany Bonn, May 5, 1955

58. The Three High Commissioners (from left: André François-Poncet, France; James B. Conant, U.S.A.; Frederick R. Hoyer Millar, Great Britain) sign the Proclamation Revoking the Occupation Statute

PROCLAMATION

WHEREAS a new relationship between the French Republic, the United States of America, and the United Kingdom of Great Britain and Northern Ireland, on the one hand, and the Federal Republic of Germany, on the other, has been established by the Convention on Relations between the Three Powers and the Federal Republic of Germany and the Related Conventions which were signed at Bonn on 26 May 1952, were amended by the Protocol on the Termination of the Occupation Regime in the Federal Republic of Germany signed at Paris on 23 October 1954, and enter into force today,

NOW THEREFORE, We,

André Francois-Poncet, French High Commissioner for Germany,

James B. Conant, United States High Commissioner for Germany,

Frederick Robert Hoyer Millar, United Kingdom High Commissioner for Germany,

Acting on behalf of, and duly authorised by our Governments, DO HEREBY JOINTLY PROCLAIM. THAT the Occupation Statute is revoked; and

THAT the Allied High Commission and the Offices of the Land Commissioners in the Federal Republic are abolished.

This Proclamation shall take effect at noon on the fifth day of May 1955.

Done at
BONN, Mehlem, this fifth day of May 1955.

ANDRÉ FRANÇOIS-PONCET
J. B. CONANT
P. R. HOYER MILLAR

PROCLAMATION

ATTENDU que de nouvelles relations entre la République Francaise, les Etats-Unis d'Amérique et le Royaume-Uni de Grande-Bretagne et d'Irlande du Nord, d'une part, et la République Fédérale d'Allemagne, d'autre part, ont été établies par la Convention sur les Relations entre les Trois Puissances et la République Fédérale d'Allemagne et les Conventions rattachées qui ont été signées à Bonn le 26 Mai 1952, amendées par le Protocole sur la Cessation du Régime d'Occupation dans la République Fédérale d'Allemagne, signé à Paris le 23 Octobre 1954, et qui entrent en vigueur aujourd'hui,

NOUS,

André Francois-Poncet, Haut Commissaire de la République Française en Allemagne,

James B. Conant, Haut Commissaire des Etats-Unis en Allemagne,

Frederick Robert Hoyer Millar Haut Commissaire du Royaume-Uni en Allemagne,

Agissant au nom de nos Gouvernements et dûment autorisés à cet effet. PROCLAMONS CONJOINTEMENT :
QUE le Statut d'Occupation est abrogé et

QUE la Haute Commission Alliée et les Commissariats de Land en République Fédérale sont abolis.

Cette Proclamation prend effet le 5 Mai 1955 à midi.

Fait à
BONN, Mehlem, le cinq mai 1955.

ANDRÉ FRANÇOIS-PONCET
J. B. CONANT
F. R. HOYER MILLAR

PROKLAMATION

In Anbetracht des neuen Verhältnisses zwischen der Französischen Republik, den Vereinigten Staaten von Amerika und dem Vereinigten Königreich von Großbritannien und Nordirland einerseits und der Bundesrepublik Deutschland andererseits, das durch den am 26. Mai 1952 in Bonn unterzeichneten Vertrag über die Beziehungen zwischen der Bundesrepublik Deutschland und den Drei Mächten und seinen Zusatzverträgen geschaffen ist, die durch das am 23. Oktober 1954 in Paris unterzeichnete Protokoll über die Beendigung des Besatzungsregimes in der Bundesrepublik Deutschland geändert wurden und heute in Kraft treten,

VERKUNDEN Wir,

André François-Poncet, Hoher Kommissar der Französischen Republik in Deutschland,

James B. Conant, Hoher Kommissar der Vereinigten Staaten für Deutschland,

Frederick Robert Hoyer Millar, Hoher Kommissar des Vereinigten Königreichs für Deutschland,

gemeinschaftlich im Namen und in Vollmacht unserer Regierungen,

DASS das Besatzungsstatut aufgehoben ist und

DASS die Alliierte Hohe Kommission und die Dienststellen der Landeskommissare in der Bundesrepublik aufgelöst sind.

Diese Proklamation tritt am 5. Mai 1955 mittags 12 Uhr in Kraft.

Ausgefertigt in
BONN, Mehlem, den fünften Mai 1955.

ANDRÉ FRANÇOIS-PONCET
J. B. CONANT
F. R. HOYER MILLAR

59. The Proclamation Revoking the Occupation Statute

Bonn

The Federal Republic of Germany: Partner in the Western Defense

60. Agreement on the Status of NATO Forces in Germany: The Negotiating Table in the Bonn Foreign Office

61. August 3, 1959: Signing of the Agreement in the Bonn Foreign Office (on the far right, the American Ambassador David Bruce. Behind him the Author)

We agreed in Bonn that May 5, 1955, would be the date on which the agreements should become effective. The date "5.5.55" could easily be remembered, we thought. The historic event needed to be given prominence in a special way.

On the same day the Allied High Commission met for the last time. The meeting place was the large conference room of the Office of the United States High Commissioner (now of the American Embassy) in Bonn-Mehlem. Along the southern wall of the room the press, radio and television cameras had taken up their positions. Facing them was a long table with chairs for the three high commissioners and their staff.

The French High Commissioner, François-Poncet, in his capacity as the senior high commissioner, opened the proceedings. He was followed by Dr. James B. Conant, the United States High Commissioner, and Sir Frederick Hoyer Millar of Great Britain.

The last action of the high commissioners was the signing of the "Proclamation Revoking the Occupation Statute and Abolishing the Allied High Commission and the Offices of the Land Commissioners in the Federal Republic of Germany."

Film cameras buzzed; the glare of the lights from the photographers' stand fell upon the faces of the high commissioners as they put their names to the Proclamation. From my place behind Dr. Conant I could see the clock above the door of the room. It showed twelve noon. From across the river church bells could be heard as they struck the noon hour. At this moment the Proclamation and the Paris Agreements entered into force.

The occupation regime was terminated. Germany was released from the bondage to which she had become subject after the deepest fall in her history. Under the terms of the agreements the Federal Republic had regained "the full authority of a sovereign state over its internal and external affairs." The high commissioners changed hats. From viceroys of the Allies they became the first ambassadors to the Federal Republic of Germany.

All of us who were present at the ceremony felt that the mantle of history had touched us, that we had witnessed a momentous turning point in European politics.

During the last months in the life of the High Commission I had been chairman of the legal committee. In this capacity I tendered to my colleagues a farewell lunch in the American Club in the project. In my speech, I reminded them of the many trials and tribulations we had gone through together over the last few years to reach the goal of the present day.

On May 5, 1980—I happened to be in Germany on this day— all public buildings were decorated with the black-red-golden flag of the Federal Republic. No poll was taken to ascertain how many people understood the significance of these flags. Twenty-five years ago the Paris Agreements had entered into force. Germany had been reborn as a free, sovereign state.

In letters exchanged between the German foreign minister and his American, British and French colleagues to commemorate this anniversary, reference was made to Article 7 of the Bonn Convention on Relations which proclaims as the common aim of the signatory states "a reunified Germany enjoying a liberal-democratic constitution, like that of the Federal Republic, and integrated within the European community."

Article 7 is valid international law; the political conception it embodies of a reunified Germany still remains a binding, unalterable aim of the common policy of the three Western Allies and the Federal Republic of Germany.

Epilogue

This book of memoirs shall end with May 5, 1955, the day when the door to a new political future was opened to Germany.

It was May again in Bonn, a glorious spring day like the day in 1952 when the foreign ministers of the three occupying powers met in Bonn with the federal chancellor to sign the Bonn Conventions. This climax of postwar policies was followed by years of doubt and uncertainty. Yet in these years the determination of all concerned to end the occupation regime and to return Germany to the community of free nations never faltered.

On May 5, 1955, the great work was done. *Tantae molis erat.* . . . Vergil's words about the toils of founding the Roman nation are also applicable to the reconstruction of Germany after World War II.

The German people had won their way back to an honorable place among the free and peace-loving nations of the world. As Secretary of State James Byrnes had stated in his Stuttgart speech of September 6, 1946, it had been the wish of the American people to help Germany attain this goal. The wish had been fulfilled. I had contributed my share to this endeavor in the service of the people and government of the United States.

What I felt on May 5, 1955 can best be described in the words of my friend, the historian and professor at Yale University, Hajo Holborn. In a speech responding to the award of the Inter-Nations Prize in Bonn—one day before his death in 1969—he talked about his fate which was similar to mine. It had been one of the happiest experiences in his life, he said, that he had always been able "to move in the fullest identity of his American duties with his German past."

After May 5, 1955, I remained in Bonn for fourteen more years. During the last few years I was as the legal advisor of the American embassy, and sole "survivor"—a friend of mine once called me "the last of the Mohicans"—of about 150 staff members of the Office of the General Counsel in the United States High Commissioner's Office. My service had been extended for five years beyond the mandatory retirement age after the secretary of state had certified that my continuation in office was required "in the public interest of the United States."

One of my first assignments after the accession of the Federal Republic to NATO was to participate in the negotiations on the adjustment of the Bonn Forces Convention to the Treaty on the Status of NATO Forces. The negotiations began in Bonn in November 1955 and, insofar as length is concerned, took a record time of more than three and a half years to conclude—after many crises and much painstaking work. The Supplementary Agreement to the NATO Status of Forces Agreement was signed on August 3, 1959. I had been in on the negotiations from an almost euphoric start to a finish that left everyone exhausted.

Otherwise, the years from 1955 up to my retirement in 1969 were filled with work in connection with the liquidation of matters arising from the war and the occupation. Among my duties was the preparation of decisions on the fate of foreign nationals, mostly from Eastern Europe, who had been brought to Germany during the war. After the war, many of them had committed serious crimes, chiefly murders, for which they had been sentenced in the first years of the occupation by American Military Courts. Those condemned to prison terms were confined in German prisons. After the Federal Republic had become a sovereign state, the federal government agreed to continue holding them under German control.

Decisions on the termination or reduction of sentences, paroles, pardons or other acts of clemency with regard to these prisoners were the prerogative of the United States. It was exercised by the American ambassador. He could, however, act only after he had obtained recommendations from a Mixed Clemency Advisory Board consisting of an American and a German member. For many years I was the American member of the board. Together with my German colleague, Ministerial Counselor in the Baden-Württemberg Ministry of Justice Dr. Bogenrieder, I frequently visited the German penal institutions where the prisoners were detained in order to interview them preparatory to recommendations for submission to the American ambassador. The murders had been committed largely by people who, after being released from detention camps

Bonn

62. November 27, 1968: American, British, French and German Colleagues say farewell to the Author on his Retirement

63. The American Embassy in the Mehlemer Aue

64. Stimson Memorial Chapel in the American
Housing Project

at the end of the war, had been roaming the country in quest for booty or perhaps also for revenge. This did not mitigate their often brutal deeds. In many cases we were able to have the homelands of the prisoners take them back.

From the occupation stemmed the right of the three Allies to take all appropriate measures to protect the security of their forces if threatened by serious disturbances of public security and order (emergency powers). This right, which the Allies retained under the Convention on Relations lapsed in the event that German authorities obtained similar powers under German legislation. It took almost fourteen years, until 1968, before an emergency law was adopted in the Federal Republic which resulted in the abrogation of the Allied powers. Article 48 of the Weimar Constitution, which vested dictatorial powers in the Reich president in the event of an emergency, had cast a shadow on this hotly debated issue of German domestic politics. The German-Allied negotiations on the lapse of the Allied rights presented similar difficulties. Important security interests were at stake; it was my duty, in cooperation with my military colleagues, to uphold them for the American side. Among other matters within my domain were questions in connection with commitments of the Federal Republic, under the Settlement Convention, to compensate victims of Nazi persecution. One such question concerned the payment of damages to Polish women and girls who had suffered grievous injuries to their health from medical experiments in German concentration camps. I was able to settle the question with my German counterpart after it had lain dormant for years.

In February of 1969, a few months before my retirement, when my successor had already arrived in Bonn, I was sent for a short time to the American Mission in Berlin to take the place of the legal advisor who had been transferred to Washington.

In the office building of the Mission in Berlin-Dahlem in the Clay-Allee, the former Kronprinzenallee, I found myself installed in the same office that I had occupied from 1946 to 1948 as a member of the Legal Division of OMGUS. I had returned to the point where more than twenty years before I had begun my service with the American authorities in Germany. My postwar career in Germany had come full circle.

On July 2, a day after my retirement from the United States Foreign Service, Federal President Heinemann awarded me the Commander's Cross of the Order of Merit of the Federal Republic of Germany "in recognition of the meritorious service I had rendered the Federal Republic of Germany" in the peaceful reconstruction of Germany and the strengthening of good relations between the American and the German people. An award by the secretary of state on the occasion of my retirement ascribed to me an "enduring contribution to German-American understanding."

If I reflect on the changes in my life—from a Prussian civil servant and "non-Aryan" in the Third Reich to a law student at Yale Law School, and then a member of the armed forces of the United States and an officer in the service of American authorities in postwar Germany, I am reminded of the words in Goethe's *Hermann and Dorothea* which have stayed in my memory ever since I had first seen them painted in large letters in the reception hall of the World Economics Institute in Kiel during my student years:

A man who in unstable times is himself of unstable mind
Magnifies the evil and spreads it farther and farther.
But he who is of unbending spirit
Will be the master of his destiny.

ABOUT THE AUTHOR

by
William Royall Tyler
Former Assistant Secretary of State
for European Affairs, and Ambassador

I first met Joachim von Elbe in January 1958, when I arrived in Bonn as Political Counselor, when David Bruce was the Ambassador.

During my preparation for this assignment, my colleagues in the State Department's Bureau of German Affairs had frequently mentioned his name in terms of the highest respect. He was considered by them to be the most knowledgeable Embassy official, not only on German affairs in general, and Berlin in particular, but on U.S. policy toward Germany since the war. Given his reputation and influence, his title of Legal Advisor was singularly inadequate, as illustrated by the following excerpt from a letter to him on the occasion of his eightieth birthday, in June 1982, from Ambassador Burns:

> You worked for the United Government in Germany during a very dynamic period. I imagine that many statesmen would envy the formative influence you had over the many international agreements on which you worked between 1946 and 1969. The Convention on Relations between the Three Powers and the Federal Republic of Germany and the Supplementary Agreement to the NATO Status of Forces Agreement continue to constitute the legal foundation for the United States relationship with the Federal Republic of Germany. Of course, your unique dual professional qualifications and personal perspective were invaluable in this work.

Dr. von Elbe served under the first five American Ambassadors to the Federal Republic: James B. Conant, David

K. E. Bruce, Walter C. Dowling, George C. McGhee, and Henry Cabot Lodge.

His principal role was that of an advisor, but with an unusually extensive authority. He dealt directly with his British, French and German colleagues in developing working positions on legal and legislative issues. His knowledge, discretion, and personal qualities were highly appreciated and respected by his colleagues, foreign as well as American. As a senior official of the British Embassy once said to me, "I don't know what we'd do without your chap von Elbe." His political acumen and soundness of judgment reflected his immense store of historical and legal knowledge which encompassed not only Germany and the United States, but also France. While his outlook was thoroughly American, he displayed an objectivity and moderation in policy issues which were invaluable.

The data of Dr. von Elbe's remarkable career give an incomplete idea of his intellectual and cultural attainments, which include a lively and enlightened interest in music, and in art and literature in general. He lives by, and represents, the humanistic values and tradition. Among the memories which his many friends who served with him in the Embassy particularly treasure are those of the hospitable and stimulating evenings in his apartment, when he would give a talk on his favorite subject and field of research: *Germania Romana.* These talks were illustrated by his own excellent films in color and accompanied by a commentary as learned as it was informal, which bridged the intervening centuries and brought to life the Roman past in a way none of us had experienced in any classroom.

In 1975, he published *Roman Germany. A Guide to Sites and Museums.* In 1977, after revision and expansion by the author, it appeared in German under the title *Die Römer in Deutschland*, with a masterly introduction by Rudolf Pörtner who also wrote a Foreword to the book in which he says of Dr. von Elbe: "Love of history, particularly that of *Germania Romana*, he considers an heritage from his Rhenish homeland, and as something innate in him. He first wrote this book for his fellow countrymen across the ocean in order to provide them with a guide for their historical travels in the Federal Republic," and concludes that it should soon become ". . . an indispensable handbook for all those who love, and are knowledgeable about *Germania Romana*, as well as for those engaged, through travel and study, in the discovery of that unknown country called Germany."

These books were taking shape during those evenings when he opened the eyes of so many of his fellow Americans to the wonders of the Roman legacy to Germany's past; as well as expeditions with them to the *Limes*, to Cologne, Trier, and other great Roman sites.

Thus, in addition to his contributions to the establishment of the constitutional and institutional framework within which the Federal Republic developed after the war, Dr. von Elbe also made a lasting contribution to the increased awareness and knowledge, both by Americans and Germans, of Germany's Roman past. He must derive great satisfaction from the fact that this is realized by all those on both sides of the Atlantic who are devoted to the cause of German-American relations.

In the letter, already mentioned above, Ambassador Burns also writes:

> I am familiar with your books on the Romans in Germany and believe their acclaim to be well deserved. Frankly, we in the Embassy take not inconsiderable pride in our association with the creator of these authoritative works. I understand that you are working on your memoirs. Let me encourage you in this endeavor. From what I understand of your life you will be producing a book that is as useful as it is interesting.

I will now close with a paragraph on which, in deference to Dr. von Elbe's extreme modesty, I shall forebear from elaborating:

In ancient China, the properties of the bamboo were considered to symbolize five virtues inherent in the mind and character of those striving to live in conformity with the highest ideals. These are: first, that the bamboo grows straight, as one's character should be; second, that it is evergreen, thus retaining all its life the freshness of youth; third, that it bends, but never breaks before the winds of adversity; fourth, that it is light, as one should not be a burden to one's friends; and finally, that it keeps within itself an empty space, as a human should, for constant accumulation of knowledge and wisdom.

Index

Sources of Illustrations

Bundesarchiv, Koblenz, Federal Republic of Germany 1, 2, 3, 4, 12, 16, 17, 18, 19, 20, 21, 22, 23, 24, 25, 26, 27, 28, 29, 30, 31, 42, 43, 44, 45, 46, 47, 48, 49, 50, 51, 52, 53, 54, 55

Fürstlich Wiedisches Archiv, Neuwied on the Rhine, Federal Republic of Germany 5, 6, 7, 11

Presse- und Informationsdienst der Bundesregierung, Bundes-bildstelle, Bonn, Federal Republic of Germany 61

Culver Pictures, Inc. (CPI), New York, U.S.A. 36, 41

Brown University Library, Providence, Rhode Island, U.S.A. 13

Hedwig von Harnier, Bonn, Federal Republic of Germany 9, 63, 64

Private Photographs 8, 10, 14, 15, 32, 33, 34, 35, 37, 38, 39, 40, 56, 57, 58, 59, 60, 62